SECOND EDITION

APPLIED BEHAVIOR ANALYSIS IN THE CLASSROOM

Patrick J. Schloss
Bloomsburg University

Maureen A. Smith
SUNY College at Buffalo

Allyn and Bacon
Boston • London • Toronto • Sydney • Tokyo • Singapore

Series Editor: Ray Short
Series Editorial Assistant: Karin Huang
Vice President, Education: Nancy Forsyth
Marketing Manager: Kathy Hunter
Sr. Editorial Production Administrator: Susan McIntyre
Editorial-Production Service: Omegatype Typography, Inc.
Composition Buyer: Linda Cox
Manufacturing Buyer: Suzanne Lareau
Cover Administrator: Jenny Hart
Electronic Composition: Omegatype Typography, Inc.

Library of Congress Cataloging-in-Publication Data

Schloss, Patrick J.
    Applied behavior analysis in the classroom / Patrick J. Schloss,
Maureen A. Smith. — 2nd ed.
      p. cm.
    Includes bibliographical references and indexes.
    ISBN 0–205–19683–7
    1. Behavior modification. 2. Behavioral assessment of children.
3. Classroom management. 4. Problem children—Education.
I. Smith, Maureen A. II. Title.
LB1060.2.S34 1998
371.39'3—dc21   97–30862
                                           CIP

Printed in the United States of America
10 9 8 7 6 5 4 3   RRD 04 03 02 01 00 99

Contents

Preface

As teachers, we are faced with a monumental task: to ensure that our students acquire skills that will contribute to their ability to lead full and productive lives. We must accomplish this task, despite the fact that our resources are shrinking and our students are becoming more diverse (Carnine, 1992). Further complicating our efforts is the stress our students face as they deal with drastic changes in their families and neighborhoods. School officials are now in the difficult position of having to develop and implement programming that goes beyond the traditional "Three Rs" (Fantuzzo & Atkins, 1992).

State boards of education have gone to great lengths to develop curricula that identify and sequence objectives whose mastery will enhance success in adulthood. Traditional curricula have also been altered dramatically by technological and social changes. Computer literacy, whether taught separately or in conjunction with the content areas, will be essential if students are to meet the challenges of the twenty-first century. And the science curriculum now includes the study of ecology so that students can understand the relationship between their actions and the preservation of our environment.

Similarly, complex issues such as AIDS and substance abuse have forced the inclusion of curricular areas vastly different from those targeted when we were children. Unfortunately, one thing that has not changed very much is the length of the average school day, and we find ourselves in the difficult position of having to provide instruction in an increasing number of diverse areas within the same time limits. Further complicating this issue are the distractions that can keep us from effectively using the time available. Unavoidable events such as assemblies, snow days, teacher or student illness, and mandatory testing play havoc with our schedules and often leave us feeling as though there will never be enough time in the day to get everything done.

Another distraction that frequently undermines our ability to do our jobs in a timely manner is student misbehavior. Although most of our students do not pose any discipline problems, the small number who do can disrupt the learning environment for everyone (Smith & Rivera, 1994). During the course of the average day, students may swear, argue, fight, be inattentive, or refuse to follow directions. As a result, valuable instructional time is lost because we may need to interrupt, delay, or postpone a lesson to deal with the misbehavior. Student misbehavior has another negative side effect. Even after the problem has been resolved, we may find ourselves less than enthusiastic about working with a particular student. Eventually, our professionalism and sense of dedication may outweigh our reluctance. However, the quality and quantity of future teacher–student interactions may be compromised.

We may not be able to exert control over assemblies, illness, snow days, and testing schedules, but we can manage student misbehavior. Generally, our supervisors and principals expect that we will manage behavior and create a positive learning atmosphere for all the students in our class. Failure to do so may jeopardize our jobs. Thus, behavior management skills are among the crucial competencies needed by all teachers, regardless of whether their focus is general or special education. All students, whether normally achieving or disabled, are capable of displaying discipline problems. The student with disruptive behavior can no longer be removed automatically and permanently from the general education classroom. The least restrictive environment mandate (LRE) contained within The Individuals with Disabilities Education Act (IDEA) requires that the general education classroom, with reasonable modifications, be considered first as a placement for all students with disabilities. Moreover, movements such as the Regular Education Initiative (REI) and full inclusion have resulted in the return of students with disabilities to the general education classroom. Thus, professionals from general education, special education, counseling, and remedial reading must be prepared to work effectively and collaboratively to meet the needs of all students.

Most teacher preparation programs include coursework related to behavior management (perhaps that's why you are reading this text!). Upon completion of these courses, you should have the skills necessary to arrange a classroom environment that promotes acceptable behaviors. You should also be able to deal with misbehavior efficiently, effectively, ethically, and with minimal disruption to the learning process. We believe the most effective way to design such a classroom is to use the principles of applied behavior analysis, or ABA.

Organization

This second edition of *Applied Behavior Analysis in the Classroom* contains 16 chapters. The first two chapters provide historical, philosophical, and methodological perspectives on applied behavior analysis. They focus on historical antecedents to current applied behavior analysis methods, ethical issues in applied behavior analysis, and major steps in developing an applied behavior analysis program.

Chapter 3 emphasizes the "applied" focus of applied behavior analysis. Topics include the selection of socially valid goals, the use of minimally intrusive behavior change methods, the establishment of both long-term and short-term program objectives, and the communication of objectives in writing.

The "behavioral" focus of applied behavior analysis is addressed in Chapters 4 through 10. Included are discussions of applying antecedent control techniques, increasing appropriate behaviors through the teaching of social skills, developing positive emotional characteristics, using consequence control to increase appropriate responses, reducing disruptive behaviors through positive methods, and reducing disruptive behaviors through aversive methods.

Chapters 11, 12, and 13 describe "analytic" methods of applied behavior analysis, and they focus on methods for data collection, graphing, and single-case experimentation.

The last three chapters are designed to assist the reader in extending the benefits of applied behavior analysis. Chapter 14 addresses external agents that may be effective in promoting program generalization. Chapter 15 considers internal agents that promote generalization. The final chapter provides an overview of methods for working effectively with parents.

Features

We have included several major features to enhance the value of *Applied Behavior Analysis in the Classroom* as both a course text and a reference book. First, the book is organized in the chronological order typically associated with designing, implementing, and evaluating an applied behavior analysis program. We begin with the selection of socially valid goals and objectives; continue through the selection of behavior change methods; and conclude with behavior recording, graphing, and reporting.

Technical jargon is avoided except where general terms are not available to convey precise meaning. Because of the importance of clear definition of terms in applied behavior analysis, we have included an extensive glossary. Words included in the glossary have distinct and essential meaning to applied behavior analysis professionals.

We have included numerous examples to support discussions of each applied behavior analysis principle. Examples are drawn from our own experiences and those of others with whom we have worked. We have attempted to extend examples to a wide range of interpersonal situations outside of special education to emphasize their general utility.

Finally, the text includes a substantial number of tables and figures. We have used illustrations extensively to summarize or display essential content. Many can also be copied and will provide ready forms or protocols to assist in your own applied behavior analysis programming.

A Word of Thanks

We are grateful to the people who have made the writing of this text possible. Our deepest appreciation is extended to Ray Short, editor at Allyn and Bacon. Ray's editorial leadership has helped to focus the content and style of the text. His editorial assistant, Karin Huang, has provided substantial assistance in the technical aspects of manuscript preparation.

We thank Gay Goodman, Ph.D., from the University of Houston, for her review of this edition of the text, and Cynthia Watkins, Ph.D., from Northern Iowa University at Cedar Falls, and her students for their careful review of the first edition. We also acknowledge the students in our courses who have used this text since its original publication, particularly Joseph Franjoine of the Arcade School District in Arcade, New York. The comments and suggestions from all of these individuals were invaluable as we prepared this edition. We are grateful to David Hofius for preparing the glossary and to Charles Green for preparing the Instructor's Manual with Test Items.

P. J. S
M. A. S.

References

Carnine, D. (1992). Expanding the notion of teachers' rights: Access to tools that work. *Journal of Applied Behavior Analysis, 25,* 13–19.

Fantuzzo, J., & Atkins, M. (1992). Applied behavior analysis for educators: Teacher centered and classroom based. *Journal of Applied Behavior Analysis, 25,* 37–42.

Smith, D. D., & Rivera, D. P. (1995). Discipline in special education and general education settings. *Focus on Exceptional Children, 27*(5), 1–14.

1

APPLIED BEHAVIOR ANALYSIS: DEFINITION AND THEORY

Applied Behavior Analysis versus Behavior Modification

As you read through this text, you will probably encounter some terms and procedures that are familiar to you. You may have even referred to these terms and procedures as "behavior modification." Unfortunately, because of misunderstanding and misuse, this phrase has acquired a negative connotation, as is exemplified by people who perceive behavior modification to be the use of M & Ms to reward good behavior. At the other end of the continuum, and equally narrow in their interpretation, are those individuals who perceive behavior modification to be the use of electric shock to control bad behavior. Scenes from *One Flew Over the Cuckoo's Nest* come to mind. Also contributing to the misuse of this phrase are procedures for changing behavior that are not representative of the theoretical model underlying behavior modification; for example, drugs and counseling can alter behavior, but these techniques are typical of medical and psychodynamic models.

The misuse of techniques traditionally associated with behavior modification has also contributed to its bad reputation. Occasionally, newspapers and popular magazines have reported incidents in which students either have been at risk for, or have actually experienced, neglect or injury as a result of teacher misuse of a behavior modification technique, such as incorrect use of the time-out procedure. Obviously, we should be very concerned about the misuse of a technique and should do everything in our power to rectify the situation and prevent additional problems. It could be argued that in the interest of sensationalism and selling copies, some publications fail to describe accurately and completely all facets of a situation. What is not debatable is the fact that these reports supply information used by the public to form opinions. Parental apprehension surrounding use of a specific technique could extend unfairly to other procedures associated with the model.

1

Misunderstanding of the concept and misuse of techniques have tarnished the reputation of behavior modification. In response, professionals have explored alternative terminology that precisely conveys the nature of management techniques used with students. In addition, they continue to develop new techniques and to refine those currently in use. Their ongoing efforts increase the number of options we have for managing student behavior and ensure their accurate and appropriate use. The result of these efforts has been the development and application of techniques based on principles of applied behavior analysis.

Definition of Applied Behavior Analysis (ABA)

The phrase **applied behavior analysis** was first defined by Baer, Wolf, and Risley (1968) in the inaugural issue of the *Journal of Applied Behavior Analysis* as the "process of applying sometimes tentative principles of behavior to the improvement of specific behaviors and simultaneously evaluating whether or not any changes noted are indeed attributable to the process of application" (p. 91). They elaborated by defining each word within the phrase. The term "applied" means that the behavior targeted for change is socially relevant or important. As will be discussed, B. F. Skinner, a pioneer in behaviorism, demonstrated principles of reinforcement in laboratory settings with animals. Although these investigations were essential to the development of his theory, we and our students do not function in a laboratory. Living in the real world offers us real challenges that must be met efficiently if we are to acquire the tremendous body of skills that enables us to live productive and enjoyable lives. Therefore, classroom behaviors increased by use of applied behavior analysis principles include paying attention, volunteering responses, solving math problems correctly, and making and keeping friends. Similarly, we can apply these principles to decrease or eliminate behaviors that undermine a student's progress such as swearing, fighting, and destroying property. Table 1.1 contrasts clinically important behaviors with their socially important counterparts.

TABLE 1.1   Clinically Important Behaviors versus Socially Important Behaviors

We want to change behaviors that will make a difference in the quality of our students' lives. Compare the following clinically important behaviors to their socially important counterparts.

Clinical Behaviors	Socially Important Behaviors
Results of a self-concept inventory completed by Tom	Number of positive or negative comments Tom makes about himself
Kate's attitude toward peers with handicaps	Number of times Kate initiates a conversation with a peer who is handicapped
Laura's ability to solve a problem as measured by completing a maze	Laura's ability to find the shortest distance on a map
Bridget's finger dexterity as measured by a pegboard task	Bridget's typing or handwriting skills

The term **behavior** refers to events that are observable and measurable. Individuals who use applied behavior analysis define the behavior so precisely that there is no question about what is being changed. For example, you may want to raise a student's low self-concept. Before attempting to do so, you will need to specify clearly what you mean. A student with a low self-concept probably does not feel very good about himself, but are the feelings observable and measurable? Will you always be able to tell when the student is wrestling with a low self-concept? You can detect a low self-concept by identifying discrete behaviors that suggest a student has a poor opinion of self. For example, does the student make negative self-statements such as "I can't do anything right" or "Nobody likes me"? Is the student in fact experiencing academic difficulties or lacking friends? Do other people notice and compliment the student's positive traits? Answers to these questions enable you to identify clearly the strengths and weaknesses in the student's behavioral repertoire prior to intervention. They also serve as a backdrop against which the results of an intervention program will be measured. Table 1.2 includes additional samples of observable and measurable classroom behaviors.

The term *analysis* refers to the process by which the effects of a behavior change program are measured. We want to make sure that the intervention program we

TABLE 1.2 Measureable, Observable, Classroom Behaviors

Compare student descriptions in Column A and Column B. Which descriptions are easier to verify?

Column A		Column B
"Tricia is smart."	versus	"Tricia was in the 90th percentile on a norm-referenced reading test."
		"All of the answers Tricia volunteers are correct."
"Pat is a self-starter."	versus	"Pat does all of his work with no teacher assistance."
		"Pat always has things to do in his spare time."
"Eric is nice."	versus	"Eric helps other students."
		"Eric has many friends."
"Luke writes well."	versus	"Luke uses a variety of syntactic structures."
		"Luke uses topical sentences that clearly identify the main idea."
"Andrew is in a bad mood."	versus	"Andrew is swearing."
		"Andrew is refusing to complete his math sheet."
"Charles is not paying attention."	versus	"Charles has not completed his math worksheet."
		"I have to repeat my directions for Charles."
"Jim is hyperactive."	versus	"Jim is out of his seat every two minutes."
		"Jim doesn't work on a task for more than three minutes."
"Mary is unpopular."	versus	"No one sits with Mary at lunch."
		"No one selected Mary to work on the team project."

designed and implemented is the only reason a student's behavior changed. For example, you may notice that a student in your first grade class is beginning to throw temper tantrums during which she screams, swears, and destroys property. You consider this behavior unacceptable and identify a strategy to deal with it. After four weeks, you notice the student no longer has tantrums, and you naturally attribute this change to your clever strategy. At the next parent conference, however, you discover that her mother and father had experienced marital difficulties, separated briefly, but recently reconciled. You note that the dates of separation and reconciliation correspond to the onset and termination of tantrum behavior. Now the question arises: Did the student's behavior change as a result of the implementation of your strategy or as a result of her parents' reconciliation? You have no idea just how effective your strategy was or if it will work with other students in similar predicaments. That is why it is essential to verify the relationship between instructional practices and a student's progress. Appropriate analysis allows us to identify and retain effective methods and materials for future use.

As you can see, use of the phrase *applied behavior analysis* offers several advantages over use of the phrase *behavior modification*. It suggests that clearly defined behaviors are selected for change based on their social importance to students and teachers, not on their convenience for clinical researchers. Applied behavior analysis also implies that a specific body of carefully described techniques will be used and the effects clearly documented.

Historical Foundations of Applied Behavior Analysis

As suggested earlier, applied behavior analysis has its roots in behavioral theory, which states that most behaviors are learned responses to environmental stimuli. Behavioral theory can be traced to Watson's and Pavlov's work in the area of classical or respondent conditioning. Watson and Rayner (1920) paired the emission of a loud sound and the presentation of a small, woolly animal to a young child. Eventually, the child demonstrated fear in the sole presence of a small, woolly animal. Pavlov (1927) simultaneously presented food and the sound of a bell to a dog. As a result of repeated pairings, the dog salivated when only the sound of the bell was presented.

B. F. Skinner (1953) extended behavioral theory by investigating operant conditioning. He noted that pigeons increased pecking behavior if it was followed by the presentation of food. In contrast, this behavior decreased if no food was forthcoming or if the pigeons were punished. Thus, Skinner demonstrated three important principles of operant conditioning: reinforcement, extinction, and punishment. Another major contributor to the foundations of behaviorism was Albert Bandura (1965; 1977), who demonstrated that individuals could learn new behaviors by watching others engage in those behaviors. For example, a student who is unable to perform simple functions on a computer may observe another child who is able to do so. After repeated observations, the student begins to demonstrate basic computer skills. Bandura's work on model learning has received a great deal of attention; you may already be familiar with studies describing the effects of televised aggression on young viewers.

Respondent conditioning, operant conditioning, and model learning have contributed greatly to the foundations of behaviorism and the development of applied behavior analysis principles. The purpose of this text is to describe how these principles can assist you in establishing and maintaining a classroom atmosphere that enhances your students' academic and social development. However, you should be aware that there are other theoretical models which suggest alternative intervention techniques. We believe a review of some of these models will highlight the usefulness of applied behavior analysis. Our review will be brief; for more information, see Morse and Smith (1980) and Newcomer (1993).

The Psychodynamic Model

The psychodynamic model is based on the works of Sigmund Freud. He argued that behavior was motivated by an individual's life history and by internal forces that were sexual and aggressive in nature. (You have no doubt heard of the id, the ego, and the superego.) More recent contributors to the model include Carl Rogers (1961) and Abraham Maslow (1968), who believed human behavior is motivated by the need to satisfy positive internal forces such as love and concern.

Proponents of the psychodynamic model maintain that behavior can be changed if the individual learns to control internal forces. Techniques to facilitate control include individual and group counseling to gain insights into behavior and identify appropriate alternatives. Similarly, family counseling helps participants to understand why the affected individual behaves in a particular manner and to identify ways to interact more positively. Other techniques include art, music, or dance therapy, which provide nontraditional ways of expressing negative feelings.

In theory, psychodynamic techniques assist the individual in understanding what motivated inappropriate behavior; therefore, subsequent changes should be pervasive and longlasting. Unfortunately, there are no data supporting the effectiveness of psychodynamic approaches. This lack of documentation suggests that these techniques may not be the most efficient use of valuable teacher and student time. In addition, there are several reasons why we may be at a distinct disadvantage when implementing these techniques in our classroom. First, most of us have not received training in counseling as part of our teacher preparation program. We may either feel inadequate in the role of counselor or feel that counseling is not a responsibility teachers should assume. Second, the lack of standardized procedures may hinder the efforts of those who have accepted the responsibility of providing services within a psychodynamic model. For example, when counseling, what do you do first? How do you respond to a negative comment? Do you contradict? Redirect? If asked for an opinion, what do you say? Even if a set of procedures were developed and used successfully with one student, would it be useful with another? Third, any pervasive and longlasting changes may require a great deal of time to achieve. The school year may not be long enough to accomplish these changes. Fourth, what is the teacher supposed to do while waiting for these changes to occur? Psychodynamic techniques do not offer immediate solutions to everyday classroom problems. Finally, students need to be skilled communicators to participate in individual or group counseling. Not all students currently have the language necessary for them to benefit from these techniques.

The Medical Model

Proponents of the medical model believe biological factors are responsible for human behavior. While more extreme advocates maintain that all unacceptable behaviors can be traced to abnormal physiology, the more popular view is that some behaviors can be linked to physical factors while others are linked to environmental conditions. Certainly, there can be no question that how we feel influences how we behave. A cold that cheats us of a good night's sleep may leave us irritable during the day. Hay fever or other allergies may keep us from venturing outside during particular months of the year. Other biological conditions are associated with more serious problems. The presence of an extra chromosome causes Down syndrome. A brain injury or a tumor can cause epilepsy. Insulin deficiency causes diabetes. Consumption of milk products by individuals unable to metabolize them causes phenylketonuria (PKU), a disorder associated with severe mental retardation. Biological factors are suspected in conditions such as hyperactivity, schizophrenia, and depression.

A biological cause suggests a biological intervention and, in some instances, this approach has been useful. For example, insulin injections help people with diabetes. Similarly, elimination of milk products reduces the effects of PKU. Even when we are unsure of the cause, we know that medication can relieve some of the symptoms of hyperactivity, schizophrenia, and depression, vastly improving the quality of life for affected individuals and their families. The medical model has even proven useful to those individuals whose medical condition could not be prevented. For example, the removal of architectural barriers enables people using wheelchairs to have access to many public buildings.

While the medical model offers technology that can change behavior, it is not the model of choice for typical classroom problems. First, it explains only a small percentage of unacceptable behavior. Second, within the medical model, the role of the teacher is restricted to referring students for possible medical evaluation and monitoring behavior while students are on medication. While there are exceptions, physicians usually do not ask the teacher's opinion when prescribing or continuing medication. Third, drug therapy may not be sufficient treatment. While it may change a student's behavior, gains are not maintained when medication is suspended. A more effective treatment program combines medication with other therapeutic techniques, such as those based on applied behavior analysis. Fourth, although a medical model may remove blame for a problem, it may also remove responsibility for change from students, parents, and teachers. Parents and teachers may lower expectations for the student because they believe nothing they do will alter the child's biological status. Similarly, students may believe their medication has more control over their behavior than they do.

The Ecological Model

Advocates of psychodynamic and medical models attribute behavior to internal factors such as impulses and physiology. As discussed earlier, those supporting a behavioral model believe behavior is a function of environmental stimuli. Proponents of the ecological model recognize the influences of both internal and external forces on an individual's behavior. Specifically, they believe an individual's behavior interacts with environmental conditions. The appropriateness of a behavior is determined by how closely it matches the standards of the setting in which it occurs. For example, calling out is generally normal on the playground, but unacceptable in most classrooms. On a more serious note, behaviors such as stealing and vandalism may be required to maintain membership in a gang, but they are unacceptable within society at large.

The goal of ecological interventions is to maximize the match between an individual's behavior and the demands of the setting. Because the ecological model emphasizes internal and external forces, intervention techniques focus on changing the individual, the environment, or both. Because internal and external forces are considered, intervention techniques may resemble those suggested by other models. A classic example of an ecological intervention is Project Re-Ed (Hobbs, 1966), in which students demonstrating serious academic and social problems were removed from public school to a residential setting. During the week, students received instruction to improve their academic and social skills. Parents, with the assistance of social workers, identified community resources that could assist the family in meeting the child's needs. Weekends were spent together at home. A liaison teacher worked with school officials to ensure a smooth and speedy transition back to the regular classroom.

An ecological model encourages us to examine all internal and external factors that may contribute to a student's problem and to identify a variety of resources to solve it. Unfortunately, this strength is also a weakness. Identification and coordination of diverse resources may require more time, expertise, and money than a school district can afford.

As you can see, there is a variety of alternatives to applied behavior analysis. Although each model has something of value to offer, we believe that teachers and students will benefit most from the use of applied behavior analysis techniques.

Advantages of ABA over Other Models

The use of applied behavior analysis techniques offers distinct advantages over other models when developing and implementing classroom management programs. First, by virtue of their training, classroom teachers and paraprofessionals are qualified to use applied behavior analysis. School personnel unfamiliar with ABA techniques can learn them relatively quickly with some coursework and supervised practice. Interventions suggested by the medical and psychoanalytic models require substantial training and typically fall outside the educator's responsibilities. Second, applied behavior analysis requires us to evaluate the techniques and materials we use. Evaluation allows us to maximize valuable teacher and student time because we can retain effective techniques and materials, and revise or discard those that are ineffective. Third, ABA techniques have proven effective with students who have limited communication skills, unlike some psychoanalytic strategies that require verbal ability. Fourth, on a related note, use of ABA techniques has changed a variety of behaviors demonstrated by individuals with diverse backgrounds (Sulzer-Azaroff & Gillat, 1990).

Using ABA, teachers have increased students' level of participation (Mason & Egel, 1995) and time on task (Adair & Schneider, 1993); and improved verbal language (Matson, Sevin, Fridley, & Love, 1990), social skills (Fad, Ross, & Boston, 1995), play skills (Capone, Smith, & Schloss, 1988), academic skills (Belfiore, Skinner, & Ferkins, 1995), independent living skills (McKelvey, Sisson, Van Hasselt, & Hersen, 1992; Pattavina, Bergstrom, Marchand-Martella, Martella, 1992; Schloss, Alexander, Horning, Parker, & Wright, 1993; Schloss, Alper, Watkins, & Petrechko, 1995), and leisure activities (Davis & Chittum, 1994). ABA techniques have been used among the general population to increase use of seat belts (Barry & Geller, 1991) and designated drivers (Brigham, Meier, & Goodner, 1995) and to decrease calls to directory assistance (McSweeny, 1978). They have also decreased inappropriate behaviors such as noncompliance (Mace, Hock, Lalli, West, Belfiore, Pinter, & Brown, 1988), stealing (Switzer, Deal, & Bailey, 1977), and aggression (Bay-Hinitz, Peterson, & Quilitch, 1994). Particularly notable is the elimination of longstanding and severe problems such as self-abuse (Schloss, Smith, Smaldino, Field, Tiffin, & Ramsey, 1983) and self-stimulation (Repp, Felce, & Barton, 1988). Prior to intervention using applied behavior analysis, many of these problems had been considered untreatable. Individuals participating in these studies ranged in age from very young (Capone et al., 1988) to secondary school age (Adair & Schneider, 1993) and were identified as nonhandicapped (White & Bailey, 1990) or handicapped by mental retardation (Hughes & Rusch, 1989), or as having behavior disorders (Neef, Shade, & Miller, 1994), a hearing impairment (Rasing, 1993), a learning disability (Adair & Schneider, 1993; Belfiore, Skinner, & Ferkins, 1995), autism (Matson et al., 1990), traumatic brain injury (Davis & Chittum, 1994), or multiple problems (McKelvey et al., 1992). Finally, applied behavior analysis techniques have been used successfully in public school classrooms (Adair & Schneider, 1993; Belfiore, Skinner, & Ferkins, 1995), residential schools (McKelvey et al., 1992), hospitals (Capone et al., 1988), recreational facilities (Schloss, Smith, & Kiehl, 1986), the community (Pattavina et al., 1992), and work environments (Hughes & Rusch, 1989).

Criticisms of Applied Behavior Analysis

Fantuzzo and Atkins (1992) observed that users of ABA have documented the range and effectiveness of these techniques for a variety of problems demonstrated by children and youth. Further, they identified several factors that make schools the perfect setting for helping those who have academic and behavioral difficulties. First, teachers have access to students for several hours each day, five days a week, 40 weeks a year. Second, teachers also have access to norms for acceptable performance in that they work with students who have acceptable academic and behavior skills. Third, the typical school day provides many opportunities for teachers to note student strengths and weaknesses in a variety of academic and social situations. Despite the availability of these techniques and their suitability for use in the classroom, Fantuzzo and Atkins (1992) noted that ABA techniques are used inconsistently by teachers and have been subjected to much criticism. As with any method or material, you should be aware of these criticisms and be prepared to address them with a colleague or parent. The following discussion identifies common criticisms of ABA and offers suggestions for responding to them.

Teachers Have No Right to Control Behavior

Some people argue that an individual has a free will that allows him or her to choose how to behave. Therefore, use of applied behavior analysis to change an individual's behavior is a violation of his or her free will. However, as Smith (1993) pointed out, users of ABA are not alone in their efforts to control the behavior of other people. Advertising executives design campaigns to influence the choices we make at the supermarket, the movie theater, and the car showroom. Politicians carefully craft their speeches to influence our behavior on election day. Smith noted that users of applied behavior analysis may be more susceptible to criticism because ABA is a systematic approach that targets behavior displayed by a specific individual. However, teachers try every day to change specific student behavior. As Martin and Pear (1996) suggested, changing a student's behavior is a primary goal of education. As teachers, we assume the responsibility for developing in our students those behaviors needed to succeed in the world. For example, one of our basic responsibilities is to teach a child to read, a form of behavior change that few would challenge.

On a related note, the concept of free will implies that an individual has a menu of behaviors from which he or she can choose a response. For example, when criticized, you can choose to apologize if the complaint is warranted, defend an action by arguing its appropriateness, or ignore the comment altogether. An individual with few alternatives may have no choice when responding to criticism. We know a young man who became highly physically aggressive when criticized. Because he was unable to respond appropriately and predictably, the young man was confined to a mental health facility. Some may argue that he chose to become aggressive; however, we maintain that aggression was his only choice, a choice that severely limited his ability to function in the community. A person with limited options is not free. As teachers, it is our responsibility to expand our students' repertoires of academic and social behaviors so that they can choose appropriate responses that enhance their standing in the community.

ABA Employs Dangerous Techniques

As mentioned in our discussion of behavior modification, the use of techniques such as time-out has aroused concern among the general public. Some people are concerned with the way in which a technique is used, while others question whether some techniques should be used at all.

The possibility that a technique is being misused should be of deep concern to all of us. We believe you should make it clear, when discussing this issue, that a technique has been selected only after careful consideration of several factors (e.g., the student's age, the severity and longevity of the problem, the nature of previous efforts to solve it, and the effectiveness of the technique in solving similar problems). In addition, you should point out that use of the technique will be monitored and evaluated.

You can make similar points when discussing the use of a specific technique with a parent or colleague. Of particular concern to parents and colleagues are techniques to decrease behaviors, or punishers. Some people maintain that punishment has no place in the public schools. You can reassure them by pointing out that techniques generally perceived as punishment vary in their intensity. For example, a teacher reprimand is generally sufficient to stop many undesirable student behaviors. It is unlikely that anyone would argue this form of punishment has no place in the classroom. Other stronger punishments are available, but their use is warranted only after careful consideration of factors mentioned previously. The strongest forms of punishment are used in extreme situations with a very small group of individuals whose problem behaviors are health- or life-threatening. In all situations, you should describe how more positive strategies are being used simultaneously, identify specific guidelines being followed to guarantee the student's safety, and ensure that punishment techniques will be faded as soon as possible.

The Behaviors Changed Are Not in the Students' Best Interests

Winett and Winkler (1972) argued that the best interests of students are not always the primary consideration when selecting behaviors to be changed. We may have as our top priority the elimination of behaviors that make our professional lives difficult and interfere with the daily management of classrooms. Our efforts result in a group of children who are "being forced to spend almost their whole day not being children, but being quiet, docile, and obedient 'young adults'" (p. 500). In a rebuttal, O'Leary (1972) pointed out that Winett and Winkler's (1972) conclusions were based on a small number of studies from a single journal. He reviewed these studies and concluded that applied behavior analysis techniques had been used to reduce disruptive behaviors of some students, behavior that impeded either their performance or that of their peers. O'Leary (1972) cited additional studies in which use of ABA techniques enhanced desirable behaviors such as academic skills, spontaneous speech, and social skills. In summary, the use of applied behavior analysis helped teachers reduce or eliminate inappropriate behavior and increase behaviors that allowed students to learn essential skills. Teachers could spend less time disciplining and students could spend more time learning.

It is important to remember that the behavior targeted for change should be for the student's good, not your convenience. Weiss (1990) offered the following criteria that can help you decide if a behavior should be changed.

1. Is the student's behavior currently or potentially dangerous?
2. Does the behavior interfere with the student's ability to learn essential skills?
3. Does the behavior limit the student's ability to participate in other activities?
4. Does the behavior limit integration into the community?
5. As a result of this behavior, is the student more dependent on other people?
6. Is medication or another restrictive measure necessary to manage the behavior?
7. Do other people agree that this behavior should be changed?

Teachers Are Bribing Students

Some people have described ABA techniques such as primary reinforcement (e.g., edibles or tokens) as bribery. They maintain that students should behave themselves or complete certain tasks simply because they are the right things to do. If you are confronted with this argument, we suggest that your response include two points. First, by definition, bribery involves paying someone in advance to do something that is wrong or illegal. Edibles and tokens are used after a desired behavior has been demonstrated to increase the likelihood that it will occur again. They are comparable to the paychecks we receive from our employers for doing our jobs. As Smith (1993) noted, "all employees work for pay...but most would resent the implication that they are working for a bribe" (p. 279). Second, we agree that students should behave themselves and complete tasks because they are the right things to do and they enable students to acquire essential skills. With occasional reminders, most students will accomplish these goals; therefore, edibles and tokens are not required. Unfortunately, a small group of students, such as those who are very young or disabled, will require assistance in learning to behave and complete their work. In these instances, teachers can use edibles and tokens to enhance learning. You should point out that use of these techniques will be faded over time and replaced with events that occur naturally in the classroom. For example, edibles will be presented simultaneously with a smile. Eventually, the smile will be sufficient reward for a job well done.

The Language of ABA Is Unappealing

Not only do people object to some ABA techniques, some take exception to the terms we use to describe them. Axelrod (1992) pointed out that many of the terms used in ABA conflict with ideals espoused within the American culture. In a culture that values freedom and independence, use of terms such as "control, reinforcement, and punishment...[is] seen as coercive and controlling" (p. 31). We do not advocate that use of such terms be abandoned. As is true for any science, applied behavior analysis must have a vocabulary that allows its users to communicate in a precise manner. We encourage you to understand and use the language of applied behavior analysis correctly. When working with parents, colleagues, and paraprofessionals, we also recommend you carefully explain what you mean by these terms and provide examples. The phrase "time-out" will raise fewer eyebrows if you elaborate by saying, "If he teases his neighbor, William must sit in a study carrel for two minutes. He will be allowed to rejoin the group if he is in control of his behavior, offers an apology, and indicates he is ready to work." By using appropriate vocabulary to describe correctly implemented procedures, you can do much to dispel misperceptions about applied behavior analysis.

Changes Don't Carry Over

A great deal of time and effort may be invested in designing and implementing an ABA program to change a student's behavior. At first, the program may be successful; however, after a short time, the teacher may note that gains were not maintained, that is, the student reverted back to his or her old ways. Similarly, the teacher may observe that the gains demonstrated in one setting or with one adult did not occur in another setting or with another adult. Obviously, such outcomes are disappointing to the hardworking teacher. They also create the impression that ABA does not produce benefits that are long-lasting or that generalize to other settings or people. Two factors can account for these outcomes. First, in some cases, an expert other than the teacher has developed and implemented the ABA program. Having "made it happen," the expert leaves the teacher with the responsibility of "making it work" (Fantuzzo & Atkins, 1992, p. 39). Second, any intervention that does not consider at the outset how to ensure maintenance and generalization across settings was poorly planned in the first place.

We address these problems in several ways. First, the purpose of this book is to provide you with the information you need to use ABA techniques appropriately and effectively. Reading this text, completing a course in ABA, and participating in supervised activities will allow you to develop the skills you need to handle most of the academic and behavioral challenges you will encounter in the classroom. While a particularly unusual problem may require the assistance of an outside consultant, you should have the skills necessary to incorporate any program into your classroom. Second, throughout this text, we describe specific steps you can take to build in maintenance and generalization. For example, in Chapter 7, we describe how to change the frequency of a reinforcement program so that a student learns to behave for a longer period of time for fewer rewards. Finally, Chapters 14 and 15 present techniques that further promote maintenance and generalization.

Rather than undermining the use of these principles, critics have prompted ABA proponents to examine thoroughly the reasons they change certain behaviors. In addition, guidelines for selecting and using specific techniques have been developed, along with safeguards to ensure appropriate use. The purpose of this text is to assist you in acquiring the expertise to change student behavior and to use this knowledge ethically.

Ethical Use of Applied Behavior Analysis

Ethical use of techniques based on applied behavior analysis was implied in our responses to criticism. We believe you should change behaviors based on their importance to students and their families, and on their ability to increase a student's options in the community. We also believe that such techniques should be used only as long as necessary, at sufficient strength, and with appropriate safeguards.

Many authors have discussed ethical use of applied behavior analysis (Alberto & Troutman, 1995; Association for the Advancement of Behavior Therapy, 1987; McDonnell, 1993; Sajwaj, 1977; Van Houten et al., 1988). Chapters in this book in which behavior change techniques are described include measures that you can take to use applied behavior analysis responsibly and ethically; however, we believe these measures are so important that they warrant a separate, comprehensive discussion.

Clearly Identify Goals

The goals of an intervention program should be clearly identified, with the behavior you wish to increase or decrease described completely in objective and measurable terms. This precaution allows all interested parties to have a complete understanding of the behavior that will be changed. Such clarity also simplifies the evaluation process because it is easier to observe and record any changes in behavior. If you are planning to eliminate a behavior completely, it is essential that you identify what alternative behavior or skill the student will learn to demonstrate. For example, you may want to change the behavior of a student who throws a tantrum when teased by peers. As inappropriate and disruptive as the tantrum is, you may be targeting for elimination the only option the student has in his repertoire. If you don't teach him a more appropriate response to teasing, the student will likely display another equally unacceptable behavior, such as physically attacking his peers. Thus, your goal for this student should be twofold: to eliminate his tantrums and increase assertiveness.

We discussed earlier the importance of making sure the behavior being changed is "applied," that is, socially relevant or important. Wolf (1978) urged us to verify the social importance of goals with "significant others," that is, parents, colleagues, and, where possible, the student. You should ask other people concerned about the student's development if targeted goals are important and will make a difference (see Chapter 3).

Obtain Permission

The nature of the program you wish to implement may require more than just consulting significant others. For example, it may be your opinion that a child who displays a severe or long-standing problem such as self-abuse may benefit only from a complex program that includes positive reinforcement and punishment. It is extremely likely that you will need to obtain **informed consent** in writing prior to program implementation. Informed consent refers to the individual's ability to make informed decisions regarding any treatment or services he or she will receive. It requires that you explain to the individual the goals of the program you have designed and the techniques you plan to use. Most often, you will be working with children and youth, some of whom may not have the ability to understand this information and make a decision about participation (Smith, 1993). Therefore, you will need to obtain informed consent from the parents. You should share all aspects of the program with parents, including the behaviors you want to change, the techniques you will use, the rationale for their selection, safeguards, and a method for evaluation. Seeking parental input and permission is required for special education students by the **Individuals with Disabilities Education Act (IDEA)**, but it is also common sense. Parents who know, understand, and approve of their child's educational program maximize its success and minimize misunderstanding and misinformation. We will discuss this further in Chapter 16.

Be Competent

As a teacher, you will be responsible for the design, implementation, and evaluation of a behavior change program. To perform in an ethical and responsible manner, you should be competent in all aspects of program development and implementation. As we discussed earlier, techniques based on applied behavior analysis can be learned with relative ease by school personnel. However, we do not mean to suggest that mastery of these techniques can be accomplished with little effort on your part. On the contrary, you should use applied behavior analysis only after sufficient coursework that, at a very minimum, addresses: (a) conceptual issues, (b) techniques for increasing and decreasing behaviors, (c) rationale for selection, (d) safeguards, (e) design and evaluation, (f) fading to natural conditions, and (g) communicating with parents and other professionals. In addition, your first few attempts to use applied behavior analysis should be monitored by a colleague or supervisor to make sure you are using it correctly and ethically. Every chapter in this text contains information that will increase your competency.

Provide a Humane, Caring Learning Environment

We have to guarantee to our students and their parents that the educational environment is comfortable and safe. By an "educational environment," we mean both the classroom and the teacher who is managing it. The classroom should be a relaxed, nonthreatening place where students can participate in a variety of enjoyable activities. Similarly, you as the teacher should be warm, friendly, and nonjudgmental. Applied behavior analysis requires you to carry out some aspects of a behavior change program in an objective and efficient manner; however, that does not mean you should become a cold, unfeeling robot. Your students should perceive you as a person who encourages and praises, but who is also fair and consistent. Chapters 7 and 8 will assist you in achieving and maintaining this delicate balance.

Carefully Select ABA Techniques

Selection of an ABA technique or combination of techniques should reflect thorough consideration of several factors. We mentioned some of these previously, including the student's age, the severity and duration of the problem behavior, the nature of techniques already used, and the efficacy of this new technique in solving other, similar problems. There are other considerations. You should use a technique or a combination of techniques that is sufficiently strong to deal with the problem, but you should avoid overkill. For example, perhaps you can solve a student's problem by carefully combining positive reinforcement techniques. In this case, use of punishment procedures is unwarranted and a waste of valuable teacher time. When you select a technique, you should also make sure that it will be implemented within approved guidelines. For example, use of one form of time-out requires you to meet specific standards of safety. If you cannot adhere to these standards, then you should not use this technique. Information you need to select appropriate techniques will be presented in Chapter 9.

Prepare the Program in Advance

The behavior change program should be developed fully in writing in advance of implementation. Sections should include complete descriptions of goals and target behaviors, behavior change techniques, rationale for selection, safeguards, program evaluation, and fading. Advanced planning offers you many advantages. First, you can seek the input of parents and colleagues and obtain their permission. Second, thorough examination of the problem and its solution minimizes the need for on-the-spot decisions that may compromise the program's integrity. Third, written descriptions of how techniques will be used and who will use them reduces misuse and misunderstanding. Finally, complete program descriptions ensure that student safety has been considered. We will discuss home–school communication in Chapter 16.

Ensure Confidentiality and Maintain the Dignity of the Student

The behavior change program should be conducted in a confidential manner. Granted, other students will be aware of a program, as will colleagues who participate in your classroom. However, one student's problems are not fair game for discussion in the faculty lounge during lunch or with parents of other students during school conferences. In addition, implementation of a program should not result in public humiliation of the student. Even when reprimanding a student for inappropriate behavior, you can get your point across without subjecting the student to ridicule or exposing him or her to punishment that exceeds the crime.

These seven ethical considerations are listed in Table 1.3 on page 16. As Alberto and Troutman (1995) pointed out, it is important that we demonstrate ethical use of applied behavior analysis techniques in our classrooms. Although we should do so

TABLE 1.3   Ethical Considerations

Safe and effective use of applied behavior analysis requires that you adhere to the following guidelines:

1. **Clearly identify goals**—Make sure you select and describe completely socially important goals that increase the quality of your students' lives. Share these goals with significant others and ask for their input.

2. **Obtain permission**—Request permission from parents or guardians and your supervisor or administrator, particularly if you plan to decrease behaviors with techniques such as time-out or something more intrusive.

3. **Be competent**—Complete the coursework and practicum necessary to make sure you understand how to use applied behavior analytic techniques safely and effectively.

4. **Provide a humane, caring learning environment**—Make sure you are pleasant to work with and that your classroom is a safe, enjoyable place.

5. **Carefully select applied behavior analytic techniques**—Select a technique based on its appropriateness for the student's age and problem. Make sure your behavior change program rewards appropriate behavior, especially if you are using techniques to decrease inappropriate behavior.

6. **Prepare the program in advance**—Before implementing your program, describe it in writing in as much detail as possible. This step forces you to think of all the contingencies that may come up. Written descriptions can help minimize misunderstandings because they can be shared with parents and other school officials.

7. **Ensure confidentiality and maintain the dignity of the student**—A student's problems and your plans for managing them should not be discussed outside formal settings with individuals not directly involved. Similarly, using procedures should not make the student the object of ridicule and scorn.

primarily because we have the best interests of our students at heart, failure to behave ethically also encourages noneducators to obtain greater control over what happens in our classrooms.

Summary

The increasing amount of curricular material that must be addressed within the school day requires that you arrange and use classroom time efficiently and effectively. By creating and managing learning opportunities, you help your students acquire skills they need to participate fully and enjoyably in a complex society. One threat to the creation of a positive classroom environment is student misbehavior.

As a teacher, you have several options for addressing behavior problems and we briefly reviewed some of them. It is our opinion that of all the options presented, applied behavior analysis is most suited to the needs of teachers and students because it offers the largest number of proven techniques for handling the diverse problems students can demonstrate. However, using these techniques to change behavior requires sufficient study and supervised practice. Inadequate preparation leads to misunderstanding and misuse of applied behavior analysis. Therefore, the purpose of this text is to present you with the information you need to use applied behavior analysis effectively and safely with your students.

References

Adair, J. G., & Schneider, J. L. (1993). Banking on learning: An incentive system for adolescents in the resource room. *Teaching Exceptional Children, 25*(2), 30–34.

Alberto, P. A., & Troutman, A. C. (1995). *Applied behavior analysis for teachers* (4th ed.). Columbus, OH: Merrill.

Association for the Advancement of Behavior Therapy (1987). *Ethical issues for human services.* New York: Association for the Advancement of Behavior Therapy.

Axelrod, S. (1992). Disseminating an effective educational technology. *Journal of Applied Behavior Analysis, 25,* 31–35.

Baer, D. M., Wolf, M. M., & Risley, T. R. (1968). Some current dimensions of applied behavior analysis. *Journal of Applied Behavior Analysis, 1,* 91–97.

Bandura, A. (1965). Influence of model's reinforcement contingencies on the acquisition of imitative responses. *Journal of Personality and Social Psychology, 1,* 589–595.

Bandura, A. (1977). *Social learning theory.* Englewood Cliffs, NJ: Prentice-Hall.

Barry, T. D., & Geller, E. S. (1991). A single-subject approach to evaluating vehicle safety belt reminders: Back to basics. *Journal of Applied Behavior Analysis, 24,* 13–22.

Bay-Hinitz, A. K., Peterson, R. F., & Quilitch, H. R. (1994). Cooperative games: A way to modify aggressive and cooperative behaviors in young children. *Journal of Applied Behavior Analysis, 27,* 435–446.

Belfiore, P. J., Skinner, C. H., & Ferkins, M. A. (1995). Effects of response and trial repetition on sight-word training for students with learning disabilities. *Journal of Applied Behavior Analysis, 28,* 347–348.

Brigham, T. A., Meier, S. M., & Goodner, V. (1995). Increasing designated driving with a program of prompts and incentives. *Journal of Applied Behavior Analysis, 28,* 83–84.

Capone, A. M., Smith, M. A., & Schloss, P. J. (1988). Prompting play skills. *Teaching Exceptional Children, 21*(1), 54–56.

Davis, P. K., & Chittum, R. (1994). A group oriented contingency to increase leisure activities of adults with traumatic brain injury. *Journal of Applied Behavior Analysis, 27,* 553–554.

Fad, K. S., Ross, M., & Boston, J. (1995). We're better together: Using cooperative learning to teach social skills to young children. *Teaching Exceptional Children, 27*(4), 28–34.

Fantuzzo, J., & Atkins, M. (1992) Applied behavior analysis for educators: Teacher centered and classroom based. *Journal of Applied Behavior Analysis, 25,* 37–42.

Hobbs, N. (1966). Helping disturbed children. Psychological and ecological strategies. *American Psychologist, 2,* 1105–1115.

Hughes, C., & Rusch, F. R. (1989). Teaching supported employees with severe mental retardation to solve problems. *Journal of Applied Behavior Analysis, 22,* 365–372.

Mace, F., Hock, M. L., Lalli, J. S., West, B. J., Belfiore, P., Pinter, E., & Brown, D. K. (1988). Behavioral momentum in the treatment of noncompliance. *Journal of Applied Behavior Analysis, 21,* 123–141.

Martin, G., & Pear, J. (1996). *Behavior modification: What it is and how to use it* (5th ed.). Englewood Cliffs, NJ: Prentice-Hall.

Maslow, A. (1968) *Toward a psychology of being.* Princeton, NJ: Nostrand.

Mason, S. A., & Egel, L. (1995). What does Amy like: Using a mini-reinforcer assessment to increase student participation in instructional activities. *Teaching Exceptional Children, 28*(1), 42–45.

Matson, J. L., Sevin, J. A., Fridley, D., & Love, S. R. (1990). Increasing spontaneous language in three autistic children. *Journal of Applied Behavior Analysis, 23,* 227–233.

McDonnell, A. P. (1993). Ethical considerations in teaching compliance to individuals with mental retardation. *Education and Training in Mental Retardation, 28,* 3–12.

McDonnell, J., & Ferguson, B. (1989). A comparison of time delay and decreasing prompt hierarchy strategies in teaching banking skills to students with moderate handicaps. *Journal of Applied Behavior Analysis, 22,* 85–91.

McKelvey, J. L., Sisson, L. A., Van Hasselt, V. B., & Hersen, M. (1992). An approach to teaching self-dressing to a child with dual sensory impairment. *Teaching Exceptional Children, 25*(1), 12–15.

McSweeny, A. J. (1978). Effects of response cost on the behavior of a million persons: Charging for directory assistance in Cincinnati. *Journal of Applied Behavior Analysis, 11,* 47–52.

Morse, W. C., & Smith, J. M. (1980). *Understanding child variance.* Reston, VA: Council for Exceptional Children.

Neef, N. A., Shade, D., & Miller, M. S. (1994). Assessing influential dimensions of reinforcers on choice in students with serious emotional disturbance. *Journal of Applied Behavior Analysis, 27,* 575–583.

Newcomer, P. L. (1993). *Understanding and teaching emotionally disturbed children and adolescents* (2nd ed.). Austin, TX: PRO-ED.

O'Leary, K. D. (1972). Behavior modification in the classroom: A rejoinder to Winett and Winkler. *Journal of Applied Behavior Analysis, 15,* 505–511.

Pattavina, S., Bergstrom, T., Marchand-Martella, N. E., & Martella, R. C. (1992). Moving on: Learning to cross streets independently. *Teaching Exceptional Children, 25*(1), 32–35.

Pavlov, I. P. (1927). *Conditioned reflexes: An investigation of the psychological activity of the cerebral cortex.* New York: Dover.

Rapport, M. D., Murphy, A., Bailey, J. S. (1982). Ritalin vs. response cost in the control of hyperactive children: A within-subject comparison. *Journal of Applied Behavior Analysis, 15,* 205–216.

Rasing, E. J. (1993). Effects of a multifaceted training procedure on the social behaviors of hearing impaired children with severe language disabilities: A replication. *Journal of Applied Behavior Analysis, 26,* 405–406.

Repp, A. C., Felce, D., & Barton, L. E. (1988). Basing the treatment of stereotypic and self-injurious behavior on hypotheses of causes. *Journal of Applied Behavior Analysis, 21,* 281–289.

Richman, G. S., Reiss, M. L., Bauman, K. E., & Bailey, J. S. (1984). Teaching menstrual care to mentally retarded women: Acquisition, generalization, and maintenance. *Journal of Applied Behavior Analysis, 17,* 441–452.

Rogers, C. (1961). *Becoming a person: A therapist's view of psychotherapy.* Boston: Houghton Mifflin.

Sajwaj, T. (1977). Issues and implications of establishing guidelines for the use of behavioral techniques. *Journal of Applied Behavior Analysis, 10,* 531–540.

Schloss, P. J., Alexander, N., Horning, E., Parker, K., & Wright, B. (1993). Teaching meal preparation vocabulary and procedures to individuals with mental retardation. *Teaching Exceptional Children, 25*(3), 7–12.

Schloss, P. J., Alper, S., Watkins, C., Petrechko, L. (1995). I can cook! A template for teaching meal preparation skills. *Teaching Exceptional Children, 28*(4), 39–42.

Schloss, P. J., Smith, M. A., & Kiehl, W. (1986). Rec club: A community centered approach to recreational development for moderately retarded adults. *Education and Training of the Mentally Retarded, 21,* 282–288.

Schloss, P. J., Smith, M. A., Smaldino, S. E., Field, M., Tiffin, R., & Ramsey, D. K. (1983). Social learning of treatment of self-injurious behaviors of a hearing impaired youth. *Journal of Rehabilitation of the Deaf, 17*(2), 16–22.

Skinner, B. F. (1953). *Science and human behavior.* New York: Macmillan.

Smith, M. D. (1993). *Behavior modification of exceptional children and youth.* Boston: Andover Medical Publishers.

Sulzer-Azaroff, B., & Gillat, A. (1990). Trends in behavior analysis in education. *Journal of Applied Behavior Analysis, 23,* 491–495.

Switzer, E. B., Deal, T. E., & Bailey, J. S. (1977). The reduction of stealing in second graders using a group contingency. *Journal of Applied Behavior Analysis, 10,* 267–272.

Van Houten, R., Axelrod, S., Bailey, J. S., Favell, J. E., Foxx, R. M., Iwata, B. A., & Lovaas, O. I. (1988). The right to effective behavioral treatment. *Journal of Applied Behavior Analysis, 21,* 381–384.

Watson, J. B., & Rayner, R. (1920). Conditioned emotional reactions. *Journal of Experimental Psychology, 3,* 1–14.

Weiss, N. (1990). Positive behavioral programs. In J. F. Gardner & M. S. Chapman (Eds.), *Programming issues in developmental disabilities.* Baltimore: Paul H. Brookes.

White, A. G., & Bailey, J. S. (1990). Reducing the disruptive behaviors of physical education students with Sit and Watch. *Journal of Applied Behavior Analysis, 23,* 353–359.

Winett, R. A., & Winkler, R. C. (1972). Current behavior modification in the classroom: Be still, be quiet, be docile. *Journal of Applied Behavior Analysis, 5,* 499–504.

Wolf, M. M. (1978). Social validity: The case for subjective measurement or how behavior analysis is finding its heart. *Journal of Applied Behavior Analysis, 11,* 203–214.

2

THE BIG PICTURE

No doubt, you have been a guest at a big event such as a wedding, a 50th anniversary celebration, or a 100th birthday party and enjoyed yourself immensely. You probably noticed and complimented your hosts on the excellence of the food, the distinctiveness of the music, and the creativity of the decorations. However, you probably cannot truly understand the care and thought that goes into such an event until you have assumed full responsibility for planning every detail. Those who have arranged such occasions may emphasize the importance of beginning work well in advance of the big day: reading magazines and party planners; budgeting resources; and asking the opinions of friends, relatives, and professional consultants. Despite having made and verified arrangements, on the day of the big event the hosts may be so fraught with worry that they do not relax until the final guest has gone home. It is no wonder that some couples look back on their wedding day as one of the worst of their lives. Having organized an event of this magnitude, however, allows them to appreciate more fully the efforts of other people who have planned an enjoyable and memorable occasion.

Planning and implementing an applied behavior analysis (ABA) program also requires considerable thought and attention to detail. While a traditional wedding is a once-in-a-lifetime thing (we hope!), we believe teachers will have numerous opportunities to plan and implement applied behavior analysis programs during their professional careers. The purpose of this text is to assist you with this undertaking. Just as planning major social events requires coordination of many activities, so too does the formulation of an applied behavior analysis intervention. There are many factors that can increase the effectiveness of ABA; there are also many pitfalls that can weaken it. Knowing how to orchestrate these subtle features increases both the success of your program and your incentive to invest additional time and effort in subsequent endeavors.

When you are preparing students for a lesson, you may describe for them the sequence of activities they will complete. Providing such an advanced organizer helps students anticipate information and keeps them focused on important concepts. The purpose of this chapter is to serve as an advanced organizer for the wealth of information we will present in subsequent chapters. Here we will provide a sampling of some of the most important factors you should consider when using applied behavior analysis. We hope this preview will help you appreciate the complexities of this technology and will highlight the importance of carefully reading this text.

Developing an Applied Behavior Analysis Intervention

We will discuss procedures that will enable you to establish a classroom environment in which all students can learn the academic and behavioral skills they need to maximize their potential. This does not mean that your classroom will become highly regimented and austere; quite the contrary. Applied behavior analysis assists you in creating and maintaining an enjoyable setting in which your students can learn and grow.

The procedures we will describe can be used to address any of the problems you may encounter. We expect that most teachers will use these techniques to solve common classroom problems such as inattention, noncompliance, and verbal and physical aggression. Applied behavioral analysis can also be used to address more unusual behaviors demonstrated by a small percentage of individuals. In fact, one advantage of applied behavior analysis is that it has been used successfully with problem behaviors previously considered extremely difficult to treat (Morse & Smith, 1980). For example, some students with severe disabilities demonstrate self-injurious behaviors such as hitting, pinching, biting, and hair-pulling. Careful use of ABA techniques has dramatically decreased these behaviors and increased the use of skills that enhance the quality of life for these individuals.

Granted, the techniques used to address common behavior problems differ dramatically from those used to treat more serious problems. Nonetheless, the steps you follow in creating and implementing an ABA program are the same for all students, regardless of the exact nature of their difficulties. The sequence of steps we recommend you follow is presented in Table 2.1 on page 22. In the next sections, we provide an overview of each step in the order in which it occurs. Subsequent chapters in this book are devoted to each step in the sequence.

Selecting Goals and Objectives

The first two steps in the sequence focus teacher attention on the selection of goals and objectives for applied behavior analysis programs. We are confident that the terms *goal* and *objective* are not new to you. Goals are global expectations for behavior that are typically developed over a long period of time. They can be broken down into objectives, or short-term statements, that focus on the development of specific behaviors. For example, good citizenship is typically a goal for students. Objectives based on this goal include maintaining employment, paying taxes, and voting. (Actually, any of these objectives can be broken down further. Maintaining

TABLE 2.1   A Flowchart of the Steps in Developing Applied Behavior Analysis Interventions

Step 1   Select long-term goals and short-term objectives that have social validity.
a. Precisely define the behavior you think should be changed using measurable and observable terms.
b. Identify a technique for measuring how often or how long the behavior presently occurs.
c. Use the measurement technique to compare current levels of the student's performance to that of competent individuals.
d. Solicit the opinion of significant people in natural settings regarding goals.
e. Solicit the opinion of significant people in other settings regarding training procedures.
f. After training, ask if the level of improvement is acceptable.

Step 2   Develop behavioral objectives.
a. In addition to describing the target behavior in measurable, observable terms, specify conditions and criteria.
b. Identify excessive behaviors that must be reduced.
c. Identify deficit behaviors that must be increased.
d. Establish priorities.

Step 3   Select antecedent control techniques.
a. Identify and maintain factors that contribute to appropriate behavior.
b. Identify and eliminate factors that contribute to inappropriate behavior.
c. Fade to naturally occurring antecedents.

Step 4   Develop related personal characteristics.
a. Teach skills that increase students' ability to meet environmental demands.

Step 5   Develop consequence control.
a. Develop and clearly describe how appropriate behaviors will be reinforced.
b. Develop and clearly describe how inappropriate behaviors will be reduced.
c. Share your plan with significant others and obtain informed consent if necessary.
d. Fade to naturally occurring contingencies that occur at normal rates.

Step 6   Collect data.
a. Use the measuring system developed in Step 1 to record the level of student performance before and after implementing the ABA program.

Step 7   Graph data.
a. Convert raw table to a graph.

Step 8   Use a design.
a. Establish a functional relationship between the intervention procedures and changes in behavior.

Step 9   Plan generalization and maintenance.
a. Select generalization strategies for use before, during, and after an intervention.
b. Probe for generalization.

Step 10   Teach self-management.
a. Identify self-management strategies.
b. Teach self-management using established guidelines.

Step 11   Communicate with others.
a. Use formal and informal communication methods.

employment requires students to develop job skills and identify and obtain suitable work.)

Careful selection of the goals and objectives of an applied behavior analysis program is essential. Nothing else that follows will matter much if goals and objectives are inappropriate or poorly stated. For example, you may devote a great deal of time and energy to developing and implementing a program that teaches agricultural skills. It may be successful, but how useful is this goal in an urban setting? Similarly, you may teach students to read basic sight vocabulary words with 100 percent accuracy, but how acceptable is this criterion if it takes them two minutes to read each word?

Step 1: Ensure the Social Validity of Your Goals

While we want students to behave in school and complete their assignments, we also want to make sure that their daily and weekly efforts contribute to the mastery of long-term goals. Broadly defined goals of general education typically include the development of appropriate social, emotional, academic, and vocational characteristics (Schloss, Smith, & Schloss, 1995). Applied behavior analysis techniques can assist students in developing and retaining skills in each of these key areas. Skills targeted by ABA intervention programs should be immediately useful to students, yet ultimately contribute to their ability to live and work successfully in community settings. A comprehensive applied behavior analysis program can enhance student achievement of these goals only if we ensure the targeted skills are socially valid; that is, they are valued by society at large.

The first step in using applied behavior analysis is to make sure the problems the students demonstrate or the skills they lack are significant and will interfere with mastering goals valued by society. Of course, you are a member of society; you may also have several years of experience with children. Therefore, you may feel confident that your opinions regarding what is important or how well things should be done represent the prevailing beliefs of the community at large. Relying on the opinion of one person, however, could result in well-intentioned but misguided programming. Occasionally, you may have encountered a person whose idea of appropriate behavior or whose standards for acceptable performance were very different from yours. Idiosyncratic behaviors or standards may result in students appearing more out of place than they did prior to instruction.

There are different options for ensuring the social validity of the goals and objectives of an intervention program. We encourage you to exercise these options prior to implementing a program to ensure that its goals are worth the time and effort to attain. Options we will describe include social comparison, subjective evaluation, and procedure acceptability.

Step 2: Develop Behavioral Objectives

Having verified that student behavior is interfering with the development of socially important skills, your next step is to write objectives that precisely describe what students will be able to do after the intervention program has been implemented. Failure to write objectives, or objectives that are poorly written seriously undermine the use of applied behavior analysis. You cannot use a technique consistently if you do not know which behaviors should prompt it. Similarly, you cannot know when to discontinue the use of a technique if you are unsure of the performance level that indicates it is no longer necessary.

You are probably very familiar with behavioral objectives; perhaps you have written substantial numbers of them for academic lesson plans. If this is the case, then you are already aware of the importance of describing the conditions under which measurable, observable behaviors will occur and identifying the criteria that indicate mastery. You may be relieved that previous experience may reduce the amount of effort you have to put into this step; however, we must remind you that your earlier efforts may have focused exclusively on deficits in your students' *academic* skills. You will need to write objectives and develop interventions that address other areas of your students' *behavior*, both deficit and excessive. For example, you may write an objective for a student whose extremely withdrawn behavior suggests a social skill deficit. You may have another student who argues and uses obscene language with adults and peers. Obviously, these behaviors are excessive and should be reduced; however, they are probably the result of performance deficits in social skills and negotiating skills, or at least deficits in the motivation to use them. An objective targeting these deficits is appropriate.

An analysis of students' excessive and deficit behaviors may lead to the development of several objectives. Each of the objectives may be important and appropriate; however, implementing an intervention program to deal with all of them simultaneously is probably unfair. You may remember the frustration you felt on New Year's Day trying to keep all the resolutions you made on New Year's Eve. Therefore, it is essential to prioritize objectives and move systematically from one to the next as student improvement dictates.

Integrating Three Entry Points

Having written precise, socially important objectives, you are ready to move on to Step 3 in the development of an applied behavior analysis program. With Steps 3 through 5, focus your attention on the selection of techniques that will increase deficit behavior and decrease excess behavior demonstrated by your students. The suggestions offered in this text expand the work of Schloss (1984) and are a marked contrast to traditional methods for dealing with problem behaviors.

We will begin with an example. Perhaps when you were in high school, you behaved in some way that violated your math teacher's expectations. Perhaps you did not complete your homework. As a result, the teacher yelled at you, assigned more homework, and threatened to send a note home to your parents if you did not shape up. This outcome illustrates the traditional disciplinary model, which is presented in Figure 2.1. The traditional discipline model has only one entry point or one opportunity for teachers to change inappropriate student behaviors, specif-

Behavior ⟶ Aversive Consequences

Behavior that violates
the expectations of
the educator

Unpleasant condition
expected to deter the
future occurrence of
the behavior

FIGURE 2.1   The Traditional Discipline Model

In Schloss, P. J. (1984). *Social development of handicapped children and adolescents.*
Rockville, MD: Aspen. Reprinted by permission of PRO-ED, Inc.

ically, aversive consequences. The success of this model is measured by three outcomes: the problem behavior should occur less often, improvements should be noted in other settings, and they should continue to be noticeable over time. Your teacher's actions would have been considered successful if you never again forgot your math homework, if you began completing all assignments given by other teachers, and if you consistently turned in homework for the remainder of the school year. Although commonly used, the traditional discipline model has a major drawback: Teachers merely react to student behavior, which limits their ability to influence, refine, and shape desirable behaviors. Basically, teachers who rely on the traditional model put all their eggs in one basket. Table 2.2 presents other examples of how the traditional discipline model works.

In this text, we will describe a multifaceted model that includes three major entry points or opportunities for teachers to change student behaviors. This model is illustrated in Figure 2.2 on page 26. It includes antecedent control, related personal characteristics, and consequence control. You may note some similarities between the traditional model and the multifaceted model. Both models include students' behaviors and consequences. However, the consequences in the multifaceted model are broader, in that they can include pleasant events to increase behaviors. The multifaceted model also adds two more entry points which we believe give the teacher more influence over the nature of the target behavior students will display.

TABLE 2.2   Examples of the Traditional Discipline Model in Action

Behavior	Aversive Consequences
Max teases a classmate.	Max is reprimanded by the teacher.
Andrew swears on the playground.	Andrew is sent to the principal's office.
Stephen hits a classmate.	Stephen is sent to in-school suspension.
Bart is noncompliant.	Bart writes "I will listen to my teacher" on the board one hundred times.
Samantha throws food in the cafeteria.	Samantha is not allowed to eat in the cafeteria for a week.
Olivia is late for class.	Olivia stays after school.

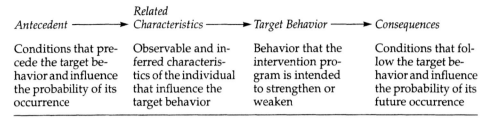

Antecedent	Related Characteristics	Target Behavior	Consequences
Conditions that precede the target behavior and influence the probability of its occurrence	Observable and inferred characteristics of the individual that influence the target behavior	Behavior that the intervention program is intended to strengthen or weaken	Conditions that follow the target behavior and influence the probability of its future occurrence

FIGURE 2.2   The Multifaceted Model

In Schloss, P. J. (1984). *Social development of handicapped children and adolescents*. Rockville, MD: Aspen. Reprinted by permission of PRO-ED, Inc.

We will use an example from medicine. Perhaps you have high blood pressure. A doctor putting all of his or her eggs in one basket may only write a prescription. (A worst-case scenario is the doctor who advises no special course of action and waits until you have a stroke to intervene.) This example is analogous to the traditional discipline model. Not satisfied with this course of action, you may see another doctor who, in addition to writing the same prescription, recommends a specific diet and regular exercise. This example is analogous to the multifaceted model. A variety of techniques are being combined to greatly reduce your risk of suffering the ill effects of high blood pressure. Table 2.3 provides examples of how the multifaceted model works in classrooms.

We cannot emphasize strongly enough the importance of using a powerful program that provides many avenues for bringing about change. There are two aspects of power that must be considered. First, teachers who use antecedent control have the power to influence behavior by removing factors that contribute to problems

TABLE 2.3   Examples of the Multifaceted Model in Action

Before an ABA program

Antecedent	Related Characteristics	Target Behavior	Consequences
William is teased by classmates.	William is immature and unable to ignore his peers.	William throws a tantrum.	William is reprimanded and sent to time-out. Peers are reprimanded.

After an ABA program

Antecedent	Related Characteristics	Target Behavior	Consequences
William is teased by classmates.	William counts to ten and finds something to do.	William remains on task, ignoring peers.	William finishes his work and is praised. Peers are reprimanded.

and presenting those that support appropriate alternatives. Similarly, teachers using related personal characteristics have the power to make substantial changes in students' repertoires of skill. The second aspect of power is concerned with the selection of specific techniques to enhance antecedent and consequence control and the development of related personal characteristics. Chronic, severe problems require powerful strategies; mild problems require less powerful strategies.

We strongly recommend that teachers address all three entry points when preparing to use applied behavior analysis. Omitting any one of them limits your power to deal effectively and efficiently with problem behaviors.

Step 3: Select Antecedent Control Techniques

Antecedent control is synonymous with prevention. Of the three entry points, it is the one most under the teacher's control. To use antecedent control, a teacher analyzes the environment and identifies those factors that contribute to appropriate and inappropriate student behavior. Those that enhance performance are retained; those that contribute to the occurrence of problems are eliminated. For example, perhaps the teacher notices that student misbehavior increases during unstructured time. Limiting the length of free time and requiring students to choose from a menu of carefully designed activities could reduce or eliminate inappropriate behavior.

It is possible that only one or a small number of your students are experiencing problems that require a special applied behavior analysis program. Knowing the power of a multifaceted approach, you establish antecedent control and make modifications to the classroom. Although you had only one or a few students in mind, any changes made will probably benefit everyone in your class. For example, developing and posting classroom rules make your expectations clear to all of your students, not just those directly involved in a behavior change program.

Finally, a tight antecedent control program may alter the frequency of both acceptable and unacceptable behavior to within tolerable levels. While this is a wonderful outcome, we strongly advise that sufficient attention be given to the other entry points. Just as it is inappropriate to rely solely on consequence control, it is not wise to rely solely on antecedent control to change behaviors. It has been our experience that students continue to test limits and that teachers should have a comprehensive package for dealing with challenging behaviors.

Step 4: Develop Related Personal Characteristics

As we stated earlier, a primary goal of education is to influence the development of positive social, emotional, academic, and vocational skills, which enhance our students' ability to control their own lives. Traditionally, teachers are always working on at least one related personal characteristic, specifically, academic skills. For example, teaching students how to read opens up tremendous opportunities for them. Students who can read can master the content areas more easily, advance to higher education, find suitable employment, and develop a wider variety of leisure skills.

Although it is no small undertaking, sole reliance on academic skills may be insufficient to deter the inappropriate behavior that gets some students into trouble. You may be familiar with some students whose academic skills are quite advanced, yet they have no friends. You may know other students for whom limited academic skills is the least of their problems. Perhaps they become withdrawn or verbally and physically aggressive at the slightest provocation. For these students, you will need to teach more diverse related personal characteristics, such as social skill training, systematic desensitization, and progressive muscle relaxation. The goal of teaching related personal characteristics is to equip students with the skills they need to effectively meet the demands of the environments in which they function and to avoid using behaviors that result in unpleasant consequences.

As is true for academic skills, students who are learning other related personal characteristics will need occasional reinforcement of their efforts. Other students who experience lapses in their ability to handle environmental demands will need to face the consequences of their actions. In either case, teachers must be prepared with adequate contingency management programs.

Step 5: Develop Consequence Control

This entry point is probably most frequently associated with applied behavior analysis. Certainly, there is an abundance of techniques available for teachers who need to reward appropriate student behaviors and decrease unacceptable responses. As suggested previously, consequence control techniques vary in the power they offer teachers. Desirable behaviors can be followed by something as innocuous as a smile or as powerful as food. Similarly, undesirable behaviors can be followed by something as mild as a quiet verbal reprimand or as powerful as overcorrection. The power of the technique used to reward or punish is a function of how new and strong a student's behavior is.

Some students simply need to increase their use of a newly acquired skill. Teachers have several options for strengthening these behaviors, including primary reinforcers, social reinforcers, token economies, and contingency contracts. Other students, however, need to decrease or eliminate use of unacceptable behaviors. Under such circumstances, teachers can use differential reinforcement, extinction, verbal reprimands, response cost systems, or the presentation of aversive consequences. As will be emphasized in subsequent chapters, a few cautions are in order. First, as we mentioned in Chapter 1, inappropriate application of some consequences has resulted in the establishment of specific guidelines governing their use. Teachers must be aware of these guidelines and plan accordingly. Second, the approval of parents or guardians may be necessary before using consequences for inappropriate behavior. Third, consequences should be used in combination with positive approaches. Obviously, teachers must be sensitive to the many subtle aspects of this entry point.

We offer one final note. As valuable as consequence control techniques are, we must remind you that, with few exceptions, they merely control or suppress behavior; they do not teach. This limitation emphasizes the importance of using a multifaceted approach when dealing with problem behaviors. Applied behavior analysis programs that integrate antecedent control, the teaching of related personal characteristics, and consequence control are much more powerful in producing and maintaining positive changes in student performance.

Evaluating the Effectiveness of ABA

Are you feeling a little overwhelmed yet? Actually, you are about at the halfway point in the sequence for developing an applied behavior management program. By now, we hope you have begun to appreciate the complex nature of the task. Having gotten a feel for the amount of work required, you will no doubt understand the importance of making sure all your time and effort have not been wasted. As we mentioned in Chapter 1, the term *applied behavior analysis* stipulates that we analyze the impact a program has had on student performance. The next three steps in the sequence satisfy this requirement.

Step 6: Collect Data

We return to the medical example discussed earlier. We argued that a multifaceted intervention program integrating medication, proper eating, and regular exercise would have a greater impact on high blood pressure than just the use of medication. There are several pieces of information we could use to support our claim. Proper eating and regular exercise will probably reduce weight as measured by a standard scale. Exercise will also change the results of a stress test. All three components should reduce blood pressure as measured by standard medical equipment. These data, coupled with anecdotal comments regarding general well-being, should provide ample support for the effectiveness of a program.

We also need data to evaluate the effectiveness of applied behavior analysis. We cannot rely on our subjective impressions of student performance because they are too easily influenced by factors such as mood, time of day, and memory. Therefore, the sixth step in the sequence of activities is to record student behaviors before, during, and after implementation of an applied behavior analysis intervention. Several options are available that vary according to the behavior they can measure, the accuracy of the information they supply, and the ease with which they are used by busy teachers engaged in all phases of instruction.

Step 7: Graph Data

The piles of data sheets you accumulated in Step 6 may contain the support you need for the efficacy of your program. However, scanning one sheet and comparing it to the next may not give you a true indication of what you have accomplished with your intervention program. Decisions regarding effectiveness are facilitated when teachers have a fast and easy way to organize and present their data. Graphs are probably the best format available.

Adhering to simple guidelines can make a graph extraordinarily helpful in showing both teachers and students how much progress has been made toward the mastery of an objective. These guidelines include suggestions for labeling behavior strength and teaching sessions, separating phases, and drawing data points. Completed graphs are essential for the decision you will make in Step 8 regarding the effectiveness of an intervention program.

Step 8: Use a Design

You have, no doubt, read many articles in professional journals that reported the results of empirical investigations. You may remember that prior to presenting the results, the authors discussed the design they followed that enabled them to draw conclusions about the effect of a treatment on a behavior. Many of these designs were suitable for use with large groups of participants. Applied behavior analysis can be used with large groups as well; however, the largest group of people most teachers are concerned about is the students in their classes. This circumstance does not excuse us from maintaining some degree of scientific rigor in our work with small populations; rather, it challenges us to identify other ways to document the effectiveness of our intervention programs.

Single-subject design methodology is the perfect solution because it is sensitive to the changes in behaviors that result from the use of ABA with small numbers of students. It allows us to rule out alternative explanations and draw conclusions about the relationship between our intervention program and subsequent changes in student performance.

Extending the Benefits of ABA

Another way to make sure our efforts to change student behavior have not been wasted is to document that positive changes continued over time and were noticed in the presence of different individuals in novel settings. Put simply, we are hoping that generalization has occurred. Most of you are familiar with students who forget an old skill the minute a new one is introduced or who think that skills learned in one situation have no bearing on the next. We know a student who was angry that his teacher deducted points on his science test for each term that was spelled incorrectly. He maintained that correct spelling had nothing to do with science!

We risk substantial waste of teacher, student, and financial resources if we do not take steps to ensure that improvements in behavior are stable and pervasive. In fact, as we noted in Chapter 1, the lack of generalization and maintenance is a major criticism of applied behavior analysis. Planning for generalization and maintenance is a relatively recent addition to the field of applied behavior analysis. Early efforts in the development of this technology were directed toward documenting its ability to influence behavior. More recent efforts have focused on extending the benefits. Measures for enhancing generalization and maintenance comprise the final three steps in our sequence.

Step 9: Plan Generalization and Maintenance

Let's go back to our medical example. Perhaps being overweight was one reason for your high blood pressure. Adhering to a low-calorie diet has resulted in weight loss and lower blood pressure. Having lost the weight, you want to make sure you keep it off. Although you no longer need to adhere to the low-calorie diet you were using, you cannot go back to your old eating habits. Instead, you develop a healthy diet that will allow you to maintain your current weight. Applied behavior analysis works the same way.

Just as you have planned your original intervention program, so too must you plan for continued use of newly acquired skills by your students. It would be a shame to see hard-won gains in student performance revert back to pretreatment levels. In Step 9 of the sequence, teachers are encouraged to identify and implement specific generalization strategies before, during, and after use of ABA. It is also necessary for teachers to assess the impact of the generalization strategies, just as they did for original intervention procedures.

Step 10: Teach Self-Management

In Step 10, you assume the responsibility for making sure students used newly acquired skills in all relevant settings. It might seem strange, but one of your goals as a teacher should be to teach your students to not need you anymore. No, you do not want to do yourself out of a job, but you do want to move on to other equally important curricular areas. It is easier to move on if you know that hard-won gains are still apparent in student behavior. The best way to accomplish this is to teach your students to manage their own behavior so that they continue to use their skills appropriately when you are not around.

Few of you have been systematically taught self-management skills. Despite the lack of formal training, you juggle your schedule so that you can manage many responsibilities at work and at home. Generally, you carry out these responsibilities with few reminders and, occasionally, have a few hours to enjoy some leisure activities. However, many students typically in need of ABA programs will also need to learn how to manage their own behavior. There are several self-management techniques you can choose from, and guidelines have been developed to ensure they are taught adequately.

Step 11: Communicate with Others

Another way to extend the benefits of an ABA intervention program is to publicize it. We are not suggesting you need to crank out a manuscript and submit it for publication in a professional journal. However, there are several individuals who would be interested in your efforts. You can use formal and informal methods to communicate relevant aspects of your work, particularly the purpose of your program, the specific procedures used, the results, and any recommendations. Practicing good communication skills keeps others informed of your work, and lets students know that different people now have the same expectations for behavior. It is also a great way to show how efficiently and effectively you have used existing resources. Finally, teachers are notorious pack rats, saving everything in the event it will be needed again sometime before retirement. A permanent description of your program will be extremely useful if you should encounter another student with similar characteristics.

Summary

Our intention was to provide you with an advanced organizer for subsequent chapters of the book. We hope that you have come to appreciate the complexity of the task undertaken by anyone developing an applied behavior analysis intervention. We also hope we have not discouraged you. Competent use of applied behavior analysis takes reading and practice but, when implemented correctly, it should offer substantial benefits to teachers and students. However, we cannot emphasize strongly enough that cutting corners, neglecting entry points, or eliminating steps in the sequence will undermine its effectiveness.

Now that we have given you a flavor for the complexities of ABA, it is time to begin. While many things are happening simultaneously in the real classroom, adequate preparation begins with one topic at at time. The following chapters provide detailed explanations of each of the steps listed in the sequence in Table 2.1.

References

Morse, W. C., & Smith, J. M. (1980). *Understanding child variance*. Reston, VA: Council for Exceptional Children.

Schloss, P. J. (1984). *Social development of handicapped children and adolescents*. Rockville, MD: Aspen.

Schloss, P. J., Smith, M. A., & Schloss, C. N. (1995). *Instructional methods for secondary students with learning and behavior problems*. Boston: Allyn and Bacon.

3

BEHAVIORAL OBJECTIVES

One student or many students in your class may be displaying a behavior that you think must be changed. For example, a student may be out of his seat so often that he fails to complete his work. In addition, his out-of-seat activities may distract his classmates, making it difficult for them to finish their assignments in a timely manner. Another student may not follow reasonable teacher directives. She always seems to be testing your authority. Two other students may get in fistfights frequently. Finally, many students in your class may fail to turn in homework that is accurate or on time. In all of these examples, the behaviors in need of change are clear. Having identified a behavior to change, you need to describe it in clear, unequivocal terms and make sure that it is "applied" or socially important. As discussed in Chapter 1, a concise description helps students, parents, and other school personnel understand exactly what behavior or skill is being targeted. In addition, a concise description makes subsequent behavior changes easier to measure, which is a valuable tool when evaluating the effectiveness of an intervention program.

There are two purposes of this chapter. The first purpose is to help you write clear, precise objectives for behavior change programs. You may be familiar with writing objectives for academic areas; procedures for writing objectives for behavior change programs are similar. We will distinguish between long-term goals, short-term objectives, and instructional objectives. We will identify essential features of instructional objectives and discuss them in detail. Several examples of objectives for increasing and decreasing classroom behaviors will be provided. The second purpose is to help you ensure that the goals you establish and the objectives you write have social importance—that is, social validity. We will discuss a rationale and several methods for selecting behaviors, standards, and procedures that make a difference in your students' quality of life.

Long-Term Goals versus Short-Term Objectives versus Instructional Objectives

Basically, an objective is a goal to be achieved by your students. Objectives can vary according to their specificity and the amount of time required for mastery. Long-term goals are very broadly stated and generally require an academic year to master. Goal areas usually correspond to subject matter such as reading, mathematics, and written language. As you shall see, they should also include increasing appropriate behaviors and decreasing inappropriate behaviors. Short-term objectives (STOs) are derived from goals and are completed in a much shorter time span that can range from two weeks to three months. Instructional or lesson plan objectives (LPOs), in turn, are derived from short-term objectives and can be mastered within a single lesson. As illustrated in Figure 3.1, goals, short-term objectives, and instructional objectives are strongly related.

A small number of long-term goals should generate several short-term objectives, which should suggest even more instructional objectives. For example, your long-term goal may be that your students will read at the third grade level. Short-term objectives based on this goal may include recognizing sight vocabulary; identifying unknown words through the use of phonics, structural analysis, and context clues; and comprehending written material at literal, inferential, and critical levels. Any one of these short-term objectives should suggest several instructional objectives. Phonics, for example, can be broken down into the rules for single initial and final consonants, short and long vowels, vowel digraphs, and consonant blends. Tables 3.1 on page 35 and 3.2 on page 36 present additional examples of goals, STOs, and LPOs.

You can also have long-term goals, short-term objectives, and instructional objectives that target social behaviors. You may have as your long-term goal the de-

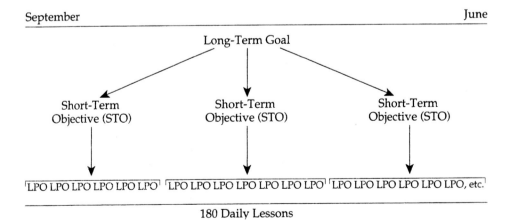

FIGURE 3.1   **The Relationship between Goals, Short-Term Objectives, and Instructional Objectives**

TABLE 3.1 **Examples of the Relationship between Long-Term Goals, Short-Term Objectives (STOs), and Lesson Plan Objectives (LPOs) for Academic Content**

Long-term goals drive short-term objectives that in turn drive lesson plan objectives. Examine the following example. See how specificity increases as the time to master them decreases.

Long-Term Goal	Short-Term Objective	Instructional Objective
Develop creative writing skills	Develop cursive writing skills	(a) Given a close point model, paper, and pencil, Jim will write *l, i, e,* and *t* in cursive with 100% legibility. (b) Given a close point model, paper, and pencil, Jim will write *u, v,* and *w* in cursive with 100% legibility. (c) etc.
	Use mechanics	(a) Given unpunctuated sentences, Jim will use a period, a question mark, and an exclamation point with 100% accuracy. (b) Given sentences without capital letters, Jim will capitalize the beginning of each sentence and all proper nouns with 100% accuracy. (c) etc.
	Improve content	(a) In a small-group setting and given a topic, Jim will identify orally two relevant ideas to write about. (b) In a small-group setting and given a list of ideas, Jim will organize a semantic map in writing. (c) Given a topic and a semantic map, Jim will write a paragraph that consists of a main sentence and two sentences containing supporting details. (d) etc.

velopment of appropriate social skills by your students. This goal can be broken down into short-term objectives that include initiating, maintaining, and terminating conversations; giving and receiving compliments and criticisms; and asking and answering questions. Instructional objectives can include complimenting peers or authority figures on their appearance, possessions, or unique skills.

For some students with more severe problems, you may find it necessary to decrease unacceptable behaviors. For example, you may have as your long-term goal the complete elimination of tantruming behavior. Short-term objectives may be focused on decreasing the length, frequency, and severity of tantrums. Because it is important to teach socially appropriate alternatives for unacceptable behavior, you may have as your instructional objectives that the student will learn to count to ten before saying or doing anything, to respond to criticism in socially appropriate ways, to ignore people who are bothering him, or to ask for help from an authority figure. At first, you may devote a lesson or a series of lessons solely to the

TABLE 3.2   **Examples of the Relationship between Long-Term Goals, Short-Term Objectives (STOs), and Lesson Plan Objectives (LPOs) for Behavior Management**

Long-Term Goal	Short-Term Objective	Instructional Objective
Increase time on task	Increase time on task during Sustained Silent Reading	(a) Given a reading task at her ability level, Cassandra will stay at her seat and read silently, keeping her eyes on the story for 10 minutes. She will orally summarize the main point correctly. (b) Given a reading task at her ability level, Cassandra will stay at her seat and read silently, keeping her eyes on the story for 15 minutes. She will orally answer two comprehension questions with 100% accuracy. (c) etc.

development of these skills. Subsequent lessons may have multiple objectives: those that focus on academic skills and those that focus on maintaining appropriate behavior.

You may already be familiar with these concepts, particularly if you are preparing for a career in special education. The Individuals with Disabilities Education Act (IDEA) guarantees that each student enrolled in special education will receive a free and appropriate public education (FAPE). One way to ensure the appropriateness of an educational program is the Individual Education Plan (IEP). This document is a contract between a school district and the student and his or her parents that, among other things, identifies long-term goals and short-term objectives. As you can see, identifying goals and objectives may not be just good teaching; it may be a legal necessity.

Features of an Instructional Objective

An instructional objective can target an academic skill such as reading or mathematics, an affective skill such as establishing friendships or expressing opinions tactfully, or a psychomotor skill such as keyboarding skills or athletic development. An objective is written correctly if it includes four features: student orientation, behavioral terminology, a criterion, and a statement of condition. Each of these features will be discussed separately.

Student Orientation

The first important feature of an objective is that it identifies a skill that will be performed by your students, not you. We have seen many lesson plans written by education majors in which the goal was "to teach fire safety" or "to review long and short vowels in one-syllable words." Such objectives are inappropriate because they are teacher-oriented, implying that the behavior could be more important to you than to your students. In keeping with the principles of applied behavior analysis, these objectives should be revised to clarify their importance and usefulness to students. "To teach fire safety" should be written "identify fire safety rules"; "to review long and short vowels" should be written "read aloud, correctly, words that contain long or short vowels"; "to teach homework completion" should be written "to turn in every homework assignment on time and completed with 90 percent accuracy."

Behavioral Terminology

The revisions we just suggested illustrate the second feature of an objective: It should be behavioral, clearly identifying how students will perform in measurable and observable terms. In the first chapter, we emphasized the importance of precisely describing behaviors we wish to change, and we provided examples of measurable, observable classroom behaviors. We should point out that some curricular areas are more easily described than others. Bloom (1956) recognized this difficulty when he developed the *Taxonomy of Educational Objectives*. Using the classification schemes for plants and animals as a model, he identified three domains of learning: cognitive, affective, and psychomotor (we alluded to these in the first paragraph in this section). Each domain included categories of objectives arranged in hierarchical order from simplest to most complex. For example, the cognitive domain emphasized intellectual outcomes and was broken up into knowledge, comprehension, application, analysis, synthesis, and evaluation. Finally, Bloom (1956) provided behavioral terms for each category of objectives.

Two points need to be made here. First, it is highly probable that objectives representing lower levels of cognitive ability are identified most easily by classroom teachers. For example, "reads aloud the first grade list of Dolch sight words" and "recites the multiplication tables" are objectives selected frequently for elementary students. We do not argue the importance of these skills; proficiency is essential if your students are to master more difficult material in subsequent lessons. It is because they are so easily identified and described that teachers may devote a majority of instructional time to knowledge-based skills and ignore those that require higher levels of cognition. Make sure you develop and implement lessons that enable your students to acquire competence at all levels of cognitive ability.

The second, related point is that even teachers who plan lessons to enhance all levels of cognition may neglect skills from the other two domains identified by Bloom (1956). Certainly appropriate lessons that incorporate relevant material will enhance your students' academic abilities and reduce the possibility that they will misbehave out of frustration or boredom. This is an antecedent control technique that we will discuss in detail in Chapter 4. Nonetheless, the psychomotor and affective domains include skills that are essential to your students' overall development. You should assume responsibility either for teaching these skills directly or for ensuring they are addressed by other school personnel. For example, the psychomotor domain includes gross and fine motor skills. The physical education teacher probably assumes most of the responsibility for this domain, although fine motor skills receive attention in penmanship and keyboarding lessons you develop or in drawing lessons planned by the art teacher. Similarly, the affective domain has been associated with the evaluation and appreciation of the fine arts. It also includes many of the skills emphasized in subsequent chapters of this text, such as social skills and self-management. By selecting and teaching skills that represent the full range of each domain, you increase your students' ability to participate successfully in home, school, work, and community settings.

As teachers, it is our responsibility to change cognitive, affective, and psychomotor skills to enhance the quality of our students' lives. For all students, "change" means "increase." For example, we will increase their competency in traditional curricular areas such as language, reading, and math. Most of us will also increase our students' cognitive awareness of topics such as substance abuse and sexuality, and provide them with the affective education necessary to make fully informed decisions about these issues. Finally, we will increase students' motor abilities through activities such as athletic events, art lessons, and dance instruction.

For some students, however, "change" will also mean "decrease." Behaviors students need to decrease are those that interfere with their development in other areas. For example, a student may overgeneralize the "*i* before *e*" rule and write "sceince" for "science" or "sciene" for "scene." Another student may be holding a pencil improperly, resulting in dark, thick strokes that rip the paper. In both instances, cognitive and psychomotor skills will be analyzed and errors eliminated so that the students will spell correctly and write legibly.

TABLE 3.3   **Appropriate Alternatives for Behaviors That Should Be Decreased**

Part of your responsibility as a teacher is to decrease or eliminate behaviors that interfere with a student's progress and to increase appropriate alternatives. You should be proficient at describing both undesirable behaviors and their desirable alternatives in measurable, observable, and repeatable terms. Compare the inappropriate behaviors listed in the first column with the appropriate behaviors listed in the second column.

Inappropriate Behaviors	Appropriate Alternatives
Bill calls out answers.	Bill raises his hand.
Ann takes objects that do not belong to her.	Ann requests permission to borrow items by using the owner's name, making her request, and saying "please."
Peter expresses his anger with peers by throwing breakable items.	Peter counts to ten, and then asks a peer to discuss a problem.
Mary cries each time she is given a teacher directive.	Mary follows one-step directions given by her teacher.

We believe that insufficient or inappropriate affective behaviors can be major impediments to student progress. Managing these affective behaviors is our primary concern in this book. Although we will demonstrate how cognitive and psychomotor skills can enhance your efforts, we will focus much attention on increasing affective behaviors that enhance student development and decreasing those that interfere. At this point, we simply want you to be aware that some student behaviors will need to be decreased or eliminated and suitable alternatives developed in their place. Therefore, your repertoire of behavioral terminology should include words that allow you to discuss increasing and decreasing behavior. Table 3.3 is a list of target behaviors that should be decreased and appropriate alternatives that can be increased.

Finally, we think it may be useful in some instances to refine further the terminology used in an objective by providing lists of inclusionary and exclusionary behaviors. Inclusionary behaviors are examples of the target behavior. Exclusionary behaviors do not reflect the target behavior. For example, the list of inclusionary behaviors that represent "engaging in cooperative play," a behavior we want to increase, contains playing a board or computer game with one or more peers and a one-on-one basketball match. The list of exclusionary behaviors contains playing solitaire and reading a book silently. Table 3.4 contains samples of inclusionary and exclusionary behaviors for swearing, a behavior we want to decrease.

TABLE 3.4 Objectives Containing Inclusionary and Exclusionary Behaviors

You can increase the precision of the terminology contained in instructional objectives by including samples of what does and does not exemplify the behavior you are changing. The following lists clarify what does and does not constitute swearing (White & Koorland, 1996).

Objective: During independent, small-group, or large-group activities in the classroom or on the school grounds, Andrew will not swear ever.

Swearing Includes	Swearing Excludes
1. Verbal assaults such as "F___ you," and "Go to h___."	1. Use of substitutes such as "darn," "shoot," "heck," etc.
2. Profanity or religious contemptuousness such as "Jes__ Chr__t!"	
3. An obscenity or word not permitted legally in certain contexts.	
4. Epithets or outbursts of anger such as "D___ it!"	
5. Scatology or verbalizations that refer to human excrement.	
6. Use of hand or finger gestures to convey any of the above.	

Criterion Level

The third feature of an objective is a criterion level, which specifically states how well a student must perform or behave. You should consider four factors when establishing a criterion. First, it can be stated in many different ways, depending on the exact nature of the skill being targeted. There are at least four types of criteria useful to teachers: percentages, steps or components, rate or frequency, and time. A percentage or level of accuracy is useful when developing academic skills. A series of steps or components that make up an acceptable answer is useful when learning an academic strategy and identifying responses within social settings. The rate or frequency of a behavior is particularly important when using applied behavior analysis. Typically, we want to increase behaviors that do not occur often enough or decrease those that occur too often. Finally, a criterion may involve time, in that a student should initiate or complete an activity within a certain interval. You may find it convenient to combine types of criteria when developing an objective. For example, a student may need to read aloud 44 first grade sight words with 100 percent accuracy in two minutes or less. Table 3.5 contains examples of criterion levels suitable for the variety of skills students must master.

Second, the criterion must reflect the importance of the skill. Basic skills such as math facts or sight word vocabulary should be mastered with 100 percent accuracy because students need them in order to learn other, more complex skills. We can be more flexible in other academic areas. For example, computerized spell checkers have reduced the need for students to spell with 100 percent accuracy; perhaps a criterion of 80 percent is more realistic. Just as some academic skills vary in their importance, so do affective skills. For example, you may be annoyed by a student who tries to get your attention by calling out rather than raising her hand. However, establishing a criterion of zero call-outs may be unrealistic because it does not allow for informal discussions, the natural exuberance of youth, or emergency situations. A reasonable criterion for this student may be no more than four call-outs per day. Other behaviors with more serious repercussions require stricter standards. For example, most people would agree that the classroom is not the place for highly aggressive behavior and would set the frequency of occurrence at zero.

The third factor to consider is the student's age. Objectives and criterion levels that are appropriate for one segment of the student population may be inappropriate for another. For example, a young child who destroys a textbook may be expected to apologize, but an older child would be expected to apologize and repair or replace the book. It is easier to identify appropriate criterion levels if you observe other students of comparable ages perform the skill in the natural environment. Such observations prevent you from establishing criterion levels that are either too high and frustrating for your students or too low and boring.

A fourth factor in criterion selection is what significant others in your students' lives believe or do. The criterion you specify may reflect your background and values; however, other people who know and interact with your students may not share your opinions or adhere to your standards. For example, perhaps you are

TABLE 3.5   Sample Criterion Levels

An instructional objective must identify a standard for students to meet so that you can be certain they have mastered the skill. Below are several examples of criterion statements. You can see how different types of criterion statements can be used to describe increases or decreases in student behavior across cognitive, affective, and psychomotor domains.

Percentage

After silently reading a passage from a fourth grade basal text, the student will orally answer comprehension questions with 90 percent accuracy.

Steps/Components

When requesting assistance, the student will

1. use an attention getter such as the person's name,
2. ask the question, and
3. use a social amenity such as "please."

Rate/Frequency

Given a computer, a word processing program, and a handwritten document, the student will type *with a minimum of 35 words per minute.*

During daily small- and large-group lessons, the student will decrease call-outs to *no more than three times a day.*

Time

During lunch and free play periods, the student will increase peer interaction time by one minute each.

After arrival at school, the student will hang up her coat, gather her materials, attend to personal needs, and be prepared to begin the scheduled morning activity *within 10 minutes.*

---

teaching students to respond to a compliment about a new article of clothing. You may think it is necessary both to say thank you and to extend the conversation by telling where and when the article was purchased. Colleagues and parents, however, may tell you they think this criterion is overkill. Further, you may notice that students whose behavior you think is appropriate respond to compliments simply by saying "thanks." Selecting a criterion that is too high or elaborate wastes valuable teacher and student time. We encourage you to verify your criterion selection by asking other people their opinions or watching what they do. We will elaborate on these ideas later in this chapter.

Condition

The fourth feature of an objective is a statement of the conditions under which the behavior will be performed. The condition statement identifies any and all material or resources to which the student will have access or circumstances to which he or she will be exposed. Conditions can describe academic, affective, or psychomotor skills. For example, "Given a dictionary and a list of vocabulary words..." is an appropriate condition statement for developing dictionary skills. "Given a paper, pencil, and a word followed by a sentence..." is appropriate for a spelling test. Affective objectives targeting social skill development can begin with "When greeted by a peer..." or "When an adult denies a request...." A psychomotor objective for handwriting could begin "Given ¾-inch lined paper, a standard writing instrument, and a list of ten dictated sentences...."

A condition statement should reflect the age and ability level of a student. For example, we expect elementary students to master basic math facts with 100 percent accuracy. However, memorization may not be the most efficient use of the instructional time available to a secondary student in special education. In fact, he has probably tried and failed to memorize this information on several occasions. An objective for this student should begin with a condition such as "Given a calculator and a problem-solving activity...."

Having presented the components of objectives and discussed them in detail, we want to make sure you can recognize objectives that are correctly written and locate errors. Table 3.6 lists nine objectives. Examine them carefully and see if you can identify those written properly. Can you pinpoint and correct the errors?

Selecting Relevant and Reasonable Long-Term Goals, Short-Term Objectives, Lesson Plan Objectives, and Procedures

We hope the information in the previous section made you aware of the intricacies of developing goals and expanding them into short-term objectives and lesson plan objectives that are comprehensive and stated clearly. As we mentioned in Chapter 2, developing goals and objectives is just the first step in creating an ABA program. Although you may be starting to feel overwhelmed by this step, we need to offer one more point for your consideration. The four components for writing goals and objectives are not the only things you need to address. Equally important to the development of goals and objectives is the concept of social validity. *Social validity* was introduced by Wolf (1978), who defined it as the social significance of our goals, the social appropriateness of our procedures, and the social importance of their effects. In this section, we identify the components of social validity, and describe different techniques for ensuring that goals and objectives reflect this important concept.

Social Validity of Goals

The **social validity of our goals** is the most frequently assessed form of social validity. Basically, we are asking ourselves, "Are the goals of our educational program what society really wants?" Hawkins (1991) questioned the use of the term *social validity* because it suggests that society wants us to address and solve large-scale problems and solutions. Perhaps it does. As we noted in Chapter 1, state education

TABLE 3.6   Self-Check

Read each of the following instructional objectives. Decide if it is correctly written. If not, make any corrections you think are necessary.

1. At the end of the lesson, the student will write the spelling of 10 single-syllable words featuring the long *a* sound, with 80 percent accuracy.

   ____ The objective is written correctly.

   _✓_ The objective is written incorrectly and should be rewritten:

   _____

   _____

2. Given a calculator, a pencil, and a set of word problems, the teacher will explain and demonstrate a strategy for solving them, including all four steps each time.

   ____ The objective is written correctly.

   _✝_ The objective is written incorrectly and should be rewritten:

   _____

   _____

3. During lunch and snack times, the student will refrain from throwing food. She will eat, then properly dispose of leftovers, every day.

   ____ The objective is written correctly.

   ____ The objective is written incorrectly and should be rewritten:

   _____

   _____

4. When entering the classroom, the student will greet his teacher every morning.

   ____ The objective is written correctly.

   ____ The objective is written incorrectly and should be rewritten:

   _____

   _____

5. Given ¾-inch lined paper, a pencil, and 10 dictated sentences, the student will reproduce each sentence in cursive with 100 percent legibility.

   ____ The objective is written correctly.

   ____ The objective is written incorrectly and should be rewritten:

   _____

   _____

6. After viewing a videotape on recycling, the students will identify and discuss its main points. Each student will contribute at least one relevant comment.

   ____ The objective is written correctly.

   ____ The objective is written incorrectly and should be rewritten:

   _____

   _____

Continued

TABLE 3.6 *Continued*

7. Given a story written at the third grade level, the student will read silently with 90 percent comprehension.

    _____ The objective is written correctly.

    _____ The objective is written incorrectly and should be rewritten:

    _____

    _____

8. Given a story written at the third grade level, the student will read silently and answer five comprehension questions in writing with 80 percent accuracy.

    _____ The objective is written correctly.

    _____ The objective is written incorrectly and should be rewritten:

    _____

    _____

9. Given a list of instructional objectives, the student will judge the accuracy and completeness of each by identifying four essential features contained in each. Objectives written incorrectly will be rewritten in the appropriate format. The student will complete this task with 100 percent accuracy.

    _____ The objective is written correctly.

    _____ The objective is written incorrectly and should be rewritten:

    _____

    _____

Answers

1. Incorrect. You should have rewritten the condition statement to describe materials the student will have access to during the course of the lesson.

2. Incorrect. You should have rewritten the objective so that it has a student orientation.

3. Correct.

4. Incorrect. You should have rewritten the objective to clarify "greet." There are many ways to acknowledge a teacher in the morning, but not all of them are appropriate and acceptable.

5. Correct.

6. Correct.

7. Incorrect. You should have rewritten the objective so that "silent reading" is measurable and observable, perhaps by adding something about responding to oral comprehension questions.

8. Technically, this objective is correct because it does include all the components. However, a student who can silently read and comprehend may have difficulty with written expression. His comprehension may be evaluated as poor—not because he doesn't understand the passage but because he has limited written language skills. This objective could be rewritten so that the student answers five comprehension questions orally with 80 percent accuracy.

9. Correct. We hope you met the objective.

departments have expanded the traditional curriculum to include topics such as drug use and sexuality in the hope that heightened knowledge and awareness will enable students to make informed decisions. But teachers must deal with society one child at a time and, as Van Houten (cited in Geller, 1991) pointed out, what benefits one child will probably benefit society at large. For example, a student who learns about the negative effects of drug use is more likely to avoid using drugs, saving taxpayers the money necessary for a rehabilitation program. Similarly, just as one student benefits when she is taught to locate and maintain employment, so too do other members of society benefit as fewer tax dollars will be needed to support her in the future.

The question now arises: "Whom do we ask?" Schwartz and Baer (1991) recommended asking "direct" and "indirect" consumers (p. 193). Direct consumers are those individuals who receive our services; in our case, the students. Indirect consumers are persons who, by virtue of interacting with direct consumers, are affected by the behavior changed during an educational program or an intervention technique. In our case, indirect consumers include our students' family members and peers. We can also ask the opinions of members of the immediate community in which our students live, including those who interact regularly with direct and indirect consumers, such as the school bus driver and the cafeteria worker. Finally, we can poll members of the extended community, which includes people who probably do not know direct or indirect consumers but who live or work in the same area. Examples include employers and store managers.

Suppose you want to develop a social skills program. You know what you think is important, but you need to make sure your goals and expectations are valued by other people. You have limited time and money available for this program so you do not want to waste either by teaching skills that are not important. In keeping with Schwartz and Baer's (1991) suggestion, you should ask your students what kinds of problems they have and what they would like to learn. (Later, we will deal with responding to students who indicate they have no problems and therefore do not need to learn anything.) Next, ask your students' parents for their opinion about the way their children interact with other people and for ideas about improving behavior. Then, seek input from other people who see your students frequently, such as other teachers, the librarian, the bus driver, and the cafeteria worker. Finally, talk with clerks in a convenience store or the manager of a movie theater. They may not know your students, but they can offer insights into behavior they expect from children in a particular age group.

A related factor in the social validation of your goals is the standard established for students to achieve. In an earlier example, we discussed setting the criterion for accepting a compliment. The original idea was to teach students to say "thank you," then extend the conversation. Social validity requires that we make sure this is a reasonable standard to achieve. One way to validate this standard is to observe how competent students respond to compliments. If their response is a simple "thank you," the original criterion should be adjusted. Another way to ensure the social validity of the standards included in goals is to survey current or future environments in which students will participate. Perhaps you are preparing a student currently placed in a separate special education setting for an inclusive placement. In the special education class, you offer several verbal reminders regarding homework assignments. An observation in the general education setting indicates that the teacher merely makes notes of assignments in a corner of the blackboard. An objective targeting homework skills should reflect this difference in conditions.

We recognize that extensive measures such as observing people and other settings may be unnecessary in that the social importance of many skills is already widely recognized. No one disputes the importance of reading or managing money. However, these measures are warranted if the importance of goals and standards is less clear. Social validation of your goals and standards also reduces the amount of time and resources devoted either to teaching skills that are not important or to attaining an excessively high level of mastery. In addition, we suggested in Chapter 1 that you obtain permission to provide special or unique programming. Social validation of your goals and standards can make it easier for you to obtain that permission. Obviously, your students' parents or guardians can provide informed consent only after receiving a complete description of what your goals are, how they were established, and how their attainment will make a positive difference in their child's ability to function effectively in a community setting. Hawkins (1991) suggests asking parents to "imagine it is a year from now and this goal has been achieved. How much better is _____'s life, in terms of what she can do, how easy is life for her, how many pleasant things happen to her..." (p. 208).

We caution you to use feedback you receive from students, family members, and members of the community wisely and to make necessary adjustments in your goals and standards. Otherwise, respondents will wonder why you ever bothered to ask and why they ever bothered to answer (Schwartz & Baer, 1991).

We have one final point to make about the social validity of goals. Some respondents may indicate there is no problem to solve or skill to learn. Unfortunately, some individuals are not always right and do not always know or do what is good for them. Many of us would prefer not to wear seat belts because they are at times uncomfortable. We occasionally drive faster than dedicated state troopers prefer, to get where we are going sooner. Our students are similar. They would rather continue behaving in certain ways and not accept the challenge of acquiring information or learning skills that ultimately make life better and easier. This does not entitle us to bully students and their parents into accepting goals and participating in programs simply because we know what is good for them. To the contrary, we are obligated to explain to students and their parents the immediate and extended benefits of learning new skills (Schreibman, in Geller, 1991).

Social Validity of Procedures

Having established socially valid goals and standards, you will need to select and implement ABA techniques for facilitating student mastery. We are not jumping the gun by discussing these techniques now; Chapters 4 through 10 will provide you with the information you need to choose from among the many options available. At this point, we only want to point out that, just as goals and standards must be socially valid, so too must the procedures we use to change behaviors. Kazdin (1980) referred to this concept as *treatment acceptability*. In Chapter 1, we advised you to explain to students, parents, and other important individuals the exact nature of techniques to be used for increasing learning and changing behavior prior to their enactment. Despite your explanation, it is possible that students and parents still object to the educational program. Obviously, their response should concern you because students who do not like their educational program "may avoid it, or run away, or complain loudly" (Wolf, 1978, p. 206).

Social validity of procedures encourages you to go beyond mere explanations of the relationship between instructional procedures and subsequent changes in academic and affective behaviors. You must show how your instructional program will enable students to become more independent, mature, and self-confident; and demonstrate how your procedures will enhance the students' personal dignity and freedom (Bailey, in Geller, 1991).

Before your meeting with students and parents, make sure you have done your homework. Be familiar with the variety of techniques available, and make sure that you have selected those that have been proven effective either in the professional literature or through previous professional experience. During the meeting, discuss the advantages and limitations associated with any educational procedures you plan to use and identify how you will protect students from possible negative side effects. Include examples of how this technique worked in the past for other students with similar learning and behavior problems. Describe how you plan to evaluate the program and modify it in light of the results.

The concerns of students and parents are not the only ones you may need to address. School officials may express concern for an instructional program, either because of its nature or its expense. Of course, your choice of techniques should reflect district policies or you may face legal repercussions. Discussions with supervisors can include the points made in the meeting with students and parents. Objections to the expense of an instructional program can be addressed by pointing out that money and effort invested now may prevent the need for additional, more costly programming in the future.

We offer a final point. Just as people may believe a goal is irrelevant, so too they may object to an intervention program. You may feel inconvenienced by a daily regimen of moderate exercise and medication to lower your blood pressure, but that "inconvenience" will probably contribute to a longer, happier life. Students and parents may judge as poor a program that ultimately succeeds. Hawkins (1991) cautioned that a student's or parent's opinion is not a sufficient condition for social validation; it is merely a second opinion from another viewpoint. You are advised, however, to listen to students and parents, and to incorporate their suggestions for making a program more humane and acceptable.

Social Validity of Effects

Hopefully, socially acceptable procedures have enabled students to achieve socially valid goals and procedures. It is not sufficient to point out that academic skills have improved and that acceptable behavior increased while unacceptable behavior decreased. **Social validity of effects** requires a demonstration that the results of our educational program increased the quality of our students' lives. For example, you may have reduced the duration of a 10-year-old student's tantruming behavior from two hours to ten minutes per week. Everyone will agree that this is a step in the right direction, but someone may ask if it is ever appropriate for a student that age to throw a tantrum.

Wolf (1978) identified two strategies for evaluating the social validity of the effects of an educational program. One strategy is **social comparison,** in which you compare the academic and behavioral gains made by your students to the levels demonstrated by competent peers. Perhaps you are working on increasing fluency or the number of words your students use in their creative writing. Ask another teacher if you may borrow samples of the writing produced by students in her class. Count the number of words per sample, average them, and compare them to the number produced by your students. This comparison is a measure of the social validity of the effects of your writing program.

Subjective evaluation is the second strategy for measuring the social validity of the effects of an instructional program. Sometimes, the importance of your effects is a matter of judgment that members of the community are qualified to make. You may find it unusual to ask your students and their parents how they like a program or whether or not a skill was useful to them. You, like Wolf (1978), may assume "Of course they like it. After all, we are doing it to them for their own good, aren't we? And even if they don't like it, we know what is best for them" (p. 206). However, the feedback you receive may provide information that enables you to improve your instruction.

You can ask parents, peers, or other teachers to rate student behavior before and after an instructional program is implemented. You will have more confidence in your findings if you use a rating device such as a Likert scale that has clearly defined points. Make sure you provide instructions that are free from bias so that raters do not anticipate your expectations.

We caution you that subjective evaluation can be abused. It is difficult to tell if your respondents are providing honest opinions. However, just because we know the system can be manipulated does not excuse us from gathering this information. We advise you to ensure that individuals providing subjective evaluations are guaranteed confidentiality. Use your professional judgment to make appropriate modifications to your instructional program. Subjective measurements are a supplement to objective evaluation, not a substitute. Evaluation of a program cannot rest solely on opinion; rather, you must document effectiveness by gathering information from objective sources.

Issues in Writing Instructional Objectives

Although we believe that socially valid instructional objectives are essential to change academic and affective behaviors effectively and efficiently, we recognize that the process of selecting and writing them may be challenging. Several objections to writing instructional objectives have emerged in the professional literature. We will discuss each objection briefly and offer a response that highlights the benefits of continuing this practice.

Writing Instructional Objectives Is Time-Consuming

We agree that appropriate instructional objectives take time to identify and define, particularly for beginning teachers. But at the risk of sounding trite, the more instructional objectives you write, the more skilled you become and the easier the task. Of course, we all know that teachers never throw anything away; so, after writing a series of objectives, file them away for future use as your students' needs dictate. Even as you are struggling to produce and perfect instructional objectives, remember the benefits they offer you and your students. First, instructional objectives help everyone (including colleagues, parents, and your students themselves) understand clearly what you want your students to do. Second, they identify clearly the standard your students must achieve to demonstrate mastery of the skill. Such specificity is extremely valuable when developing testing instruments. Third, instructional objectives that are carefully selected and well written assist with material selection (Mager, 1984). The condition statement included in your objective should suggest materials that should be available to students during the course of the lesson.

You may have access to computer programs that allow you to select from an extensive bank of objectives. Such programs are appealing because they include many curricular areas, and all the work appears to have been done for you. We advise you to use these programs with caution. Goals and objectives you select from these banks should reflect the standards we have discussed in this chapter. In addition, it is unlikely that even the most extensive program will provide objectives for all the cognitive, affective, and psychomotor behaviors you want to change. Such programs should allow you to modify existing objectives and develop new ones that meet your students' needs.

Not All Areas Are Easily Broken Down into Instructional Objectives

We admit that some curricular areas are more easily "operationalized" than others (a good example is written language). We described this situation earlier in our discussion of Bloom's taxonomy, where we noted that most teachers direct their efforts toward teaching skills that represent the lowest levels of the cognitive domain and frequently ignore higher-level cognitive skills or skills from the affective and psychomotor domains. Such a narrow focus on low-level skills is increasingly inappropriate as our ever-changing society demands more and more from its members. Similarly, deficits in the affective and psychomotor domains may pose major problems for some of our students. Ignoring these domains may undermine student progress and violate the concept of a free and appropriate education. We encourage you to expand the depth and breadth of the curricular areas you address during the school day. Continued practice makes you more skilled in writing instructional objectives suitable for all skill levels within each domain, particularly if you work cooperatively with colleagues.

Instructional Objectives Are Not Related to Teaching

Lovitt (1977) reported that one objection to writing instructional objectives was that they were not related to teaching. If you find that is still true, then you have not been reading very carefully! Each feature of a correctly written objective has direct bearing on the teaching process. The condition statement assists in the selection of appropriate instructional materials; the statement of behavior is student-focused and clearly identifies a socially relevant skill in measurable and observable terms; and finally, the criterion statement should suggest a method of evaluation. Surely, we can agree that materials, skills, and evaluation are directly related to teaching.

Instructional Objectives Impose Values

Lovitt (1977) also reported some concern that instructional objectives force the teacher's value system upon the students. Again, if you still believe this, then you need to reread the previous discussion of social validity. We emphasized the importance of making sure the goals and objectives you select are socially relevant and capable of making a difference in the lives of your students. We encouraged you both to discuss objectives with parents, your colleagues, and, when possible, your students; and to verify the appropriateness of the criterion by subjective evaluation or social comparison.

Some teachers may continue to argue that it is not appropriate to require a student to learn a skill or perform in a particular way simply because other members of the community do so. We are not advocating that all your students become replicas of each other. We are advising you to make sure that your students have the skills they need to function effectively in their community and that they are aware of the positive and negative ramifications of their choices. As discussed in Chapter 1, freedom of choice and human dignity are enjoyed by the student whose actions are the result of conscious decisions, rather than his or her inability to behave in any other way.

Errors in Writing Instructional Objectives

In this chapter, we discussed at length how to write instructional objectives correctly and have provided several examples. Despite our efforts, you will probably make some mistakes, particularly if you are writing objectives for the first time or if you are writing them for areas that are new to you. We have identified some common errors teachers make when writing instructional objectives. (We know because we have made them.) Keeping them in mind while you write may prevent you from making them.

Not Using Behavioral Terminology

It has been our experience that using nonbehavioral terminology is the error made most frequently when writing instructional objectives. Mager (1984) noticed that some objectives "have the appearance of objectives but contain no performances" (p. 89). He provided an example of such an objective in which the students were to "demonstrate a comprehension of the short-story form" (p. 89). The language contained in this objective does not describe anything that is measurable, observable, or repeatable. Make sure that the instructional objectives you develop clearly specify what your students will do by the end of the lesson.

Omitting a Feature

Occasionally, when reviewing lesson plans written by teachers, we have noticed that one of the four essential features of an instructional objective is missing. For one reason or another, the feature most likely to be omitted is either the condition statement or the criterion. At the beginning, you may find it helpful to always write instructional objectives in the same format: that is, the condition statement, followed by the behavior, and finally the criterion. This idea may be helpful until writing complete instructional objectives becomes second nature.

Using a Teacher Orientation

Some teachers make the mistake of writing an objective that describes what *they* will do, not what their students will do. Remember, the goal of your lesson should not be that you have taught a specific skill, but rather that your students have learned it.

Using a Vague Condition

Mager (1984) refers to this problem as a "false given" and illustrates it with an objective that begins, "Given three days of instruction…" (p. 90). Such a statement gives you no clue as to what materials the student will have access to or the conditions under which learning will occur. Make sure that the condition statements you write specify these important details.

Eliminating a Problem Behavior without Developing an Appropriate Alternative

Some of you will use the information presented in this text to address severe or long-standing behavior problems demonstrated by some of your students. While this is a commendable decision, we need to remind you about a point we made in Chapter 1. You cannot eliminate an inappropriate behavior without providing the student with the opportunity to develop appropriate alternatives. For example, we know a young man who used to bang his head against walls, desks, and other hard surfaces when school personnel would not comply with his wishes (e.g., a request for a soft drink in the middle of a reading lesson). Surprisingly enough, the individual did not appear to sustain any injuries during these episodes; however, this behavior was unacceptable and had to be eliminated. It occurred to us that head banging was the only way this young man could express his displeasure. Eliminating it without providing an appropriate substitute may have resulted in the development of other equally undesirable behaviors. We devised two sets of objectives: the first set dealt with the elimination of head banging and the second set focused on the development of social skills.

Not Writing Socially Valid Objectives

The instructional objectives you write could be absolutely perfect in the sense that they are written from your students' perspective and contain all the essential features. They could also be completely inappropriate in that they are focused on skills that do not reflect your students' ages, interests, or abilities. This problem is more likely to occur when you are working with older students. One of the authors of this text made that mistake early in her teaching career. She decided to work on multiplication and division of fractions with a 17-year-old student because the results of formal and informal math tests indicated deficits in these skills. She quickly realized that, with the exception of doubling a recipe, fractions were not as important to a student preparing to graduate as managing personal finances was. She then developed new instructional objectives that addressed handling bank accounts, using credit cards responsibly, and figuring out taxes. We again refer you to our earlier discussion of social validity, where we discussed the importance of developing skills that will make a qualitative difference in the lives of your students.

Writing Objectives That Lack Depth

We already discussed this problem when we noted that some teachers may write objectives only for lower-level skills such as knowledge and comprehension. Although we understand that it is easier to write objectives for such skills, we encourage you to consider skills that represent higher levels of functioning such as application, analysis, synthesis, and evaluation.

Writing Objectives That Lack Breadth

We also noted earlier that some teachers write objectives only for cognitive skills. Please remember that the affective and psychomotor domains contribute substantially to your students' overall development. Make sure their educational program balances skills from all three domains.

Writing Objectives with Mismatched Components

Item 8 in Table 3.6 illustrates a mismatch between the target behavior and the criterion. In this example, reading comprehension is assessed by performance on a writing task. This is an unfair assessment method because students who comprehend what they have read may be unable to express their knowledge in writing. A mismatch can also occur between the condition and the criterion. For example, a student who is given five sentences is required to punctuate them using a period, a question mark, or an exclamation point with 90 percent accuracy. This criterion is unattainable because there are only five sentences. Just one mistake reduces the student's score to 80 percent. For the sake of clarity, we discussed the components of short-term objectives and lesson plan objectives separately. However, you must consider how all four components work together.

Summary

In this chapter, we have distinguished between long-term goals, short-term objectives, and instructional objectives. We have presented the components you need to write objectives appropriately and have provided many examples. We also discussed in detail the concept of social validity and its implications for the selection of goals, objectives, standards, and procedures. Attention to the four components of writing objectives and to all facets of social validity will make goals and objectives comprehensive and appropriate. Finally, we have responded to several objections to instructional objectives and have identified ways to avoid the errors that occur when writing them. Armed with this information, you are ready to continue to the next step in developing a positive classroom environment. In the next chapter, we discuss antecedent control techniques that can enhance learning and can prevent many typical classroom problems from occurring.

References

Bloom, B. S. (1956). *Taxonomy of educational objectives*. New York: David McKay Associates.

Geller, E. S. (1991). Where's the validity in social validity? *Journal of Applied Behavior Analysis, 24*, 179–184.

Hawkins, R. P. (1991). Is social validity what we are interested in? Argument for a functional approach. *Journal of Applied Behavior Analysis, 24*, 205–213.

Kazdin, A. E. (1980). Acceptability of alternative treatments for deviant child behavior. *Journal of Applied Behavior Analysis, 13*, 259–273.

Lovitt, T. C. (1977). *In spite of my resistance, I've learned from children*. Columbus, OH: Merrill.

Mager, R. F. (1984). *Preparing instructional objectives*. Belmont, CA: Pittman.

Schwartz, I. S., & Baer, D. M. (1991). Social validity assessments: Is current practice state of the art? *Journal of Applied Behavior Analysis, 24*, 189–204.

White, R. B., & Koorland, M. A. (1996). Curses! What can we do about cursing? *Teaching Exceptional Children, 28*(4), 48–52.

Wolf, M. M. (1978). Social validity: The case for subjective evaluation or How applied behavior analysis is finding its heart. *Journal of Applied Behavior Analysis, 11*, 203–214.

4

USING ANTECEDENT CONTROL TECHNIQUES

Now that you have selected the skills you want your students to develop and have written them in a clear and concise format, your next task is to identify strategies you will use to teach them effectively and efficiently. You have at your disposal three sets of techniques. The first set includes antecedent control techniques, the focus of this chapter. Other sets include related personal characteristics and consequence control techniques, which will be presented in subsequent chapters. To facilitate comprehension, we are presenting these topics in separate chapters; however, you will find that an instructional program is more effective if techniques from each of the three sets are selected carefully and combined into a comprehensive package. As mentioned in Chapter 1, such a program simply gives you more "power" or options to assist students in overcoming learning and behavior problems. This philosophy is similar to the one you may have followed when trying to get into shape. A proper diet helps, and a good exercise program helps, but you will probably get faster results by combining proper nutrition and good exercise.

Antecedent Control Defined

An antecedent is an event that precedes a behavior and influences the probability that it will recur in the future. It can cue either appropriate or inappropriate behavior (Munk & Repp, 1994). Your task is to identify those events or antecedents present in your class that cue students either to learn or not learn, or to behave or misbehave. Obviously, you want to alter antecedents that lead to poor learning or inappropriate behavior and keep those that enable your students to progress toward academic and social goals.

Examples of Antecedents

Actually, we are all under the influence of antecedents. There are some things that most of us respond to uniformly. For example, a letter from the Internal Revenue Service questioning last year's tax return is very likely to put you in a terrible mood and send you scurrying for your receipts. As the day or hour of your appointment with the IRS approaches, others may notice that you are nervous, distracted, and short tempered. Other antecedents that prompt negative feelings and behaviors for most of us include receiving a traffic citation for speeding, overdrawing on a checking account, and arguing with a spouse.

Antecedents can also foster good moods and cue desirable behaviors. You will probably be in a very good mood if the IRS audit finds in your favor and the agent gives you a sizable refund check. Everyone at home and at work will probably notice that you are more pleasant and that you are getting more things done with fewer mistakes. Other antecedents that promote positive feelings and behaviors for most of us include winning the lottery, getting a raise or promotion, hearing about a snow day that closes down schools, and having a surprise party given in our honor.

In addition, each of us may have little "idiosyncracies," that is, little things that either annoy or please us that do not seem to affect other people the same way. For example, you may hate waiting in line at the grocery store, while someone else may use it as an opportunity to scan the headlines of all the scandal sheets. You may enjoy driving long distances because it gives you the chance to view beautiful scenery. Someone else may be willing to pay the expense of flying because he or she thinks long stretches behind the steering wheel are a waste of time.

Just as antecedents in our everyday environment affect us, there are antecedents particular to the classroom that affect our students and their performance. Your task is to identify and use those antecedents that promote student learning and minimize or eliminate those that interfere. There is a group of antecedent control techniques that we believe are predictable, that is, they will probably have the same effect on all of your students. Each of these techniques is discussed in detail in this chapter. We firmly believe that you should consider the impact of each technique on your students and make every effort to incorporate them into your classroom. The techniques should be used consistently. Not to do so, in our opinion, would constitute poor teaching that could undermine your students' chances for success. Things like schedules, classroom rules, and established routines should be events you plan for in your classroom, not things that evolve haphazardly.

Words of Caution

There is another set of antecedents that is less predictable, and as such, deserves special attention. While the techniques we will present shortly affect most students the same way, they do not account for every single antecedent that can influence all students' behavior or learning. Just as we adults have our idiosyncracies, some students also have unusual "triggers" that influence them to learn and behave in certain ways.

In Chapter 3, we mentioned a student who banged his head against hard surfaces when denied a request. Actually, the student reacted this way whenever we used "no," "not," "don't," "can't," "stop," or any word or phrase with a negative connotation. You can imagine the strain such reactions placed on his teachers and peers. His teacher developed a multistep program to assist the student in learning more appropriate behaviors. First, she assumed sole responsibility for teaching the student on a one-to-one basis. Second, she eliminated all negative words and phrases from her vocabulary. Naturally, the student no longer demonstrated head banging behavior, but did this constitute a "cure"? Not really. You see, although the student no longer banged his head, he was only interacting with one individual who granted his every wish. This situation was not only costly, but very unrealistic and unethical. Ultimately, we do the student no favor by creating an environment so dissimilar to the community in which he will eventually have to live. Fortunately, his teacher was aware of this problem. While assuming sole responsibility for instruction, she implemented a social skill program and relaxation training to help the student develop appropriate alternatives to aggression. She also developed a program of consequences to use when the student demonstrated inappropriate behavior. During the third step of the program, she alone used negative words and phrases. As you would predict, the student banged his head. The teacher implemented the consequences and, eventually, the student accepted negative words and phrases appropriately. Then other teachers began presenting lessons that involved the participation of other students. After some time, the student's head banging episodes were eliminated and the special program was faded.

We use this example to highlight two precautions you must take when addressing unusual and less predictable antecedents to a student's learning and behavior problems. First, while they must be controlled to some degree at the beginning of your intervention program, it is essential that they be dismantled as soon as possible in favor of the more traditional antecedent control techniques that prevail in your classroom. This precaution keeps you from maintaining a classroom environment that is unnecessarily restrictive. Second, this example highlights the importance of carefully combining techniques that address related personal characteristics and consequence control. These combined elements produced a much more effective and efficient instructional program.

Antecedent Control Techniques

As we mentioned earlier, several antecedent control techniques have a predictable effect on most students' learning and behavior (Schloss, Smith, & Schloss, 1995; Smith & Misra, 1992). These techniques are listed in Table 4.1, and we will describe and illustrate each one separately. We encourage you to examine your classroom and make sure these techniques are in place. If they are lacking, you may wish to incorporate them, especially in light of Schloss and Sedlak's (1986) evaluation of their importance; they referred to antecedent control as "prevention" (p. 179). We stated earlier that the power of an instructional program is increased by using antecedent control techniques in conjunction with the development of related personal characteristics and the use of consequence control techniques. While you may be prepared to use techniques from all three sets, you may find you do not have to because antecedent control techniques can prevent several learning and

TABLE 4.1   Predictable Antecedent Control Techniques

When evaluating your classroom or establishing a new one, you should make sure the following antecedent control techniques are present.

1. *Classroom rules.* A carefully selected list of rules and consequences helps students understand what will and will not be tolerated in the classroom.

2. *Classroom routines.* Telling students in advance how to handle simple academic and nonacademic routines increases their independence and reduces their need to interrupt you or their peers.

3. *A classroom schedule.* A well designed schedule ensures that important curricular areas receive sufficient attention and allows everyone to predict what will occur during the school day.

4. *Time management.* Consider how to increase allocated and engaged time and decrease transition time.

5. *Teacher–student interactions.* Positive teacher–student interactions foster mutual respect.

6. *Peer interactions.* Interactions with peers can be a positive influence on student performance.

7. *Modeling.* Arrange for students to model the appropriate behavior demonstrated by a peer they like and respect.

8. *Systematic instruction.* Careful selection and use of teaching procedures such as task analysis, shaping, and prompting reduce student boredom and frustration and motivate them to stay on task.

9. *Rate of success.* Avoid problems that result from boredom and frustration. Make sure you have taught important skills and have documented your students' level of mastery.

10. *Functional, age-appropriate activities and materials.* Such activities and materials make lessons more interesting and enhance students' ability to function in community settings.

11. *Review of the educational program.* This is particularly important for teachers of special-needs students who must make sure goals and objectives are appropriate and being mastered at the expected rate.

12. *Physical arrangement.* Carefully organize the physical layout of your classroom to encourage appropriate student behavior.

behavior problems from ever occurring. Obviously, it is more efficient to prevent a problem than to try to solve it after it has occurred.

Classroom Rules

You probably remember having rules in some or all of the classrooms in which you were a student. You may even remember what they were or that you contributed to their development or that you broke a few. A list of rules is still a good idea and can contribute to a positive classroom atmosphere, when properly developed and stated. The benefits include clearly established expectations for student behavior. Standards for behavior that have been discussed in advance help students understand what will and will not be tolerated in the classroom (Munk & Repp, 1994).

TABLE 4.2   Steps in Developing Classroom Rules

Follow these steps to ensure that the list of rules governing your classroom is fair and appropriate.

1. *Select a limited number of rules.* More than seven rules may be too many for your students to remember.

2. *Seek student input on the rules included on the list.* You may increase their commitment to following them.

3. *State classroom rules using clear, precise language.* This will help students to know exactly which behaviors are important.

4. *Accentuate the positive.* State rules positively to help students identify the acceptable behavior they should demonstrate.

5. *Establish consequences for rule infractions.* Consequences should be reasonable and planned in advance to ensure that fairness is not compromised because of anger.

6. *Teach rules.* Use standard instructional practices to teach rules. Provide examples of following and breaking rules.

7. *Post rules in a permanent place in an age-appropriate format.*

8. *Monitor adherence.* Reinforce students for following rules. Administer predetermined consequences to students who break the rules.

A list of rules also defines consequences clearly. Students who violate a rule will know in advance what the consequences of their actions will be. Properly constructed, rules also develop self-regulation, that is, students follow rules based on feelings of necessity for behavior and treating others in a certain way (DeVries & Zan, 1995–96).

Finally, a list of rules promotes a sense of fairness. Rules and consequences are established when everyone is feeling calm and relaxed. Should you have to implement consequences, you can do so matter-of-factly, knowing that you are not being mean, harsh, or overly demanding. (A student who claims otherwise can be reminded of this after a problem has been resolved.)

A list of appropriate rules does not develop by accident. It requires careful planning on your part prior to the arrival of your students or immediately at the beginning of school term. We suggest you follow the eight steps listed in Table 4.2 when establishing your list of classroom rules. They are elaborated on here.

Select a Limited Number of Rules

Different authors vary in their recommendations for the specific number of rules you should have. The number ranges from four (Shores, Gunter, Denny, & Jack, 1993) to seven (Schloss, Smith, & Schloss, 1995) although there is general consensus that the list should be short (Smith & Rivera, 1995). We recommend that you try to limit the number of rules to seven. Any more than seven may be more than your students can remember, particularly if they are young or disabled. This step requires that you examine carefully your expectations for student behavior and identify only those that are truly important. Additional sources for important rules include your supervisor or principal. Check with them to see if your school has any specific requirements regarding student behavior. For example, it may be school policy that all students walk in the halls or carry hall passes when traveling independently from one part of the building to another. If such policies exist, make sure they are reflected in your classroom rules.

You may think it particularly challenging to limit the number of rules to seven. One mistake we see teachers make is that they include rules that aren't really important. DeVries and Zan (1995–96) advised that rules be specific responses to real or potential problems in your classroom. You need to ask yourself what behaviors are essential to the day-to-day functioning of your classroom and develop rules accordingly. We also see statements that aren't really rules at all. For example, "everyone can learn" is a great philosophy but a poor rule. It can be displayed in your class as a motto but not as a rule. A third mistake we frequently see teachers making is that they develop several related rules. DeVries and Zan (1995–96) provided an excellent example of such a problem. A kindergarten teacher and her students devoted five rules to kicking, fighting, pinching, slapping, and hitting. After some thought, these five rules were consolidated into one rule about not hurting anyone. We recommend that you examine your list very carefully and eliminate any redundancies.

Seek Student Input on the Rules Included on the List
It may be possible for your students to contribute to the development of the rules for the classroom (Smith & Rivera, 1995). In fact, DeVries and Zan (1995–96) believe that involving students in the creation of rules is a powerful way to promote their ability to self-regulate. The extent of their involvement is up to you. Some teachers prefer to develop rules in advance and present them to students along with a rationale for their inclusion. The original list may be modified in light of discussion with students. Other teachers prefer to wait until school begins and develop rules as a group activity. This may prove to be an eye-opening experience. As strict as you think you are, you may find that your students can make up rules more rigid and consequences more severe than you ever imagined. Knowledge of your students' ages and abilities makes you the best judge of which path to follow. Some student input or discussion is desirable because it allows them to feel as though they have made a contribution to the list of rules they will have to obey. In addition, student involvement in the establishment of rules may increase their commitment to obeying them. They also show greater interest in enforcing rules among classmates (DeVries & Zan, 1995–96).

State Classroom Rules Using Clear, Precise Language
This step makes sure that students understand exactly what behavior is being described. You may have already learned that students are very good at finding exceptions to rules. We know a group of teachers who had established for all their classrooms the rule that students were to use polite language when talking to each other. Shortly thereafter, they overheard students saying things like, "You're such a four" and "You're acting like an eight." Confusion reigned until a teacher found a notebook left in the student lounge that listed numbers and their corresponding obscenity. (Sorry, we will not list these in table form!) Technically, the students had

not violated the letter of the law, just its spirit. Such problems may be avoided by a frequent review of clearly stated rules that includes a discussion of behaviors that do and do not constitute violations.

Accentuate the Positive
State rules positively so that students know what they are supposed to do (DeVries & Zan, 1995–96; Shores, Gunter, Denny, & Jack, 1993; Smith & Rivera, 1995). Unfortunately, many of our students already know what to do to get themselves in trouble; therefore, a rule should remind them of the appropriate alternative. For example, a rule such as "No shouting" could be rewritten "Use a quiet voice when talking in class."

Establish Consequences for Rule Infractions
Just as you identify rules early in the school year, you should identify consequences in advance of needing them (Shores, Gunter, Denny, & Jack, 1993). Already knowing how to respond to infractions keeps you from imposing harsher and potentially unfair penalties in the heat of the moment.

Teach Rules
It is not sufficient merely to establish a list of rules. To make sure your students understand and follow them, we recommend teaching rules just as you would teach any other academic material. You can begin on the first day of school (Prater, 1992).

Discussion should begin with the importance of rules and the identification of rules students already follow in other settings. For example, most students should be familiar with rules for crossing busy intersections and the rationale for following them. You can draw an analogy to the classroom, indicating that rules are also necessary in this setting to make sure everyone can learn in a safe and friendly environment. Next, either present each rule on your list or have students volunteer rules they think are important. Discuss the relative importance of each rule (remember, you want to keep your list at seven), ways to show it is being followed or broken, how it should be stated on your final list, and consequences for breaking it. End the discussion with a final review of the rules selected for inclusion on the list. This final review is not the last time students will see or discuss the rules. The rules should be reviewed frequently during the first week or so of the semester and occasionally during the remainder of the school year. The first day after an extended school break or the arrival of a new student in your class are perfect times to review rules.

Post Rules in a Permanent Place Using an Age-Appropriate Format
Rules should be on permanent display in an obvious place in your room so that you and your students can refer to them. We recommend reserving a bulletin board or a large section of a classroom wall for your rules.

Monitor Adherence
Finally, make sure you monitor how well your students follow the rules. A comprehensive, clearly stated list of rules contributes nothing to a positive classroom

atmosphere if you ignore infractions or do not act on them in the agreed-upon manner. Prater (1992) and Smith and Rivera (1995) advised teachers to attend to students who follow the rules, not just those who break them.

Classroom Routines

Another antecedent control technique that you can think about before the first day of school is the establishment of classroom routines, that is, procedures for handling regularly occurring events. For example, a student assigned a worksheet may have a question. Does he interrupt you if you are teaching another group? If so, how does he get your attention? Where does he put the worksheet when he is done? Establishing routines to handle such classroom events increases efficiency. Thinking about the solutions to problems before they occur helps your classroom run more smoothly and increases your students' ability to function more independently. The more your students are involved in these procedures, the less you need to be involved (Prater, 1992). Routines also help to reduce interruptions during important instructional time, increasing students' time-on-task (Prater, 1992).

There are two types of classroom routines for you to consider: academic and nonacademic. Academic routines are related to ongoing lessons and include tasks such as obtaining or returning books, worksheets, and other materials; and procedures for acquiring assistance during seatwork. Nonacademic routines contribute to the efficient management of your classroom but are not directly related to ongoing lessons. Examples include assigning and completing classroom chores, obtaining a hall pass or permission to go to the bathroom, collecting milk money, using free time, turning in homework, and borrowing books from the classroom library. You may come up with additional examples for each category after analyzing your needs and the needs of your students. You may not be able to anticipate all needs on the first day of school, but advanced planning for as many as possible minimizes confusion.

We suggest that you examine your expectations for your students when developing classroom routines. Although your goal for very young students may be that they increase their independence, it is unreasonable to expect them to carry out a large number of sophisticated routines. Start out with a small number of simple but important routines and build from there. Generally, your expectations can be higher for older students. Again, consider school-wide policies when establishing routines, such as the need for a hall pass when traveling in the building. Because it is impossible for us to identify the unique needs of your classroom, it is difficult to establish solid recommendations for creating and managing specific routines. Table 4.3 on page 62 presents some ideas for handling some of the routines discussed in this section, but they are only a springboard for further thought. We do recommend, however, that whatever routines you establish be taught and practiced just as systematically as rules and academic material. For example, perhaps the routine for obtaining assistance requires each student to have a cylindrical container, one-half of which is painted red and the other half is painted green. Teach your students to keep the green half on top until they are experiencing difficulty with an assignment. They can turn the container so that the red half is on top, but

TABLE 4.3   Ideas for Classroom Routines

While we cannot anticipate every routine you may need to establish your classroom, here are some ideas for younger and older students.

Classroom Need	Young Students	Older Students
Requesting help	Paint the top half of a cylinder red, the other half green. Students place the red portion on top when they need help.	Have a sign-up sheet
Getting a hall pass	Have a wooden pass with your name engraved on it	Students complete hall pass form with all but your signature
Chores	Assign to students on a rotating basis	Assign to students on a rotating basis
Book and material distribution	Make this a regularly assigned chore	Students are entirely responsible for their own materials
Milk money	Brought from home in labeled envelope and placed in specially marked box	(Not applicable)

they should also move on to the next question, item, or page until you are able to assist them (Prater, 1992).

A Classroom Schedule

The third antecedent control technique, the development of a classroom schedule, can also be food for thought prior to the first day of school. You may remember having a schedule of activities in classrooms you were in as a child. Even now, you may still write down tasks that must be done today or this week and feel a sense of accomplishment when crossing them off upon completion. A schedule can provide you and your students with the same sense of organization and accomplishment.

The importance of a classroom schedule has grown as demands on teacher time have increased. As Smith (1985) pointed out, a well organized classroom schedule offers two distinct benefits. First, it assists with the allocation of instruction time. Important curricular areas are given sufficient instructional time during the school day or week. Second, it enhances predictability because it allows the teacher, students, and other professionals to predict what will happen during a school day. Such organization and predictability may increase a student's motivation to participate in school activities and complete them at high rates of success. Smith (1985) suggested eight guidelines to develop an appropriate classroom schedule, which are included in Table 4.4 and discussed separately.

Seek Student Input

As with the establishment of rules, you may think it appropriate to get your students involved in the development of a class schedule. We advise you to consider two factors. First, you may not have complete control over the time some activities

TABLE 4.4   Guidelines for Schedule Development

Smith (1985) recommended the following guidelines to develop a schedule that will meet your needs and the needs of your students.

1. *Seek student input.* If possible, get students involved in the planning of their daily schedule. It may increase their commitment to their educational program.

2. *Display schedules in a permanent, prominent place.* A schedule should be in a format your students understand and readily available for a quick reference.

3. *Alternate activities.* Students may be more motivated to complete a difficult lesson if they know it will be followed by an activity or curricular area they enjoy.

4. *Be sensitive to the length of activities.* Younger and less able students will probably need shorter activities. Older, more sophisticated students should be able to work for longer periods of time.

5. *Avoid revising a schedule.* Adhering to your schedule as closely as possible maximizes its benefits.

6. *Reinforce student effort to complete the assigned tasks.* Students should be praised for how much they accomplished.

7. *Motivate students to participate.* Have fun, related activities preplanned in case you finish a lesson earlier than anticipated.

8. *Keep parents informed.* Sending a copy of the schedule home to parents keeps them more involved in their child's education.

Reprinted from Smith, M. A. (1985). Scheduling for success. *Perspectives for Teachers of the Hearing Impaired, 3*(3), 14–16. Reprinted by permission of *Perspectives in Education and Deafness.*

occur. For example, your supervisor or principal will probably inform you of the lunchroom schedule. Similarly, the speech therapist and the physical education teacher, by virtue of the number of students they serve, may have limited flexibility in their schedules. Because activities such as lunch, therapy, and physical education are nonnegotiable, you should write them in the correct time slot on a rough draft of the schedule so that students will know to work around them. Second, you should have a list of activities or curricular areas that must be included on the schedule. It should come as no surprise that if left to their own devices, some students may choose to eliminate completely from a schedule those activities or areas they find difficult to do. We will discuss a technique for handling this problem shortly.

Display Schedules in a Permanent, Prominent Place
As with rules, you must make sure that your class schedule is displayed permanently and prominently in your room. It is a reference tool that helps you and your students adequately prepare for and participate in the day's activities. Of course, the schedule's format must reflect the students' ages and abilities. We know a primary grade teacher who used a computer software program to generate pictures that represented each activity on the schedule. She pasted each picture to a large index card, then placed it in a slot chart with two other cards. One card bore the printed name of the activity; the other stated and illustrated the time it began. This format was ideal for young children learning to read and tell time. Elementary and

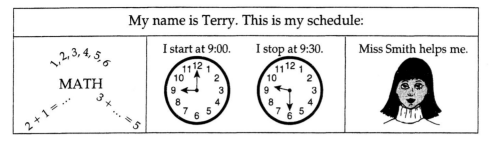

My name is Terry. This is my schedule:			
1, 2, 3, 4, 5, 6 MATH 2 + 1 = ··· 3 + ··· = 5	I start at 9:00.	I stop at 9:30.	Miss Smith helps me.

Name _____ Date _____

Schedule	Activity	AA	OT
8:30 – 9:00	_____	5	5
9:00 – 9:30	_____	5	5
9:30 – 10:00	_____	5	5
10:00 – 10:30	_____	5	5
10:30 – 11:00	_____	5	5
11:00 – 11:30	_____	5	5
11:30 – 12:00	_____	5	5
12:00 – 12:30	_____	5	5
12:30 – 1:00	_____	5	5
1:00 – 1:30	_____	5	5
1:30 – 2:00	_____	5	5
2:00 – 2:30	_____	5	5
2:30 – 3:00	_____	5	5

Total Points Earned ____ ____
Total Points Spent ____ ____
Points To Be Banked ____ ____

FIGURE 4.1   Schedules Can Vary in Format to Reflect the Students' Ages and Abilities

Reprinted from Smith, M. A. (1985). Scheduling for success. *Perspectives for Teachers of the Hearing Impaired, 3*(3), 14–16. Reprinted by permission of *Perspectives in Education and Deafness.*

intermediate level students may prefer a chart that lists each activity and the time it starts and stops. Teachers who are working with older students may simply have them keep their schedules taped inside notebooks. One school district we are familiar with requires all students to purchase and carry a notebook that includes a page for a schedule. Other formats are presented in Figure 4.1.

Alternate Activities
Premack (1959) suggested that individuals are more likely to engage in a less enjoyable activity if they know that it will be followed by something they enjoy do-

ing. You may have already noticed that you use this principle when planning a busy day. Perhaps you go to class, have lunch with friends, study at the library, watch a favorite daytime television show videotaped earlier, work out at the gym, and then have dinner and a quiet evening. Just as you alternate activities to get through the day, so too can students benefit from such an arrangement. Earlier, we mentioned that some students may not want to schedule any activity that is difficult for them. While you obviously cannot allow this to happen, you can suggest they "sandwich" something they do not enjoy between two more pleasant activities. This arrangement helps them stick with more difficult subject matter because they know it will be followed by an activity or subject they enjoy.

Be Sensitive to the Length of Activities

Just as the format of a schedule is sensitive to students, the length of an activity must also reflect their ages and abilities. If you work with younger or more disabled students, schedule activities in smaller blocks of time, perhaps no more than 20 or 30 minutes. Older students can be expected to participate in activities that last 45 or 50 minutes. If you think your students are not working long enough in a particular curricular area, you can conduct some social comparison by checking with teachers of other students and examining their schedules. Increasing time on a particular task may be added to your students' goals.

Avoid Revising a Schedule

We recognize that events such as snow days, field trips, teacher illness, personal time, fire drills, and assemblies are not easily predicted and are frequently unavoidable. Nonetheless, these events can be disruptive because they undermine your students' ability to predict what will happen during the day or week. Therefore, we encourage you to adhere to the schedule as closely as possible. Inform students of special events as soon as you can. The teacher we mentioned earlier was able to accommodate last-minute schedule changes simply by moving the index cards on the slot chart.

One word of caution is in order. Sometimes a student may use inappropriate behavior to escape or avoid activities that are difficult. Obviously, this is one situation for which it is desirable to have prepared in advance a consequence technique to manage the student's behavior. Once order has been restored, the student should resume the activity at the point of disruption and complete it. It would be ideal if all activities missed as a result of inappropriate behavior could be made up, but other teacher responsibilities may preclude such a measure. You may have to settle for the student's completing small portions of the work missed. The bottom line is that a student will learn that he or she has nothing to gain through misbehavior and that all scheduled activities will eventually be completed.

Reinforce Student Effort to Complete the Assigned Tasks

When teaching strategy courses, we strongly encourage preservice and inservice teachers to overplan, that is, to have more related activities prepared than they will probably have time for in a single lesson. It has been our experience that it is better to run out of time than to run out of things to do. As a result, it is likely that students will not finish everything even though they paid attention. Should this occur, we advise you to review and summarize points covered and reinforce student effort in addition to task completion.

Motivate Students to Participate

Despite careful planning, it just may happen that your lesson does not take as long to complete as you thought it would. It is a good idea to have planned in advance a number of activities that are related to the curricular area emphasized in your lesson. For example, you may have finished a lesson on basic subtraction skills earlier than anticipated. Give your students a ditto that requires them to solve basic addition and subtraction problems; the answers will be used to decode a secret message or color a picture. This is a fun activity that keeps your students working on the scheduled curricular area.

Keep Parents Informed

Once the classroom schedule has been developed, it can be copied and sent home to parents to keep them informed of classroom activities. You may wish to attach a copy of the schedule to the Individualized Education Plan of a student receiving special education services.

Time Management

Closely related to a schedule is time management. You have carefully divided the day and the week into time periods that will allow you to cover all the curricular areas for which you are responsible. Now you need to make sure that you adhere to the schedule as closely as possible so that you make efficient and effective use of your time with your students. Effective time management requires that you handle three major types of classroom time: allocated time, engaged time, and transition time.

Allocated Time

Allocated time is the amount of time you set aside for specific instructional activities and is a direct reflection of your classroom schedule. It is not surprising that there is a high correlation between the amount of time teachers allocate to instruction and the subsequent achievement demonstrated by their students (Prater, 1992). Obviously, the more time you spend teaching, the more your students will learn. We already mentioned that several unanticipated events can disrupt the schedule; however, you should try to adhere to it as closely as possible so that students have access to the instruction they need to achieve goals and objectives.

Engaged Time

Engaged time refers to the amount of time students are actually involved in the curricular activities specified on the schedule. Prater (1992) identified several teaching behaviors that can increase engaged time. First, she encouraged teachers to use specific signals to obtain student attention prior to beginning any lesson. In addition, student attention can be maintained by using an introduction to the lesson that is motivating, such as posing a problem or relating the lesson to students' immediate needs. Second, Prater (1992) recommended questioning students frequently during a lesson. Posing the question, then pausing, then calling on a student randomly keeps the entire class on its toes. We know several elementary teachers who keep on their desks a jar of popsicle sticks, each stick bearing the name of one student. They ask a question, pause, then draw a stick at random. Not knowing who will be called on motivates all of their students to think of an appropriate response or a correct answer. Third, Prater (1992) suggested that teachers scan the rooms frequently and establish eye contact with students. Such visual contact may keep students on task, even those doing independent assignments rather than participating in the teacher's lesson. Fourth, Prater (1992) encouraged teachers to have all of their materials and supplies ready before the lesson begins. We are familiar with a student teacher who realized, in the middle of a cooking lesson, that she didn't have any bowls handy and that a few of the key ingredients were missing. She lost valuable teaching minutes because she had to run to the Home Ec room, then recapture her students' attention upon her return. We advise you to get into the habit of not leaving school at the end of the day until you have everything ready for the next day. Fifth, Prater (1992) encouraged teachers to manage behavior effectively. Obviously, disruptions seriously undermine the amount of engaged time for the misbehaving student and his or her classmates. One of our goals in writing this book is to help you not only prevent disruptions, but to deal effectively with them should they occur.

Transition Time

Obviously, you need to move from one lesson to another several times a day. You may even have to move from one part of the school building to the next. Time devoted to getting materials or putting them away, lining up for lunch, or moving from one subject or room to another is called transition time. Transition time is unavoidable; most middle schools and high schools plan for it specifically by having a brief period during which students and teachers move to their next class. Smith and Rivera (1995) believe transition time within or between lessons can be minimized with careful planning. Prater's (1992) suggestion to have all materials and supplies ready in advance not only increases engaged time, but it also reduces transition time. Teachers who are prepared can move more quickly and smoothly from one lesson to the next. Another technique is to warn students of an impending transition. Keep your eye on the clock. Two minutes before the next scheduled activity is to begin, advise students that they have two minutes to finish what they are doing and get ready. Smith and Rivera (1995) recommended further that teachers tell students how a transition will be made. For example, students can line up by rows, from tallest to shortest, or by the color of the shirts or blouses. You should also make sure that your behavioral expectations are clear. For example, students are to stay in line and there should be no talking.

Teacher–Student Interactions

The four antecedent control activities we have presented so far were concerned with things you can begin working on before your students ever set foot in your classroom. With our discussion of teacher–student interaction, we begin to describe several antecedent control techniques that you will find helpful once your students have arrived and begin their instructional day.

You probably are pursuing a career in education because you find working with children and youth rewarding. You certainly want all of your students to like and enjoy working with you and eventually consider you their friend. Similarly, you begin the new year expecting to like each one of your students. Although things usually work out this way, you may find after a while that there are one or two students you cannot get along with, no matter how hard you try. This may be particularly true if the students in question have experienced frequent failure in their school careers. You may be bearing the brunt of their frustration with the entire education system. For these reasons, Schloss and Sedlack (1986) proposed six guidelines to enhance teacher–student interactions, which are listed in Table 4.5. Following their suggestions should increase your ability to communicate effectively with all of your students, not just those who seem to rub you the wrong way. With continued use of the guidelines, you will find that mutual respect has developed between you and your recalcitrant students; you may even find yourselves liking each other.

Show Respect for a Student's Age and Abilities

We know a young speech therapist who, in the final stages of her master's program, was assigned to work with an older gentleman who had suffered a stroke.

TABLE 4.5   Guidelines for Enhancing Teacher–Student Interactions

Schloss and Sedlak (1986) suggested six techniques for improving the quality of your interactions with students.

1. *Show respect for a student's age and abilities.* Use appropriate vocabulary, syntax, vocal inflections, and body language.
2. *Speak in concrete terms.* Avoid frequent references to past and future events that may confuse young or disabled students.
3. *Balance praise and criticism carefully.* Students need to know what they are doing right in addition to what behaviors they must change.
4. *Provide objective feedback.* Use clear, precise language when praising or criticizing. Students will know exactly which behaviors are acceptable and can be repeated. Similarly, the will know suitable alternatives to inappropriate behaviors.
5. *Encourage students to solve their own problems.* This measure increases your students' independence.
6. *Assist students who are unable to solve problems.* This measure helps students who continue to misbehave because they are currently unable to identify reasonable solutions to their problems.

He was left with very few expressive language skills and was temporarily confined to a wheelchair. Although he understood perfectly everything that was said to him, his ability to express himself orally was limited to "Uh-huh," accompanied by vigorous nodding of his head. Keep in mind that this gentleman was a well educated, highly respected, and visible member of the community, and, prior to his health problems, had earned a substantial salary. The speech clinician was observed greeting him in the following manner. She stooped over, looked him in the eye with a big smile, and, using vocal inflections reserved for a one-year-old, said, "Mr. _____! How are you? How is your wife? Are we ready to do some work?" While she may not have intended to do so, her questions, vocabulary, tone of voice, and stance suggested to all present that she had little respect for the gentleman's age and ability.

As teachers, we need to be aware of how our vocabulary, syntax, tone of voice, and body language affect our students. We need to use these features to communicate to students our acknowledgement of and respect for their age and ability. While you may find it necessary to modify your vocabulary and syntax to accommodate the language characteristics of some students, you can accomplish this without talking down to them. Students will resent and avoid teachers who use intonation patterns or body language that are more appropriate for younger children.

Speak in Concrete Terms

With very young or disabled children, you may find it necessary to avoid frequent references to past or future events. Generally, receptive language skills are better developed than expressive skills; that is, children will understand more than they can say. Use vocabulary and syntax slightly more sophisticated than the children are producing to discuss topics of current and concrete interest.

Balance Praise and Criticism Carefully

Obviously, children do not show up at the classroom door with all the skills they need to succeed. If they did, they would not need to attend school at all. It is your job to provide your students with opportunities to develop these skills, although not all will do so in a predictable manner. You need to praise their accomplishments and provide constructive criticism when they fall short. The danger lies in providing too little praise and too much criticism. Teacher–student interactions are enhanced when students perceive you as a warm and caring individual who knows and understands their strengths and weaknesses. We encourage you to praise student effort and accomplishment, and we offer guidelines for doing so in Chapter 7. We also advise you to balance carefully your use of praise and your use of criticism. Some students may have so many learning and behavior problems that trying to address them simultaneously would result in a constant barrage of criticism. Pick your battles. Select for immediate change a small number of behaviors that can make a difference in a student's life, and limit your criticism to times when these behaviors occur. As students improve, you can add more behaviors to the list.

Provide Objective Feedback

In Chapter 3, we discussed the importance of describing students' learning and behavior goals in measurable, observable terms. This allows everyone involved to have a clear understanding of what is being accomplished. Similarly, you should use clear, objective terminology when discussing strengths and weaknesses with students. As will be discussed in Chapter 7, praise should include the use of the student's name, a brief description of what was accomplished, and a compliment. Praise delivered in this manner clearly identifies what was done and increases the probability of a repeat performance. Critical comments should also include the student's name, a brief description of the problem, and either a request or a suggestion for an alternative behavior. Criticism delivered in this manner clearly identifies the student's mistake and asks for or offers suggestions for how performance can be improved.

Encourage Students to Solve Their Own Problems

We believe a good teacher teaches students to not need him or her anymore. One way to do this is to encourage students to identify solutions to their own problems. We alluded to this earlier when we suggested that, when criticizing, you ask students to identify alternatives to improve their performance. Students who develop their own solutions may assume more responsibility for changing their behavior.

Assist Students Who Are Unable to Solve Problems

Unfortunately, not all students are capable of identifying reasonable solutions to their problems and, left to their own devices, will either do nothing to improve performance or pursue options that are useless. For example, we know a teenager who, when she encountered academic difficulty, began to talk to God out loud. She told us she thought he could help her. Far be it from us to rule out divine intervention, but we did not think this technique would work on a regular basis. We suggested she read more attentively, complete her homework, and consult her teacher when needed. In similar instances, you may find it necessary to identify appropriate solutions for your students. Such occurrences should suggest to you the need to develop a student's related personal characteristics, an area that will be covered in Chapters 5 and 6.

Peer Interactions

Just as the quality of teacher–student interactions can prevent many learning and behavior problems, so too can interactions with peers influence your students' performance. You may already recognize the importance of this antecedent to student behavior. Perhaps you have witnessed the effect that one student in a bad mood has had on his peers. You may have noticed that it is not too long before other students are grumpy, complaining, and noncompliant. The moral is to take advantage of the appropriate behavior of the students in the class. Careful use of praise can encourage a student to use or maintain a positive attitude or an appropriate behavior. It may be infectious.

Peer interactions are particularly important to teachers involved with special education students. Interaction with nonhandicapped peers should occur as often as possible. In fact, the Individualized Education Plan requires teachers to identify how a student in special education will participate in activities designed for students in regular education. Such interaction is essential because it provides special-needs students with the opportunity to observe and learn from nonhandicapped students.

Modeling

We all have our heroes or idols—people we admire because of their convictions, actions, achievements, or appearance. Your students are also likely to have heroes or idols they imitate occasionally to enhance their own status. You can look around your classroom and probably identify the pop star currently in vogue simply by the way your students are dressed. Capitalize on your students' desire to imitate individuals they respect by using it to increase their desire and ability to demonstrate appropriate behavior. This antecedent control technique is called **modeling** and it can have a powerful effect on student behavior if you follow three guidelines. (In Chapter 5, we will discuss how modeling can be used as one component in a social skills intervention to enhance students' related personal characteristics.) First, make sure the student you want others to model is indeed someone they like and admire. The student you have in mind may be ideal by your standards, but that does not mean peers perceive him or her the same way. Second, make sure the student you select as a model is praised for appropriate behavior in the presence of others. This step allows other students to identify the rewards associated with specific behaviors. Finally, make sure your students are capable of performing the behavior being demonstrated by the model. Motivation to perform a skill is an essential but not sufficient condition for modeling to succeed. For example, wanting to turn in homework assignments does not mean a student has the skills necessary to complete them. This step requires you to have considered the influence of related personal characteristics on a student's ability to perform or behave. You may have to teach some skills prior to using modeling as an antecedent control technique.

Systematic Instruction

Rules, routines, schedules, and time allocation are antecedent control techniques that could be planned prior to the arrival of students. Teacher–student interactions, peer interactions, and modeling obviously require the presence of students, but they can occur throughout the instructional day. We now turn our attention to antecedent control techniques that you can address during instruction itself.

The eighth antecedent control technique is systematic instruction. Creating and teaching lessons that reflect student strengths and promote success can increase your students' academic repertoire and reduce the possibility that they will misbehave out of boredom and frustration. Systematic instruction is also a technique for enhancing related personal characteristics because through it students acquire new skills that enable them to respond to and manage their environment more effectively.

A number of teaching models are available to assist you in the development and implementation of systematic instruction. They include learning strategies, cooperative learning, and activities-based instruction. We have had a great deal of success using *Direct Instruction*. This model has been described as the direct measurement of a student's performance on a learning task and the accompanying arrangement of instructional programs and procedures for each child (Haring & Gentry, 1976). Over the years, several graphic representations of the sequence of activities based on Direct Instruction have emerged. Schloss and Sedlak (1986) incorporated them into the Sequence of Instructional Activities, which is presented in Figure 4.2.

As you can see, the second and third steps of this sequence require the identification of goals and objectives, areas already discussed in Chapter 3. The fourth step is designing instruction. It includes the selection of strategies that assist students in acquiring new skills. Several options are available to you. Each enhances your ability to provide systematic instruction because you teach students skills they need at a pace that will not frustrate or bore them. Three of these techniques are particularly relevant in the implementation of applied behavior analysis: task analysis, shaping, and prompting.

Task Analysis

Task analysis is the process of breaking down a complex behavior into its simplest components. Each component is demonstrated and discussed during a lesson or over a series of lessons. Students are provided ample opportunities to practice each component until they are able to perform the entire task unassisted.

Task analysis is more easily conducted in some domains than in others. For example, psychomotor tasks such as handwriting, dancing, and preparing a meal are easily broken down into several smaller steps. Table 4.6 on page 74 presents a task analysis for working at the register at a popular fast food restaurant. In keeping with our discussion of social validity in Chapter 3, we developed this task analysis by conducting several observations in a fast food restaurant.

Many skills from the cognitive domain can be task analyzed also. For example, if you inspected most basal reading series, you would probably find that the authors have listed several component skills necessary to master and use phonics. Many mathematics skills are also easily broken down, as illustrated by the task analysis for coin use presented in Table 4.7 on page 75. Other cognitive areas, such as writing an essay, and many affective skills are not as readily task analyzed.

Shaping

It is likely that learners who are very young or disabled may experience difficulty when learning new skills. You may have conducted a task analysis, but some students still may not learn at the rate you had anticipated. For these students, we suggest you try a technique called **shaping**, which is the process of reinforcing successive approximations of a skill until the student can perform it accurately each time. Shaping occurs frequently in our daily experiences. For example, parents may

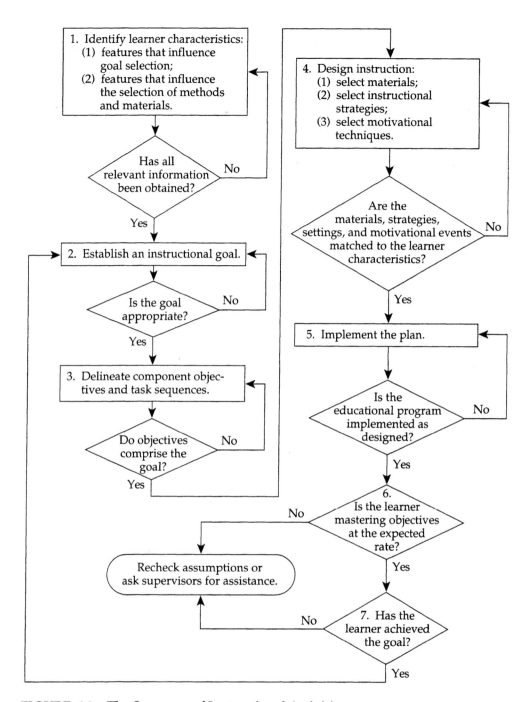

FIGURE 4.2   The Sequence of Instructional Activities

Adapted from P. J. Schloss and R. A. Sedlak, *Instructional Methods for Students with Learning and Behavioral Problems.* Copyright © 1986 by Allyn and Bacon. Used by permission.

TABLE 4.6   A Task Analysis for Working a Register at a Fast Food Restaurant

Skill

1. Stands in front of the register
2. Smiles at the customer
3. Greets the customer
4. Asks to take the customer's order
5. Describes an item upon customer request
6. Locates the item label, symbol, or price on the register
7. Presses the corresponding key
8. Suggests any special item
9. Repeats the order to the customer
10. Tallies the order
11. Asks "For here or to go?"
12. States the total cost and adds "please"
13. Gets a tray or bag of the appropriate size
14. Gets items in the following order: beverages, sandwich/breakfast items, cookies/pies, fries/hash browns, ice cream
15. Orders any special grill item
16. Places items on the tray or in the bag
17. Provides any condiments the customer requests
18. Obtains money from the customer
19. Counts the money given
20. Presses the corresponding register keys
21. Presses "amount tendered"
22. Places money into appropriate sections
23. Identifies change due to the customer by reading the register
24. Selects bills/coins that represent the correct change
25. Gives the change to the customer, identifying the amount
26. Presses "print" if the customer requests a receipt
27. Gives the tray/bag and any change to the customer
28. Thanks the customer and asks him or her to come again
29. If necessary, asks the customer to wait for a special order
30. Repeats Steps 1–29 with the next customer
31. Brings a special order to a customer
32. Thanks the customer for waiting
33. Assists other crew members when not busy

TABLE 4.7   A Task Analysis for Coin Use

1.0 Money Skills
    1.1 Identifies coins by name
        1.1.1 Identifies penny
        1.1.2 Identifies nickel
        1.1.3 Identifies dime
        1.1.4 Identifies quarter
        1.1.5 Identifies half-dollar
        1.1.6 Identifies silver dollar
    1.2 Identifies coin by value
        1.2.1 Identifies penny
        1.2.2 Identifies nickel
        1.2.3 Identifies dime
        1.2.4 Identifies quarter
        1.2.5 Identifies half-dollar
        1.2.6 Identifies silver dollar
    1.3 Identifies coins by head or tail
    1.4 Identifies value of groups of coins
        1.4.1 Identifies values up to 5 cents
        1.4.2 Identifies values up to 10 cents
        1.4.3 Identifies values up to 25 cents
        1.4.4 Identifies values up to 50 cents
        1.4.5 Identifies values up to 99 cents

accept unusual pronunciations of words, such as "poon" for "spoon" from their toddler. As their child grows, however, parents expect the child to say "spoon" and perhaps "please" before giving it to him. This example illustrates two essential components for shaping identified by Becker, Englemann, and Thomas (1975): differential reinforcement and shifting criterion. *Differential reinforcement* means that only behaviors meeting a certain standard are recognized and reinforced, while others not meeting that standard are ignored. A *shifting criterion* approaches the standard of acceptable behavior. In the previous example, parents originally accepted and reinforced "poon" but expected and rewarded more complex language as their child developed.

The following guidelines will increase the effectiveness of a shaping program.

1. State program objectives in clear and complete terms.
2. Identify clear and discrete approximations of the terminal objective.
3. Match the first approximation with the entry skill level of the student. Subsequent steps should be sufficiently small to ensure success, but sufficiently large to avoid boredom and wasted instructional time.
4. Identify prompting and reinforcing procedures (as described in Chapters 5 and 7) to be used in the shaping process. Whenever possible, use natural prompts and reinforcement.
5. Describe to the student in advance all procedures and the sequence of instruction.

6. Prompt and reinforce the target approximation on each occurrence.
7. Move to the next approximation only when the previous one is mastered.
8. Fade prompts and reinforcement once the overall objective is achieved.
9. Encourage the student to practice the new skill in a variety of settings.
10. If the shaping procedure is not effective, evaluate the appropriateness and strength of the prompt and reinforcement as well as the size of the criterion change.

Used appropriately, shaping can be a valuable teaching strategy. Cognitive skills such as creative writing can be taught by shaping your students' ability to select an increasing number of novel vocabulary words and to write complex sentences. Shaping can also be used to help students master affective goals. For example, a student who does not know how to apologize for making a mistake can be taught to apologize and eventually to offer an explanation and a remedy for the situation. Similarly, you can use shaping to decrease unacceptable behavior as illustrated by the teacher who accepts five call-outs on Monday, four on Tuesday, and so on. Effective use of shaping requires excellent task analysis skills. You must be able to break down a behavior into steps that match your students' ability. Steps that are too small waste valuable instructional time and bore your students; steps that are too large frustrate them. Both can lead to undesirable behavior.

Prompting

Occasionally during a lesson, a student may hesitate or incorrectly answer a question or perform a skill. You may assist by providing any one of several **prompts** or cues that increase the probability that student will answer or perform correctly. Schloss and Sedlak (1986) arranged prompts in a hierarchical order from least to most intrusive. Their list included:

1. *A cue.* This is a simple command or directive that advises the student that a response is now required. For example, you can instruct a student to write a *q*.
2. *A graphic product.* To use this prompt, provide the students with an example of the skill or product. For example, during a handwriting lesson, refer to the chart usually posted above the chalkboard.
3. *A graphic process.* Demonstrate for the group how to make a *q*.
4. *A verbal prompt.* State a rule or verbally describe for students how to complete a task. Give verbal instructions for writing a *q*.
5. *Modeling.* Identify the correct answer or perform the behavior for the student having difficulty. Write a *q* on the student's paper while he or she observes.
6. *A physical prompt.* Physically guide the student through the task. Put your hand over the student's and physically write a *q*.

It is a good idea to interrupt the student who is making an error because he or she is practicing mistakes that can only strengthen undesirable behaviors. When a student is having difficulty, use a prompt sufficiently strong enough to get the desired response. For example, a student who is having trouble producing a *q* in cursive writing may only need to be referred to the handwriting chart. Pause briefly to see if that prompt was sufficient. If so, continue with the lesson; if not, give the next level of prompting. Automatically assuming the student needs a detailed explanation or physical assistance is a waste of valuable instruction time. Such overkill also has the disadvantage of fostering a student's dependence on the teacher. We advise you to pair more intrusive prompts and less intrusive prompts. For example, while physically guiding a student as she draws a *q*, verbally describe what you are doing. Over time, you should be able to fade the physical prompt in favor of the verbal. More information about prompts is presented in Chapter 5.

Rate of Success

A fairly common problem teachers must deal with is the student who fails to complete independent assignments. For example, you may have a student who never does her homework. You may try to solve the problem by requiring the student to maintain an assignment notebook or by writing notes home to enlist the aid of her parents. Despite these efforts, however, the student still may not complete homework assignments. Similarly, another student may never complete the math worksheet required from those not involved in the reading group you are currently instructing. In both instances, you may have overlooked one very important prerequisite to completion of independent assignments: Does the student have the skills necessary to do the task?

We have observed several student teachers conducting lessons that unfortunately consisted primarily of the distribution and completion of worksheets with little or no instruction. During the conference afterwards, the student teachers have expressed alarm at their pupils' performance on the worksheet and their behavior during the lesson. Their reaction prompts us to ask, "When during your lesson did you actually teach something?"

On the other hand, you may assign independent work to students, assuming it will take them 30 minutes to complete. To your surprise, the students are done in 10 minutes. To your dismay, they are now engaged in horseplay that is disrupting other students.

The point of these examples is that many problems occur because tasks assigned to students are either too hard and frustrating, or too easy and boring (Smith & Rivera, 1995). It has been our experience that, of the two problems, assigning tasks that are too difficult is more likely to occur. Shores, Gunter, Denny, and Jack (1993) summarized several studies in which students demonstrated escape or avoidance behavior in the presence of tasks that were too difficult.

We recommend you give adequate consideration to the students' rate of success, the ninth antecedent control technique. We have mentioned several times in this chapter that undesirable behavior may result when students are bored or frustrated. Munk and Repp (1994) summarized the results of several studies that indicated that the level of task difficulty can be an antecedent to inappropriate behavior. You can prevent such behaviors by carefully attending to four levels of mastery identified by Schloss and Sedlak (1986) when selecting student assignments: 100 percent mastery, 90 to 99 percent mastery, 70 to 90 percent mastery, and less than 70 percent mastery.

One Hundred Percent Mastery

Students who demonstrate this level of proficiency have mastered a skill and no longer require additional practice in subsequent teacher-directed lessons. These skills are the focus of homework assignments and independent worksheets that are completed with no errors. They are frequently the basis for very interesting, entertaining independent activities. For example, students who have mastered high-level fraction skills can plan and prepare their favorite recipes for a class party.

Ninety to Ninety-Nine Percent Mastery

This level of proficiency indicates that students have learned the material but occasionally make errors. Work at this level frequently takes the form of worksheets. You need to make sure your students understand the concepts included on the worksheet and the specific directions for completing it. This level is the focus of games or drill and practice activities during which the students will have access to a teacher who can provide timely feedback on their performance. Even at this rate of success, a student may need assistance. Prater (1992) advises that you should not need to spend more than 30 or 40 seconds with a student. Longer than this suggests that the level of difficulty is too high or that instruction was not adequate.

Seventy to Ninety Percent Mastery

This level of proficiency indicates that students have not completely mastered the material. Left to their own devices, students will probably make and practice errors. This information is the focus of additional teacher-directed activities and should never be presented during independent activities such as homework or worksheets, as it may increase students' frustration and tendency to misbehave.

Less than Seventy Percent Mastery

Material on which the students are experiencing a rate of success lower than 70 percent is too difficult, even when given in the presence of a teacher. This material should be broken into smaller instructional units, perhaps via task analysis, which become the focus of additional teacher-directed lessons. It should never be included on independent worksheets or homework assignments.

Functional, Age-Appropriate Activities and Materials

In Chapter 3, we described a mistake made by the second author who selected the wrong objective for a 17-year-old student. As you may recall, she chose to work on multiplication and division of fractions rather than more relevant mathematics skills such as personal finances. Before realizing the error of her ways, she planned and implemented several lessons in which the student was presented with a series of problems to be solved. As you can imagine, none of them went over very well. The student was not very motivated to participate, and his readiness to give up suggested the tasks were frustrating.

   This incident highlights the importance of planning and implementing lessons that include functional, age-appropriate activities. This is the tenth antecedent control technique. We have already discussed the importance of selecting functional goals and objectives that can make a difference in your students' lives. We now encourage you to take time at the beginning of your lesson to help students see the relevance of the information you are about to present. Students who understand how this information will be useful to them are more motivated to participate in the lesson.

In addition, make sure you are sensitive to the age of your students when designing activities. A teacher of young students and a teacher of older students may each plan to review addition and subtraction skills. The first teacher can use a ditto that requires students to solve problems and use their answers to decode a secret message. The second teacher can provide a calculator and have students balance a checkbook.

We also advise you to consider your students' ages and abilities when selecting or developing instructional materials. These characteristics should be carefully matched to features of teacher-made or commercially developed materials. Such features include prerequisite knowledge base; the relevance of concepts presented; the sequence of skills; readability level; pace; the number and nature of pictures, diagrams, and illustrations; and the amount of practice provided. A mismatch between learner characteristics and features of materials could result in students being bored or insulted by materials that are too easy, or being frustrated by materials that are too hard. Either scenario increases the probability of inappropriate behavior.

Review of the Educational Program

The eleventh antecedent control technique we will discuss is a review of the educational program. Actually, this technique is primarily of concern to teachers involved in special education. IDEA mandates that the Individualized Education Program of each child receiving special education services be reviewed at least once a year. We encourage more frequent informal reviews to ensure that goals and objectives selected for development are still appropriate for the student and that he or she is mastering them at the expected rate.

Physical Arrangement

Standard equipment in most classrooms includes desks for the teacher and students, file and storage space, bulletin and chalkboards, audiovisual and computer equipment, and textbooks and supplies. Shores, Gunter, Denny, and Jack (1993) indicated that it is important not only to have such materials but to arrange them appropriately and neatly. The physical arrangement of your classroom can influence your students' behavior. Poor seating arrangements or congested traffic patterns increase student misbehavior. They create opportunities for students to talk to each other at inappropriate times, initiate physical contact, and be disruptive even during seemingly innocuous events such as sharpening a pencil. Smith and Rivera (1995) recommended that teachers (a) observe traffic patterns and note whether there are problematic, high-frequency areas, (b) keep work areas separate, (c) provide plenty of space to decrease interactions and increase time-on-task, and (d) make sure different areas of the rooms are easily accessed by students.

Summary

In this chapter, we defined and illustrated antecedents and described how their control can contribute greatly to the establishment of a pleasant classroom environment in which students achieve learning and behavioral goals. We discussed antecedent control, a major component in the establishment of a pleasant environment that is conducive to learning. We presented twelve techniques, discussed each technique in detail, and suggested when it could be most useful during the course of the school day.

Proper attention to antecedent control has many advantages. Used properly, the techniques we described can prevent the occurrence of disruptive behaviors and minimize the need to use other components of your comprehensive behavior management plan. Although we strongly recommend use of antecedent control, we also advise you not to rely solely on it. There are times when antecedent control techniques alone will be insufficient to produce appropriate learning and behavioral outcomes. The formula for an effective classroom management system contains other components. We turn our attention to the next component, related personal characteristics, in the following chapter.

References

Becker, W. C., Englemann, S., & Thomas, D. R. (1975). *Teaching II: Cognitive learning and instruction.* Chicago: Science Research Associates.

DeVries, R., & Zan, B. (1995–96). Rule making in the classroom. *The Constructivist Educator, 5*(1), 1–3.

Haring, N. G., & Gentry, N. D. (1976). Direct and individualized instructional procedures. In N. G. Haring & R. L. Schiefelbusch (Eds.), *Teaching special children.* New York: McGraw-Hill.

Munk, D. D., & Repp, A. C. (1994). The relationship between instructional variables and problem behavior. *Exceptional Children, 60,* 390–401.

Prater, M. A. (1992). Increasing time-on-task in the classroom. *Intervention in School and Clinic, 28,* 22–27.

Premack, D. (1959). Toward empirical behavior laws: I. Positive reinforcement. *Psychological Review, 66,* 219–233.

Schloss, P. J., & Sedlak, R. A. (1986). *Instructional methods for students with learning and behavior problems.* Boston: Allyn and Bacon.

Schloss, P. J., Smith, M. A., & Schloss, C. N. (1995). *Instructional methods for secondary students with learning and behavior problems* (2nd ed.). Boston: Allyn and Bacon.

Shores, R. E., Gunter, P. L., Denny, R. K., & Jack, S. L. (1993). Classroom influences on aggressive and disruptive behaviors of students with emotional and behavioral disorders. *Focus on Exceptional Children, 26*(2), 1–10.

Smith, D., & Rivera, D. P. (1995). Discipline in special education and general education settings. *Focus on Exceptional Children, 27*(5), 1–14.

Smith, M. A. (1985). Scheduling for success. *Perspectives for Teachers of the Hearing Impaired, 3*(3), 14–16.

Smith, M. A. & Misra, A. (1992). Discipline of special education students in regular setting. *Elementary School Journal, 92,* 353–371.

5

INCREASING APPROPRIATE BEHAVIOR THROUGH RELATED PERSONAL CHARACTERISTICS

The preceding chapter described antecedent control strategies that promote positive social behavior. These procedures involved structuring the environment so the student has fewer opportunities to engage in disruptive behavior. Unfortunately, we are seldom able to structure environments so that all potentially provoking situations are prevented. Many of our students are provoked into disruptive social behavior by the simple presence of another student. Others are likely to act out any time they are not in close proximity to an authority figure. Still others lose control when they are unsuccessful in a competitive situation. It is not possible to eliminate all situations in which students interact with others, are not directly supervised by adults, or run the risk of losing in a competitive event.

Even when possible, it is often undesirable to remove or eliminate some antecedents. For example, we may be able to separate a student from other individuals with the use of an isolated room or partition. We recognize, however, that the benefits of reduced disruptive behavior that result from isolation do not outweigh the disadvantages associated with removing the learner from interpersonal contact with others. Similarly, we could remove all possible sources of failure and negative feedback. Doing so, however, would also remove the individual from significant achievement opportunities.

Acknowledging that it is not possible or desirable to remove a student from all provoking antecedents, we must develop skills that allow the individual to face such challenges without becoming disruptive. In general, these abilities are described as **related characteristics.** We address three major related characteristics in this text. The first, *social skills,* is the focus of this chapter; the second, *emotional control,* is addressed in Chapter 6; and the third, *self-management,* is addressed in Chapter 15.

Importance of Social Skills

Muscott and Gifford (1994) pointed out that schools, along with families and religious institutions, have been a major force in the development and refinement of socially skillful behavior by students. They noted that, unfortunately, the erosion of the family unit and the declining influence of organized religion may force school officials to assume an even larger role in the social development of their students. They advised teachers to target the development of social skills in order to promote the development of psychological health among students. Muscott and Gifford's review of the literature highlighted the negative outcomes for students who are socially unskillful. They face academic underachievement and failure, a greater risk for dropping out of school, a lack of friends, and unsuccessful employment. Muscott and Gifford's comments were about students without disabilities. They noted that legal mandates such as the least restrictive environment (LRE) contained within the Individuals with Disabilities Education Act (IDEA) and philosophies such as the Regular Education Initiative (REI) and full inclusion may result in the placement of more students with disabilities in general education settings. Hundert (1995) noted that physical proximity to nonhandicapped students does not guarantee that students with disabilities in general education settings will develop much-needed social skills.

Social skill development may be particularly important for individuals with disabilities. Parker and Asher (1987) have concluded that a strong relationship exists between school achievement and peer relations. The authors also noted a relationship between deficient interpersonal skills in childhood and juvenile/adult crime, and between childhood social skill deficits and adult psychopathology. Other research results indicate that teachers reacted more favorably to students who exhibited positive social behaviors. These students were more likely to obtain high evaluations even when producing work comparable to a less socially skillful individual (Heavy, Adelman, Nelson, & Smith, 1989; Shinn, Ramsey, Walker, Steiber, & O'Neill, 1987).

Gresham (1982) studied the relationship between social skills and success of individuals with disabilities in mainstream settings. His review produced the following conclusions:

1. Mainstreamed handicapped children interact less frequently and more negatively with nonhandicapped children.
2. Mainstreamed handicapped children are poorly accepted by their nonhandicapped peers.
3. Mainstreamed handicapped children do not model the behaviors of nonhandicapped peers as a result of increased exposure to them (p. 332).

Schloss, Smith, and Schloss (1995) reviewed the literature pertaining to social skills and adult adjustment, and supported the importance of social skill development in individuals with disabilities. Social skills were better predictors of successful adult adjustment than academic achievement and intelligence (Kelly & Drabman, 1977; Martin, Rusch, Lagomarcino, & Chadsey-Rusch, 1986; Schloss & Schloss, 1987). Social skill deficits were more likely to cause termination from employment than specific performance problems or other factors (Greenspan & Shoultz, 1981).

Finally, Schloss, Smith, and Schloss (1995) reported that social skill development programs have the potential to support the integration of individuals with disabilities into less restrictive educational and community settings. Other researchers emphasized the positive impact of integrating social skill objectives into educational and behavior management programs (Blackbourn, 1989; Carter & Sugai, 1988; Nelson, 1988).

Defining Social Skills

We have repeatedly emphasized the importance of identifying specific objectives for applied behavior analysis procedures. This is particularly important in the area of social skills because there is so much potential for disagreement on what constitutes a socially skillful response. We suggest that teachers consider both general and specific approaches for defining the social skills important to their students.

Cartledge and Milburn (1986) defined social skills as "socially acceptable learned behaviors that enable a person to interact in ways that elicit positive responses and assist in avoiding negative responses" (p. 7). General definitions such as this one include broad areas of social development and emphasize two essential concerns. The first concern is that social skill responses produce, enhance, or maintain positive outcomes for the student. For example, negotiating may produce a favorable settlement in a dispute with another student. The second concern is that social skills maximize reciprocal positive effects for individuals with whom the student is interacting. These two criteria highlight the complexity of social skills. In the presence of a provoking antecedent, the socially skillful student is able to express himself or herself in a manner that assures positive outcomes. A socially skillful child, for example, is able to respond to a class bully in a way that avoids future confrontation and may even earn respect. A less skillful child, conversely, may have no alternative but to enter into conflicts with the bully.

This general definition of social skills is useful for establishing the general curriculum area. Teachers planning for social skill development are able to develop or select very broad curriculum guides. They are also able to describe to parents, administrators, and students the general focus of social skill development activities.

It is important to note, however, that the general definition of social skills does not lend itself easily to social skill training. The general definition of social skills is difficult to translate into behavioral objectives. There are many responses that may fulfill the standards suggested by our definition (e.g., ability to compliment others, appropriate responses to criticism, participation in heterosexual interactions, etc.). Further, the general definition does not relate specific settings to appropriate interpersonal responses. A set of responses cannot be categorically described as socially appropriate without knowing the surrounding events. For example, the highly animated behavior of a basketball coach during half time of a crucial game may be viewed as being socially skillful. The same interactions, if continued throughout the season, may be viewed as nonproductive. Finally, the general definition does not provide criteria for acceptable performance. As emphasized above, a response cannot be considered to be inherently skillful or unskillful. We must consider the extent to which the behavior is used (e.g., too little or too much).

Readers who have the good fortune of watching *Leave It to Beaver* reruns may recognize Eddie Haskel as a young man who is "socially skillful" to the extreme. A careful appraisal would reveal that Eddie is not socially skillful because extreme "sugar coating" makes his efforts highly transparent to Wally, Beaver, and their parents.

Specific definitions of social skills are needed to increase the specificity of applied behavior analysis programs. They go beyond the general definitions by including three major elements: (a) a precise and objective description of the social skill, (b) the conditions under which the skill is expected to occur, and (c) the criteria for acceptable performance.

Precise and objective descriptions have been well developed for research purposes by Turner, Hersen, and Bellack (1978), who defined interpersonal skills as the ratio of eye contact to speech duration, rate of spoken language, intonation, and affect. Bornstein, Bach, McFall, Friman, and Lyons (1980) defined specific social skills as speech latency, posture, enunciation, speech content, loudness, and rate of speech.

Conditions under which the social skills are used are also found in the professional literature. Kelly, Wildman, and Berler (1980) suggest social skills for employment interview settings. Kelly, Furman, Phillips, Hathorn, and Wilson (1979) suggest social skills for conversational contexts. Schloss, Schloss, and Harris (1984) suggest social skills for classroom situations.

The criteria for acceptable performance are established in a number of social skill demonstrations. As discussed in Chapter 3, the effectiveness of a program may be judged by the extent to which a student's behavior approaches ranges observed in adaptive students. In one demonstration, Schloss and Wood (1990) established the following conversational goals for students with mental retardation: asking nondirected questions, answering nondirected questions, asking directed questions, and answering directed questions. The criteria for effective performance was established by monitoring nonhandicapped youths in similar conversational situations. The criterion for asking both types of questions was asking between one or two in a 20-minute discussion. The criterion for answering both types of questions was 100 percent for the 20-minute discussion.

Social Skills Curriculum

Schloss and Sedlak (1986) proposed the development of a matrix of interpersonal skill competencies that serves as the foundation of a curriculum guide (see Figure 5.1). The vertical axis includes elements from Rinn and Markle's (1979) tax-

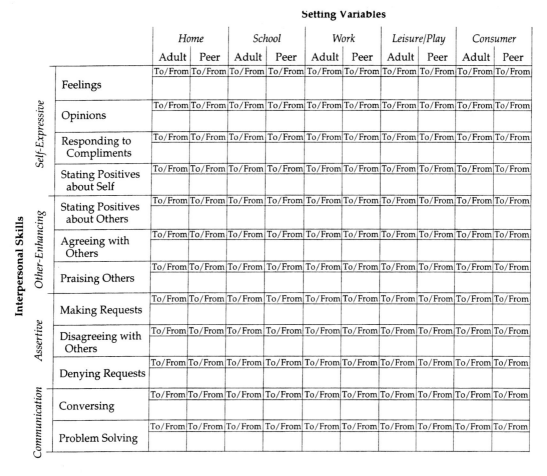

Setting Variables

	Home		School		Work		Leisure/Play		Consumer	
	Adult	Peer	Adult	Peer	Adult	Peer	Adult	Peer	Adult	Peer
Feelings	To/From	To/From	To/From	To/From	To/From	To/From	To/From	To/From	To/From	To/From
Opinions	To/From	To/From	To/From	To/From	To/From	To/From	To/From	To/From	To/From	To/From
Responding to Compliments	To/From	To/From	To/From	To/From	To/From	To/From	To/From	To/From	To/From	To/From
Stating Positives about Self	To/From	To/From	To/From	To/From	To/From	To/From	To/From	To/From	To/From	To/From
Stating Positives about Others	To/From	To/From	To/From	To/From	To/From	To/From	To/From	To/From	To/From	To/From
Agreeing with Others	To/From	To/From	To/From	To/From	To/From	To/From	To/From	To/From	To/From	To/From
Praising Others	To/From	To/From	To/From	To/From	To/From	To/From	To/From	To/From	To/From	To/From
Making Requests	To/From	To/From	To/From	To/From	To/From	To/From	To/From	To/From	To/From	To/From
Disagreeing with Others	To/From	To/From	To/From	To/From	To/From	To/From	To/From	To/From	To/From	To/From
Denying Requests	To/From	To/From	To/From	To/From	To/From	To/From	To/From	To/From	To/From	To/From
Conversing	To/From	To/From	To/From	To/From	To/From	To/From	To/From	To/From	To/From	To/From
Problem Solving	To/From	To/From	To/From	To/From	To/From	To/From	To/From	To/From	To/From	To/From

(Rows grouped under *Interpersonal Skills*: Self-Expressive, Other-Enhancing, Assertive, Communication)

FIGURE 5.1 **Interpersonal Skill Competency Matrix Used for Curriculum Planning**

onomy of social skills. Major components include self-expressive skills, other-enhancing skills, assertive skills, and communication skills. These competencies are referenced against setting variables suggested by Bernstein (1981). Setting variables include home, school, work, leisure/play, and consumer. Relationship variables including adults and peers are identified within each setting.

You should consider each cell in the matrix for possible curriculum objectives. Cells may be identified based on an assessment of the student's abilities and on the most critical demands of the setting. Sample objectives may include the following:

1. Increased expression of opinions with adults in school.
2. Increased complimenting of peers during play.

3. Decreased disagreements with peers at work.
4. Increased conversations with adults at home.
5. Increased requests of adults in consumer settings.

Age Appropriateness

It is important that social skill objectives be age appropriate. Social skills for young children may involve interactions during play (Knapczyk & Yoppi, 1975; Lancioni, 1982; Whitman, Mercurio, & Caponigri, 1970). Adolescent responses may include conversational skills (Hall, Sheldon-Wildgen, & Sherman, 1980; Matson, Kazdin, & Esveldt-Dawson, 1980). Adult responses may include vocational social skills (Hill, Wehman, & Pentecost, 1980).

The *Manual on Terminology and Classification in Mental Retardation* of the American Association on Mental Retardation (Grossman, 1973) provides additional guidance for the selection of age-appropriate interpersonal skills. Chronological ages and appropriate social characteristics are described as follows:

3 years—interacts with one or two other children in basic play activities unless guided into group activity; demonstrates a preference for interacting with some individuals more than others.

6 years—participates in larger group activities and plays basic group games; engages in expressive activities, including art and dance; and interacts with other children in simple play activities, such as "store" and "house."

9 years—is a spontaneous participant in group activities; participates in competitive games, such as dodge ball, tag, and races; may establish friendships that are sustained over weeks or months.

12 years—interacts cooperatively and competitively with others.

15 years to adult—along with cooperative and competitive interactions, initiates some group activities for social or recreational purposes; may belong to a local recreation group or religious group.

Assessment of Social Skills

The preceding curriculum matrix is useful for providing a reference point from which objectives can be drawn. Actual objective selection should be based on an analysis of the student's characteristics and other ecological factors. Several instruments and procedures may be used for this purpose.

Interviews

Formal or informal interviews can provide information regarding the interpersonal skill development history of the student (Bellack & Hersen, 1979). Van Hasselt,

Hersen, Whitehall, and Bellack (1979) cautioned that interviews conducted for the purpose of obtaining historical information may be biased by the selective recall of the student, parents, or teachers. We suggest that you interview several individuals on the same topics. Information from parents, the child, and teachers will provide a more comprehensive, balanced, and accurate view of the student's social skill history and needs. Validity of interviews can also be enhanced by using data with other assessment methods.

In addition to obtaining information from the student, an interview also gives you an actual sample of the student's interpersonal behavior. Responses such as speech latency, eye contact, affect, vocabulary, and turn taking can be monitored during the interview situation. Also, you may "test" the student's responses to specific questions or comments. You may criticize, compliment, engage in small talk, or ask for information. The student's response may serve as a foundation for selecting training priorities and procedures.

Self-Report Inventories

Self-report inventories may provide an economical and efficient source of information about an individual's self-perceptions (Bellack, 1979; Glassi & Glassi, 1979). Figure 5.2 on pages 88–89 includes sample items from a self-report inventory based on our curriculum matrix (Figure 5.1). Each of the entries is based on the skill and setting variables identified in the matrix. Note that the "work," "leisure," and "consumer" settings are combined into a single "community" setting for the sake of brevity. Students are asked to use the three-point scale (ranging from effective to ineffective) to indicate self-perceptions of specific skills.

Our inventory can be completed independently by mature students with reasonably good reading ability. Less capable students may respond orally to items as you read them. We recommend that the inventory be scored by assessing performance on each item as opposed to producing an overall score. This allows the teacher to identify specific problem areas that may subsequently become the focus of training.

It is important to note that self-report methods have the same methodological limitations as interviews. Self-reports require an accurate self-appraisal of personal performance. The complexity of social interactions may not be easily quantified and reported by the student. The questions raised and accompanying responses may have different meanings for the student and others. What a student intends to mean and what is interpreted may be very different. Responses on a self-report inventory may be influenced by your expectations of the student. The student may alter responses to conform to your expectations for mature and polite behavior.

Ratings by Others

An assessment method that may be particularly useful for identifying social skill objectives is performance rating. A number of instruments have been developed to

Please rate your ability to express the following while at home:

	Effective	Average	Ineffective
Feelings			
Opinions			
Responses to Compliments			
Positives about Self			
Positives about Others			
Agreement with Others			
Praising Others			
Requests			
Disagreement with Others			
Denying Requests of Others			
Small Talk			
Problem Solving			

Please rate your ability to express the following while at school:

	Effective	Average	Ineffective
Feelings			
Opinions			
Responses to Compliments			
Positives about Self			
Positives about Others			
Agreement with Others			
Praising Others			
Requests			
Disagreement with Others			
Denying Requests of Others			
Small Talk			
Problem Solving			

(continued)

FIGURE 5.2   Social Skill Self-Rating Inventory

Please rate your ability to express the following while in the community:			
	Effective	Average	Ineffective
Feelings			
Opinions			
Responses to Compliments			
Positives about Self			
Positives about Others			
Agreement with Others			
Praising Others			
Requests			
Disagreement with Others			
Denying Requests of Others			
Small Talk			
Problem Solving			

FIGURE 5.2 *Continued*

provide standardized data for this purpose. These include sociometric rating, direct observation, interview, and questionnaire formats (Gresham & Elliott, 1989).

Van Hesselt, Hersen, Whitehall, and Bellack (1979) have identified four advantages to these methods: (a) they can be used quickly and economically, (b) the data are easily quantified, (c) a wide range of responses may be evaluated, and (d) they can be used as a reliable independent variable in research studies. As with the preceding methods, however, they may be influenced by the expectations of the rater.

Social skill rating scales can be constructed using the following procedures:

1. Determine the scope of social skill information expected to be obtained from the scale. This may include the specific nature of social skills, the settings in which they should be demonstrated, and the reactions of others to the performance of these skills.

2. Identify specific behaviors that are characteristic of the social skill responses. For example, one may be concerned that a student is overly withdrawn in class. Specific behaviors may include answering your questions and participating in conversations with peers.

3. Establish a two- to seven-point scale or continuum that reflects varying levels of performance for each behavior (e.g., from frequently to infrequently, or excellent to poor).

4. Place behavioral entries in a logical order. This may be from first to last occurrence during the day, easiest to most difficult, or least to most important.

5. Provide instructions for completing the scale. They should include a description of the general social skills being assessed and the method by which choices are indicated.

In Vivo Observation

Possibly the most valid and reliable method is the in vivo observation of relevant social responses in natural settings. Frequency recording may be used to determine the extent to which the student engages in discrete social behaviors. Moore, Cartledge, and Heckaman (1995) gave their students a self-monitoring form and instructed them to record the number of times they did or did not perform a skill. Duration recording may be used to establish the duration of social responses. Task analysis recording may be used to determine the extent to which specific components of appropriate social responses are used. Finally, interval recording may be used to estimate both the frequency and duration of social responses. Specific information on the development and use of these methods is presented in Chapter 11.

Analogue Observation

A related method is the use of analogue observation. The major difference is that observations in the natural setting assess the student's performance when faced with ongoing situations. Analogue observation involves structuring or simulating frequent and important occurrences. For example, you may observe a student's response during role-play arguments with peers as opposed to waiting for an actual argument to occur. The advantage of analogue observations is that they can be staged to include the precise performance demands you expect. The disadvantage is that performance during contrived situations may not accurately reflect actual performance in natural settings.

Both direct and analogue observation require substantially more time and effort than the other approaches. Also, direct and analogue recording methods may limit the breadth of data being collected; for example, a frequency recording method designed to record the number of times polite greetings are being used may ignore a child's reactions to criticism. Therefore, alternative methods may be more appropriate for the initial purpose of establishing social skills objectives. An observational system may then be used to assess progress toward the mastery of the objectives.

Social Skill Development Procedures

Social skill development demonstrations generally use treatment packages that include several social learning procedures. Procedures most often included are providing a rationale, modeling, prompting, shaping, behavior rehearsal, feedback, social reinforcement, practice in natural environments, and fading (Clees & Gast, 1994; Langone, Clees, Oxford, Malone, & Ross, 1995; Moore, Cartledge, & Hecka-man, 1995). Each of these approaches will be described in the following sections.

Rationale

Just as you would for any academic lesson, provide students with a rationale for learning a particular social skill. A rationale can include a description of the skill and how its use will benefit students. During the first step of their program to teach game-related social skills, Moore, Cartledge, and Heckaman (1995) defined the skills and told students why they were important to learn. They provided students with a scenario in which a young man reacts in a hostile manner when criticized about his clothes in front of his peers. His reaction was punished by school author-ities and his parents. In their rationale, Moore, Cartledge, and Heckaman (1995) discussed why the young man needed to learn more constructive ways to handle unpleasant situations. Broome and White (1995) recommended showing students videotapes of their behavior. They described one student who was unaware of the aggressive tone he used when making a request, and its impact on others. After watching himself on tape, he was able to see how he behaved and how he affected others. He had developed a very clear rationale for changing his behavior.

Modeling

One of the most common and effective methods for developing social skills in-volves modeling. As discussed in Chapter 4, **modeling** is used by arranging con-ditions so that students are able to observe and imitate socially skillful behavior (Bandura, 1969). Modeling can be arranged in three ways. The first and most nat-ural method is *in vivo modeling,* in which students observe functional individuals engaging in the desired social skills during unstructured daily activities. For exam-ple, students can go on a field trip to a large department store to observe how clerks use their salesmanship skills. The clerks are observed performing everyday activities in natural circumstances.

The major advantage of in vivo modeling is that students are more likely to ac-cept the credibility of natural models in functional situations. Students are not only able to see the desirable social skills but they are able to witness relevant natural cues and reinforcement. The disadvantage is that we cannot always predict precise behaviors that will be demonstrated by the models.

The second and less natural method is *analogue modeling,* in which students ob-serve structured role-play situations. Appropriate social behavior can be acted out by the teacher or other students. These procedures ensure that specific responses occur through the modeling sequence. Further, the teacher is able to control the number of opportunities for students to observe the desirable behavior. Finally, role-played behavior can be interrupted if verbal instruction, feedback, and rein-forcement are needed. The disadvantage is that staged modeling in unnatural cir-cumstances may be less credible to the observers.

The third and least natural method is *symbolic modeling*, which uses books, media, or other technology. Symbolic modeling can be arranged by having students observe characters in dramas or instructional media. Similarly, students may read biographies or fictional accounts of characters with distinguished social characteristics. Finally, students can watch videotapes of people engaging in desirable social skills while in natural settings.

The major advantage of symbolic modeling is that the media can be prepared to show very specific social skills under specific circumstances. The sequence of events is stored permanently and can be repeatedly replayed for students. The disadvantage is that symbolic modeling may not be as credible as in vivo approaches.

Each of the three modeling strategies can be used for three purposes. First, they can be used as part of a larger intervention package to teach new social skills not currently in the student's repertoire. A student can learn to play a board game by observing others. Second, they can increase the strength or frequency of a previously acquired social skill. A student can be more vocal because he notices another child receiving a substantial amount of adult attention from his verbal interactions. Finally, modeling can reduce excessive social behaviors. A youth may reduce excessive eating when he notices the results of a diet on one of his friends.

It is important to note that as with all applied behavior analysis principles, modeling can influence the development and persistence of both appropriate and inappropriate responses. Students may imitate another youth, a television character, or a sports figure, regardless of whether the social responses are adaptive or aggressive. We advise you to restrict the availability of disruptive social models.

Early research evaluated factors that influenced the likelihood that students would benefit from modeling (Bandura, 1971a; Bandura, 1971b; Kazdin 1973; Ross, 1970; Stevenson, 1972; Zinzer, 1966). The results suggested five student characteristics that influence the effectiveness of observational learning, including whether the student: (a) expects to be successful in acquiring reinforcement for the modeled behavior, (b) views the model's behavior as being applicable to situations that he or she encounters, (c) has a positive self-concept, (d) is easily influenced by external cues, and (e) has been successful in using the modeled behavior in similar circumstances.

Characteristics of the model may also influence his or her effectiveness. Goldstein, Heller, and Sechrist (1966) and Bandura (1971a) report that individuals who are warm, nurturing, powerful, and competent may be more effective models. Also, individuals of the same sex are likely to have a stronger influence on the observer. Finally, the behavior of individuals perceived by the learner as having high status is more likely to be modeled.

External factors may also influence the effectiveness of a model. Specific events described by Bandura (1971a) include reinforcement of the model following the target behavior, increased status of the model as a consequence of performing the target behavior, discrete situations in which the target behavior is appropriate and likely to be reinforced, and assurance that the target behavior is within the observer's capability. Table 5.1 summarizes the preceding discussion by identifying

TABLE 5.1   Principles That Enhance the Effectiveness of Modeling When Used for Social Skill Development

1. Clearly and completely identify the social skills expected to be developed through modeling.

2. Arrange in vivo, analogue, or symbolic situations in which the student is able to observe high status models engage in the social skill.

3. Ensure that the model in reinforced (or his or her status improves) following the demonstration of the social skill.

4. Prompt and reinforce the student for modeling the social skill.

5. Vary models and settings in order to enhance the generality of the behavior change.

five principles that enhance the effectiveness of modeling when used for social skill development.

Prompting

Prompts are stimuli that influence the occurrence of socially skillful behavior. A red light, for example, is a prompt for stopping and a timer bell is a prompt for removing food from the oven. Prompts can be natural or engineered, and both may have value in social skills instruction.

Natural Prompts

Natural prompts occur as an ongoing part of the environment. They are neither structured nor embellished. There are many examples of natural prompts. One person's question is a natural prompt for another person's answer. An extended hand is a natural prompt for hand shaking. The final person being seated at a dinner table may be a natural prompt for beginning to eat the meal.

Student reaction to natural prompts ensures that they will generalize from social skill training sessions to more functional environments. For this reason, social skill instruction should always assist students in identifying the relationship between the skill and the natural prompts. It is not enough to teach a student to be assertive independent of natural prompts. Assertive behaviors should be referenced to the natural prompts that may cue these skills outside of school (e.g., when a coworker is critical of something done well, or when another person's behavior causes harm).

At first, natural prompts may not promote the appropriate social skill. For this reason, engineered prompts may be required during early phases of instruction.

Engineered Prompts

Engineered prompts are used during instruction to encourage initial acquisition of the socially skillful responses and to facilitate near errorless learning (Clees & Gast, 1994). It is important, however, that these contrived prompts be well matched to the instructional needs of the student. Only as much support should be used as is required to ensure student success. As reported by Lawrence (1975) and Mercer and Snell (1977), overly intrusive prompting may result in overdependence on external cues by the student.

In addition, a plan should be developed to gradually fade engineered prompts so that the student increasingly learns to rely on natural prompts. Rigid adherence to engineered prompts without fading to natural prompts may reduce the extent to which social skills generalize to functional settings (Schloss, 1986).

Schloss (1986) has described an engineered prompting method that ensures the appropriate level of prompting is available during instruction and is faded once skills are acquired. The system of least prompts is conducted through the following steps:

1. Write the social skill objective as discussed in Chapter 3. It includes the target responses, conditions under which they are expected to be performed, and criteria for success.

2. Identify the task sequences by conducting a task analysis. An objective addressing phone usage, for example, may be broken down into a task sequence that includes lifting the receiver, saying hello, responding to the caller, and so on.

3. Identify a hierarchy of least to most intrusive prompts for the responses in the task sequence. From least to most intrusive, these may include: a *cue* (after which students perform on their own), *verbal prompt* (teacher provides verbal instruction), *modeling prompt* (teacher demonstrates the skill), and *physical prompt* (teacher manually guides the student through the skill).

4. Begin each social skill instruction trial with a teacher demonstration of the skill, followed by a request for student performance.

5. If the student is unable to self-initiate any step, provide a verbal prompt and wait three seconds for correct performance.

6. If after three seconds the student does not perform to criteria, provide a modeling prompt for the correct behavior.

7. If the student is still unable to perform the behavior within three seconds of the modeling prompt, provide a physical prompt.

8. If the student is able to perform the subskill during any point of the preceding process, give verbal praise and emphasize positive aspects of performance.

Figure 5.3 illustrates the system of least prompts.

Shaping

Shaping is an antecedent control procedure that is used to develop new skills. It involves the identification of a hierarchy of successively closer approximations of the desired social skills. Early in the shaping process, the most primitive or imperfect approximation is prompted and reinforced. Once the imperfect response occurs consistently, the next approximation on the hierarchy is prompted and reinforced

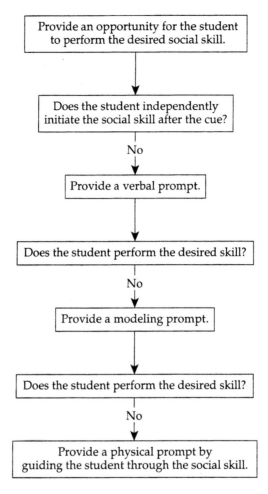

FIGURE 5.3   System of Least Prompts

while attention is withdrawn from the less perfect response. This process continues through successive approximations until only the terminal response (the behavior identified as the major goal) is prompted and reinforced.

The major value of shaping in social skill development programs is its ability to ensure success for the student. This is particularly important in view of research indicating the negative effects of frustration and failure on subsequent performance of students with disabilities (Mercer & Snell, 1977). Correctly implemented, the shaping process ensures that initial steps are appropriately matched to the entry skills of the student. Each subsequent step reflects the increased ability of the student. Instruction seldom focuses on excessively difficult or overly easy skills.

Behavior Rehearsal

This strategy for teaching social skills may include modeling, prompting, shaping, and social reinforcement. In general, you identify the adaptive social response that the student is expected to learn. If necessary, you establish approximations of the behavior and identify situations in which they should be practiced. Then model the desired social skill and prompt the student to rehearse the behavior.

Analogue and in vivo behavior rehearsal can be used. Analogue involves structuring role plays under artificial circumstances. In this case, the student would rehearse the desired social skill during simulated social conditions. Moore, Cartledge, and Heckaman (1995) used analogue modeling to present both positive and negative examples of game-related social skills. Students observed the distinct differences between appropriate and inappropriate ways to handle situations and were encouraged to be more creative and perhaps realistic when choosing socially appropriate responses. To be optimally effective, the simulated conditions should be as close as possible to the natural conditions. In vivo behavior rehearsal occurs under the natural conditions and at times in which it is actually desirable to use the social skill.

You may even videotape your students as they rehearse newly acquired skills. In their discussion of how to teach social skills safely, Clees and Gast (1994) recommended use of videotaping, and Broome and White (1995) described why and how to use videotaping during social skill instruction. It is a dramatic touch that adds vitality to the lesson. Videotaping provides an objective recording that can be played back to students, enabling them to evaluate their performances more accurately. Before videotaping, secure student permission and assure them that the tapes will be used only for instructional purposes. Demonstrate the equipment and allow them to handle it. Be aware that students may clown around during early attempts to videotape; this will subside as they adapt to the presence of the equipment. Have students view their performances and evaluate them on a scale (e.g., 1 = poor, 5 = excellent). Occasionally, have someone else view the tape and use the same scale to see if students self-appraised fairly. Disagreements about a student's performance can be resolved more easily using videotape because it is a permanent product that can be viewed repeatedly.

Both analogue and in vivo behavior rehearsal can be effective in assisting the student to practice social behaviors. They also help the student identify environmental conditions under which the behavior is expected to occur. Behavior rehearsal helps the student recognize natural cues that should prompt the behavior as well as natural consequences of the behavior.

The following procedures may be followed when using in vivo behavior rehearsal to teach social skills:

1. Identify social skill objectives for the behavior rehearsal procedure as described in Chapter 3.

2. Identify natural prompts for the social skill being rehearsed.

3. Identify natural consequences for the social skill.

4. Using in vivo behavior rehearsal, establish times in which the social skill is to be practiced around natural antecedents and consequences. Using analogue behavior rehearsal, establish social skill situations that simulate real life conditions.

5. Establish and follow a plan for rehearsing the social skill that employs modeling, prompting, shaping, feedback, and reinforcement.

6. Fade the structure surrounding the behavior rehearsal procedures as the student becomes more proficient.

Feedback

Feedback is crucial to the acquisition, maintenance, and generalization of social skills (Clees & Gast, 1994). **Feedback** is the process of providing evaluative information to a student for the purpose of maintaining or improving future responses. Most individuals try to meet the expectations of others; they continually monitor their own behavior and adjust to the standards set by others.

Unfortunately, many responses are difficult to self-monitor, and any variance may not be detected by the individual. Feedback augments an individual's perceptions and indicates how his or her performance is different from expected standards. It is assumed that students will modify their performance when they learn how it departs from the expectations of others. Several guidelines can be followed to improve the quality and effectiveness of feedback. These guidelines will be discussed separately.

Feedback Should Be Clear and Objective

Effective feedback statements provide clear and complete information about observable aspects of social skill performance. Statements should leave little doubt as to qualitative or quantitative aspects of the student's performance. Observational recording systems as described in Chapter 11 may be used as a source of objective information for feedback. Videotape, audiotape, and other media may also be used to make feedback more clear.

Feedback Should Be Current

Ideally, feedback should be given during or immediately after the critical incident. The more time between the student's actual behavior and the feedback statement, the less likely it is that the student will benefit from the feedback.

Feedback Statements Should Be Based on Current Objectives

To be most effective, students should be aware of the social skills that are being monitored by the teacher. Feedback statements should reflect those specific responses. This guideline reduces the number and variety of feedback statements given. Less frequent and more focused feedback statements are likely to be more useful.

Feedback Statements Should Be Consistent

Feedback statements should be similar when they are referring to the same objective. A student is more likely to benefit from "standard" statements than from highly variable statements.

Positive Feedback Should Balance Corrective Feedback

As mentioned in Chapter 4, students are likely to avoid or discount teachers who continually provide negative feedback. A majority of all feedback statements should describe positive behavior. This approach makes the student more responsive to the less frequent corrective feedback. This guideline will also help to maintain gains that are the target of positive feedback.

Feedback Should Be Provided by Peers as Well as Teachers

When possible, peers should be instructed to provide feedback. Peer feedback may not only improve the performance of the target student, but it may also improve the social skills of the observer. Also, some students may be more likely to respond favorably to information provided by supportive peers than adult authority figures (Jones, 1980). Implementation of this guideline may require instruction so that peers deliver feedback effectively.

Social Reinforcement

Feedback and social reinforcement are often used in combination. *Social reinforcement* is the use of interpersonal interactions to increase the consistency with which behaviors occur. Reinforcement is identified only through its function in influencing the target behavior. Social interactions that do not increase the likelihood that a student will perform the target skill are not socially reinforcing. Those that do predictably increase the extent to which responses occur in the future are socially reinforcing.

Social reinforcement is particularly useful for social skill development programs. The first major advantage of the procedure is that no special apparatus or materials are required. Social reinforcement requires very little time and effort and can be administered concurrent with prompt and feedback statements. Social reinforcement is natural to most educational and community settings. One can expect that performance gains that depend on social reinforcement may continue after intervention since individuals in the natural setting are likely to continue socially reinforcing the individual. Finally, socially reinforcing behavior and the positive behaviors of the individual being reinforced are likely to be modeled by others in the setting.

We propose the following guidelines for enhancing the effects of social reinforcement in social skill training programs:

1. Relate behaviors likely to produce social reinforcement to objectives and discuss them in advance with the student.
2. Label both process (e.g., requesting politely) and product behaviors (e.g., having the request acknowledged).

3. Use the individual's name to personalize the social reinforcement statement.
4. Evaluate the effects of interpersonal interactions presumed to be socially reinforcing. If they do not result in enhanced performance of the behavior, use more intrusive reinforcers.
5. Encourage peers, parents, other teachers, and individuals who observe the student's positive social interactions to socially reinforce the student.
6. Early in the social skill training program, use social reinforcement liberally. As skills are performed consistently, the teacher should gradually fade social reinforcement.

Practice in Natural Environments

Under ideal circumstances, social skill instruction should occur in natural environments. Training under the precise conditions in which the social skills are expected to occur reduces the need for generalization from the classroom. Unfortunately, it is not often practical to conduct social skill training in natural settings. Travel requirements, availability of community facilities, and other factors may make classroom-based training more feasible.

Even when classroom-based training is used, it is important that experiences be provided to ensure that generalization to the natural community settings occurs. One approach to accomplishing this is to assign practice activities in the functional setting, that is, assign homework. Moore, Cartledge, and Heckaman (1995) provided their students with supplemental worksheets that directed them to use the skill with someone outside of class and record the outcome. Students were also required to describe the situations and their feelings before and after using the skill, and to evaluate their effectiveness. Homework assignments were discussed at the beginning of the next lesson.

Additional sample activities are suggested in Table 5.2 on page 100. Depending on the capabilities of the student, these activities may initially be supervised and later conducted independently. The following guidelines may facilitate this process:

1. Assign natural environment activities once acquisition occurs in the classroom.
2. Work with the student to develop appropriate natural environment practice activities.
3. Give the student a clear description of the practice activity. Methods for self-evaluating performance should also be discussed.
4. Depending on the ability of the student, the teacher may provide a written description of the activity along with a form for evaluating performance. The form should include a description of the assignment and an area for self-evaluation.
5. Initially, use modeling, prompting, and feedback through natural environment activities. When few prompts are required, the teacher may encourage the student to independently engage in the natural environment activities.

TABLE 5.2   Sample Activities for Practicing Social Skills in Natural Settings

Purchase a pair of socks from the local department store and make a comment about the quality of the store's clothing.

Ask an unfamiliar person for directions to a theater.

Initiate a conversation about career goals with a person of the opposite sex.

Compliment a person of the opposite sex for his or her choice of clothing, hair style, or jewelry.

Using the phone, request information about a position vacancy.

Provide constructive feedback to a friend regarding his appearance, school work, or other behavior.

Fading

Continued reliance on teacher prompts, models, social reinforcement, and feedback reduces the likelihood that skills will generalize to natural settings when adult assistance is not provided. This is contrary to the ultimate goal. We want the student to use positive responses at appropriate times and places without any assistance. Therefore, it is essential to **fade** components of social skill training programs.

We must proceed carefully because abrupt removal of program procedures without a thoughtful fading plan often results in the loss of positive social responses. This effect may be the result of the program not being conducted sufficiently long to ensure mastery and retention of skills; the immediate loss of prompts that were necessary for consistent performances; the immediate loss of attention and reinforcement for the desirable social behaviors; or the failure of the program to instill self-control skills. Fading strategies should account for each of these possibilities.

The first consideration in developing a fading plan involves the planned *duration of the program*. The social skill development procedures should be carried out long enough to ensure that the learner develops a comfortable association between naturally occurring prompts/consequences and the target social skills. Over a period of time, the new social skills are likely to be sustained because of the learned relationship between the interpersonal responses and reinforcers in the natural setting.

The second consideration involves *building self-control strategies* into the social skill program. Early in training, the teacher may be required to identify situations in which specific social skills are used. The teacher may also need to encourage the student by identifying positive consequences associated with using proper social responses. Toward the end of training, the student should be able to identify important antecedents and probable consequences. This knowledge should help the student identify situations in which the social skills should be used. It should also provide self-motivation to engage in the skills.

The third consideration is the *gradual removal of unnatural prompts and reinforcers*. Dependency on these instructional aides should be gradually diminished as natural prompts and reinforcers exert control over the socially skillful behavior. Initial acquisition of skills may require continuous reinforcement and use of unnatural incentives. While this is the most effective approach for developing new social skills, responses maintained under the continuous schedule of reinforcement are especially prone to deterioration following the abrupt withdrawal of reinforcement. Consequently, the schedule of reinforcement should be thinned during the final stages of the training program. We discuss fading and thinning in further detail in Chapter 7.

The final consideration is closely related to the importance of practice in natural settings. Prior to the termination of the program, the student should have *numerous opportunities for practice under natural conditions.* As was discussed earlier, this approach ensures that the student learn the circumstances in which use of the social skill is most beneficial. Practice under natural conditions ensures that a link is established between training and the situations in which the social skills should be used.

Summary

Analysis of a student's learning and behavioral features is conducted to establish program goals and intervention strategies. Our initial target area was antecedents, where teachers modify the educational setting so that disruptions are prevented and positive social behaviors are more likely to occur. We emphasized that modification of antecedents as a behavior management strategy is not always possible or desirable.

As an alternative, educators must be concerned with developing related characteristics that allow the learner to display positive social behavior even when faced with provoking events. One particularly important related characteristic is social skill development. Individuals with positive social skills are able to work through provoking situations in a manner that produces satisfaction for all concerned, including the individual with disabilities.

Persons with disabilities may be particularly important targets for social skill development. Students with well developed social skills, regardless of disability, are more likely to be mainstreamed into regular educational settings and to receive positive evaluations. A brief review of adult adjustment literature indicates that social skill deficits may be associated with adverse outcomes in adulthood including criminal behavior, psychopathology, and poor employment success.

Given the applied nature of social skills, we suggested the development of a curriculum using ecological analysis methodology. Specifically, social skill objectives should be referenced to skill demands (e.g., self-expressive skills, other-enhancing skills, assertive skills, and communication skills), setting variables (e.g., home, school, work, leisure/play, and consumer), and relationship variables (e.g., adult and peer).

This chapter included a number of strategies for assessing the social skills of individuals with disabilities. We recommended less direct measures for initially establishing objectives. These may include interviews, self-reports, and ratings by others. Direct and analogue observations were recommended for monitoring the success of individual social development programs.

Finally, we discussed a number of methods for developing interpersonal skills. Particular attention was given to the use of prompting, shaping, modeling, behavior rehearsal, feedback, social reinforcement, practice in natural environments, and fading.

References

Bandura, A. (1969). *Principles of behavior modification.* New York: Holt, Rinehart, & Winston.

Bandura, A. (1971a). *Psychotherapy based on modeling principles.* In A. E. Beugin & S. L. Garfield (Eds.), *Handbook of psychotherapy and behavior change.* New York: John Wiley.

Bandura, A. (1971b). *Social learning theory.* Englewood Cliffs, NJ: Prentice-Hall.

Bellack, A. S. (1979). Behavioral assessment of social skills. In A. S. Bellack & M. Hersen (Eds.), *Research and practice in social skills training.* New York: Plenum.

Bellack, A. S., & Hersen, M. (1979). *Research and practice in social skills training.* New York: Plenum.

Bellack, A. S., & Hersen, M. (1977). *Behavior modification: An introductory textbook.* Baltimore: Williams & Wilkins.

Bernstein, G. S. (1981). Research issues in training interpersonal skills for the mentally retarded. *Education and Training of the Mentally Retarded, 1,* 70–74.

Blackbourn, J. M. (1989). Acquisition and generalization of social skills in elementary-aged children with learning disabilities. *Journal of Learning Disabilities, 22,* 28–34.

Bornstein, P. H., Bach, P. J., McFall, M. G., Friman, P. C., & Lyons, P. D. (1980). Application of a social skills training program in the modification of interpersonal deficits among retarded adults: A clinical replication. *Journal of Applied Behavior Analysis, 13,* 171–176.

Broome, S. A., & White, R. B. (1995). The many uses of videotape in classrooms serving youth with behavioral disorders. *Teaching Exceptional Children, 27*(3), 10–12.

Carter, J., & Sugai, G. (1988). Teaching social skills. *Teaching Exceptional Children, 54,* 68–71.

Cartledge, G., & Milburn, J. A. (1986). *Teaching social skills to children: Innovative approaches* (2nd ed.). Boston: Allyn and Bacon.

Clees, T. J., & Gast, D. L. (1994). Social safety skills instruction for individuals with disabilities: A sequential model. *Education and Treatment of Children, 17,* 163–184.

Glassi, J. P., & Glassi, M. D. (1979). Modification of heterosocial skill deficits. In A. S. Bellack & M. Hersen (Eds.), *Research and practice in social skills training* (pp. 131–187). New York: Plenum.

Goldstein, A. P., Heller, K., & Sechrist, L. B. (1966). *Psychotherapy and the psychology of behavior change.* New York: John Wiley & Sons.

Greenspan, S., & Shoultz, B. (1981). Why mentally retarded adults lose their jobs: Social competence as a factor in work adjustment. *Applied Research in Mental Retardation, 2,* 23–38.

Gresham, F. M. (1982). Misguided mainstreaming: The case for social skills training with handicapped children. *Exceptional Children, 48,* 422–433.

Gresham, F. M., & Elliott, S. N. (1989). Social skills assessment technology for LD students. *Learning Disability Quarterly, 12,* 141–152.

Grossman, H. J. (1973). *Manual on terminology and classification in mental retardation.* Baltimore: Garamond/Pridemark.

Hall, C., Sheldon-Wildgen, J., & Sherman, J. A. (1980). Teaching job interview skills to retarded clients. *Journal of Applied Behavior Analysis, 13,* 433–443.

Heavy, C. L., Adelman, H. S., Nelson, P., & Smith, D. C. (1989). Learning problems, anger, perceived control, and misbehavior. *Journal of Learning Disabilities, 22,* 46–50, 59.

Hill, J. W., Wehman, P., & Pentecost, J. (1980). Developing job interview skills in mentally retarded adults. *Education and Training of the Mentally Retarded, 15,* 179–186.

Hundert, J. (1995). *Enhancing social competence in young students: School-based approaches.* Austin, TX: PRO-ED.

Jones, V. F. (1980). *Adolescents with behavior problems: Strategies for teaching, counseling, and parent involvement.* Boston: Allyn and Bacon.

Kazdin, A. E. (1973). The effects of vicarious reinforcement on attentive behaviors in the classroom. *Journal of Applied Behavior Analysis, 6,* 71–78.

Kelly, J. A., & Drabman, R. S. (1977). The modification of socially detrimental behavior. *Journal of Behavior Therapy and Experimental Psychiatry, 8,* 101–104.

Kelly, J. A., Furman, W., Phillips, J., Hathorn, S., & Wilson, T. (1979). Teaching conversational skills to retarded adolescents. *Child Behavior Therapy, 1,* 85–97.

Kelly, J. A., Wildman, B. G., & Berler, E. S. (1980). Small group behavioral training to improve the job interview skills repertoire of mildly retarded adolescents. *Journal of Applied Behavior Analysis, 13,* 461–471.

Knapczyk, D. R., & Yoppi, J. O. (1975). Development of cooperative and competitive play responses in developmentally disabled children. *American Journal of Mental Deficiency, 80,* 245–255.

Lancioni, G. E. (1982). Normal children as tutors to teach social responses to withdrawn mentally retarded schoolmates: Training, maintenance, and generalization. *Journal of Applied Behavior Analysis, 15,* 17–40.

Langone, J., Clees, T. J., Oxford, M., Malone, M., & Ross, G. (1995). Acquisition and generalization of social skills by high school students with mild mental retardation. *Mental Retardation, 33,* 186–196.

Lawrence, E. A. (1975). Locus of control: Implications for special education. *Exceptional Children, 41,* 483–490.

Martin, J. E., Rusch, F. R., Lagomarcino, T., & Chadsey-Rusch, J. (1986). Comparison between nonhandicapped and mentally retarded workers: Why they lose their jobs. *Applied Research in Mental Retardation, 7,* 467–474.

Matson, J. L., Kazdin, A. E., & Esveldt-Dawson, K. (1980). Training interpersonal skills among mentally retarded and socially dysfunctional children. *Behavior Research and Therapy, 18,* 419–427.

Mercer, C. D., & Snell, M. E. (1977). *Learning theory research in mental retardation.* Columbus, OH: Merrill.

Moore, R. J., Cartledge, G., & Heckaman, K. (1995). The effects of social skill instruction and self-monitoring on game-related behaviors of adolescents with emotional or behavioral problems. *Behavioral Disorders, 20,* 253–266.

Muscott, H. S., & Gifford, T. (1994). Virtual reality and social training for students with behavioral disorders: Applications, challenges, and promising practices. *Education and Treatment of Children, 17,* 417–434.

Nelson, C. M. (1988). Social skills training for handicapped students. *Teaching Exceptional Children, 20,* 19–23.

Parker, J. G., & Asher, S. R. (1987). Peer relations and later personal adjustment: Are low-accepted children at risk? *Psychological Bulletin, 102,* 357–389.

Rinn, R. C., & Markle, A. (1979). Modification of social skill deficits in children. In A. S. Bellack & M. Hersen (Eds.), *Research and practice in social skills training* (pp. 107–129). New York: Plenum.

Ross, D. M. (1970). Effect on learning of psychological attachment to a film model. *American Journal of Mental Deficiency, 74,* 701–707.

Schloss, P. J. (1986). Sequential prompt instruction for mildly handicapped learners. *Teaching Exceptional Children, 18,* 181–185.

Schloss, P. J., & Schloss, C. N. (1987). A critical review of social skills research in mental retardation. In S. E. Breuning, J. L. Matson, & R. P. Barrett (Eds.), *Advances in mental retardation and developmental disabilities: A research annual* (pp. 107–151). Greenwich, CT: JAI Press.

Schloss, P. J., Schloss, C. N., & Harris, L. (1984). A multiple baseline analysis of an interpersonal skills training program for depressed youth. *Behavioral Disorders, 9,* 182–188.

Schloss, P. J., & Sedlak, R. A. (1986). *Instructional methods for students with learning and behavior problems.* Boston: Allyn and Bacon.

Schloss, P. J., Smith, M. A., & Schloss, C. N. (1995). *Instructional methods for handicapped adolescents* (2nd ed.). Boston: Allyn and Bacon.

Schloss, P. J., & Wood, C. E. (1990). The effects of self-monitoring on the maintenance and generalization of conversational skills in persons with mental retardation. *Mental Retardation, 28*(2), 105–115.

Shinn, M. R., Ramsey, E., Walker, H. M., Steiber, S., & O'Neill, R. E. (1987). Antisocial behavior in school settings: Initial differences in an at risk and normal population. *Journal of Special Education, 21,* 69–84.

Stevenson, H. W. (1972). *Children's learning.* New York: Appleton-Century-Crofts.

Turner, A. S., Hersen, M., & Bellack, A. S. (1978). Social skills training to teach prosocial behaviors in an organically impaired and retarded patient. *Journal of Behavior Therapy and Experimental Psychiatry, 9,* 253–258.

Van Hasselt, V. B., Hersen, M., Whitehall, M. B., & Bellack, A. S. (1979). Social skill assessment and training for children: An evaluative review. *Behavior Research and Therapy, 17,* 413–437.

Whitman, R. L., Mercurio, J. R., & Caponigri, V. (1970). Development of social responses in two severely retarded children. *Journal of Applied Behavior Analysis, 3,* 133–138.

Zinzer, O. (1966). *Imitation, modeling and cross-cultural training.* Aerospace medical research laboratories. Wright-Patterson Air Force Base, OH: Aerospace Medical Division.

6

INFLUENCING EMOTIONAL CHARACTERISTICS

The elementary school career of the first author was less than distinguished. His matriculation through a parochial school in Illinois was marked by poor grades, conduct problems, and a general disinterest in activities that his parents and teachers considered to be important. No sooner than eight weeks into the first grade he earned several swats from the principal for rowdy behavior. Despite many similar trips, he never quite got used to his visits with the principal. By eighth grade, no single event was more likely to raise his blood pressure; shorten his breath; and produce moisture on his palms, forehead, and eyes, than a swift walk to the office.

Fortunately, his high school experience was substantially more pleasant. While he never visited the office for special privileges or recognition, he also managed to avoid trips to the office that resulted from disciplinary problems. By college, he had attained "serious student" status and graduated from a state university without even learning the location of the office or name of the department chair. This special interest in education led him to obtain teaching certificates in learning disabilities, behavior disorders, and mental retardation. He acquired a position teaching students with severe behavior disorders.

Six weeks into his new position as a Special Education teacher at Minonk-Dana-Rutland Junior/Senior High School, a discipline problem occurred that required the principal's attention. Eight years after his last grade school march to the principal's office, he again was "hand-in-hand" with an individual walking toward the office.

Differences in the two experiences were fairly clear. Eight years ago, he had broken school rules. This time, he was fulfilling professional responsibilities. Eight years ago he expected punishment upon arrival at the office. This time, he anticipated administrative support upon arrival. Eight years ago, he was uncertain as to the extent of aversive consequences to be administered in the office. This trip was routine and predictable. Finally, eight years ago he was an adolescent with few experiences or capabilities that would assist in managing the pending situation. This time he was a young adult with a wider repertoire of skills that would be effective in working through the situation. It was certain *not* to include aversive elements for the author.

Despite these obvious and substantial differences, the author developed the same physiological reaction to the trip. He experienced a rise in blood pressure, shortness of breath, and excessive perspiration. This curious reaction provoked serious second thoughts about his career choice. As a child, few things were more unpleasant than a trip to the principal's office. The same unpleasant emotions appeared to continue in reaction to trips to the office as an adult.

With each passing trip to the office, the emotional reactions gradually diminished. By the end of the school year, six trips to the office following the initial trip, the author was able to proceed in a matter-of-fact manner. His emotional reaction was no more or less dramatic than if he were going to the store to purchase bread (on a full stomach).

In retrospect, the author had developed a strong emotional reaction toward going to the principal's office. Initial changes in conditions associated with going to the office and the passage of eight years without an "office-related" experience did not alter this emotional reaction. Discussion about the experience and insight alone would not change the reaction. Only repeated experiences in which trips to the office were not associated with aversive events caused the initial emotional reactions to subside.

The author's experience is common to the formation of all human emotions. Few principles of learning have been studied as extensively as that of *association.* Also, few principles are as directly applied to and frequently experienced by the general population. When you hear a siren and view the red flashing lights of a police vehicle emerging from a median, your pulse and blood pressure are certain to increase. The smell of fresh-baked bread and roasted turkey is likely to result in increased production of gastric juices and saliva. The sight and sound of large crowds at a shopping mall are likely to produce feelings of agitation or anticipation.

Discussion and insight may be effective methods for understanding and modifying emotional reactions. However, they cannot stand alone in the emotional learning process. Consider the introductory story. Repeated trips to the principal's office were associated with unpleasant feelings. Consequently, these trips were soon able to independently yield negative emotional reactions. Insight-oriented discussions allowed the author to learn more about his reactions; however, as long as the trips and aversive events were paired, emotional reactions continued.

Time alone is also not an effective aid in modifying emotional reactions. The advice to return as soon as possible to the diving board following a belly flop is commonly provided to novice swimmers. We recognize that the association of pain from the bad dive with the diving board will continue until several successful and painless dives occur. The best strategy for overcoming the fear of riding horses that results from falling off of a horse is to get back on the horse. Time off the horse will do nothing to reduce fear of the horse.

In this chapter we describe the principles that underlie the development of emotional reactions. We also discuss how you can use these principles to change the emotional reactions your students may demonstrate in the classroom. In keeping with the applied behavior analytic nature of this text, we base our discussion on respondent conditioning. This body of literature offers techniques for working with students that are data-based and consistent with classroom settings.

Emotional Learning

Researchers have noted a high prevalence of emotional reactions in school populations (Misra & Schloss, 1989). Pappy and Spielberger (1986) emphasize the serious management problems associated with anxiety disorders among school-aged populations. School phobia, or the avoidance of school due to excessive anxiety, affects about 2 percent of the population (Kennedy, 1965), and general anxiety disorders appear to affect up to 10 percent of the population (Cass & Thomas, 1979; Graham, 1979).

Numerous disorders (e.g., autism, mental retardation, and physical handicaps) clearly result from biological limitations over which professionals have little control. Biological problems do, however, interact with environmental events to increase or decrease the ultimate impact of the disability. Mental retardation, for example, may result from a lack of oxygen at birth. Although professionals cannot replace nerve tissue lost, it is possible to assist the individual in developing appropriate social skills, functional academic capabilities, and essential personal management and care skills. Under less favorable conditions (e.g., large ward institutional care), the individual may not develop such skills.

Most nature/nurture discussions in the professional literature focus on the development of academic skills and intelligence. What may be equally important is the development of appropriate emotional characteristics. In view of this, we recommend that professionals carefully consider the following:

Biological and constitutional factors interact with the environment to produce emotional characteristics.

Learning and behavior disorders predispose an individual to develop maladaptive emotional characteristics through the association of learning tasks with failure and punishment.

Professionals and family members must exercise extreme care in establishing attainable expectations and rewards that produce appropriate emotional characteristics.

Generally, your responsibility to provide for your students' appropriate emotional development is best viewed by considering the role of association in emotional learning. *Activities and events that are associated with satisfying initial conditions and outcomes will be approached in the future with satisfying emotional expressions. Those that are associated with unpleasant conditions and consequences are likely to be avoided with a degree of anxiety or hostility.* For example, a student who consistently experiences success and rewards in math class through the first few grades will approach math class in subsequent grades with enthusiasm. A student who consistently fails math and is often reprimanded or embarrassed is likely to avoid subsequent classes. When class attendance is mandated, he or she is likely to be disinterested, fearful, or angry.

The role of association in emotional learning has been discussed very generally to this point. We now provide a more detailed view of the association of emotion with environmental conditions.

Operant versus Respondent Learning

Most of the systematic intervention procedures designed by teachers are based primarily on the **operant conditioning** or learning paradigm. The basic premise of this paradigm is that behavior is influenced by its consequences. Behavior that is maintained by positive consequences is said to be *positively reinforced.* Behavior that is maintained by the removal or avoidance of unpleasant consequences is said to be *negatively reinforced.* Finally, behavior that decreases as the result of unpleasant consequences is said to be *punished.* Not all behavioral reactions can be explained through operant learning. Emotional behaviors, in particular, are better understood by using an alternative learning paradigm.

Learning that results from the environment eliciting an emotional response is described as **respondent conditioning.** This term is synonymous with **classical conditioning** and **Pavlovian conditioning.** Figure 6.1 illustrates the difference between operant and respondent conditioning. Note that in operant conditioning, voluntary, controlled behavior produces predictable consequences. Speeding produces a fine, work produces payment, pleasant greetings produce a response from others. In respondent conditioning, an event produces or elicits an uncontrollable response. For example, aggression from another individual produces fear, receiving an award produces pride, wet pants produce embarrassment.

It is important to emphasize that complex behavior patterns generally result from both respondent and operant learning. A young man's initial reaction to pending athletic competition is uncontrolled anxiety (respondent). Increased anxiety motivates the youth to increase his training regimen. Increased training improves the skill and physical condition of the youth, resulting in enhanced performance and subsequent victory (operant). He continues to train rigorously in anticipation of future contests. To increase the clarity of explanations, the remainder of this chapter will address respondent learning as an isolated phenomenon. Other chapters will integrate emotional learning strategies with operant procedures.

Learned and Unlearned Emotional Responses

Not all emotional reactions are learned. At birth, a few events that satisfy basic needs automatically produce emotional responses. These *unlearned* emotional re-

OPERANT CONDITIONING

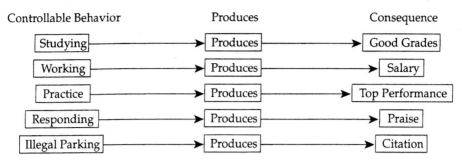

RESPONDENT CONDITIONING

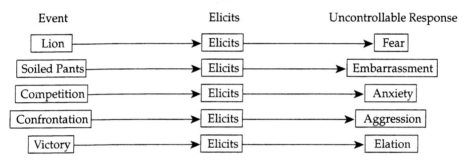

FIGURE 6.1   Relationship between Operant and Respondent Conditioning

sponses are reflexes that occur without the benefit of instruction. Dissatisfaction is produced automatically by unpleasant events such as hunger, extreme temperatures, loud noises or bright lights, and physical irritants. On the other hand, satisfaction is produced by food, warmth, soft noise, dim lights, and removal of irritants.

Feelings of pride in accomplishment, anxiety over failure, anger toward someone who is aggressive, envy toward others' accomplishments, and so on, are not experienced by the newborn. As the child grows older, these new events begin to produce emotional responses. The emotional response becomes more subtle and variable. These differentiated responses to new events are described as *learned* emotional reactions.

All of us are born with the same limited set of unlearned emotional responses. Learned emotions vary among people as a result of their learning histories. Our initial example in which the principal's office elicited anxiety is a commonly acquired emotional reaction that is not present at birth. Only those for whom the principal's office has been paired with unpleasant events (real, observed, or imagined) are likely to possess that uncontrollable emotional reaction.

	At Birth	Initial Pairing	After Multiple Pairings
Mother's Voice	Neutral	Neutral	Satisfaction
Food	Satisfaction	Satisfaction	Satisfaction

FIGURE 6.2   Illustration of the Relationship of a Neutral Stimulus (Mother's Voice) to an Unlearned Emotional Response (Satisfaction) before, during, and after Pairings in Respondent Conditioning

Figure 6.2 further illustrates the manner in which association causes an unlearned emotional reaction (those present at birth) to produce a learned emotional reaction (those developed through life experiences). Note that repeated pairings of unlearned emotional reactions with a neutral stimulus eventually enable the neutral stimulus to produce the same reaction.

For most students entering elementary and secondary schools, unlearned emotional responses are seldom used to produce emotional responses. Initial emotional learning causes language to develop strong emotional control through its pairing with unlearned emotional reactions (e.g., parent's voice with food, removal of irritants, and presentation of unpleasant consequences). As one matures, these language-based learned emotional responses are paired with neutral stimuli to produce emotional reactions from the neutral stimuli (e.g., praise with good grades, compliments for achievement, and threats with disruptive behavior). This process, referred to as *higher order conditioning,* serves as the basis from which spoken language exerts emotional control over people. It may be the most important emotional learning event associated with school motivation as we generally use language to prompt students' desirable emotional behavior. Further, teachers' spoken language may be one of the more frequent elicitors of disruptive emotional behavior.

Both desirable and undesirable emotional responses are learned through routine interactions with the environment. Students who have grown up in warm and supportive environments, been encouraged to establish and maintain mutually supportive relationships, and experienced positive events are likely to possess appropriate emotional responses. Students deprived of positive events, who have repeatedly faced unpleasant stimuli, whose interactions with adults are characteristically aversive, and who are frequently isolated from supportive social situations are likely to develop undesirable emotional features.

Principles that govern the acquisition, reduction, or modification of emotional reactions are provided in subsequent sections of this chapter. Knowledge of these principles will assist you in developing classroom environments that promote positive emotional expression. Further, they will assist you in designing intensive emotional learning programs that reduce the ability of an event to elicit inappropriate or excessive emotional reactions.

Development of Emotional Responses

We noted earlier that at birth very few events produce emotional reactions. Those that are produced are restricted to satisfaction and dissatisfaction. The basic rule of emotional learning explains the ability of a previously neutral event to provoke emotional reactions. This basic rule is that *a neutral event repeatedly paired with an emotionally provoking event will begin to produce the same emotional response as the provoking event when the previously neutral event is presented alone.*

The classic illustration of this rule is Pavlov's dog. The sight and smell of food prompted the dog's reaction or emotional response (salivation). The bell, however, was a neutral event that produced no reaction in the dog. Both events were presented simultaneously (paired), and eventually, salivation occurred in the presence of the bell alone. Another example is the manner in which a mother's voice develops emotional control over her infant. We can assume that at birth the mother's voice is a neutral stimulus. It produces neither satisfaction nor dissatisfaction to the newborn. Shortly following birth, however, the mother begins to nurture the child by providing warmth (holding in a blanket), providing food (breast or bottle feeding), and removing irritants (diapering). She talks to the child repeatedly during the activities that produce the unlearned emotional reaction of satisfaction. Repeated pairings of the neutral event, mother's voice, with the unlearned emotional reaction, satisfaction, eventually result in the mother's voice independently producing the satisfying emotional reaction.

The associations used in the preceding examples are obvious and direct. Direct associations occurred between aversive events and the principal's office. The bell was paired with the sight and smell of food. The mother's voice was directly paired with feeding and comforting the baby. Many associations are not as direct or apparent. Several less direct methods of association include vicarious conditioning, emotive imagery, stimulus generalization, and semantic generalization. Each of these extends the basic rule of emotional learning.

Vicarious Conditioning

An emotional reaction to a neutral stimulus may result from observing another individual's emotional response to a similar stimulus. Many children and adults, for example, are afraid of events with which they have had little or no experience. Usually people's fears can be attributed to their observation of others being harmed by the events. Few people have had direct experience with poisonous reptiles. Yet, one would expect the average person to become fearful if locked in a room with a snake. It is not common for people to experience a shark attack. However, a shark alert in a swimming area would be certain to provoke a degree of panic. In both cases, emotional learning has not occurred through direct experience but through vicarious conditioning, the observation of others.

Vicarious conditioning can occur though direct observations or through media. Television shows, photographs, radio reports, and written and verbal accounts of emotionally provoking incidents can develop similar emotional reactions in the observer. For example, few people have experienced the excitement of blasting through the atmosphere in an Apollo capsule. Yet people uniformly display a degree of excitement when touring the air and space exhibits at the Smithsonian Institution. It is likely that a majority of this excitement results from media reports of NASA's activities over the past decades.

Emotive Imagery

Beyond direct experience and observing media accounts, a person's mental image of an event can condition an emotional reaction. Simply "imagining" a provoking situation can produce an emotional response that is similar to actually being in the situation. We have all experienced dreams that were emotionally laden. You may note that upon waking up from such dreams, you exhibit the same emotional reaction that occurs in actual life. We wake up in a "good mood" from a dream in which we won a lottery or have an enjoyable date with a desirable individual. We wake up in a "bad mood" from a dream in which we had a car accident or were rejected by a friend.

Emotive imagery is used to condition positive emotions by therapists and teachers alike. Knowing that a student is very apprehensive about taking a test, the teacher may ask that she place her head on the desk, close her eyes, and imagine sailing through the exam with few errors. The confident feelings that this produces may extend into the actual test-taking situation. Athletes are often instructed to form a mental image of a successful competition. This image is expected to reduce anxiety and increase confidence so that actual performance is enhanced.

Stimulus Generalization

An object or event does not have to be identical to the provoking event for the same emotional reaction to occur. Stimulus generalization results when emotional reactions extend beyond a specific set of conditions to similar conditions. The classic example of stimulus generalization is found in Watson and Rayner's (1920) work with a toddler named Albert. You may recall that Watson paired presentation of a loud sound (an emotionally provoking event) with a white toy rabbit (neutral stimulus). After several pairings, the presence of the toy was enough to make Albert cry (a learned emotional reaction). Watson reported, however, that Albert also cried in the presence of other white furry objects—including another stuffed animal, cotton, and even Watson's beard.

The more similar the objects or events, the more likely it is that generalization will occur. Highly similar objects such as two different rattlesnakes are more likely to produce common emotional reactions than only moderately similar objects such as a rattlesnake and a garden snake. Dissimilar objects such as a rattlesnake and a rabbit are unlikely to produce comparable emotional reactions.

Stimulus generalization accounts, in part, for students developing pervasive negative emotions and attitudes toward all schools, teachers, and instructional materials. The pairing of helplessness, frustration, and failure with a few teachers, sets of books, or schools is likely to generalize to all subsequent teachers, books, and schools. Conversely, positive experiences in primary grades are likely to produce a similar positive outlook upon entering secondary and post secondary grades.

Semantic Generalization

Objects or events that are described with the same verbal labels may produce similar emotional reactions despite their appearance or function of being dissimilar. A youth may have a generalized dislike for authority figures described as "principals," "police officers," or "teachers." The presence of an individual described with these labels may produce the same negative emotional reaction despite the person's having different stature, sex, or attire. The initial dislike for principals, police officers, or teachers may have resulted from several bad experiences with one or more of the authority figures. Subsequently, any individual described with these labels immediately elicits the same emotional reaction.

Strength and Persistence of Emotional Reaction

The rules we have just described account for the development of emotional responses. They do not, however, address the intensity and persistence of a student's emotional reactions. This section outlines rules that govern the development of intense and persistent emotional reactions.

Children and youth differ not only in the range of emotional expression but in the intensity of that expression. Physical threats may produce mild agitation in one child and debilitating fear in another. Similarly, a testing situation may cause one youth to be slightly anxious and another to be physically ill. Two related rules account for the strength and persistence of learned emotional reactions. The first addresses the intensity of the emotionally provoking response that is paired with the neutral event. The second addresses the frequency of pairings between the provoking event and the neutral event. These rules will be considered separately.

Intensity of the Paired Response

The stronger the emotional response produced by the paired event, the stronger the emotional response that will eventually develop in reaction to the previously neutral event. In other words, when events that produce very intense emotional reactions are paired with neutral events, the neutral events will develop similarly strong emotional reactions. An event that produces a very mild emotional response will produce at most a mild response to the paired event.

For example, a few years ago a severe storm hit southern Illinois. One family's mobile home was lifted from its pad, destroying the unit and its contents. In addition, one child was critically injured. It is not surprising that subsequent severe storm warnings, tornado sightings, weather alerts, and so on are likely to produce extreme stress and fear reactions in the family members. Another family suffered only minor property damage (e.g., fallen tree limbs and slight damage to roofing). All family members were safely sheltered from the storm. Given the minor intensity of the event, storm-related experiences that follow are likely to produce only mild emotional responses in this family.

Frequency of Pairings

Frequent associations of the neutral event with an emotionally provoking event will enhance the strength and persistence of the eventual emotional response to the neutral event. Peer rejection occurring only a few times a year through grade school will do little to condition a negative emotional response to social interactions. Daily or weekly episodes of peer rejection are likely to result in the child developing a persistent aversion to social interactions. Similarly, a teacher who continually pairs requests for work with support and satisfying outcomes will eventually produce positive emotional expression in her students without the use of more tangible consequences.

Students placed in educational settings characterized by the *frequent association of intensely favorable* emotional events are likely to develop persistent and strong positive reactions to school. These reactions are also likely to generalize to many of the activities and events associated with school. Conversely, students with educational histories characterized by *frequent exposure to intensely negative* emotional events such as corporal punishment, deprivation of privileges, public failure, and reprimands are likely to develop persistent and strong negative reactions to school. Likewise, these reactions may generalize to all school-related settings and activities.

The importance of these principles to preventing the development of negative emotional reactions should be clear. Unfortunately, many children and youth enter our classes with well-established negative emotional reactions to school events. Therefore, it may be equally important to recognize how these principles relate to altering disruptive emotional expression. The following section will describe rules that govern the modification of existing emotional characteristics.

Developing Alternative Emotional Responses

We have emphasized that children's and youths' behavioral characteristics change over time. We can expect that as students grow older and are exposed to a variety of learning experiences, their responses will change. Experiences that are well conceived produce changes that enhance the child's or youth's adaptability to the school and community. Just as behavioral repertoires develop over time, so also do emotional features. We are all familiar with people who were traumatized with the prospect of swimming, public speaking, or playing aggressive sports who later became highly accomplished at these activities. Similarly, we are aware of individuals who, despite early positive dispositions toward school, dropped out prior to finishing high school.

In most cases, changes in emotional responses occur through chance experiences. As teachers, you can be much more systematic. You would not leave the development of academic skills to chance. Similarly, you can take a more proactive role in your students' development of appropriate emotional responses.

In Chapter 4, we encouraged you to use antecedent control techniques to increase the likelihood that students will demonstrate appropriate classroom behavior. We also warned you that it is unwise, not to mention impossible, to exercise such tight control that your classroom becomes unnatural. A major part of your teaching responsibilities is to assist your students in developing the skills they need to control their behavior, regardless of the circumstances surrounding them. Two principles for developing alternative emotional responses will be considered in the following sections. The first, **extinction,** is used to simply diminish an excessive emotional response without providing an alternative form of emotional expression. The second, **counterconditioning,** provides for the replacement of a disruptive emotional reaction with a more adaptive reaction.

Extinction

Respondent extinction is used to reduce or eliminate acquired emotional reactions. As noted earlier, neutral events develop the ability to elicit emotional responses through repeated pairings with provoking events. Neutral events that have become provoking will lose their ability to produce acquired emotional reactions if they subsequently occur in the absence of the paired provoking event.

For example, an adolescent who has repeatedly experienced failure in school is likely to develop negative emotional reactions to the school setting (and related stimuli). Subsequent resource room and consultation services can result in more appropriate standards for success as well as increased student performance. As a result, failure experiences will occur substantially less often. Because failure is no longer paired with the educational setting, the educational setting loses its ability to provoke the negative emotions.

Be advised, however, that this technique takes time to work. Students' negative emotional reactions have developed over time; therefore, you will need to be consistent and persistent as you provide educational services that are more appropriate for students' needs.

Counterconditioning

Counterconditioning is similar to extinction except that rather than pairing a provoking event with neutral stimuli, the provoking event is paired with stimuli that produce incompatible positive emotions. An event that has acquired negative emotional properties is paired with an event that yields stronger positive emotions. The original event will lose its ability to elicit the original response and may begin to produce the incompatible positive emotion.

There is a long tradition of barbers providing lollipops to children during a haircut. Negative emotional reactions are likely to occur in the barber chair as haircutting is paired with provoking events (e.g., loud noise, hair pulls, irritating vibrations, and the appearance of sharp instruments). The lollipop is an unlearned stimulus for the unlearned emotion of pleasure and satisfaction. Pairing the lollipop (satisfying emotion) with haircutting (negative emotion) is intended to minimize the formation of negative emotions and possibly increase positive emotions associated with haircuts.

Counterconditioning requires that the incompatible response be more intense than the negative response. Failure to consider the relative strength of the two emotional responses could result in the incompatible event losing its ability to elicit positive emotions because of its association with the stronger negative emotional reaction. In the previous example, it is possible that the child dislikes haircuts more than he likes lollipops. If this were the case, then the lollipop would have no effect on the child's emotional reaction to getting his hair cut. In fact, it is possible that presenting a lollipop while getting a haircut may make the child hate lollipops. A procedure for counterconditioning negative emotional reactions for which there are no stronger positive emotions will be discussed later in this chapter.

The rate of extinction or counterconditioning is determined by the magnitude of previous conditioning trials. As noted previously, pairings with highly noxious stimuli will be more resistant to change. Also, emotions developed through numerous pairings will be more resistant to change. Frequent and consistent presentation of the learned emotional event without the paired provoking event will result in extinction of the learned emotional event more quickly than if the paired provoking event is allowed to occur occasionally. Finally, in counterconditioning, the stronger the paired incompatible response, the quicker the change in the negative emotional reaction.

It is important to note, for the sake of clarity, that rules of emotional learning, extinction, and counterconditioning have been described as isolated events. In real life, they often occur simultaneously. For example, it is best to use counterconditioning while using extinction. The most rapid change in negative emotional expression will occur if the unpleasant event is removed (extinction) at the same time that an event that produces incompatible positive emotions is introduced (counterconditioning). For example, perhaps you have a sixth grader who is a very poor reader. As a result, he hates to participate in reading lessons, particularly those that involve oral reading. You should use your expertise to identify specific areas of weaknesses and design appropriate instruction that will enable him to make progress. Involve him in these lessons and ensure success. Praise his efforts and refrain from criticizing him after oral reading (extinction). At the same time, use a variety of written materials about activities he enjoys rather than a basal text (counterconditioning). Over time, his reading skills will improve and he will be less likely to avoid reading. In fact, he may start to enjoy it.

Finally, there is no evidence that time alone alters negative emotional reactions. Students who have negative feelings toward school in the spring are likely to continue to dislike school in the fall in the absence of extinction or counterconditioning experiences. Students who drop out of school at age 16 are not likely to gladly return to school at the age of 18 unless intervening events change their emotional reactions toward school. Students do not outgrow their negative emotions. These emotions change because during the passage of time, planned or unplanned counterconditioning or extinction trials occur.

We assume you are concerned about the positive emotional development of your students; therefore, you must recognize how emotions are formed. Based on this understanding you should design educational programs that consistently pair classroom activities with events that produce positive emotions. Recognition that a student has developed negative emotional reactions to the school environment should result in the development of extinction and counterconditioning programs. The following sections will describe specific procedures that can be used to ensure the development of positive emotions and elimination of disruptive emotions.

Emotional Development Strategies

We have emphasized that influencing emotional characteristics of students with learning and behavior disorders is as important as promoting desirable social, academic, personal, and vocational skills. In some ways it may be more important, because a person's emotional disposition underlies his or her motivation to develop all subsequent skills. A youth who enjoys school is likely to approach educational activities with enthusiasm and care. A student who does not like school is likely to avoid educational activities whenever possible. Clearly, the student with a positive outlook is most likely to achieve to his or her highest potential. Conversely, the disinterested student will quickly be labeled as an underachiever or at risk for dropping out of school.

Strategy #1: The Basic Rule of Emotional Learning

The first strategy useful for influencing the emotional characteristics of children and youth follows from the basic rule of emotional learning. It is appropriate for the development of new positive emotional reactions for students who do not possess an appropriate range and intensity of emotional expression. This strategy is appropriate for withdrawn students who are not interested in school activities considered enjoyable by the general population, as well as for aggressive youths who are apathetic toward specific educational activities. The basic strategy for promoting the development of new emotions is as follows:

1. Identify events that produce positive emotional responses for the student.
2. Identify specific school-related events that fail to produce the same emotional response.
3. Structure the school day so that the two events occur simultaneously on numerous occasions.

For example, you notice that a withdrawn preschooler becomes very excited and animated when playing "Simon Says," eating lunch or snacks, and throwing a ball with the teacher. You notice that while the preschooler appears happy when engaged in these activities with you, he is disinterested and bored when engaged in any activities with peers. Arrange for the student to play games and eat snacks with you and other students. By pairing the neutral event (playing with peers) with the positive event (eating snacks and playing games with you), other children will acquire the ability to produce the same positive emotional response in the withdrawn child.

Strategy #2: Vicarious Conditioning

A similar strategy that follows from the rule of vicarious conditioning can be used to develop positive emotional reactions to neutral events. The strategy is similar to the previous approach except that the new emotional reaction is developed through observations of other individuals rather than direct participation. Vicarious conditioning is conducted as follows:

1. Identify events in which the student fails to exhibit positive emotional responses.
2. Identify situations in which other children or youth produce a positive emotional response to the same event.
3. Arrange for the child or youth to observe (and/or participate with) the other students in these situations.

For example, arrange for a student to watch several soccer games prior to encouraging him to try out for the team. Change a student's class placement so that he will be with students who show enthusiasm for the material. Arrange a seating assignment so that a "disinterested" child is able to interact with children who are excited about class activities.

Emotional Reduction Strategies

The previous strategies are useful for developing positive emotional reactions in students who show little or no emotional reactions to enjoyable situations. As teachers, you will also be dealing with students who have excessive emotional reactions. Generally, your goal is to diminish or eliminate these excessive reactions.

Strategy #1: Counterconditioning

The rule of counterconditioning forms the basis of emotional reduction procedures. The basic strategy includes repeatedly pairing the emotionally provoking event with an event that produces a more intense incompatible positive response. Basic procedures for reducing negative emotionality include the following:

1. Identify stimuli that elicit negative emotional responses.
2. Identify stimuli that elicit stronger incompatible emotional responses.

3. Structure the classroom environment so that the negative and positive stimuli occur together. Alternately, arrange for the positive stimuli to precede the negative stimuli.

For example, a preschooler who is afraid of the water may refuse to go into a swimming pool. The smart swimming instructor will allow the child's mother to accompany her into the water. Her love for and trust in her mother outweigh her fear of the water. Once in the water, the swimming instructor can teach the skills necessary for a child to become a confident, competent swimmer.

Strategy #2: Vicarious Counterconditioning

Counterconditioning can also occur through the use of vicarious conditioning. The following procedures illustrate the manner in which vicarious counterconditioning can be used:

1. Identify situations that elicit negative emotional reactions.
2. Identify situations in which other students demonstrate incompatible positive emotions to the same event.
3. Structure the educational environment so that the child or youth frequently observes other students demonstrating positive emotional reactions to the provoking event.

For example, you can reduce a child's fear of water by encouraging her to sit on the deck of a pool and watch others play in the water. A parent may reduce his daughter's fear of separation by having her watch other children enjoy treats shortly after their parents leave the daycare center. Anger toward authority figures following criticism may be reduced by watching films in which workers use the feedback to increase production and salary.

Strategy #3: Systematic Desensitization

We have repeatedly emphasized that counterconditioning must involve the presentation of a *stronger* incompatible emotional response. Many negative emotional reactions are so provoking that events producing equally strong positive emotional responses cannot be identified. To accommodate these situations, researchers have developed a method called *systematic desensitization.*

It is possible for a single event to produce such an excessively strong emotional reaction that it is difficult to handle in the classroom. With systematic desensitization, you can arrange for events to happen that resemble the original event. These events should be arranged in a hierarchical order from least to most provoking. Present the least provoking event and allow the initial minor reaction to subside. Gradually move through the hierarchy until emotional control is established. Specifically, systematic desensitization involves the following steps:

1. Interview the student and others who are aware of the problem to identify events associated with the excessive negative emotional reactions. Prioritize these events from least provoking to most provoking. This ranking for a school-phobic student may begin with preparing for school, going to the bus stop, boarding the bus, leaving the bus, entering the school building, entering class, and taking the assigned seat.

2. Identify an event that produces an incompatible positive emotional reaction. In the school phobia example, this may include the emotive imagery and progressive muscle relaxation exercises that are discussed later in this chapter.

3. Pair the least provoking event in the hierarchy identified in step one with the event producing the incompatible emotional reaction. This association continues until the event fails to produce a negative emotional reaction.

4. Pair the second, slightly more provoking event in the hierarchy with the event producing the incompatible emotional reaction. Again, this association continues until the student is no longer aroused by the event.

5. Pair the third, more provoking event in the hierarchy with the event producing the incompatible emotional reaction until the student is able to remain calm through the event.

6. Continue this process through each subsequent event on the hierarchy until the most provoking event fails to produce an excessive negative reaction.

Schloss, Smith, Santora, and Bryant (1989) demonstrated the use of systematic desensitization in reducing excessive agitation and aggression of an individual with mental retardation. Interviews with the youth and his parents identified three areas that produced excessive emotional reactions. These included "joking," "criticism," and "heterosexual talk." The youth and his parents also assisted in establishing a hierarchy of situations in each area that were increasingly likely to produce agitation. The heterosexual talk hierarchy, for example, included the following steps: telling a story that included a woman described as being pretty, talking about pretty girls, talking about marital relations, discussing physical contact with women in the form of hand holding, and discussing physical contact with women in the form of hugging and kissing.

The young man was taught to engage in progressive muscle relaxation as described in the following section. When he was able to produce a state of relaxation, the first stimulus in the hierarchy was introduced. This continued through each session until he was able to remain relaxed throughout the session. At that time, the next step on the hierarchy was introduced. This process continued until he was able to remain relaxed through the most provoking stimulus (i.e., discussing physical hugging and kissing).

Establishing Positive Emotions

The foundational strategies for developing and altering emotional characteristics rely on pairing situations that yield neutral or negative emotions with events that produce incompatible positive emotions. In most of our early examples, positive emotions were encouraged by arranging for a student to engage in a specific activity that produced these positive reactions. Events discussed included game playing, eating, participating in social interactions, and so on. Approaches for producing incompatible positive emotions that are independent of environmental contexts are also important to systematic efforts to alter emotions. The major advantage of these approaches is that they can be used by a student regardless of the surrounding physical conditions.

Emotive Imagery

Probably the most pragmatic method for producing a positive emotional response is to use emotive imagery. Emotive imagery involves the student imagining situations in which positive emotional responses are likely to occur. A child or youth may be encouraged to imagine playing on the beach, sinking a game-winning free throw, listening to a favorite comedian, or spending a large sum of money. Reese, Howard, and Reese (1978) described the use of emotive imagery in the following passage:

> One 14 year old boy with an intense fear of dogs had a burning desire to own an Alfa Romeo and race it at the "Indianapolis 500." During the course of therapy he imagined owning the car as the therapist vividly described its beauty and action. Gradually, the anxiety producing stimulus was introduced: " ...The speedometer is climbing into the 90's; you have a wonderful feeling of being in perfect control; you look at the trees whizzing by and you see a little dog standing next to one of them—if you feel any anxiety, just raise your finger." Eventually, the child imagines that he is showing off his car to a crowd of envious people in a strange town when a dog comes up and sniffs at his heels. (p. 195)

This description illustrates the highly structured and carefully planned use of emotive imagery. It is important to note, however, that emotive imagery can be used more spontaneously. For example, Olympic diving and gymnastic athletes often talk about combating preroutine anxiety and pessimism by cognitively rehearsing a "perfect" dive or routine. Professional golfers often visualize the flight of the golf ball directly toward the hole in anticipation of a difficult shot. Similar approaches can be used with students who become angry when asked to complete academic assignments. Upon receiving a request, they may be encouraged to imagine completing the assignment, being praised by the teacher, and receiving predetermined privileges.

Progressive Muscle Relaxation

An alternative approach to producing positive emotional responses is progressive muscle relaxation. This method was pioneered by Jacobsen (1938) and promoted more recently by Wolpe (1958). Progressive muscle relaxation involves actively relaxing each of the major muscle groups. Relaxed muscle groups are then compared with groups that have not yet become the focus of relaxation exercises.

Bernstein and Borkovec (1973) have suggested the following procedures for using progressive muscle relaxation:

1. Request that the student lie down on a mat or bed. Arms should lie naturally at the side with hands about six inches from the side and palms facing up.

2. The student should be instructed to use "deep breathing." Air should flow though the nose by depressing the diaphragm (as opposed to expanding the chest). Air exchange should be slow and rhythmic.

3. The student should be instructed to "let go" of all tension and become limp.

4. Initial levels of relaxation can be evaluated by raising one of the student's hands or arms and letting it fall to the mat. A natural fall unrestrained by muscular activity suggests a reasonable level of relaxation. A more likely outcome early in the relaxation process is a jerky or forced movement of the hand to the mat.

5. Relaxation of the arms begins by requesting that the student clench and hold the right fist for six seconds. Next he or she is asked to raise the right arm and dig the elbow into the mat for six seconds. The student is asked to compare the relaxed right arm with the more tense left arm, and the preceding steps are repeated for the left arm.

6. Relaxation of the neck and shoulders begins by requesting that the student pull both shoulders up to the center of the body and hold for six seconds, then requesting that the student force his or her chin into the chest and hold for six seconds. Finally, ask the student to pull his or her head back, raising the chin as far as possible, and hold for six seconds. Again, the now relaxed muscles may be compared to other tense muscles. The student may also be asked to compare pre and post feelings of the muscles.

7. Relaxation of the face is conducted initially by asking the student to raise his or her eyebrows for six seconds. Next, ask the student to make a big smile that shows all teeth for six seconds, then request that the individual close his or her eyes as tightly as possible while raising the jaw. This position is held for six seconds. As with all muscle groups, the student may be asked to make comparisons between the now relaxed muscles and tense muscles.

8. The relaxation process moves to the legs by requesting that the student keep his or her right knee straight, stretching the right toes and ankles down from the leg for six seconds. Next, the legs are relaxed by asking the student to twist the right toes to the left for six seconds. The student is then asked to compare the relaxed right side with the left side. Finally, the preceding steps are repeated with the left side.

9. Relaxation is completed by guiding the student through a self-relaxation process. The student is asked to concentrate on each of the body parts and determine whether or not all stress has been removed from the muscle group. The student is asked to focus on the toes, ankles, calves, thighs, buttocks, abdomen, chest, neck, fingers, wrist, forearm, biceps, shoulders, cheeks, and forehead. He or she should be encouraged to self-induce relaxation when tension is detected.

Summary

A majority of attention in the professional literature and applied behavior analysis texts focuses on operant learning principles. As was emphasized early in this chapter, however, respondent learning may be equally important to overall school adjustment and more important for general emotional development. We noted that students with handicaps may possess biological or constitutional features that interact with the environment to produce negative emotional characteristics. The features may produce a high rate of failure and punishment in school, home, and community settings. The association of unpleasant events with these settings increases the likelihood that these settings independently produce dysfunctional emotions. Professionals, family members, and others must be careful to ensure that all important environments become associated with positive and supportive emotions.

As a general rule, activities and events associated with satisfying conditions and outcomes will be approached by a student in the future with feelings of challenge, success striving, confidence, and attainment. Those that are associated with unpleasant conditions and outcomes will be avoided with feelings of anxiety, apprehension, and possible hostility. Consequently, educators should strive to ensure that the school environment is replete with success striving and success attainment activities. There should be a consistent association between the educational environment and satisfying events.

For very young children and some students with more severe cognitive handicaps, school activities may need to be paired with unlearned emotional events such as physical comfort and food. These associations will develop positive emotional reactions to the school events. Special attention should also be paid to developing the emotional control of language. This is accomplished by pairing the unlearned emotional events with the verbal interactions from the teacher.

Older students are likely to have established learned emotional responses. They are likely to feel good about praise and other adult interactions. Certain activities such as games and television watching are also likely to produce positive emotional reactions. When this is the case, these secondary emotional events should be paired with neutral events from which similar emotional expressions are desired. Pairing competitive activities that a student enjoys with drill and practice exercises may increase positive emotional expression toward the drill and practice exercises.

Unfortunately, many students have developed negative emotional characteristics. In most cases, events that should elicit neutral or positive reactions actually elicit negative reactions. We recommend the use of counterconditioning to change these emotional reactions. In general, counterconditioning is accomplished by pairing the event producing the negative emotional reaction with events that produce *stronger* incompatible positive reactions. When events cannot be identified that produce stronger reactions, we encourage the use of systematic desensitization. This is accomplished by pairing approximations of the negative event with a positive event.

Finally, we recommended two major strategies for producing positive emotional reactions. Emotive imagery involves encouraging the student to imagine a situation in which positive emotions are likely to be elicited. The second, progressive muscle relaxation, involves tensing and releasing all of the major muscle groups. These procedures are encouraged for use in conjunction with counterconditioning and systematic desensitization.

Early in the chapter we noted that the principles of emotional learning were closely associated with operant principles discussed throughout this text. We purposefully treated these principles as being distinct from operant principles to enable a more clear description of the rationale for and practice of emotional learning practices. Two discrete relationships between the two learning paradigms should be clear at this point.

First, the operant paradigm relies on the use of satisfying and aversive events as consequences for behavior. Operant strategies for students with poorly developed emotional characteristics must rely on primary reinforcements (e.g., using food and comfort as a positive consequence for good behavior). Operant strategies for students with well developed emotional characteristics can employ more natural and age normative secondary reinforcing events (e.g., social praise as a consequence for good behavior). The goal of emotional learning programs to develop the strength of events such as social praise and achievement opportunities benefits the conduct of operant procedures. Emotional development leading to the strong influence of normative secondary reinforcing events allows the use of more natural reinforcers.

Second, well conceived operant programs also accommodate respondent principles and goals. For example, an operant program with attainable objectives and satisfying consequences ensures the pairing of those satisfying consequences with the events identified in the objective. These events (e.g., work completion or social participation) are likely to be neutral or negative at the start of the program. Because of the repeated pairing of these events with the satisfying consequences, the events are likely to attain the same positive emotional value as the consequences.

In conclusion, this chapter has provided a foundation for the development of positive emotional reactions. We have emphasized the role of a positive and supportive environment in fostering the development of positive emotional reactions. We also identified specific strategies for altering dysfunctional emotions. Finally, we presented specific strategies for promoting positive emotions.

References

Bernstein, D. A., & Borkovec, T. D. (1973). *Progressive relaxation training: A manual for the helping professions.* Champaign, IL: Research Press.

Cass, L. K., & Thomas, C. B. (1979). *Childhood pathology and later adjustment: The question of prediction.* New York: Wiley.

Graham, P. J. (1979). Epidemiological studies. In H. C. Quay & J. S. Werry (Eds.), *Psychopathological disorders of childhood* (2nd ed.). New York: Wiley.

Jacobsen, E. (1938). *Progressive relaxation.* Chicago: University of Chicago Press.

Kennedy, W. (1965). School phobia: Rapid treatment of fifty cases. *Journal of Abnormal Psychology, 70,* 285–289.

Misra, A., & Schloss, P. J. (1989). Respondent techniques for reducting emotions limiting school adjustment: A quantitative review and methodological critique. *Education and Treatment of Children, 12*(2), 174–189.

Pappy, J. P., & Spielberger C. D. (1986). Assessment of anxiety and achievement in kindergarten and first and second grade children. *Journal of Abnormal Child Psychology, 14,* 279–286.

Reese, E. P., Howard, J., & Reese, T. W. (1978). *Human operant behavior: Analysis and application.* Dubuque, IA: William C. Brown.

Schloss, P. J., Smith, M., Santora, C., & Bryant, R. (1989). A respondent conditioning approach to reducing anger responses of a dually diagnosed man with mental retardation. *Behavior Therapy, 20,* 459–464.

Watson, J. B., & Rayner, R. (1920). Conditioned emotional reactions. *Journal of Experimental Psychology, 3,* 1–14.

Wolpe, J. (1958). *Psychotherapy by reciprocal inhibition.* Stanford, CA: Stanford University Press, 1958.

7

INCREASING APPROPRIATE
BEHAVIOR THROUGH
CONSEQUENCE CONTROL

We emphasized in the preceding chapters that interventions focused on related characteristics help students learn appropriate skills. These skills provide students with alternatives to disruptive responses. For example, prior to participation in relaxation and social skill training, a student may have no alternative but to argue or fight when challenged by a classmate. Following successful development of related characteristics, the student may be able to remain relaxed and negotiate rather than argue and fight. Whether or not the student will *choose* the socially appropriate action cannot be assured through intervention on related characteristics alone. A child who has learned to relax and negotiate when confronted may still choose to become angry and fight.

Consequences are events that follow a specific behavior and influence the likelihood that a student will use the behavior in the future. Therefore, while attention to related characteristics may develop positive alternatives to disruptive social behaviors, consequences help to ensure that students use these behaviors in the place of disruptive responses.

Rotter (1975) proposed a social learning model that highlights the importance of consequences. He contended that the likelihood that a behavior will be used is determined by the student's expectation for reinforcement and the perceived value of reinforcement to the student. The following formula denotes the relationship of these variables:

Behavioral Potential = Expectancy and Value of Reinforcement

Rotter's formulation has several major implications for applied behavior analysis interventions. *First, students who engage in disruptive social behaviors may not possess positive social responses expected to be effective in producing valued reinforcement.* Research by a number of authors indicates that individuals with disabilities are less likely to possess appropriate social responses (Blackbourn, 1989; Carter & Sugai, 1988; Martin, Rusch, Lagomarcino, & Chadsey-Rusch, 1986; Nelson, 1988; Schloss & Schloss, 1987). Instruction in related characteristics is intended to correct this problem by providing these alternative prosocial skills. However, because of past learning history, the student who is now socially competent may still believe that disruptive responses will produce greater or more immediate satisfaction.

Second, students who engage in disruptive social behaviors may prefer reinforcement produced by these responses over those available through positive behavior. In our previous example, reinforcement expected from the disruptive responses may include peer approval and unconditional compliance from the classmate. The socially skillful response may only produce praise from the teacher and conditional compliance from the classmate. If the student values the former set of consequences over the latter, you can expect disruptive responses to be used over socially skillful responses.

Third, students who engage in disruptive social behaviors may have *increased expectancy for reinforcement* following these responses when contrasted with positive social responses. The student may believe, based on past events, that being argumentative and engaging in fighting will consistently produce the desired effects (i.e., reinforcement). Social skills, however, may produce satisfying effects only intermittently.

Each of these factors highlights the importance of developing appropriate consequences for positive behaviors. Antecedents may set the stage for appropriate behaviors to occur, and may also prevent the occurrence of disruptive behaviors. Related characteristics help the student acquire new alternative positive responses. Consequences, however, ensure that the student will choose to use the positive social behaviors over other options. This assurance results from the increased preference for items or events that result from positive social behavior as well as the increased expectancy that these items or events will be obtained.

Reinforcement

Definition of Reinforcement

Reinforcement is a process through which a target behavior is strengthened (i.e., increasing the frequency, duration, or magnitude) as the result of its effect in producing specific consequences. Reinforcement describes a contingency (if/then relationship) in which the contingent presentation of a consequence increases the likelihood of future occurrences of the behavior. *Reinforcers* include satisfying consequences that are effective in increasing the strength of a behavior. These satisfying consequences can include attainment of positive events or the avoidance/removal of negative events. The difference between these two conditions is described in the following section.

Positive versus Negative Reinforcement

Positive reinforcement strengthens behavior through a contingent relationship with a satisfying consequence. Our students study for tests because good performance results in social praise and special privileges from parents. Praise and privileges are satisfying events that increase the likelihood that studying occurs in the future. Professional athletes train diligently for sports competitions because of the expectation for success, financial reward, and public acclaim.

     Negative reinforcement strengthens behavior through a contingent relationship involving the removal or avoidance of dissatisfying events. An employee may behave very positively toward her employer because of the employer's reputation for firing staff members that he does not like. Behaving positively is negatively reinforced because it serves the function of avoiding work termination. A child may cry whenever her diapers become filled. Upon hearing the crying, her father and mother change the diapers. Crying is negatively reinforced by its effectiveness in removing irritants.

     It has been our experience that negative reinforcement is frequently confused with the concept of punishment. Cipani (1995) and Justen and Howerton (1993) attributed this confusion to the aversive elements of negative reinforcement. People mistakenly assume that negative reinforcement is used to reduce behavior. We have heard many teachers label procedures they use to increase behaviors as positive reinforcement and the procedures they use to decrease behaviors as negative reinforcement. The correct term for the latter group of procedures is punishment. Positive and negative reinforcement are not opposites; in fact, they both involve procedures that increase behavior. Punishment, on the other hand, decreases behavior.

     The same event can be influenced by both positive and negative reinforcement. For example, think of the reason you observe posted safety limits or wear a seat belt. The more civic-minded response is that you are positively reinforced by the satisfaction you feel from obeying the law. A more honest response is that you are negatively reinforced by avoiding a ticket or injury in a serious accident. Positive and negative reinforcement also influence your students' behavior. Studying produces good grades and the occasional special privilege (positive reinforcement) and allows students to avoid failure (negative reinforcement). Table 7.1 provides additional examples of positive and negative reinforcers.

Establishing Reinforcement Strength

Reinforcers can also be described by their strength. A strong reinforcer is one for which a child or youth has a marked preference. A weak reinforcer is one for which the child or youth is slightly more than indifferent. A parsimonious test of reinforcement strength involves simply observing what the child does when given a range of alternatives.

     We have numerous opportunities to observe reinforcer preference every day. For example, the television guide includes all possible television shows that we

TABLE 7.1   Definition and Examples of Positive and Negative Reinforcement

Class—Positive Reinforcement
Definition—An item or event that follows or is produced by a behavior that results in the increased or sustained occurrence of the behavior.
Example—High grades for studying result in continued studying. Studying is positively reinforced by high grades.

Weight loss and improved health from aerobic exercise result in continued exercise.
Exercise is positively reinforced by weight loss and improved health.

Weekly wage and benefits from employment result in continued employment. Employment is positively reinforced by wages and benefits.

Completion of each assembly in a sheltered workshop produces a token and increased production occurs. Assembly completion is positively reinforced by tokens.

Class—Negative Reinforcement
Definition—Removal/avoidance of a noxious item or event as a consequence of a behavior that results in the increased or sustained occurrence of the behavior.
Example—Washing clothes results in the removal of unpleasant odors. Clothes washing is negatively reinforced by elimination of odors.

Negotiation results in the cancellation of a trial. Negotiation is negatively reinforced by avoidance of litigation.

Cramming for an examination results in the avoidance of a failing grade. Cramming is negative reinforced by the avoidance of failure.

Providing food for a crying baby results in the elimination of crying. Feeding is negatively reinforced by the cessation of crying.

may watch during any given period. Shows that are selected for viewing are likely to have the most reinforcing properties. The reinforcement value of clothing, food, and other purchases is evaluated in the same manner. Again, we have the opportunity to select from a range of potentially reinforcing items. Those routinely selected are likely to be the most reinforcing.

A program to change your students' behavior has a much greater chance of success if the reinforcers you are offering are in fact reinforcing. Don't leave reinforcer selection to chance. You can identify your students' preferences in a highly structured manner or through unstructured observations. Structure can be provided by giving students a specific menu or list of potentially reinforcing items or events and determining which are selected most often. The least structured approach is to simply observe the manner in which a student spends his or her free time. If, for example, it is noted that a youth is most frequently engaged in sports activities, watching television, and eating, then these three activities may be described as the strongest potential reinforcers. The same youth may seldom choose to read historic biographies, so we would describe reading of biographies as being a weak reinforcer.

Natural versus Artificial Reinforcers

Reinforcers are also categorized by the extent to which they occur naturally in the environment. *Natural reinforcers* occur without special attention or manipulation by professionals. Eating is positively reinforced by feelings of fullness and contentment, and is negatively reinforced by the removal of hunger pangs. Walking is positively reinforced by the arrival at a desired destination, and is negatively reinforced by the avoidance of events that are being left behind.

Artificial reinforcers are the result of special engineering by professionals or others. The applied behavior analysis literature is replete with demonstrations in which teachers, psychologists, parents, or others increase the strength of behaviors though the use of artificial reinforcement. For example, Matson, Sevin, Fridley, and Love (1990) provided the following description of a procedure used to increase the expressive language of three children with autism.

> *A correct imitation of the modeled response or a spontaneous response was immediately reinforced with (a) the stimulus just requested (e.g., crayon), (b) an edible reinforcer (candy, grapes, popcorn, etc.), and (c) verbal praise. In addition, at the conclusion of each session, children were allowed to play with the objects they had appropriately requested. (p. 229)*

In this case, edible reinforcers (candy, grapes, popcorn, etc.) are defined as an unnatural or artificial reinforcer because they are arranged specifically by the professional. They would seldom occur naturally as a consequence for verbal interaction. Receiving a crayon when requested may be a natural reinforcer because it is a logical result of the verbal request.

It is important to note that behavior changes that result from artificial reinforcers are likely to deteriorate once the artificial reinforcers are removed. Therefore, it is important that reinforcement programs include elements that will increase the permanence of behavior changes once the formal program is discontinued. These elements may include increased dependence on natural reinforcers while fading artificial reinforcers and promotion of self-management skills. We will discuss fading procedures later in this chapter.

Primary versus Secondary Reinforcers

A final important dichotomy is based on the relationship between the reinforcing event and past learning. An event that is reinforcing to all children at birth with no evidence of intervening learning or conditioning is defined as a **primary reinforcer.** Primary reinforcers include warmth, food, gentle pressure (caresses), and removal of irritants. Each of these events, to varying degrees, is reinforcing for all people at birth regardless of learning. A newborn will cry for food. Once fed, she will be more contented. Without learning, the newborn will suck to gain food. Finally, she will struggle to avoid irritants and will not be content until they are removed.

Secondary reinforcers are items or events that gain reinforcing properties through the individual's learning history. Learning, in this case, occurs by pairing a previously neutral event with a primary reinforcer. Secondary reinforcers may also be developed by pairing a secondary reinforcer with a neutral event. A mother's voice, for example, may acquire secondary reinforcing properties because of its pairing with warmth, caresses, removal of irritants, and food.

Identifying Reinforcers

Any event can be a negative or positive reinforcer depending solely on its relationship to the behavior of an individual. Teacher praise may be a positive reinforcer for many students, but not all. Whether or not it is reinforcing is determined solely by its effectiveness in increasing or maintaining performance.

A young child is likely to work diligently so that he will gain attention from his teacher. Teacher attention is a positive reinforcer for the child as determined through direct observation of teacher attention and behavior strength. An older adolescent may find teacher attention to be extremely childish and distasteful; and he may skip class to avoid attention from the teacher. In this case, truancy is said to be negatively reinforced by teacher attention. Another youth's behavior may not be influenced at all by teacher attention. Regardless of what the teacher says or does, the level of academic performance does not change. In this case, teacher praise is observed to be neutral (i.e., neither positively nor negatively reinforcing).

The basic method of determining whether or not an item or event is reinforcing is referred to as a **functional analysis.** Functional analysis methodology is used to determine the relationship between a behavior and environmental events. The most basic, but potentially least reliable method for conducting a functional analysis is to informally observe the student and note events that consistently follow target responses. You may hypothesize that these events reinforce the target response. A more reliable method is to manipulate events following the target responses. You know an event is a reinforcer if the target response increases in strength during periods in which it is in place and if the target response decreases in strength when it is removed.

The simple questionnaire presented in Figure 7.1 on pages 132–133 may be effective for suggesting possible reinforcers. The questionnaire may be completed by the student or someone who knows the student well, such as his or her parents. Note that the questionnaire is divided into sections based on types of reinforcers. This questionnaire is only the starting point for identifying reinforcers because they can never be identified or defined solely based on what a person says. Rather, they are selected through the functional analysis of behavior and consequences. Verbal reports may provide a starting point for beginning actual observations.

Social Reinforcement

Social reinforcement is a special form of secondary reinforcement that is effective with a wide range of responses for many students. It is defined as any interpersonal

Name: _____ Date: _____

Instructions: The following is a list of possible reinforcers. Included are primary reinforcers (food and drink) and secondary reinforcers (social relations, leisure participation, academic activity, tangible items, and general reinforcers). Identify the strength of each reinforcer by placing no check (not reinforcing) or checking minimum, moderate, maximum. Also, identify other potential reinforcers in each column. Finally, be certain to confirm the strength of each reinforcer using functional analysis methodology.

Food	Minimum	Moderate	Maximum
Candy			
Fruit			
Vegetables			
Breads			
Pastry			
Cookies			
Meats			
Other			

Drink	Minimum	Moderate	Maximum
Water			
Soda			
Fruit Drink			
Milk			
Shake			
Tea			
Coffee			

Social Relations	Minimum	Moderate	Maximum
Group Discussion			
Individual Discussion			
Members of Opposite Sex			
Members of Same Sex			
Club Membership			
Praise from Peers			
Praise from Authority			
Other			

Leisure Participation	Minimum	Moderate	Maximum
Football			
Baseball			
Basketball			
Golf			
Swimming			
Running			
Tennis			
Pool			
Bowling			
Cycling			
Hunting			
Skiing			
Other			

Continued

FIGURE 7.1 Checklist for Identifying Potential Reinforcers

Academic Activity	Minimum	Moderate	Maximum
Reading			
Math			
Science			
Social Studies			
Writing			
English			
Foreign Language			
Teaching Assistance			
Other			

Tangible Items	Minimum	Moderate	Maximum
Awards			
Ribbons			
Balloons			
Games			
Comic Books			
Toys			
Sports Equipment			
Computer Programs			
Other			

Generalized Reinforcers	Minimum	Moderate	Maximum
Tokens			
Stars			
Points			
Displays of Performance			
Money			
Other			

Identify three high-preference items or activities for each setting.

School free time:

1. _____

2. _____

3. _____

Home free time:

1. _____

2. _____

3. _____

Community free time:

1. _____

2. _____

3. _____

FIGURE 7.1 *Continued*

interaction that increases the likelihood of a behavior occurring. As with all reinforcement procedures, social reinforcement is defined only through a functional relationship in which discrete events reliably produce an increase in a target behavior. For example, a pat on the back is defined as a social reinforcer only if it increases the strength of a specific response. Also, the pat on the back is said to be socially reinforcing for only that behavior. Its value as a social reinforcer must be established for each response you want to develop.

Several factors emphasize the importance of social reinforcement in educational programs. Most important, social reinforcement may be one of the most natural of all contingency arrangements (Kaplan, 1991). A majority of adult behavior is supported by its effectiveness in producing social support. For example, luxury automobiles, designer clothes, and gold watches are very popular despite their being no more effective than less expensive alternatives for the primary purpose of providing transportation, providing warmth, and keeping time. You may speculate, however, that these alternatives are less effective in producing social attention.

Second, social reinforcement requires no special apparatus or commodities. You can implement a social reinforcement program in your class without any additional expenses.

Third, social reinforcement is natural to all educational and community settings. Problems involving the maintenance of behavior changes once the program is discontinued can be avoided since social reinforcement is generally provided (though probably not as consistently and frequently) in the absence of formal programs.

Fourth, social reinforcement is generally a public event that allows all students to observe the behavior demonstrated by the student and the corresponding social reinforcement. Based on the research of Bandura (1971), one may expect that others will model the student being reinforced and provide an additional opportunity for you to use social reinforcement throughout the classroom.

Social reinforcement can and should be used by itself whenever possible. It is not a good idea to use social reinforcement and a more tangible reward such as token reinforcers with a student who works just as hard for praise alone. Using both procedures is overkill. Unfortunately, some students are not able to work for social reinforcement alone; more intrusive procedures are required. In such cases, the delivery of tokens or other applied behavior analysis procedures should be combined with social praise. With repeated pairings over time, the reinforcing properties of the praise statement will be increased and use of more intrusive procedures can be faded.

It is important to note that social reinforcement can motivate both positive and disruptive behaviors. Gardner (1977) for example, argued that a large number of the disruptive social responses exhibited by students with disabilities may be supported through social reinforcement. Specifically:

> *Socially reinforcing events which most children obtain following appropriate behavior may become most frequently available only after some inappropriate behavior for many children with exceptional learning and behavior characteristics. For example, a child may not have the learning and behavior characteristics which the significant social environment expects and thus is provided little social attention,*

approval, or praise. The child valuing social attention from adults and peers may discover that his disruptive behavior or his excessive dependence behavior may result in the desired social attention. (p. 444)

Gardner argued that in the absence of social reinforcement for positive social responses, the child or youth may engage in any response that is effective in producing these consequences. As such, adults inadvertently reinforce disruptive behaviors by providing attention not available for positive social responding.

Careful use of social reinforcement involves two major objectives. First you must ensure that inappropriate responses are not supported by the inadvertent use of social reinforcers. This problem can be detected by using the continuous recording procedure discussed in Chapter 11. If the data indicate that disruptive responses are followed by interpersonal interactions, you may hypothesize that these interactions are reinforcing. We again must emphasize that the interactions need not be positive or supportive. As noted by Gardner (1977), even caustic and corrective interactions can be socially reinforcing.

The second objective for ensuring the careful use of social reinforcement involves structuring learning environments so that appropriate responses are supported by interpersonal interactions. Six major guidelines should be followed when using social reinforcement.

1. Identify in advance behaviors that are expected to be developed or sustained using social reinforcement. The student should be informed of responses that are likely to produce social reinforcement.

2. Include four elements in social reinforcement statements—the student's name, the process behavior, the product behavior, and a compliment. For example, a teacher may say, "Bill (name), you really worked hard on your math assignment (process). I am certain that you will do well on the exam (product). Good work! (compliment)." This pattern ensures that the statement is personalized, that the student is aware of the specific behaviors that are valued, and that he is aware of the long-term natural consequences of the behavior.

3. Use an observational procedure (see Chapter 10) to ensure that the interpersonal interactions are reinforcing. If not, use a more intrusive motivational procedure (e.g., token economy, or contingency contract). If a more intrusive procedure is used, always pair it with social praise. This may develop reinforcing properties of praise.

4. Encourage all adults and peers to use social reinforcement in relation to the target behavior. Students who know that others expect and will reinforce a behavior are more likely to demonstrate that behavior in other settings.

5. Limit social praise to a small number of discrete statements when working with students who are severely developmentally delayed, language impaired, or very young. This will aid the student in learning the relationship between the discrete statement, positive behavior, and other reinforcing events.

6. Fade the number of socially reinforcing interactions once the target behaviors reach an acceptable level. Fading may increase the likelihood that the behavior change will be maintained in the absence of high rates of social reinforcement.

Token Reinforcers

We have emphasized the importance of using natural reinforcers whenever possible. The major advantage is that natural events will continue to exist when the intervention program has ended, and consequently, one would expect maintenance of the behavior change. Unfortunately, natural reinforcers are not always sufficiently strong or available to promote many of the responses of concern to teachers.

Token reinforcement has been used to develop a wide range of responses not influenced by natural reinforcers (Odom, Hoyson, Jamieson, & Strain, 1985; Schloss, Holt, Mulveney, & Green, 1988; Watson-Perczel, Lutzker, Green, & McGimpsey, 1988). The major advantage of token reinforcement systems is the ease with which they can be administered to groups of students. A token system can account for individual differences in the reinforcement characteristics of students, and it can also be used to develop the strength of natural reinforcers. Once natural events begin to influence academic and social responses, the artificial token system can be faded.

Token reinforcers are secondary reinforcing items or events that develop reinforcement strength through conditioning (i.e., learning by pairing with another reinforcing item or event). Money, for example, is a conditioned reinforcer or token reinforcer. Throughout life, money is paired with primary and other secondary reinforcers. We exchange money for food, drink, commodities, and travel. Increasingly, money develops the same motivational influence that the paired events possess. A child may work as hard to acquire 75 cents as he would to obtain a bottle of soda. Those who watch popular game shows recognize that participants are as eager to earn cash as the actual prizes.

Tokens are not defined by their shape or size but by their value as a conditioned reinforcer. Token reinforcers may include paper or coins (as in the case of money), checks on a ledger (as in a bank account), tangible items (e.g., poker chips, game pieces, paper clips, paste-on stars, stamps), or intangible items (e.g., points). Their reinforcement value through association with other reinforcers defines them as token or conditioned reinforcers.

Several guidelines should be followed when developing and implementing a token economy. These guidelines will enhance the effectiveness of the program.

1. Token economies are fairly intrusive and may be unnatural. Also, it may be difficult to fade reliance on token economies from educational programs. Therefore, take care to evaluate more natural and less intrusive motivational approaches before concluding that use of a token economy is appropriate (Myles, Moran, Ormsbee, & Downing, 1992).

2. As with all reinforcement procedures, give tokens (or other reinforcers) to the student immediately following the target behavior. Delays between student response and reinforcement may confuse the relationship between effort and reward.

3. Always pair delivery of tokens with natural reinforcers such as social reinforcers. For example, always state the process behavior (e.g., "You worked very carefully."), the product behavior ("All of the problems are correct."), and both natural and artificial reinforcers earned ("You will get an excellent grade, and you

earned a token."). This process emphasizes the association between the token and natural reinforcers. Over time, you can expect the natural reinforcers to become more influential.

4. Use tokens that are inexpensive and easy to manage. On a related note, ensure that the physical characteristics of the token are age and ability appropriate. Older and more mildly disabled individuals may benefit from the use of a ledger that resembles a bank book. Poker chips or other manipulatives may be more appropriate for younger and less capable students. We recommend caution when selecting manipulatives for very young children. Marbles and buttons may end up in their mouths. In addition, make sure your token cannot be counterfeited.

5. Match the delay from receipt of the token to exchange for the back-up incentive with the cognitive features of the student. Waiting too long to exchange tokens may reduce the association between the token and back-up reinforcer. Too short a period may not encourage a student to delay gratification.

6. Carefully balance the economy (availability of tokens and response costs versus cost of back-up reinforcers). Overly available tokens with low-cost backups may cause the student to become satiated (i.e., the child loses interest in the reinforcers because of their ready availability). Also, a student may engage in disruptive behaviors, knowing that even a brief period of good conduct will produce reinforcement. Excessive difficulty in acquiring tokens or ease in losing tokens may frustrate the child. He or she may choose not to earn tokens because of the limited expectation for success and reinforcement.

7. Deliver tokens consistently and according to a preestablished plan. Rosenberg (1986) advised teachers to post and review rules and procedures for administering the token economy. More severely involved learners may be taught the procedure using behavior rehearsal and prompts. Failure to inform students of procedures and to follow the procedures consistently may reduce student expectations for success and reinforcement. They may become uncertain as to whether or not effort really will produce the desired consequence.

8. Establish prompts in the classroom to remind students of all contingencies under the token economy. These may include a poster stating target behaviors, reward and response cost rates, and exchange rates.

9. Make available a variety of **backup reinforcers.** The teacher should continually evaluate the effectiveness of backup reinforcers and obtain more attractive alternatives for backups with low reinforcement value.

10. Fade token economies and other unnatural reinforcement systems from the educational program as soon as possible.

Contingency Contracting

A *contingency contract* is a written description of contingency relationships involving student performance, teacher performance, and reinforcing consequences. Contingency contracts are developed through mutual negotiations between the student, teacher, and others involved in the behavior change program. This provision is particularly important as it is generally recognized by authors in the field that students involved in developing and implementing their own educational programs are more likely to comply with program provisions (McDonnell, Wilcox, & Hardman, 1991; Macht, 1990; Mercer & Mercer, 1989). Also, negotiation sessions provide excellent opportunities for you and your students to discuss personal goals and expectations, to consider alternative strategies for promoting the behavior change, and to examine the long-term consequences of current and future behavior patterns (Schloss, 1984).

Contingency contracts generally include six major provisions. First, they include a precise definition of behaviors that are expected of the child or youth. Second, they indicate all positive consequences that will result from performing the behavior to a specified criterion. Third, contingency contracts contain a clear statement of adverse consequences that will result from failing to comply with conditions of the contract. Fourth, they include a statement of your responsibilities in facilitating success for the child or youth, such as special prompts that may be provided. Fifth, they contain a statement of how maintenance of the desired behavior will be supported. Finally, the contract should have a section for student, teacher, and, if necessary, parent signatures. Signing and dating the contract enhance its importance. Contracts spanning several days may also include a date by which conditions of the contract must be met or it will expire and need to be renegotiated.

Depending on the objectives of the program, contingency contracts may include positive reinforcement, negative reinforcement, and punishment arrangements. Contracts that simply increase the strength of positive academic and social responses will typically include reinforcing elements. Those that also seek to decrease disruptive responses may also include punishing consequences. Contingency contracts that are designed to decrease disruptive behaviors with punishing contingencies should also include reinforcing consequences for alternative positive social responses. For example, if you design a program to reduce swearing using a response cost procedure (see Chapter 9), teach and reinforce assertive behaviors that can be used for the same purpose.

Clear and complete descriptions of all provisions of the contract should be provided in the written document. "Loopholes" that permit the student to avoid important educational or contingency arrangements should be avoided. All participants must be aware of the scope and precise provisions of the agreement. Clearly specifying all contract terms minimizes future controversies that may result from vague provisions.

Finally, an objective recording system should accompany the use of contingency contracts. The recording system is important for evaluating the effectiveness of the contingency contract as well as providing feedback to all participants. Data that indicate minimal progress toward the objectives of the program may suggest a revision in the contingency contract. Data indicating the success of the program may also suggest the need to initiate fading procedures.

Figure 7.2 illustrates a sample contingency contract that was developed by adhering to the guidelines listed on page 140.

Danny will comply with the following class rules:

1. Be seated prior to the start of each period and remain in seat throughout the period unless permission to move is given by Ms. Landoworski.
2. Complete assignments given by Ms. Landoworski prior to the end of each period.
3. Make corrections to assignments during study hour.
4. Record homework in an assignment folder and complete it either during study hour or at home in the evening.

Ms. Landoworski agrees to:

1. Provide assignments at the beginning of each instructional period and give sufficent direct instruction to ensure that Danny is able to successfully complete the assignment.
2. Check all assignments at the end of the period in which they were completed and identify necessary corrections.
3. Provide instructional assistance when she judges it to be necessary and when requested by Danny.
4. Award a letter grade for all classroom assignments and all homework following corrections.
5. Permit Danny to use the gym during the last period of the day if all assignments, corrections, and the previous day's homework are completed.
6. Nominate Danny to take driver education if a C or higher grade is maintained in all subjects by the end of the semester.

Danny's basketball coach, Mr. Foster, agrees to:

1. Supervise Danny in the gym at the end of the day when he has completed his assignments, corrections, and the previous day's homework.

Danny's parents agree to:

1. Supervise Danny as he completes homework.
2. Provide Danny with five dollars and allow him to go out with friends on Saturdays when all grades for the week exceed C.

Maintenance bonus:

Danny will be allowed to use the family car on Saturdays if he obtains eligibility to enroll in driver education through this agreement, earns his license, and maintains C grades or better.

Danny Aims	Date	Coach Foster	Date
Ms. Landoworski	Date	Ms. Aims	Date

FIGURE 7.2   Sample Contingency Contract between Danny Aims and Ms. Landoworski

1. The contingency contract is developed through mutual negotiation. Consider both student interests and the overall program goals when developing a contract.

2. Note participants and their responsibilities on the contract.

3. State the positive consequences of fulfilling responsibilities noted in the contract.

4. State the unpleasant consequences associated with failing to meet responsibilities under the contract.

5. Emphasize benefits associated with meeting contract terms over liabilities associated with failing to meet contract provisions.

6. Use an observational recording system (including reliability checks to ensure objectivity) to monitor progress under the contingency contract.

7. Include maintenance goals in the contingency contract to ensure that progress is sustained once the initial goals of the contract are achieved.

8. All participants, including professional staff, must strive to meet their responsibilities under the contingency contract.

Activity Reinforcers

Premack (1959) reported a series of studies that suggested a method for using desirable activities to encourage participation in unpleasant activities. As you may recall from our discussion of schedules in Chapter 4, the procedure involves pairing high-preference activities with low-preference activities to increase the likelihood that a student will participate in the low-preference activities. Homme, deBaca, Devine, Steinhorst, and Richert (1963), who actually coined the term **Premack Principle**, provided the following description of its use.

> In observing children in a preschool program, educators noted that the most preferred activities included running around the classroom, screaming, pushing chairs across the floor, and playing with jigsaw puzzles. Among the least likely behaviors were those of complying with the teacher's request to "sit down" or to attend to the teacher's instruction. The teacher then arranged for the children to engage in their high-preference behaviors of running and screaming following small amounts of the teacher-requested behaviors of sitting and attending. After some experience with this procedure of low-preference behavior leading to high-preference behavior, the children quickly acquired a range of appropriate behaviors. (p. 544)

Classroom and school environments provide numerous opportunities to formally or informally use the Premack Principle. Careful observation will reveal a range of favorite activities for students in a class. It will also reveal undesirable activities. Once these two sets of events are recognized, you can structure the educational program so that the high-preference events follow or are contingent on completion of the low-preference activities.

As discussed in Chapter 4, one very natural method for incorporating the Premack Principle into daily activities is through the careful arrangement of the class schedule. We advocated alternating pleasant and unpleasant class periods throughout the school day. A related use of the Premack Principle involves using high-interest materials and activities to teach low-interest skills and concepts (Schloss & Sedlak, 1986). One of your students may dislike math but enjoy baseball card collecting. The student's card collection can be used for math practice. For example, you may ask the student to create a team of nine players (one in each position) and compute team statistics (e.g., batting average, on base percentage, number of hits and runs, etc.). You may also ask the student to develop a spreadsheet and calculate the value of his collection. This approach reinforces math skill practice with the desirable activity of manipulating baseball trading cards. When you assign themes, develop work placements, or provide reading materials based on students' recreational interests, you are practicing the Premack Principle in a similar manner.

A more structured adaptation of the Premack Principle involves the use of a reinforcement. In this case, upon completion of an undesirable activity, the student is permitted to select from a range of desirable activities that are listed on a menu. As was discussed earlier, the use of an activity menu reduces the likelihood that a student will become disinterested through overuse of the same activity. Also, the menu is useful for accommodating individual differences since high-interest activities vary among students.

Enhancing the Effectiveness of Reinforcement Programs

The strength of a reinforcement procedure can be dramatically influenced by the way in which it is designed and administered. Clarity of objectives, selection of reinforcers, student participation in planning, availability of reinforcers outside of the program, and other factors can contribute to enhancing program effectiveness. This section includes a discussion of these variables.

Identifying Target Behaviors

The effectiveness of a reinforcement program often hinges on the careful selection and description of target behaviors. To have maximum effectiveness you should identify and define target behaviors in objective terms. There should be no question as to whether or not a behavior has been performed (and should produce reinforcement). Clear and complete performance statements such as "each time the ball is struck," "for every page completed with fewer than three errors," or "whenever the student leaves the classroom," will set the stage for consistent application of reinforcing contingencies. Vague descriptions, such as "to acceptable standards," "whenever it is appropriate," or "with the intention of hurting others," are likely to result in the inconsistent application of reinforcers.

Reliable monitoring of a reinforcement program also requires an objective description of the target behavior. Vague or subjective descriptions of target behaviors invariably lead to measurement error. For example, you may gradually shift your expectations so that any noted improvement in student behavior is actually the result of an increase in your tolerance rather than student growth.

Prompting Responses to Be Reinforced

Target behaviors should also be within the student's ability. The most influential reinforcers cannot cause a student to perform a skill that is excessively difficult. In fact, establishing a program in which positive items or events are made contingent on behaviors that are outside of an individual's repertoire is likely to produce frustration and avoidance.

Prompting may be used in combination with a reinforcement procedure to ensure that the student is able to perform the target response. A student who is not able to independently initiate the target behavior may be provided verbal, modeling, or manual guidance. The pleasant item or event may then be used to reinforce performance under the associated prompt. A system of least prompts can be used to ensure that the student becomes increasingly less dependent on prompts while continuing to perform the desired behavior.

It is important to note that the preceding discussion relates to the reinforcement of newly acquired skills. Use caution when encouraging the persistence of acquired responses with prompts. Consistently requesting that a student follow class rules so that he can earn special privileges may reinforce compliance only after verbal reminders or warnings. The goal of the intervention program, however, may be for the student to self-initiate these actions. Therefore, while it is important to ensure that students possess critical skills and are aware of contingency relationship, unnatural prompts should be replaced with self-initiated responses as quickly as possible.

Using Shaping and Chaining to Increase Program Effectiveness

A student who possesses the necessary skills to meet your expectations may still not choose to consistently display these skills. Upon evaluating a range of possible reinforcers, you may conclude that no available activity or event is sufficiently reinforcing to assure the consistent use of the response. In this case, establish more modest expectations for reinforcement. As the student consistently meets these modest expectations, the criteria for reinforcement may be elevated.

Shaping was described in Chapters 4 and 5 as a method for teaching new skills. It is also useful for establishing graduated expectations for the consistent performance of existing skills. It is used by initially reinforcing approximations of the terminal response. Once the initial approximation of the terminal response is performed consistently, the standard for reinforcement is increased. When this more rigorous standard is achieved, a closer approximation of the terminal response is required. This process continues until the student consistently performs the terminal response. For example, you may establish neat penmanship on all assignments as a terminal objective. Initially, "A" grades are provided when all letters are legible. Later, the "A" grade is provided when letters are on the line. Then the "A" grade is provided when letters are the correct size and appropriately spaced. In subsequent steps you will require the correct formation of each letter.

Chaining is used by initially reinforcing only modest portions of a complex behavior chain. As the small portion of the chain is performed consistently, the number of performance steps required for reinforcement is systematically increased until the entire complex sequence of responses must be demonstrated to produce reinforcement. For example, you may want to teach a preschooler how to dress properly for cold weather. Initially, reinforce the child for putting on a hat. Once this occurs consistently, reinforce the child for putting on a hat and mittens. Next, reinforcement may be provided for hat, mittens, and boots. Continue until the child is willing to put on all cold weather clothes.

Identifying Reinforcers

We have emphasized throughout this chapter that various events are reinforcing for different individuals. More than any other element, the effectiveness of a reinforcement program depends on the selection of activities and events that are actually reinforcing. We have discussed several strategies for evaluating and developing reinforcer effectiveness early in this chapter. We recommended the use of a reinforcer preference checklist to form initial hypotheses. Then we suggested following this up with direct observations, noting that activities and events that a student selected when given a wide choice were most likely to be strongly reinforcing. Finally, we suggested employing functional analysis methodology to objectively validate the reinforcement relationship.

Encouraging Student Participation

The effectiveness of reinforcement programs can be enhanced by encouraging student participation during design and implementation. You are in a much more tenable position to enforce contingency arrangements that have been agreed upon in advance by the student. This is particularly true for adolescents who are resistant to adult authority (Schloss & Sedlak, 1986). Regardless of attractive features of a reinforcement program, a countercontrolling student may choose to violate the contingency arrangements just to maintain control over the situation.

Students who assist in developing contingency arrangements are less likely to renege on program provisions. Earlier in this chapter, we discussed the use of contingency contracts. The culminating activity in producing a contract involves signing a statement of commitment to the process and goals outlined in writing. As noted by Martin and Pear (1996), signing a contract helps to ensure that all participants will adhere to its provisions.

Limiting Availability of Reinforcers

Deprivation increases the potency of a reinforcing activity or item. The longer the period of deprivation, the stronger the reinforcer. The shorter the period of deprivation, the weaker the reinforcer. For example, food is unlikely to be strongly reinforcing shortly after a holiday meal. For this reason, many people find it easier to initiate a diet after a period of large food consumption. Conversely, food is likely to be highly reinforcing during a severely restrictive diet. This accounts for binges that occur during or after restrictive dieting.

Similarly, students for whom reinforcers are widely available outside of the program conditions are less likely to be influenced by the reinforcers under the program. A colleague reported that her daughter Sarah did not receive a sticker on an assignment she completed in school. Undaunted, when she arrived home, Sarah simply went to her sticker collection, chose one, and affixed it to the paper herself. Finally, social reinforcement for work completion is less likely to be influential for a child who receives substantial praise throughout the school day for other activities.

While we emphasize that deprivation will increase the strength of a reinforcer, we must also note that limiting availability of some reinforcers under certain conditions may not be ethical. For example, the mental health codes of Illinois and Missouri identify the ability to own and manage personal possessions (e.g., radio, reading materials, and mail) as a basic patient right. Only under extreme circumstances, and with the approval of a behavior management review committee, can a patient be deprived of these possessions. Similarly, students should never be deprived of meals and liquids necessary for basic nutritional well-being as a component of a general school-based reinforcement program. A problem sufficiently severe to warrant the deprivation of food is best treated by an expert applied behavior analyst. Even then, the expert will rely on a program review committee to conclude that problems associated with the loss of basic liberty and potential risk of food deprivation are outweighed by the benefits to be gained from a successful program.

Another privilege frequently withheld from a student may not be a privilege at all. It is not uncommon for teachers to hold a student back from "specials" such as physical education because of misbehavior or the failure to complete an assignment. You need to check with district officials to see if activities such as physical education are state-mandated. You may be breaking the law by limiting a student's participation. Similarly, related services included on a student's Individualized Education Plan (IEP) cannot be limited or withheld because of misbehavior.

Using a Reinforcement Menu

A student may become satiated with the most potent reinforcer if the reinforcer is used excessively. We are all familiar with the excitement associated with taking our first ride on a new attraction at a local theme park. We are also aware that the excitement eventually fades as we experience more rides. Similarly, new foods and restaurants may initially be highly attractive. Over a number of experiences, the foods or establishments become less exotic and more routine. Eventually, they lose their reinforcing properties.

As we highlighted earlier, reinforcement menus are effective for avoiding satiation. While a student may become satiated with eating at one restaurant, he or she may be less likely to satiate on eating at his or her choice of restaurant. In the classroom, a child may become satiated with earning the privilege of cleaning the board. However, the reinforcement value may be sustained given a choice of privileges that included cleaning the board.

Employing Reinforcer Sampling

A number of students, particularly those from deprived backgrounds, may have limited experience with potential reinforcers. This lack of exposure may limit the strength of the reinforcer. For example, a student who has never been to a theater is unlikely to work toward a field trip to the theater simply because he or she is unaware of the fun involved in going to a show. Also, some students have limited experience in actually earning reinforcers, either because of their own misbehavior or because adults failed to follow through on the contingency arrangement. Such outcomes are most unfortunate and can seriously undermine the effectiveness of the reinforcement program. We noted earlier that the effectiveness of a contingency management program may depend on a student's expectation that he or she will earn the prescribed reinforcers

Reinforcer sampling may be effective in exposing students to potential reinforcers, demonstrating that they can be earned, and thereby increasing the likelihood that the reinforcer will be effective. Reinforcer sampling involves allowing the student to experience the reinforcer without cost prior to initiating the formal contingency arrangement. Reinforcer sampling may also involve exposing the student to a variety of possible reinforcers to determine which is most attractive to him or her. Any or all may then be made available to the student contingent on fulfilling the objectives of the reinforcement program.

A related method of employing reinforcer sampling involves the use of shaping or chaining procedures. Initially, you may have very minimal expectations for reinforcement. Expectations may be very primitive forms of the terminal behavior as in the case of shaping, or only a few easy steps in a task sequence as in the case of chaining. Once the student experiences the acquisition of reinforcement for very modest performance changes, you may increase your standard. This approach supports the student's expectations for success and reinforcement within the program.

Providing Reinforcers Immediately

Contingency arrangements are most easily learned when performance of the target behavior is followed immediately by the reinforcer. Beyond actually learning contingency arrangements, the potency of a reinforcer is enhanced by the immediacy of delivery. The same reinforcer delivered immediately after a response is more likely to promote future responses than one that follows the response by several minutes. Michael (1986), for example, cautioned that delays exceeding 30 seconds substantially diminish the impact of the reinforcer.

We have emphasized throughout this and other chapters that reinforcers should be delivered immediately upon performance of target responses to establish the contingency relationship. A youth with moderate disabilities who receives a nickel immediately after each assembly is completed at the workshop will more quickly recognize the relationship between wages and effort than the youth who is provided a biweekly paycheck based on the same piece rate. One would expect that students receiving nickels immediately after unit completion will work harder than students receiving delayed incentives.

The immediate delivery of reinforcement also avoids the development of unexpected and dysfunctional contingencies. For example, you may plan to reinforce preschoolers' work completion by providing stickers at the end of the day. However, a majority of assignments that produce stickers occur in the morning. Unfortunately, a more volatile child in the class may consistently perform a reasonable amount of work early in the day but become restless and disruptive by the afternoon. Although you believe that stickers are given to reinforce the morning's performance, you may actually be reinforcing disruptions that occurred immediately prior to the delivery of the sticker.

Avoiding Mixed and Counterproductive Contingencies

Most contingency arrangements are complex. That is, they involve multiple positive and negative reinforcers. Dieting, for example, may be supported by positive social reinforcement (e.g., compliments from others), primary reinforcement (e.g., feeling better at a lighter weight), negative social reinforcement (e.g., avoidance of social isolation), and negative primary reinforcement (e.g., avoidance of health problems). In this example, all of the contingencies work to support dieting behavior. Sometimes, however, one or more of the complex contingencies can be mixed and counterproductive.

A child may view free time upon completion of assignments as very desirable. Consequently, a reinforcing relationship is established between free time and early work completion. Jealous peers, however, may tease the child for being "teacher's pet" and getting special privileges. The value of free time as a reinforcer may be diminished by the effects of peer teasing. In this case, slow work may be negatively reinforced because it allows the student to avoid peer teasing.

When developing a reinforcement program, be sure to identify and remove any mixed counterproductive contingencies. In the preceding case, you would work with the other children to eliminate teasing. You may also deliver reinforcers that are likely to provoke other students privately. Failing to do this, you must assume that the positive reinforcer is sufficiently strong to outweigh counterproductive contingencies.

Fading Reinforcement Programs

We have purposefully avoided use of the popular term "behavior management" in writing this text. *Management* implies an effort to control behavior for a transient purpose. One may manage classroom behavior to improve deportment with little concern for the lasting changes that influence future academic experiences. For example, you can ensure desirable classroom behavior by providing a reinforcer after each period of appropriate classroom behavior. You may recognize, however, that students quickly revert to previous disruptive patterns without use of the reinforcement system.

In Chapter 1, we discussed the major criticisms of applied behavior analysis. Perhaps the criticism we hear most frequently involves the issue of bribery. As you may recall from our discussion, many people believe that students should complete tasks and behave appropriately simply because these are the right things to do; giving students rewards for doing what they are suppose to do anyway is bribery. We encouraged you to respond to such complaints by clarifying that bribery is paying someone to do something that is wrong. Completing work and behaving appropriately are desirable behaviors that should be increased. We also agreed with the idea that students should perform certain tasks and behave in certain ways because these are the right things to do. However, we recognized that, for some students, these behaviors are not currently in their repertoire. Thus, we create and implement programs with the goal of developing these behaviors in our students. Once these behaviors have been firmly established, we should plan to reduce use of contrived rewards in favor of reinforcing events that occur naturally in the classroom.

We have occasionally mentioned Scott, a student we worked with who was highly aggressive in the presence of comments with negative connotations, such as "no, "don't," "can't," and "won't." We developed a comprehensive program that included the elements discussed in this text, such as the use of antecedent control, social skills development, and progressive muscle relaxation. Scott also earned "punches" (with a hole puncher) on an index card after every two minutes of appropriate, on-task behavior. After 30 punches, he could select from a menu of reinforcers. Our efforts paid off as his aggressive outbursts decreased dramatically. As heartening as his progress was, we knew our task was not completed. Although it was effective, reinforcing Scott every two minutes was time-consuming and unnatural. We needed a plan that would allow appropriate behavior to continue under more natural conditions. In applied behavior analysis terminology, we needed to thin (change) our schedule of reinforcement. There are two broad categories of schedules of reinforcement: continuous and intermittent. We will discuss each separately before turning our attention to thinning.

Continuous Schedules of Reinforcement

A continuous schedule of reinforcement (CRF) allows a student to receive a reinforcer every time the appropriate behavior is displayed. Consequently, the new behavior should develop quickly, but there are some problems. First, if you deliver the same reinforcer every single time, the student will satiate and the reinforcer will lose its effectiveness. Circumvent this problem by using a variety of items you know the student likes. Scott was able to select from a menu of reinforcers. Second, this level of reinforcement does not help with generalization and maintenance. If we suddenly discontinued reinforcing Scott every two minutes, it is highly likely that his aggressive behaviors would have returned. Thus, continuous reinforcement is useful for establishing new behaviors but not for maintaining them. Third, this is the type of reinforcement schedule that parents and others involved with the student refer to as bribery.

Intermittent Reinforcement

With intermittent reinforcement, the student is being reinforced occasionally. Appropriate behavior continues because the student is less able to predict when reinforcement will occur. Intermittent reinforcement can involve fixed intervals (FI) of time. A student can be reinforced after a predetermined amount of time has elapsed. In Scott's case, reinforcement occurred after every two minutes. Intermittent reinforcement can also involve a fixed ratio (FR) or an amount of work. For example, a student is reinforced for every five math problems she completes. Both interval and ratio intermittent schedules can also be variable or averaged. For example, Scott could be reinforced after two minutes, again after four minutes, again after one minute, and again after one minute. On the average, Scott is on a variable interval (VI) schedule in which he is being reinforced every two minutes. Ratio schedules can be variable (VR). Intermittent and ratio schedules are not easily predicted; thus, students continue to display appropriate behavior because they are unsure of which minute or item will produce reinforcement. The New York State Lottery system has as its motto, "Hey, you never know." Just as people keep buying lottery tickets in the hope of winning big, so too will students continue to behave in anticipation of being reinforced.

Thinning Schedules of Reinforcement

Thinning involves moving students from a dense schedule during which they receive a substantial amount of reinforcement to a sparse schedule during which less reinforcement is available. If you change the schedule of reinforcement so that the student is working longer or harder for less, then you are thinning. You are reducing the student's need for reinforcement. For example, once Scott's behavior stabilized at a two-minute interval schedule, we increased the time to five minutes. There were a few episodes of aggression but his behavior stabilized quickly. We continued to increase the length of the interval until he was working for the standard 45-minute high school class period without reinforcement.

Thinning offers advantages to both teachers and students. Students demonstrate higher levels of responding for longer periods of time. Teachers can devote more time to instructional matters and less time to reinforcing behavior. However, you need to guard against ratio strain (Alberto & Troutman, 1995), which occurs when the schedule has been thinned too quickly. In essence, the student is not earning enough reinforcers to maintain the desired level of responding. Should ratio strain occur, you should return to the previous level of reinforcement until the behavior stabilizes. Thin again, but use smaller steps.

Summary

In this chapter, we defined two major types of reinforcement. Positive reinforcement occurs when favorable events follow a behavior and increase the likelihood of its reoccurrence. Negative reinforcement occurs when a behavior is strengthened through its effectiveness in removing unpleasant events. Both positive and negative reinforcement increase the likelihood that the target behavior will occur in the future. They may be effective in promoting both positive and disruptive responses.

We used several other criteria to differentiate among types of reinforcers. Weak reinforcers were distinguished from strong reinforcers based on the degree of preference given the event or item by an individual. Natural reinforcers were distinguished from artificial reinforcers by the extent to which they occur in the environment without special professional engineering. Finally, primary reinforcers were distinguished from secondary reinforcers based on the relationship between the item or event and past learning.

Several special types of reinforcers were discussed. Social reinforcement involved the use of interpersonal interaction to increase the likelihood of a behavior occurring. Interactions may include pats on the back, compliments, gestures, or other methods of communicating support. Token reinforcers are secondary reinforcing items or events that develop reinforcement strength through conditioning. Tokens may include money, chips, points, or other tangible items that are exchanged for other reinforcers. Contingency contracts are written descriptions of contingency relationships that specify all conditions under which achievement is expected as well as the reinforcers that are assured when performance occurs. We also highlighted the use of the Premack Principle as a foundation for using activity reinforcers. The Premack Principle involves pairing an undesirable activity with a desirable activity to increase the likelihood that the student will participate in the desirable activity. We concluded with a series of guidelines for increasing the effectiveness of reinforcement procedures, paying particular attention to scheduling and thinning reinforcement.

This chapter was intended to enhance your ability to increase the quality and quantity of students' positive academic and social responses. It is also important that you be able to reduce the magnitude of disruptive academic and social behaviors. Procedures discussed in the next two chapters will address this objective.

References

Alberto, P. A., & Troutman, A. C. (1995). *Applied behavior analysis for teachers* (4th ed.). Columbus, OH: Merrill.

Bandura, A. (1971). *Psychotherapy based on modeling principles.* In A. E. Beugin & S. L. Garfield (Eds.), *Handbook of psychotherapy and behavior change.* New York: John Wiley.

Blackbourn, J. M. (1989). Acquisition and generalization of social skills in elementary-aged children with learning disabilities. *Journal of Learning Disabilities, 22,* 28–34.

Carter, J., & Sugai, G. (1988). Teaching social skills. *Teaching Exceptional Children, 54,* 68–71.

Cipani, E. C. (1995). Be aware of negative reinforcement. *Teaching Exceptional Children, 27*(4), 36–40.

Gardner, W. I. (1977). *Learning and behavior characteristics of exceptional children and youth.* Boston: Allyn and Bacon.

Homme, L. E., deBaca, P. C., Devine, J. V., Steinhorst, R., & Richert, E. J. (1963). Use of the Premack Principle in controlling the behavior of nursery school children. *Journal of the Experimental Analysis of Behavior, 6,* 544–548.

Justen, J. E., & Howerton, D. L. (1993). Clarifying behavior management terminology. *Intervention in School and Clinic, 29,* 36–40.

Kaplan, J. S. (1991). *Beyond behavior modification: A cognitive behavioral approach to behavior management in the school.* Austin, TX: PRO-ED.

Macht, J. (1990). *Managing classroom behavior: An ecological approach to academic and social learning.* New York: Longman.

Martin, G., & Pear, J. (1996). *Behavior Modification: What it is and how to do it.* Englewood Cliffs, NJ: Prentice Hall.

Martin, J. E., Rusch, F. R., Lagomarcino, T., & Chadsey-Rusch, J. (1986). Comparison between nonhandicapped and mentally retarded workers: Why they lose their jobs. *Applied Research in Mental Retardation, 7,* 467–474.

Matson, J. L., Sevin, D. F., Fridley, D. & Love, S. R. (1990). Increasing spontaneous language in three autistic children. *Journal of Applied Behavior Analysis, 23,* 227–233.

McDonnell, J., Wilcox, B., & Hardman, M. L. (1991). *Secondary programs for students with developmental disabilities.* Boston: Allyn and Bacon.

Mercer, C. D., & Mercer, A. R. (1989). *Teaching students with learning problems* (3rd ed.). Columbus, OH: Merrill.

Michael, J. (1986). Repertoire-altering effects of remote contingencies. *The Analysis of Verbal Behavior, 4,* 10–18.

Myles, B. S., Moran, M. R., Ormsbee, C. K., & Downing, J. A. (1992). Guidelines for establishing and maintaining token economies. *Intervention in School and Clinic, 27,* 164–169.

Nelson, C. M. (1988). Social skills training for handicapped students. *Teaching Exceptional Children, 20,* 19–23.

Odom, S. L., Hoyson, M., Jamieson, B., & Strain, P. (1985). Increasing handicapped preschoolers' peer social interactions: Cross-setting and component analysis. *Journal of Applied Behavior Analysis, 19,* 59–71.

Premack, D. (1959), Toward empirical behavior laws: I. Positive reinforcement. *Psychological Review, 66,* 219–233.

Rosenberg, M. S. (1986). Maximizing the effectiveness of structured classroom management programs: Implementing rule-review procedures with disruptive and distractible students. *Behavioral Disorders, 11,* 239–248.

Rotter, J. (1975). Some problems and misconceptions related to the construct of internal versus external control of reinforcement. *Journal of Consulting and Clinical Psychology, 43,* 56–67.

Schloss, P. J. (1984). *Social development of handicapped children and adolescents.* Rockville, MD: Aspen.

Schloss, P. J., Holt, J., Mulveney, M., & Green, J. (1988). The Franklin Jefferson Program: Demonstration of an integrated social learning approach to educational services for behaviorally disordered students. *Teaching: Behaviorally Disordered Youth, 4,* 7–15.

Schloss, P. J., & Schloss, C. N. (1987). A critical review of social skills research in mental retardation. In S. E. Breuning, J. L. Matson, & R. P.

Barrett (Eds.), *Advances in mental retardation and developmental disabilities: A research annual* (pp. 107–151). Greenwich, CT: JAI Press.

Schloss, P. J., & Sedlak, R. A. (1986). *Instructional methods for students with learning and behavior problems*. Boston: Allyn and Bacon.

Watson-Perczel, M., Lutzker, J. R., Green, B. F., & McGimpsey, B. J. (1988). Assessment and modification of home cleanliness among families adjudicated for child neglect. *Behavior Modification, 12,* 57–81.

8

POSITIVE APPROACHES TO DECREASING INAPPROPRIATE BEHAVIOR

It is easy to recall personal experiences in which other people used unpleasant methods to change our behavior. Many of us may recall being sent to the corner for talking out in class. We may also remember occasions in which our foul language resulted in copying multiple lines from the dictionary. Even as adults, we frequently face aversive consequences for behaviors offensive to others. Employers may criticize us for being late, spouses may deprive us of affection for not fulfilling domestic responsibilities, and state troopers may fine us for violating traffic laws. These aversive approaches are usually very effective in reducing disruptive behaviors. We are confident that every rational individual who receives a speeding ticket reentered highway traffic and remained within the speed limit (at least until the police car was out of sight).

Unfortunately, while aversive consequences may be at least temporarily effective for most learners, they have been associated with a range of negative side effects. Their benefits may be highly specific and temporary. Aversive events may lead the student to avoid the individual who administers the consequences or the setting in which the consequence is delivered. The aversive consequence may cause the student to become highly withdrawn or aggressive (Azrin & Holtz, 1966). Most important, aversive consequences have *no* educative or repertoire enhancing elements. For example, a person who punishes aggressive behavior does not teach the assertive skills that should replace aggression.

According to Gardner (1977), students demonstrating exceptional characteristics may be less successful in social and academic pursuits. Students with a restricted number of opportunities for success may use higher rates of norm violating behaviors to obtain alternate reinforcers such as negative attention from peers or authority.

The isolated use of aversive consequences has two major disadvantages in light of Gardner's discussion. First, the aversive consequence may acquire reinforcing properties and simply not be effective. For example, in the absence of any attention, the child may be reinforced by reprimands. Given that a child receives little attention for being a capable student, athlete, or friend, he may seek notoriety for being aggressive.

Second, when used in isolation, aversive consequences do not promote appropriate academic and social responses that allow the student to gain acceptable forms of reinforcement. A child who is punished for swearing may not learn more appropriate verbal skills. In this case, the child is likely to use other disruptive responses to gain attention. At minimum, the child may return to the original disruptive response when the punishing consequences are no longer present.

The overriding goals of all education programs are to increase the social and academic abilities expected by society. As emphasized by Gardner (1977), the exclusive use of aversive consequences may not serve this function. Therefore, alternative methods must be employed independently or simultaneously with aversive methods. For this reason, we have divided methods for reducing inappropriate behavior into two chapters. The current chapter addresses positive approaches to reducing disruptive responses. These approaches avoid the limitations discussed above. The next chapter includes aversive procedures, with an emphasis on the careful use of procedures that minimize negative side effects.

Because reductive procedures vary in effectiveness and potential for harm, they must be selected very carefully. For this reason the two behavioral reduction chapters are organized to emphasize two major criteria. First, we give consideration to minimally intrusive yet effective reductive procedures. Second, we highlight strategies that include repertoire enhancing elements. Table 8.1 illustrates reductive procedures that are included in the following two chapters.

The initial method discussed in this chapter is referred to as *stimulus change*. The principal aim of professionals using this procedure is to identify and avoid situations that are associated with the increased occurrence of disruptive behavior.

TABLE 8.1 Categorization of Behavioral Reduction Methods

Nonaversive	Aversive
Stimulus change	Response cost
Differential reinforcement of incompatible behaviors	Satiation
	Time-out
Differential reinforcement of alternative behaviors	Overcorrection
	Presentation of conditioned aversive stimuli
Differential reinforcement of other behaviors	Presentation of unconditioned aversive stimuli
Differential reinforcement of low rates of responding	
Extinction	

Stimulus Change

Antecedent control or stimulus control procedures were discussed at length in Chapter 4; these procedures are among the most effective, yet least intrusive behavioral reduction methods. Equally important, these strategies may require minimal effort from you and your students. There is little possibility that the procedures will produce the undesirable negative effects associated with aversive methods.

An event or object that triggers or inhibits a response is a **stimulus. Stimulus control** occurs when a specific object or event consistently influences the occurrence of a response. Stimulus change involves introducing stimuli that are likely to trigger appropriate responses and/or removing responses that are likely to trigger disruptive responses.

Basic forms of stimulus control are practiced by teachers daily. For example, you reduce student discussion by flicking the lights, ringing a bell, tapping the desk, or requesting attention. Rules posted on the classroom wall provide a visual cue that cautions students against violations. Seating assignments are generally devised to separate students who cue disruptive responses in each other. Quiet periods eliminate noise that triggers inattentiveness. Finally, study carrels are used to screen out stimuli that prompt off-task behavior.

More elaborate methods have been described in the professional literature. For example, O'Reilly, Green, and Braunling-McMorrow (1990) demonstrated the use of written checklists through which young adults with disabilities modified their living environment. Modifications to the home environment reduced potential hazards.

Continuous recording (described in Chapter 11) is used in the initial development of a stimulus control program. This recording method helps you identify events that precede or cue maladaptive behavior and alternate events that cue incompatible positive behaviors. You can modify classroom conditions so that provoking cues are replaced with supportive cues. Use modeling, shaping, and behavior rehearsal along with stimulus change to develop appropriate responses to provoking cues. As these coping responses are developed, reinstate the provoking cues while gradually fading supportive cues.

We have emphasized that the major advantage of stimulus change is the ease with which it is used. Further, there are few if any negative side effects. The disadvantage of stimulus change is that it is not often possible to identify or control provoking cues. Some responses appear to occur spontaneously without reference to environmental events. Other responses are so chronic and severe that they occur in response to an exhaustive range of cues. Finally, some disruptive responses occur in reaction to cues that cannot be manipulated. For example, many behaviorally disordered youth respond aggressively to authority figures, and it is not possible to eliminate authority figures from school or society.

We must emphasize that the effects of stimulus control are likely to be temporary if repertoire enhancing procedures are not also used. A student who is unable to refrain from depressive reactions following failure is not likely to be depressed if the teacher provides easy assignments and avoids harsh grading standards. As long as failure experiences do not occur, the student's depressive reactions are likely not to occur. Unfortunately, if you do not teach adaptive responses to failure,

TABLE 8.2   Definitions and Examples of DRI, DRA, DRO, DRL, and DRD

	Definition	Example
DRI	Increase the strength of a behavior that cannot occur at the same time as the disruptive response, thereby reducing the strength of the disruptive response.	Providing special privileges to a child for walking slowly down the hall, thereby reducing running.
DRA	Increasing the strength of a (not necessarily incompatible) positive response while removing reinforcement from the disruptive response.	Praising a youth for making notes on a pad while ignoring writing in his text (writing on a pad and in a text can occur at the same time).
DRO	Reinforcing a student for failing to engage in a response during a specified period of time.	Allowing a student to use the gym at the end of a day in which there are no occurrences of verbal aggression.
DRL	Reinforcing a student for displaying a single lower level of a disruptive behavior.	Permitting a child to go to the gym at the end of each day in which there are fewer than three occurrences of talking out.
DRD	Reinforcing a student for displaying successively lower levels of a disruptive response.	Providing a dollar for each day during an initial week in which an adolescent smokes fewer than eight cigarettes; then providing a dollar for each day in which fewer than six cigarettes are smoked; next, providing a dollar for each day in which fewer than three are smoked; and finally, providing a dollar for each day in which no cigarettes are smoked.

your student is certain to experience depressive reactions when failure occurs in subsequent grades. Actively teaching and motivating acceptable responses to failure while limiting failure experiences is essential to ensuring that the reductive strategy has a lasting effect.

Differential reinforcement may be an effective procedure for developing alternative responses. It involves strengthening one set of responses in contrast to another. The objective is for reinforced responses to occur more often while the alternate disruptive responses diminish. There are many forms of differential reinforcement including differential reinforcement of incompatible behaviors (DRI), differential reinforcement of alternative behaviors (DRA), differential reinforcement of other behaviors (DRO), differential reinforcement of low rates of behavior (DRL), and differential reinforcement of diminishing behavior (DRD). Table 8.2 includes a definition and example for each of the methods.

Differential Reinforcement of Incompatible Behaviors (DRI)

Differential reinforcement of incompatible behaviors involves reinforcing a student for engaging in a response that is incompatible (cannot occur at the same time) with a disruptive response. The target behavior and the alternative response are mutually exclusive. This process should increase the strength of the incompat-ible response and reduce the disruptive response. DRI is used by teachers who re-ward students for walking down the hall (incompatible with running down the hall), coloring within the lines (incompatible with going outside of the lines), an-swering problems correctly (incompatible with answering incorrectly), and fol-lowing a dress code (incompatible with improper attire). DRI may be used without explicitly written objectives, procedures, or evaluation methods. Alternately, it may be used as part of a carefully developed and implemented behavior management program.

The development of a formal DRI program begins with the establishment of behavioral objectives. As was discussed in Chapter 3, objectives should include a clear description of the target response, the conditions under which change is ex-pected to occur, and the optimum level of performance following successful inter-vention. In the case of DRI, the objective should indicate the specific responses that will increase and diminish as well as the strength of the incompatible and disrup-tive responses following intervention. It is important that the reinforced response truly be incompatible with the disruptive response. Talking softly, for example, is clearly incompatible with yelling. It is not possible for a child to talk softly and yell at the same time. Conversely, talking softly and being aggressive are not incompat-ible. A child can tease, threaten, assault, or otherwise hurt another child while us-ing a normal conversational tone.

The next step in developing a DRI program is to identify all contingencies. Spe-cific reinforcers and schedules for their delivery should be selected. It is important to identify consequences and schedules that are likely to be effective. Reinforce-ment menus and reinforcement sampling, as described in Chapter 7, may be used for this purpose. Procedures for teaching the contingencies to the student should also be developed. It may be advisable to use prompts or cues to remind the stu-dent of contingency relationships.

Additional program elements should be combined with DRI when warranted. For example, extinction or other aversive procedures may be used when the dis-ruptive response occurs. Use behavior rehearsal, modeling, or prompting to assist the student in using acceptable forms of the incompatible behavior.

Let's use these steps to develop a DRI program for Caroline. During reading groups, Mr. MacDonald, her teacher, assigns independent activities to those not in-volved in teacher-led instruction. Unfortunately, Caroline is constantly out of her seat during independent work time, attempting to engage her classmates in con-versation. Mr. MacDonald believes this behavior is having a detrimental effect in his class. Caroline and other students are not finishing their assignments. Also, he feels as though he is constantly reprimanding Caroline, which limits the amount of instruction time for the reading group with whom he is working. His repri-mands also detract from the positive learning atmosphere he wants to create. He decides to use a DRI program that will require Caroline to be in her seat during in-dependent activities. Mr. MacDonald specifies as his objective that Caroline will re-main seated during all independent work activities. She will not leave her seat without teacher permission. Out of concern for her rate of success (discussed in

Chapter 4), he makes sure these activities are age and ability appropriate and that she understands how to complete them. He also makes sure that she has access to items she needs such as paper and a sharpened pencil, and that there is a routine in place for requesting assistance. He instructs Caroline that she must remain in her seat for the entire time. If she does, she will earn free time, during which she can talk with her peers. Mr. MacDonald observes Caroline during independent work time. At the end of the period, if she has not left her desk without permission, he awards her free time to talk with peers. If she is out of her seat without permission, he ignores her and does not award free time afterward.

As noted earlier, the major advantage of DRI is that when successful, an incompatible positive response is developed to replace the disruptive response (Friman & Altman, 1990). Unlike stimulus change and other reductive procedures, the development of replacement skills occurs without the inclusion of other program elements. This is demonstrated in a case study reported by Mace, Kratochwill, and Fiello (1983), in which they taught a severely developmentally delayed young adult to follow a six-step compliance training procedure that was incompatible with aggression. The DRI procedure increased the use of compliance training responses and substantially reduced aggression.

A related advantage is that DRI can be highly positive from the student's perspective (Friman, 1990). All reinforcers available to the student prior to intervention are available under the provisions of the DRI program. The only difference is that the student must engage in the incompatible behavior to obtain reinforcers, as opposed to obtaining the reinforcers through disruptive responses.

There is one possible disadvantage of DRI. Some responses are so intrinsically reinforcing, or are very powerful in attracting coercive reinforcement from others. The shift of reinforcers to the incompatible behavior simply may not be effective. For example, differentially reinforcing gum chewing over smoking is not likely to be effective since the intrinsic chemical effects of nicotine far outweigh any reinforcement that can be provided for gum use. Similarly, differentially reinforcing a student for being assertive rather than aggressive may be ineffective if you are unable to prevent peers from being more responsive to aggression.

Differential Reinforcement of Alternative Behaviors (DRA)

Differential reinforcement of alternative behaviors is similar to DRI in that both procedures involve the reduction of a specific response by reinforcing other responses. They differ in the relationship between the new behavior being developed and the disruptive response. In the case of DRI, the new response is selected because it represents an incompatible alternative to the disruptive behavior; the two behaviors cannot occur simultaneously. The alternative behavior selected in DRA is not necessarily incompatible with the disruptive response. The target behavior and the alternative response are not mutually exclusive. Since the alternative response can occur at the same time as the disruptive behavior, extinction of the disruptive response must occur along with reinforcement of the alternative response.

If you are currently teaching, chances are you already use DRA. You routinely praise students for completing seatwork while ignoring off-task behavior. You probably call on students who raise their hands before answering while ignoring those who yell out. One of the more common "success stories" in public education is the youth who participated in organized sports as an alternative to delinquency. In this case, athletic activity is differentially reinforced over alternative delinquent behavior. In a related but more dramatic example, a young Fidel Castro was once scouted by the pitching staff of an American League baseball team. Unfortunately, the team did not offer Mr. Castro a contract. One may question whether or not he would have embarked on a career as a Communist revolutionary if he were differentially reinforced for his pitching skills.

Using DRA begins with the development of specific behavioral objectives. In this case, the objectives should address both the alternative response being developed and the disruptive behavior being reduced. As with all objectives, the target responses should be described in clear and complete terms. Also, the conditions under which the change will occur and the criteria for success should be specified.

Having developed the objectives, you need to identify two sets of consequences. The first includes potential reinforcers for the alternative response. Careful planning should ensure that the specific activities or items are sufficiently attractive and delivered with sufficient frequency to motivate student performance. The second set includes the removal of reinforcers from the disruptive behavior.

Response cost, time-out, and other contingencies as discussed in Chapter 9 directly address the disruptive response while the alternative behavior is being differentially reinforced. We recommend combining these procedures whenever all sources of reinforcement cannot be removed from the disruptive response. Augmentative strategies may also be used when the disruptive response is highly persistent or severe.

You should use instructional procedures such as modeling, prompting, and shaping when the alternative response is not an automatic part of the student's repertoire. For example, Jayne, Schloss, Alper, and Menscher (1994) used prompting to teach two primary students with moderate disabilities how to request assistance rather than tantrum when they encountered difficulty during simple food preparation activities.

Here is an example of how to use DRA. Allan frequently calls out answers to teacher questions rather than raising his hand. Although Ms. Haug, his teacher, appreciates his enthusiasm, she wants to make sure all of her students have time to think of an answer, then raise their hands to respond to her questions. She decides to use a DRA program with Allan. Her objective is that, after hearing a teacher question in formal teacher-led instruction, Allan will pause at least five seconds, then raise his hand. He will never call out. She tells Allan that every time he pauses to think then raises his hand without calling out, she will reward him with a point. She also tells him that other children need a chance to respond, so she may not always call on him. If he calls out, she will ignore him but she will also take away two points. Points can be exchanged for activity reinforcers such as extra time in the gym or computer privileges. She implements the program, awarding a point every time

Allan pauses then raises his hand after a question. On those occasions when she does call on Allan, Ms. Haug praises his appropriate behavior. When he calls out, she simply ignores his response, deducts two points, and calls on another student whom she then praises for displaying appropriate behavior. As Allan improves, she increases the number of points required in exchange for the activity reinforcers.

DRI and DRA share a common advantage of including repertoire enhancing elements. These elements ensure that new behaviors are fostered at the same time that disruptive responses are being diminished. Since new behaviors are developed and reinforced, behavioral improvements are likely to maintain throughout the individual's life. Another common advantage is that both strategies are reinforcement generating and include no aversive elements.

The major disadvantage of DRA is that the disruptive response can occur at the same time that the alternative response is being developed. Consequently, there is no assurance that reinforcement of the alternative behavior will have the desired reductive effect on the disruptive response. In view of this, extinction, response cost, or an aversive procedure may be required. Similarly, since DRA is an indirect method of reducing the disruptive response, one cannot expect speedy results. More powerful approaches may be required for highly disruptive responses such as physical aggression, self-abuse, and so on (Cavalier & Ferretti,1980; Matson & Taras, 1989).

Differential Reinforcement of Other Behaviors (DRO)

Differential reinforcement of other behaviors is the reinforcement of the failure to exhibit a target response during a specified period of time. Sulzer-Azaroff and Mayer (1991) have referred to DRO as "omission training" since it teaches and reinforces the omission of response from an individual's repertoire. You can see from this description that while DRO is a nonaversive approach, it does not include repertoire enhancing elements. The student is reinforced for *not engaging in the target response;* however, reinforcement is not provided for engaging in alternative positive responses.

You use DRO by providing reinforcers following time intervals in which the target behavior did not occur. Using a very unobtrusive approach, you may provide free time at the end of each 30-minute schedule period in which no verbal or physical aggression occurred. A more formal program can be developed to stop thumb sucking by a preschooler by dividing the four-hour school day into 48 intervals of five minutes in length. Following each interval in which thumb sucking did not occur, you provide the child with social praise and place one piece of dry cereal into a cup. The child is allowed to eat all of the cereal in the cup at the end of each hour.

An alternative DRO approach was described by Deitz and Repp (1974) as *momentary DRO.* Rather than providing reinforcement following a whole interval in which the disruptive response did not occur, the authors advocate providing reinforcement following any random or fixed instant in which the disruptive response was absent. Momentary DRO is similar to "spot checking" to determine if a problem behavior is occurring. Reinforcement is provided if the target response is not observed during the spot check.

A simple example of momentary DRO that relies on the observation of permanent products occurs when a teacher conducts random desk checks. Students whose desks are not cluttered or written upon receive special privileges. Alternately, a teacher may prepare an audiotape that "beeps" ten times a day at random intervals. Students who are not engaging in disruptive behaviors during the beep are reinforced.

Because DRO does not include repertoire enhancing elements, it is often used in combination with skill development strategies. In the preceding example, you may actively teach academic skills that include the use of hands while reinforcing the child for not sucking her thumb. You may also wish to reinforce alternative or incompatible behaviors (e.g., finger painting, washing, eating, etc.), while reinforcing periods of time during which no thumb sucking occurred.

DRO begins with establishing an objective for reducing the disruptive response. The objective should include a reliable description of the response being reduced, the strength of the response expected following successful intervention, and the conditions under which the reduction is expected to occur. Related objectives may be written if augmentative strategies are used to teach and reinforce alternative behaviors.

Once an objective is established, you should determine if momentary or whole interval DRO is to be used. Repp, Barton, and Brulle (1983) and Barton, Brulle, and Repp (1986) have demonstrated that whole interval DRO may be more effective than momentary DRO for initial response reduction. Momentary DRO may be an effective maintenance procedure when substantial initial changes are not required.

Determine the length of the reinforcement period prior to using whole interval DRO. Brief intervals of one to ten minutes may be selected for high rate behaviors, highly variable responses, and less mature learners. Intervals up to a day in length may be used for low rate behaviors and mature students. When using momentary DRO, you should develop a procedure for signaling the moment at which the student is evaluated. The signal may occur on a fixed interval (e.g., at the end of each class period) or during random intervals (e.g., whenever an audiotape signal occurs). Random intervals are more likely to produce a substantial and consistent effect. In our work with DRO, we have found it helpful to average the times between demonstrations of inappropriate behavior, then to choose a slightly smaller length of time.

The next step in developing a DRO procedure is for you to determine the consequences of a zero response rate during the interval. As with all reinforcement programs, we encourage you to use reinforcement sampling procedures as well as a reinforcement menu to avoid satiation. Also, the least intrusive and most natural reinforcers expected to be effective should be selected over incentives not commonly found in the setting.

Next, you may select augmentative educational strategies to use with the DRO procedure. Social skills, relaxation procedures, or self-management described in

Chapters 5, 6, and 15 may be effective adjuncts. Also, DRA can be used in conjunction with DRO by reinforcing occurrences of alternative behavior as well as providing reinforcement for intervals in which a zero rate of the disruptive response occurred. Similarly, like other differential reinforcement procedures, DRO is not likely to produce rapid results. Therefore, response cost or other punishment procedures may be paired with DRO. In this case, the student may be "fined" each time a response occurs and "rewarded" each time an interval passes in which the response did not occur.

Finally, the student should be taught all program contingencies. As with other procedures, use modeling and behavior rehearsal to ensure that the student knows what to expect under the program. Also, use prompts and tangible cues to remind students of desirable behavior and the related consequences.

You may remember our discussion of Scott in the previous chapter. Scott became very aggressive whenever the words "no," "don't," "can't," or "won't" were used. To change this behavior, his teacher developed an intervention program that included DRO. Her objective was that Scott would remain relaxed and return to the scheduled activity whenever words with a negative connotation were used. Scott was never to display aggressive behaviors, such as head butting or self-biting. She observed Scott and noted the times between aggressive behaviors. Unfortunately, because such words were used frequently, Scott's level of aggression was high. His teacher averaged the times between aggressive episodes. The average time was four minutes. Wanting to increase the likelihood of catching Scott while he was behaving appropriately, she chose to reinforce every two minutes. In addition to explaining the program, the teacher taught social skills and relaxation to Scott. The DRO program was implemented. The teacher drew 30 circles on an index card. After every two minutes during which Scott was not aggressive, she punched a hole in the card. She also praised Scott for maintaining a relaxed demeanor. An hour later, after all 30 holes were punched, Scott was allowed to select from a menu of reinforcers. If Scott demonstrated aggression, the index card was destroyed and his punitive consequences were delivered. A new card was started. As his aggressive behavior decreased, the two-minute interval was increased to five minutes, then seven minutes, and so on.

The major advantage of DRO is that positive consequences are used to reduce the strength of disruptive behavior. Therefore, negative side effects associated with punishment procedures are avoided. Also, DRO promotes a success-striving attitude (e.g., "If I do not use negative behaviors, I will gain special privileges") as opposed to an aversion-avoiding attitude (e.g., "If I use negative behaviors, I will be punished").

A second advantage is that DRO can be used effectively with a wide range of responses. DRO is not dependent on any particular response topography. Aggression, withdrawal, self-abuse, avoidance, noncompliance, and any other excessive response found in educational settings may be the focus of a DRO program.

A final advantage is that DRO may produce fairly immediate, long-lasting, and generalizable behavior changes. It is important to note that the actual speed and durability of the response reduction in any applied behavior analysis procedure is a function of the characteristics of the individual and specific contingency arrangements. However, when combined with other reductive methods, DRO may be one of the more effective differential reinforcement procedures (Sulzer-Azaroff & Mayer, 1991).

The disadvantages of DRO should be readily apparent. First, even though DRO is a positive strategy, it includes no repertoire enhancing elements. Researchers have demonstrated that while DRO is effective in reducing disruptive behavior, one cannot be certain that positive replacement skills will be developed. Conversely, DRI and DRA have been shown to be effective in both reducing the disruptive behavior and increasing positive social responses (Leitenberg, Burchard, Burchard, Fuller, & Lysaght, 1977).

A related problem is that DRO provides reinforcement following an interval for any responses other than the disruptive response. Since alternative responses are not specified, responses exhibited during the interval may be as problematic as the disruptive response. For example, an individual may participate in a DRO program to reduce cigarette smoking. Results of the program may indicate that while a majority of intervals passed with no cigarette smoking, food consumption during the intervals increased to unhealthy levels.

Finally, as was demonstrated by Harris and Wolchik (1979) and Rolider and Van Houten (1984), DRO may not be effective in reducing highly satisfying responses. Also, the effects of DRO programs may fall short of the total elimination of the disruptive response (Cowdery, Iwata, & Pace, 1990; Haring & Kennedy, 1990). DRO assumes that obtaining a reinforcer for failing to engage in the target response is more desirable to an individual than satisfaction gained through the use of the response. It is likely that select responses may produce satisfaction exceeding that available from the differential reinforcement procedure.

Differential Reinforcement of Low (DRL) and Diminishing (DRD) Rates of Behavior

Differential reinforcement of low rates of behavior provides reinforcement any time an individual's response level is below a predetermined criterion for a particular period. DRL may be based on the frequency of a response during an interval (e.g., the child is provided a reinforcer for eating at a rate lower than three bites a minute). It can also be based on duration (e.g., the child is provided a reinforcer for spending less than two hours a day watching television).

Differential reinforcement of diminishing rates of behavior is a special case of DRL in which the criterion for reinforcement is gradually reduced as the learner adjusts to initial criteria for reinforcement. In DRL, the criterion for reinforcement is fixed at one level throughout the program. DRD is analogous to a shaping program in which successive approximations of the terminal objective are reinforced until the student consistently displays the desired quality and level of performance. The major difference between DRD and shaping, however, is that rather than enhancing performance, the DRD procedure diminishes performance. A related difference is that shaping generally focuses on qualitative aspects of behavior while DRD addresses behavior strength.

Original laboratory research evaluated DRD contingency arrangements in which reinforcement was applied for successively longer periods of time between the occurrence of a behavior (Ferster & Skinner, 1957). Primates received food pellets for pulling a chain following a discrete time interval. Pellets were not delivered for pulling prior to the target time. More recent demonstrations have varied the contingency arrangements so that reinforcement is delivered at the end of an interval in which a target performance level was achieved (Deitz & Repp, 1973; Deitz & Repp, 1974). In this case, a student may receive a reinforcer for class periods in which there are fewer than three talk-outs.

Begin DRL and DRD programs by establishing performance objectives. In the case of DRL, a single objective may be written that includes the target criterion level and conditions under which the behavior change is expected to occur. There are several options for selecting a criterion when using DRD. Begin by observing for three or four days and counting the number of times the behavior occurs. Your criterion can be (a) the lowest frequency you observed, (b) an average of baseline frequencies, or (c) half the average of baseline frequencies (although we believe this criterion is very strict).

In some cases, criteria can be established during a prebaseline assessment. In others, they will be set based on the student's reaction to the preceding criterion. A student who easily achieves the first criterion may have to meet a substantially more rigorous criterion in the second phase. A student who has greater difficulty with an initial criterion may have to meet a more modest second criterion. Guidelines for implementing a changing criterion research design may be useful for establishing criteria levels.

Since DRL and DRD do not include repertoire enhancing elements, we recommend the addition of objectives that promote replacement skills. As has been emphasized repeatedly, these objectives should target skills that may be used in place of the excessive response. For example, DRL that reduces the rate of math errors may include an objective for mastery of math skills. DRL that reduces the duration of crying episodes may include an objective for increasing deep breathing and using a calm voice. Finally, DRL that addresses the rate of aggressive verbalizations may include an objective for promoting assertive statements.

The next step is to clearly identify the consequences for meeting target criteria. Care should be given to selecting potential reinforcers that are likely to have the desired effect. We have emphasized the use of reinforcement menus and reinforcer sampling procedures to strengthen the reinforcement value of an item or event. It is important to note that DRL with substantial criteria changes may require a stronger reinforcer. DRD using subtle criteria changes may be used with modest reinforcers.

As noted above, repertoire enhancing procedures should be planned as adjuncts to DRL or DRD procedures. Use modeling, behavior rehearsal, prompting, and other skill development activities to promote replacements for the disruptive social response. DRI or DRA may be used to reinforce these replacement skills while simultaneously reinforcing the reduced rate of the disruptive response.

Here are examples of how DRL and DRD are used. Mr. MacDonald could use a DRL program with Caroline to reduce her out-of-seat behavior. Rather than reducing the frequency of out-of-seat behavior to zero, he may decide that being out of seat two times within a 30-minute period of independent work is acceptable. Other students who briefly leave their seats that often still complete their work and do not distract anyone. He tells Caroline that if she is briefly out of her seat for no more than two times for reasons related to her work, she can earn free time.

Depending on how often Caroline is out of her seat, Mr. MacDonald may elect to use DRD. Perhaps Caroline is out of her seat an average of 12 times during each independent activity. Requiring that she immediately decrease this number to two may be an unreasonable expectation. He decides to set his interim criterion at 10. Mr. MacDonald gives Caroline 11 tickets. He tells her that every time she leaves her seat, she has to put one ticket in a jar on his desk. If she has at least one ticket left over, she can exchange it for free time. If she has no tickets left (because she was out of her seat 11 or more times), she has no free time. Mr. MacDonald does not need to reprimand if Caroline exceeds her limits; the loss of free time should be punishment enough. As her behavior improves, Mr. MacDonald can reduce the number of ticket he gives Caroline. Nine tickets will allow her to be out of her seat only eight times before she can no longer earn free time. Figure 8.1 illustrates Caroline's progress.

A major advantage of DRL and DRD is the positive manner in which the disruptive response is reduced. A student actually receives reinforcers for continuing to engage in the behavior, although at a reduced rate. DRD can be even more positive than DRL since initial expectations may be very modest. As the student's behavior meets the initial expectation, more rigorous requirements can be imposed. Expectations can be adjusted so that the student is never expected to perform at a level exceeding his or her capability.

A related advantage of DRL and DRD is that both procedures may be used to reduce behavior strength without totally eliminating the response. Many behaviors that are subject to punishment would be appropriate if practiced in moderation. For example, watching television, eating, talking, dating, and other social/recreational behaviors are healthy responses when their frequency and duration are limited to societal norms. Unfortunately, continuously watching television, eating to excess, incessant talking, and so on are problems because they exceed social norms. Aversive procedures often communicate the need to totally eliminate the response. A preschooler who is punished for talking in class may believe that it is always inappropriate to talk in class. As an alternative, DRL and DRD may communicate to the child that talking in moderation is appropriate.

The disadvantages of DRL and DRD are similar to those of DRO. Despite being positive strategies, there are no provisions for developing prosocial replacement skills. While DRL and DRD may be effective in reducing the target response to an acceptable level, we cannot be certain that positive replacement skills will be developed for use in the absence of the excessive response.

Also, the effects of DRL and DRD may not be immediately apparent. DRD, particularly, may require an extended period of time to achieve the terminal objec-

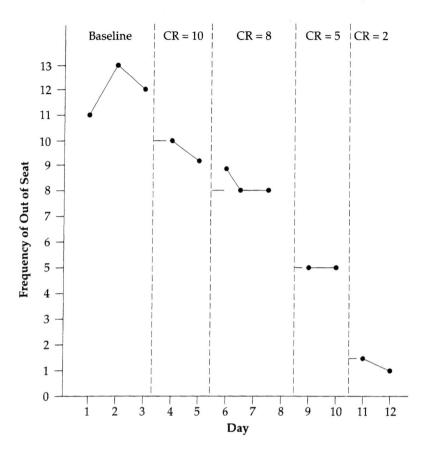

FIGURE 8.1 Data Depicting the Results of a Hypothetical DRD Program for Caroline

tive. It may not be advisable to permit some adverse responses (e.g., behaviors harmful to self and others) to continue without direct efforts to immediately terminate the behavior. Similarly, the process of reinforcing diminishing or low rates of a response can appear to others as simply reinforcing disruptive behavior. This is not important from the perspective of target students as they are actually being reinforced for low rates of the behavior. The observer who is unaware of the actual contingency relationships may model the disruptive behavior at any level to obtain similar reinforcement.

Finally, positive consequences provided through DRL or DRD may not be as attractive as reinforcers naturally resulting from the disruptive behavior. A student may choose to continue to act out in class because peer approval that is received is more desirable than teacher praise that results from meeting the DRL or DRD objective. One way to overcome this disadvantage is to limit natural reinforcers that are provided as a consequence of engaging in the disruptive behavior. An approach for reducing natural reinforcement provided to a disruptive response is through the use of extinction, which is discussed in the following section.

Extinction

Extinction is the removal of positive consequences that maintain a behavior. It is frequently referred to as planned ignoring. Extinction programs can be used to reduce disruptive social behaviors by removing reinforcers. Alternately, extinction programs can be used to maintain prosocial behaviors because they ensure that reinforcers are not removed.

Illustrating the first objective, a child who tantrums to gain parent attention is expected to stop tantruming when he recognizes that his parents no longer provide attention following tantrums. A youth who violently waves her hand so that teachers will call on her is expected to stop hand waving when it is clear that she will be overlooked unless she is sitting calmly.

Illustrating the second objective, parents may enthusiastically identify and reward achievement early in the school year. As time passes, they may lose interest in the child's educational program and discontinue the use of social praise and special privileges for success. The inadvertent removal of reinforcement, or extinction, may result in a discontinuation of high quality academic performance. A youth who initially interacts with a number of students in class hoping to establish friendships may withdraw when these efforts fail to produce positive consequences. Even for adults, a carpenter who is not paid for his labor is likely to discontinue work, and fans of the local collegiate football team are likely to discontinue going to games if there is no past history of success.

While extinction is very easy to understand conceptually, it is equally difficult to administer. Reinforcers are often difficult to identify and remove. This is particularly problematic because of the importance of removing *all* reinforcement from the target behavior. Removing only a portion of the positive consequences is likely to develop more persistent disruptive responses. This thinner schedule of reinforcement may be more resistant to future reductive efforts.

For example, most classrooms have the resident class clown whose antics usually result in laughter from his or her teachers and peers. Such antics are difficult to stop through extinction. You as the teacher may be able to control your reactions to the student's behavior but his or her classmates probably won't be able to control theirs. Even the occasional reaction from peers will be enough to sustain the clowning behavior.

The initial response to extinction is an elevation in behavior strength as the student strives to obtain lost incentives. This effect, depicted in Figure 8.2, is referred to as an *extinction burst*. The intensity of a response during an extinction burst may be sufficiently high to be dangerous to the student or others. Under these conditions, the teacher must often "give in" and provide attention or other lost reinforcers. Providing reinforcement near the peak of an extinction burst may result in the reinforcement of the disruptive response at a higher rate. Given the preceding sce-

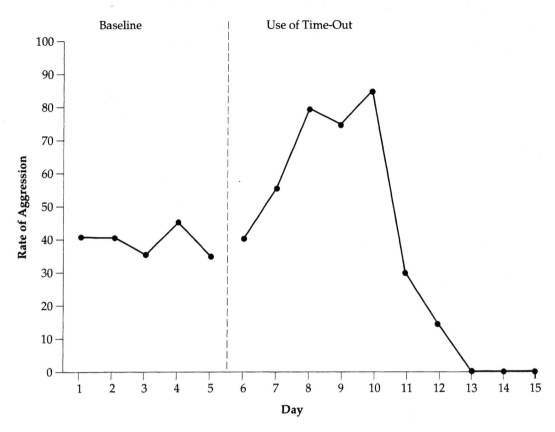

FIGURE 8.2 Data Depicting an Extinction Burst

nario, the response becomes more persistent through the ill-advised thinning of the reinforcement schedule.

Despite these issues, carefully devised and implemented extinction programs can be effective. Numerous reports appearing in the professional literature over the past several decades support the efficacy of extinction programs. The focus of these reports includes classroom discipline (O'Leary & Becker, 1967; Wilson & Hopkins, 1973); aggression (Carr, Newsom & Binkoff, 1980); sexual activity (Alford, Morin, Atkins, & Schoen, 1987); and phobias (Kaloupek, Peterson, Boyd, & Levis, 1981). While many of these demonstrations assess the isolated effectiveness of extinction, it is more common for extinction to be used in combinaton with other procedures. Extinction, for example, has been described previously as an excellent adjunct to differential reinforcement procedures.

Initiate extinction programs by establishing complementary sets of behavioral objectives. The first set should identify the reduction target and the second set should address replacement skills. It may be particularly important to specify procedures for removing all reinforcement from the target behavior within the condition statement. The condition statement may also emphasize procedures to ensure the continuation of the plan throughout the extinction burst.

Extinction does not include elements that produce replacement skills. Therefore, we recommend that a complementary objective identify target responses that will replace the behavior being extinguished. For example, the reductive objective may note that the extinction program will result in the elimination of nail biting. The complementary objective may include the development of nail care skills (e.g., cleaning, trimming, and polishing). The next step is to limit the context in which the extinction program will operate. Because of negative effects associated with the incomplete removal of reinforcement, we recommend targeting a limited number of critical settings. Unstructured environments (e.g., hall passage, recess, bus travel, etc.) may be excluded from the program because of the recognized inability to remove all sources of reinforcement. This provision is expected to promote the discrimination of settings in which the response will and will not produce reinforcement. The result will be effective response reduction in the target setting with the possibility of no effect in other settings. This is preferred to the incomplete use of extinction in all settings and the resulting development of more persistent responses in these settings.

We recommend the use of DRI or DRA procedures in conjunction with extinction. This provision will support the enhancement of behaviors that may replace the extinguished response. Similarly, use prompting, modeling, and other instructional procedures to ensure that the student is aware of contingencies in the extinction program.

Most important, establish a plan to ensure that no reinforcement is provided following occurrences of the target response. This plan may include restricting reactions of other professionals, parents, or students to the individual. It may also include modifications in the instructional setting that limit access to reinforcing events. Alterations in the instructional setting may include the use of study carrels, segregated seating, removal of desirable objects, and so on. As noted earlier, planning should reflect elevated efforts of the student to obtain reinforcement during extinction bursts. For example, if a student is likely to threaten to jump from a window (to gain attention), he may be removed to a room with no windows. Similarly, if a student is likely to be physically aggressive (to gain compliance), teachers may be trained in the use of a graduated physical guidance or other passive restraint methods (Schloss & Smith, 1987).

Finally, the extinction plan should include provision for the continuation of the program beyond the point at which the reduction objective is achieved. Skinner (1953) and Epstein and Skinner (1980) noted that extinguished responses may recur even though there has been no resumption of reinforcement. This phenomenon is described as *spontaneous recovery* or *resurgence*. Failing to continue to withhold reinforcement from the resurgent response may result in regression from performance gains made through the initial program.

The major advantage of extinction is that it can be highly effective while requiring minimal effort. Similarly, effective extinction programs avoid the use of aversive methods. Literature over the past several decades identifies a wide range of nonaversive applications with diverse behavior problems (Alford, Morin, Atkins, & Schoen, 1987; Carr & McDowell, 1980; Kaloupek, Peterson, Boyd, & Levis, 1981).

Extinction may also be effective when applied as an adjunct to differential reinforcement strategies. Used alone, the differential reinforcement approaches may result in only a gradual reduction in disruptive behavior. The combined use of differential reinforcement with extinction may accelerate the behavioral reduction.

Finally, the effects of extinction procedures can be enduring as long as the intermittent resurgence of the response is not reinforced (Epstein & Skinner, 1980). A student who stops arguing with teachers because of the teachers' efforts in avoiding the reinforcement of this behavior is likely to continue the avoidance of arguing. This is particularly true if the teachers continue to withhold reinforcement when intermittent arguing occurs.

The major disadvantage of extinction is related to the inability of teachers to continue withholding reinforcement throughout the extinction burst. As noted earlier, providing reinforcement during a higher response rate may result in more harm than was apparent prior to intervention. Not only will withholding reinforcement produce higher levels of responding but also it may produce a more persistent behavior under a thinner schedule of reinforcement.

Another important disadvantage is the difficulty in identifying and controlling all sources of reinforcement. Events that reinforce behaviors are often complex and difficult to isolate. For example, a student may smoke cigarettes to gain peer approval, to produce desirable physiological effects, to satisfy manipulatory urges, or for any number of other reasons. Each of these reasons would have to be identified and removed for an extinction plan to be effective. Similarly, a student may talk out in class to gain attention from teachers or peers, to diminish the frustration associated with difficult class work, to anger teachers, and so on. Again the effectiveness of an extinction program would hinge on the ability of the teacher to isolate and remove these consequences.

Finally, your use of extinction may lead others to believe that you condone the disruptive social behavior. This may cause other students to model the disruptive response while believing that you are not offended by the response. Similarly, adults may view the use of extinction as an indication of disinterest as opposed to active concern.

Summary

The procedures described in this chapter are positive alternatives for reducing disruptive social behaviors. Each of the procedures avoids the limitations associated with aversive consequences. Further, many of the approaches include educative components or can easily be used in conjunction with educational strategies. In view of these important features, researchers and authors have recommended the use of these nonaversive approaches prior to using more intrusive methods (Van Houten & Rolider, 1988).

It is important to note that not all disruptive responses can be altered effectively with the preceding nonaversive methods. In these cases, it may be more humane to use intrusive methods instead of ignoring persistent responding that may be harmful to the social adjustment of the individual with disabilities. Emphasizing this point, Matson and DiLorenzo (1984) have argued that "In cases where the behavior may be extremely physically harmful to the client or to others and where there is demonstration and documentation of the failure of other (less intrusive) procedures, withholding of (aversive) treatment may not be only impractical but also unethical" (p. 135).

In view of the importance of providing a range of reductive options, you should be prepared to use aversive as well as nonaversive reductive strategies. The following chapter will review aversive approaches. Special attention will be given to the careful and ethical use of these procedures.

References

Alford, G. S., Morin, C., Atkins, M., & Schoen, L. (1987). Masturbatory extinction of deviant sexual arousal: A case study. *Behavior Therapy, 18,* 265–271.

Azrin, N. H., & Holtz, W. C. (1966). Punishment. In W. K. Honig (Ed.), *Operant behavior: Areas of research and application.* New York: Appleton-Century-Crofts.

Barton, L. E., Brulle, A. R., & Repp, A. C. (1986). Maintenance of therapeutic change by momentary DRO. *Journal of Applied Behavior Analysis, 19,* 277–282.

Carr, E. G., & McDowell, J. J. (1980). Social control of self-injurious behavior of organic etiology. *Behavior Therapy, 11,* 402–409.

Carr, E. G., Newsom, C. D., & Binkoff, J. A. (1980). Escape as a factor in the aggressive behavior of two retarded children. *Journal of Applied Behavior Analysis, 13,* 101–117.

Cavalier, A. R., & Ferretti, R. P. (1980). Stereotyped behavior, alternative behavior, and collateral effects: A comparison of four intervention procedures. *Journal of Mental Deficiency Research, 24,* 219–230.

Cowdery, G. E., Iwata, B. A., & Pace, G. M. (1990). Effects and side effects of DRO as treatment for self-injurious behavior. *Journal of Applied Behavior Analysis, 23,* 497–506.

Deitz, S. M., & Repp, A. C. (1973). Decreasing classroom misbehavior through the use of DRL schedules of reinforcement. *Journal of Applied Behavior Analysis, 6,* 457–463.

Deitz, S. M., & Repp, A. C. (1974). Differentially reinforcing low rates of misbehavior with normal elementary school children. *Journal of Applied Behavior Analysis, 7,* 622.

Epstein, R., & Skinner, B. F. (1980). Resurgence of responding after the cessation of response-independence reinforcement. *Proceedings of the National Academy of Sciences, U.S.A., 77,* 6251–6253.

Ferster, C. B., & Skinner, B. F. (1957). *Schedules of reinforcement.* New York: Appleton.

Friman, P. C. (1990). Nonaversive treatment of high-rate disruption: Child and provider effect. *Exceptional Children, 57,* 64–67.

Friman, P. C., & Altman, K. (1990). Parent use of DRI on high-rate disruptive behavior: Direct and collateral benefits. *Research in Developmental Disabilities, 11,* 249–254.

Gardner, W. I. (1977). *Learning and behavior characteristics of exceptional children and youth: A humanistic behavioral approach.* Boston: Allyn and Bacon.

Haring, T. G., & Kennedy, C. H. (1990). Contextual control of problem behavior in students with severe disabilities. *Journal of Applied Behavior Analysis, 23,* 235–243.

Harris, S. L., & Wolchik S. A. (1979). Suppression of self-stimulation: Three alternative strategies. *Journal of Applied Behavior Analysis, 12,* 185–198.

Jayne, D., Schloss, P. J., Alper, S., & Menscher, S. (1994). Reducing disruptive behaviors by training students to request assistance. *Behavior Modification, 19,* 320–338.

Kaloupek, D. G., Peterson, D. A., Boyd, T. L., & Levis, D. J. (1981). The effects of exposure to a spatial ordered fear stimulus: A study of generalization of extinction effects. *Behavior Therapy, 12,* 130–137.

Leitenberg, H., Burchard, J. D., Burchard, S. N., Fuller, E. J., & Lysaght, T. V. (1977). Using positive reinforcement to suppress behaviors: Some experimental comparisons with sibling conflict. *Behavior Therapy, 8,* 168–182.

Mace, F. C., Kratochwill, T. R., & Fiello, R. A. (1983). Positive treatment of aggressive behavior in a mentally retarded adult: A case study. *Behavior Therapy, 14,* 689–696.

Matson, J., & Taras, M. E. (1989). A 20 year review of punishment and alternative methods to treat problem behaviors in developmentally delayed persons. *Research in Developmental Disabilities, 10,* 85–104.

Matson, J. L., & Dilorenzo, T. M. (1984). *Punishment and its alternatives: A new perspective for behavior modification.* New York: Springer.

O'Leary, K. D., & Becker, W. C. (1967). Behavior modification of an adjustment class: A token reinforcement program. *Exceptional Children, 33,* 637–642.

O'Reilly, M. F., Green, G., & Braunling-McMorrow, D. (1990). Self-administered written prompts to teach home accident prevention skills to adults with brain injuries. *Journal of Applied Behavior Analysis, 23,* 431–446.

Repp, A. C., Barton, L. E., & Brulle, A. R. (1983). A comparison of two procedures for programming the differential reinforcement of other behaviors. *Journal of Applied Behavior Analysis, 16,* 435–445.

Rolider, A., & Van Houten, R. (1984). The effects of DRO alone and DRO plus reprimands on the undesirable behavior of three children in home settings. *Education and Treatment of Children, 7,* 17–31.

Schloss, P. J., & Smith, M. A. (1987). Guidelines for ethical use of manual restraint in public school settings for behaviorally disordered students. *Behavioral Disorders, 12,* 207–213.

Skinner B. F. (1953). *Science and human behavior.* New York: Appleton.

Sulzer-Azaroff, B., & Mayer, G. R. (1991). *Behavior analysis for lasting change.* Fort Worth, TX: Holt, Rinehart and Winston.

Van Houten, R., & Rolider, A. (1988). Recreating the scene: An effective way to provide delayed punishment for inappropriate motor behavior. *Journal of Applied Behavior Analysis, 21,* 187–192.

Wilson, C. W., & Hopkins, B. L. (1973). The effects of contingent music on the intensity of noise in junior high home economics classes. *Journal of Applied Behavior Analysis, 6,* 269–275.

9

DECREASING INAPPROPRIATE BEHAVIOR USING PUNISHMENT

We are all familiar with students who do not respond to traditional disciplinary procedures. These students can be described in the same terms used by meteorologists to describe floods. A one-year flood (mild) describes water levels elevated to a point expected annually. A ten-year flood (moderate) describes water levels elevated to a point expected on average every decade. Finally, a twenty-year flood (severe) describes water levels that are expected every two decades. Each year, in our classes we have students whose behavior problems are sufficiently perplexing, persistent, or severe to be found in students only encountered every one, ten, or twenty years of a teaching career. For the average general or special education teaching position (excluding self-contained behavior disorders and severe disabilities), one- to five-year students usually respond to the positive strategies highlighted in the preceding chapter. These methods should always be adopted over aversive strategies when both are likely to be effective. The major features that recommend the nonaversive approaches include avoidance of the negative side effects associated with aversive stimuli and the increased likelihood that alternative prosocial behaviors may be developed through nonaversive interventions.

Unfortunately, specific disruptive responses of some students (to carry out the analogy, five- to twenty-year students) may not be easily and quickly changed using nonaversive methods. These students may require the use of aversive methods. In arguing this position, Matson and DiLorenzo (1984) state, "Punishment...is often rapidly effective in the treatment of harmful behaviors that do not respond readily to other forms of treatment" (p. 10). Cooper, Heron, and Heward (1987) further contend that it may be unethical to deprive a student of a well conceived punishment program. "Not using punishment, especially in situations where other procedures have been tried unsuccessfully, withholds a potentially effective treatment and maintains the client in a dangerous or uncomfortable state" (p. 412).

These arguments are illustrated in the treatment of self-injurious behavior (Mayhew & Harris, 1979; Singh, Beale, & Dawson,1981; Tanner & Zeiler, 1975); aggression (Azrin & Powers, 1975; Doke, Wolery, & Sumberg, 1983); and chronic self-stimulatory or stereotyped behavior (Cavalier & Ferretti, 1980; Durand & Carr, 1987; Luce & Hall, 1981). In each case the authors used aversive approaches following ineffective trials of nonaversive methods. The results substantially enhanced the quality of life for the recipient. As Baer (1971) notes, the costs of the punishment procedure in effort and pain is substantially outweighed by the avoidance of effort and pain that would result from the habitual maladaptive behavior. Repp and Dietz (1978) go on to argue that when less intrusive procedures have been used to no effect, withholding an aversive method may be both impractical and unethical.

The Doctrine of Least Restrictive Alternative

An effective philosophy governing the selection of nonaversive and aversive methods for reducing behavior problems is suggested in **the doctrine of least restrictive alternative** (Cooper, Heron, & Heward, 1987). The doctrine recognizes the advisability of using nonaversive approaches (such as response cost and time-out) whenever they are judged to be effective. Aversive methods (such as contingent electric shock) may be required, however, when systematic trials indicate that the response did not change using less intrusive means.

The doctrine of least restrictive alternative has direct relevance to information contained in this text. Specifically, we recommend that interventions using approaches described in the preceding chapter be used prior to adopting one of the more intrusive procedures presented in this chapter; the more restrictive approaches are used only when the nonaversive strategies are demonstrated to be ineffective. Even within the current chapter, we suggest that methods least likely to involve isolation, physical discomfort, or psychological distress (e.g., response cost and nonexclusion time-out) be used over those with exclusion and/or aversive elements.

In short, just as we advocate for placement in a least restrictive environment (Schloss, Smith, & Schloss, 1995) so too do we suggest that the approaches used within a particular environment be as normal as is practical. Beyond these arguments, it is important to note that the courts have consistently judged whether applied behavior analysis procedures violate the constitutional rights of a student based on the relationship of the procedure to the severity of the behavior problem (e.g., *Cole v. Greenfield-Central Community Schools*, 1966; *Dickens v. Johnson County Board of Education*, 1987; *Hayes v. Unified School District No. 377*, 1987).

Based on a rationale of minimal restrictiveness, and supported by the writings of Carr and Lovaas (1983), we suggest the following hierarchy of restrictiveness:

1. Differential reinforcement approaches (DRI and DRA) that include repertoire enhancing elements as alternative or incompatible replacements for disruptive responses. These differential reinforcement approaches are likely to be combined with extinction procedures. This is exemplified by teaching and reinforcing new social skills while ignoring confrontational behaviors.

2. Differential reinforcement approaches that provide reinforcement for gradually longer periods of time in which disruptive responses do not occur. Alternative strategies include differential reinforcement approaches that provide reinforcement for the immediate (DRL) or gradual (DRD) reduction of the behavior. These approaches should also include repertoire enhancing strategies (e.g., modeling, behavior rehearsal, and DRI/DRA). Such strategies are exemplified by reinforcing diminishing levels of the disruptive behavior while teaching and reinforcing alternative social responses.

3. Nonexclusion time-out procedures in which all sources of reinforcement are withdrawn for a brief period of time following disruptive responses. An alternative is response cost procedures in which a discrete amount of a reinforcer (e.g., loss of commissary tokens) is withdrawn following a disruptive response. These approaches are likely to be combined with repertoire enhancing teaching and differential reinforcement approaches. They are exemplified by requiring that a child place her head down on her desk for three minutes or pay ten tokens following talking out. You may then ask her to practice raising her hand and reinforce her for doing so.

4. Exclusion time-out in which a student is isolated in a room void of stimulation and interpersonal contact. Exclusion time-out is likely to be combined with repertoire enhancing teaching and differential reinforcement approaches. It is exemplified by requiring that a youth enter a time-out room for three minutes following an aggressive behavior. You may then ask him to demonstrate alternatives to aggressive behavior.

5. Overcorrection through which a student must perform extraordinary restitution following disruptive social behavior and repeatedly practice alternative positive social behavior. Depending on the nature of restitution and positive practice activities, the approach may move up the hierarchy to a minimally restrictive approach (e.g., child must apologize for dropping his books and then pick up the books), or move down the hierarchy to being highly restrictive (e.g., extended restitution and positive practice activity that require physical guidance from others).

6. Finally, presentation of aversive consequences (PAC), in which a noxious agent is presented following a disruptive behavior, may be described as the most restrictive procedure. As with other procedures that do not include repertoire enhancing strategies, PAC is likely to be combined with modeling, behavioral rehearsal, and DRI/DRA procedures. Depending on the nature of the aversive stimulus, the approach may move up the hierarchy to a minimally restrictive approach (e.g., verbal reprimand and instruction).

Well-prepared educators are able to use a variety of reductive methods. Equally important, they are able to recognize and comply with procedural standards suggested by the doctrine of least restrictive alternative. This chapter, along with the preceding chapter, will contribute resources that enable teachers to meet these standards. Specifically, we will provide a definition of punishment, which will be contrasted with the definition of aversive procedures. Next we will present an analysis of more restrictive and possibly aversive punishment methods. Then we will suggest general guidelines for maximizing the effectiveness of punishment procedures. Finally, we will discuss the limitations of punishment and suggest ethical safeguards that should govern the use of these consequences.

Punishment Defined

The technical definition of **punishment** differs substantially from the term used by the general population. Common usage suggests that punishment is the simple act of providing an unpleasant consequence following misbehavior. Typical examples include: spanking a child for soiling his pants; requiring that a youth brush his teeth with soap after swearing; scheduling a team to run multiple wind sprints following a loss; or scolding a child for being tardy. The general public may consider any aversive event that is used as a consequence for disruptive behavior to be punishment.

The technical definition goes beyond this relationship to indicate that any stimulus, whether perceived by the punisher to be favorable or unfavorable, can be a punisher. Compliments, pats on the back, written notices of performance, and so on may all be punishing. They are designated as being punishers based on their demonstrated effectiveness in reducing the target behavior (Azrin & Holtz, 1966). For example, a verbal reprimand may be a punishment for cheating if it is demonstrated to reduce the rate of cheating; and detention is a punishment for smoking if the rate of smoking is reduced after serving detention.

The following technical definition of punishment accounts for these elements:

> Punishment *is the reduction of a target behavior following the contingent presentation of a stimulus. A stimulus that consistently results in the reduction of a target behavior is said to* punish *that behavior.*

Differences between popular and technical definitions of punishment are important to teachers seeking effective methods for reducing disruptive behavior. Using only the popular definition may cause you to expose students to unpleasant learning conditions with no apparent positive influence. You may reprimand, detain, or isolate a student, and these aversive events may have no impact on the disruptive behavior. Consequently, the only effect of the popular use of "punishment" is the creation of a hostile learning environment.

Conversely, the technical definition requires that the event (aversive or pleasant) produce a reduction in the target behavior. Consequently, reprimands, detention, or isolation are used only when they function to diminish the target behavior. Selecting consequences that are in fact punishing (e.g., they do in fact reduce the rate of the target response) ensures that ineffective aversive consequences are withdrawn from the learning environment.

Classification of Punishment

The previous section classified aversive events as being unconditioned or conditioned. We emphasized that while events may be aversive, they may not be punishing. Events can be unpleasant, and yet produce no reductive effect. Further, events need not be aversive to produce a reductive effect. Considering both cases, punishment requires the demonstration of a functional relationship in which a target behavior is followed by a consequence that produces a reduction in future occurrences of the response.

Although we have been emphasizing the importance of conducting a functional analysis before designing and implementing a presumed punishment program, aversive events are generally effective punishers of the disruptive responses of many students. Recognizing this, Matson and DiLorenzo (1984) have suggested three general forms of aversive stimulation used in punishment programs, which will be discussed next.

Removal of Pleasant Events

This punishment approach involves withdrawing a desirable commodity or stimulus from an individual contingent on the occurrence of a target response, which decreases the likelihood of future occurrences of the response. A common approach is *exclusion and nonexclusion time-out*, in which all sources of reinforcement and a majority of stimulation are withdrawn from the individual. Another common approach is *response cost*, in which a specified amount of a desirable commodity (e.g., food, free time, toys; or tokens/money that represent the commodity) is assessed following a target response. Both time-out and response cost procedures will be discussed later in this chapter.

Punishment Based on Penalties and Effort

This punishment category involves requiring that an individual engage in potentially aversive physical exertion following a target response, which reduces the future strength of the target response. A common approach to punishment based on penalty and effort is *overcorrection restitution and positive practice*. These methods will be discussed in a subsequent section.

Presentation of Aversive Stimuli

This form of punishment involves producing a noxious stimulus following a target response, which decreases the likelihood of future occurrences of the response. Common approaches include placing drops of lemon juice on a person's tongue, requiring that an individual inhale ammonia, paddling, and spraying a mist of water at an individual. Specific approaches for using the presentation of aversive stimuli as well as ethical safeguards will be discussed later in this chapter.

Response Cost

A **response cost** is defined as the contingent removal of a discrete amount of reinforcers following a target response, with the result of reducing future probability of that response occurring. Actually, you have probably experienced several response cost procedures. You may have paid a fine for keeping a library book past its due date, been charged a fee for an overdrawn checking account, or received a ticket for parking or speeding. As noted earlier, a response cost is an aversive procedure. Consequently, other less restrictive strategies should be demonstrated to be ineffective prior to its implementation. Also, response cost does not include repertoire enhancing components. Therefore, it should always be paired with modeling, behavior rehearsal, and differential reinforcement procedures that develop alternative/incompatible prosocial behaviors.

Common response cost strategies include depriving the student of tangible commodities, withdrawing specific favored activities, limiting discretion over commodities or activities, and docking tokens that represent the preceding items or events as aversive consequences. The actual consequence is generally governed by the characteristics of the learner and the setting.

The first approach is the *deprivation of tangible commodities*. This method of response cost involves depriving a student of a specific item. For example, you may not allow a child to eat a cookie during morning snack because of a tantrum that occurred early in the day. Similarly, a student may not be provided playground equipment because he or she failed to return a bat and ball to the classroom after the previous recess. You may remove an edible reinforcer from a (severely disabled) student's cup every time he pushes back from the work table.

Deprivation of tangible commodities may be the most direct response cost procedure. Therefore, it may be the most useful for young and less able students. The disadvantage of using a single commodity is that a child may have previously earned sufficient amounts of the item to become satiated. For example, after earning twenty pieces of candy for work completed in the past ten minutes, the subsequent loss of candy may not be influential. Also, the loss of edible reinforcers may not be as potent following meals.

The second approach involves the *withdrawal of specific favored activities*. A response cost using the withdrawal of favored activities is exemplified by the football coach who cancels a scrimmage because players "loafed" during conditioning exercises. Similarly, you may use the withdrawal of favored activities when requiring that a child remain in his seat rather than going to recess because he tipped over his desk. (Remember that participation in some activities such as physical education or counseling may be mandated by state law or an IEP and cannot be withdrawn.)

As with the deprivation of commodities, withdrawal of favored activities is effective for younger and less capable students. Relationships between inappropriate target responses and the loss of specific activities are easier to learn than procedures using less immediate or tangible consequences such as tokens or discretionary time.

The use of specific activities also allows you to select the student's single most desirable activity.

The disadvantage of withdrawing favored activities is that a student may become bored with repeatedly earning a single activity. External conditions may also affect the attractiveness of the activity. For example, a student may not miss being able to play outside on a hot day. Consequently, the response cost procedure may not be punishing.

The third approach involves *limiting discretion over commodities or activities*. This method of response cost is exemplified by a teacher requiring that a student work on math worksheets rather than being able to select from a range of pleasant activities. Similarly, parents may punish a child for being indecisive in a fast food restaurant by specifying what will be ordered rather than allowing the child to select from the entire menu.

Limiting discretion over an activity is effective for students with a range of interests and abilities. While the relationships between inappropriate target responses and the loss of specific activities may be less clear, the loss of a range of activities avoids the boredom effect that may occur when only one item or event is withdrawn. Further, the mere loss of personal discretion and freedom may be particularly aversive to adolescents.

The last approach involves the *dockage of tokens that represent items or events*. Tokens were defined in Chapter 7 as graphic symbols or items (points, stamps, chips, tallies, etc.) that can be exchanged for back-up reinforcers (e.g., food, free time, privileges, etc.) according to a fixed menu (e.g., a candy bar costs five chips, free time is earned by producing 20 points). This response cost method involves the contingent withdrawal of tokens following a target response. For example, students may earn 10 points for completing each assignment through the day. Points can be exchanged at the end of the day for free time, snacks, special privileges, and so on. Aggressive behavior may result in a response cost of 30 points.

The loss of tokens may be the most indirect of the response cost procedures. These contingency relationships may be the most difficult for very young children or less capable learners to acquire. Conversely, they may be the most easily managed. Periods for back-up reinforcement can be delayed until convenient times during the day. Also, a variety of back-up reinforcers can be used to avoid satiation or a loss of interest.

Response cost procedures are recommended for use in carefully designed and implemented punishment programs. It is important to note, however, that a response cost can inadvertently be used to punish positive responses. You should be aware of this possibility and ensure that reinforcers are not withdrawn following the demonstration of positive social behavior. For example, you may be tempted to ask that students complete additional work if assignments are completed prior to the end of the class period. Additional work requirements may act as a response cost for early assignment completion. To avoid this and similar problems, we recommend a deliberative approach to designing and implementing response cost programs. Guidelines are discussed in the following section.

Designing and Implementing Response Cost Programs

Planning for a response cost program is initiated by conducting a prebaseline analysis. This analysis should establish that less restrictive methods have been attempted and found to be ineffective at reducing the disruptive behavior. The analysis should highlight reasonable goals for the program including an objective and reliable definition for the behavior to be reduced. Finally, the analysis should suggest potentially effective contingency arrangements. Specific items or events to be withdrawn, and the delay from onset of the disruptive response to withdrawal of the reinforcer should be determined based on the learning and behavioral features of the student.

Repertoire enhancing elements should also be built into the response cost program. You should be aware of the function of the disruptive behavior based on the prebaseline analysis. You should identify alternative/incompatible responses that serve the same function and develop them through modeling, behavior rehearsal, and differential reinforcement procedures (see Chapters 6, 7, and 8).

The student should be informed of all contingency arrangements. Contingency contracting (see Chapter 7) may be used to involve the student in developing these arrangements. Again, behavior rehearsal and modeling may be used to ensure that the student is aware of the consequences for specific responses. Also, cues (e.g., warning signs, rule sheets, etc.) may be posted to remind the student of response cost and differential reinforcement contingencies.

Just as you pair the presentation of a token with the delivery of social reinforcement, so too should you pair a response cost with a reprimand. A reprimand is a verbal statement that can be used by itself or in conjunction with another behavior reduction procedure to decrease a target behavior. Like social reinforcement, a reprimand has several components. First, it includes the student's name. Second, it instructs the student to stop engaging in a behavior. Third, it includes a rationale for discontinuing the behavior, an important component for students who do not understand the negative consequences their behavior may have. Fourth, there is a request for or the identification of an appropriate alternative to the behavior. You should encourage a student to identify a more appropriate behavior unassisted; however, we recognize that some students are unable to do so or are likely to identify an alternative that is just as inappropriate as the original behavior. An example of a reprimand is, "Cameron, you need to stop looking out the window. You won't be able to finish your work on time and go to recess. What should you be doing instead?" A student for whom a response cost system has been designed would experience the response cost and the reprimand at the same time. For example, "Andrew, you may not swear. You will lose two tokens. Instead of swearing when you are angry, you should take a deep breath and count to ten." Technically, a reprimand is a conditioned aversive event (discussed later in this chapter). However, its use is so common that few people express any concern. Nonetheless, it is important to use a reprimand correctly if it is to reduce a behavior. Table 9.1 on page 180 lists guidelines identified by Misra (1991) for using reprimands appropriately.

TABLE 9.1 Using Reprimands Effectively

Misra (1991) identified several guidelines for using reprimands. They include the following:

1. Establish priorities. Target a limited number of behaviors to reprimand.
2. Deliver the reprimand as privately as possible. No doubt, others will hear it and possibly benefit from it; however, a reprimand should not provide the opportunity for public humiliation.
3. Look the child in the eye. However, you should be sensitive to the differences in cultural backgrounds. A student may not establish eye contact during a reprimand because to do so would indicate a lack of respect for the teacher.
4. Make sure your body, facial expressions, and tone of voice deliver a consistent message. They should all "say" the same thing, that is, you are displeased by the student's violation of expectations.
5. Be specific. Use the student's name, tell him or her to stop the inappropriate behavior, and identify or request an appropriate alternative.
6. Make statements. Don't ask questions such as, "How many times have I told you not to do that?" You may not like the student's answer.
7. Make sure you use vocabulary and syntax that are understood by the student.
8. Never use judgmental language such as, "That's bad!" or "You're stupid."
9. Do not repeat a reprimand. The student will not believe that you mean what you say. If the reprimand does not stop the undesired behavior, move on to the next level in your contingency plan.
10. Remember to balance reprimands with praise. A ratio of 1 reprimand to 4 or 5 praise statements is ideal.

You should ensure that an effective balance is achieved between potential reinforcers and dockages. Too large of a dosage from a limited supply of reinforcers is likely to be ineffective as the response cost contingency is no longer in effect once the supply of reinforcers is drained (e.g., a child cannot be motivated to avoid losing tokens if all tokens have already been assessed). Too small of a dockage from an extensive supply of reinforcers is equally unlikely to be effective. A child may not be motivated to discontinue a disruptive behavior to avoid losing one token if he already possesses hundreds of tokens. For example, a response cost program in which a verbally aggressive preschooler loses her 30-minute playground time for each tantrum would be inappropriate if the baseline rate is over three tantrums an hour. In this case it may be more appropriate for the child to lose five minutes of the playground period following each verbally aggressive response. Conversely, losing only five minutes of the playground period for one offense may be inappropriate if the baseline rate is below one an hour. This minimal response cost may not be sufficiently stringent to produce a reductive effect.

The actual behavior-to-cost ratio may be developed through trial and error. As recommended by Gardner (1977), it is important that the initial response cost be presented at a level expected to be effective. Beginning at a lower level and gradually increasing until the child begins to react to the response cost may result in inadvertent acclamations of the child to progressively more stringent conditions.

Using a moderate dockage, negotiating the conditions of the response cost, and teaching contingencies used in the program may reduce the likelihood that students will become aggressive or depressed when a response cost occurs. However, students are likely to become emotional following a response cost even under the best conditions. Consequently, you must be prepared to use a back-up procedure to manage the emotional reaction.

A major mistake we see teachers make is that they allow the student to earn back all or part of the amount he or she has lost. For example, the teacher removes two stars from a chart when Jimmy crumples his paper. Jimmy sulks or starts to cry, prompting the teacher to say, "If you start working, you may have your stars back." As soon as Jimmy smoothes out the paper and starts working, the stars are redrawn. You should avoid rescinding the response cost or providing the student with an opportunity to regain lost incentives as the student becomes increasingly disruptive. Withdrawing the response cost may negatively reinforce the high rate disruptive outburst (e.g., becoming highly aggressive allows the student to avoid the response cost contingencies, thereby increasing the probability of future outbursts following response costs). In this example, Jimmy's teacher should have advised him to start working. He should be told, "If you finish your work correctly and on time, you may earn a star." We hope you see the differences in the teacher's behavior. Returning to the scheduled activity and having the opportunity to earn another star are vastly different and much more effective than backing down and giving in to students.

You must be prepared to sustain the response cost contingency regardless of the student's reaction. This may require a set of options that range in intrusiveness. You may be able to ignore mildly negative emotional reactions. You may also enforce an alternative response cost for continuing reactions. Finally, you may need to use a time-out procedure in which the student is removed from the instructional situation until he or she is calm for several minutes. Time-out is described in the following section.

Time-Out from Positive Reinforcement

Time-out from positive reinforcement involves removing an individual from all sources (as practical) of reinforcement following an inappropriate behavior. This occurs for an established period of time and must result in a reduction in the probability of future occurrences of the behavior. Cooper, Heron, and Heward (1987) identify three major elements of the functional definition of time-out.

First, there must be a discrepancy in availability of reinforcement during "time-out" and "time-in" conditions. A student may be isolated from all sources of reinforcement or selectively withdrawn from specific reinforcers. In either case, the "time-in" condition must be substantially more reinforcement rich than the "time-out" condition. The greater the disparity, the more potent the reductive effect. For example, the punishment effect of requiring a child to sit under a tree at a theme park while others are enjoying rides (assuming that the child enjoys rides and dislikes being idle) may be substantially greater than requiring a child to remain in his classroom while others go to an assembly (assuming that the child expresses little interest in the assembly).

Second, the time-out consequence must be contingent on the occurrence of a target response. Time-out is not applied haphazardly with the student being intermittently placed in the time-out condition. There must be a direct and consistent relationship between the target response and time-out. This provision requires that behaviors producing time-out from reinforcement be identified in advance. Each occurrence of the response should produce the time-out consequence.

Third, the time-out contingency must result in a reduction in the target response. Simply removing a child or youth from a reinforcing environment without evidence of a reduction in the target response is best described as isolation (Brantner & Doherty, 1983). Time-out occurs only when isolation produces a reduction in the target response (Kazdin, 1989).

The major element of time-out is the removal from reinforcement. Traditional views of time-out focus on restricting a child or youth to a "time-out" room or area. Recent discussions of time-out extend the removal from reinforcement to methods through which the learner remains in the educational setting and is not segregated or secluded. Both exclusion and nonexclusion time-out have distinct advantages and disadvantages, so each will be discussed separately.

Nonexclusion Time-Out

Nonexclusion time-out involves withdrawing all sources of satisfaction and attention from a student without restricting his or her movement. Nonexclusion time-out generally includes the combined use of three approaches. First, the student is deprived of all media or materials that may be reinforcing (e.g., television, radio, tapes, crayons, paper, pencils, and books). Second, the child or youth is withdrawn from potentially reinforcing activities (e.g., playing games, participating in discussions, and going to the student lounge). Finally, the student is deprived of all sources of adult and student attention (refer to the planned ignoring in Chapter 8).

Porterfield, Herbert-Jackson, and Risley (1976) demonstrated another approach to nonexclusion time-out. Their **contingent observation** procedure involved requiring a child to sit outside the circle of activity. This permitted the student to observe others engaging in satisfying activities without being able to participate. More recently, White and Bailey (1990) reported a similar procedure termed "sit and watch." Disruptive behaviors of children in elementary physical education classes were reduced by requiring that a child sit on the periphery of activity for three minutes following a rule violation.

Another nonexclusion time-out method, referred to as the *time-out ribbon,* has been demonstrated by Foxx and Shapiro (1978). Children in an educational program at a developmental center were provided ribbons to wear around their necks. The ribbon indicated that the child was available to receive social, edible, and activity reinforcers. Disruptive behavior resulted in the removal of the time-out ribbon for three minutes. Loss of the ribbon also signified that reinforcers normally accessible were not available for the learner.

Exclusion Time-Out

Unlike nonexclusion time-out, **exclusion time-out** involves physically removing a student from the potentially reinforcing environment to a setting void of reinforcers. The exclusion setting can range in restrictiveness from placement in a segregated setting within the classroom (e.g., sitting in a corner or behind a carrel) to an isolated room void of stimulation, classified as **isolation time-out** by some authors (Costenbader & Reading-Brown, 1995; Mace & Heller, 1990).

Consistent with the philosophy of least restrictive alternative, we suggest the use of the minimum level of exclusion necessary to produce the desired effect. Using a carrel around or near the student's existing seat is advisable if this approach can be used to effectively remove reinforcement. Conversely, if the student is able to attract reinforcement through loud verbalizations, peeking above the screen, or pushing the screen, use of a special room may be required. It is important to note that increasing the degree of isolation does not necessarily increase the procedure's effectiveness (Mace & Heller, 1990).

A room need not be specially designed for the purpose of implementing time-out programs. In fact, the most common practice may be to use a room that has another primary purpose and doubles for use in time-out programming. These accommodations may include: the blind end of a hallway, a closet, an office, a storage room, or the area below a stairwell. Whether designed for an alternative purpose or specifically for use as a time-out room, design features should account for both the safety and effectiveness of the setting.

Principal safety concerns are generally addressed in the life safety codes for educational and social service facilities in the state. Prior to use, a time-out room should be evaluated against criteria in the life safety code or other relevant regulations (e.g., mental health code, school code, etc.). Specific provisions may include:

1. The room should be of adequate size and shape to provide for comfortable access by the student and a staff member.

2. The room should have appropriate lighting and ventilation.

3. It should not be possible to block entries or exits from the room through mechanical means (e.g., bolts, locks, and door stops) that can remain in place in the absence of adult supervision. Courts have held that it is unconstitutional to leave a student alone in a locked room as punishment for disruptive behavior (*Morales v. Turman*, 1973).

4. Similarly, it should be possible for you to monitor the student without actually being in the room.

5. The room should be free of objects that may be potentially hazardous to an aggressive student (e.g., glass, unshielded light bulbs, electric sockets or switches).

6. If the student is likely to be highly aggressive and physically threatening to himself and others, the floor and possibly walls should be carpeted or otherwise padded.

7. The doorway should be sufficiently large and unobstructed to allow for the rapid and safe physical guidance of the student into the room during extreme aggressive reactions.

8. Although not an architectural concern, the student should not be deprived of basic physiological necessities while in the time-out room. These include daily meals, water, medication, exercise, and periodic access to a wash room.

Effectiveness considerations are addressed through the following guidelines:

1. The room should be void of all sources of possible reinforcement. Virtually any object can have reinforcing properties under deprivation conditions associated with time-out. Consequently, it is generally best that the room be void of objects other than a chair or mat. If an office or storage area is used for time out, objects within reach of the student should be removed.

2. Supervision should be provided through an open door. However, visual contact from student to teacher should be avoided by seating students with their backs to the doorway.

3. To the extent possible, the time-out room should be sound deadened so that the child or youth is unable to draw others into the room by disrupting other students. The ability to draw others into the room may reinforce these outbursts.

4. All responses that may draw a teacher into the room should be anticipated and the room structured accordingly. For example, a child should not be placed in a room with drywall surfaces if the child is likely to kick holes in the drywall.

5. The room should be convenient to the classroom. Some students may need to be physically guided to the room. Consequently, the longer the distance, the greater the possible struggle. Also, time-out is generally recommended for only brief time periods. Therefore, it is advisable to minimize transition time to and from the time-out room.

Designing and Implementing a Time-Out Program

As with all applied behavior analysis interventions, time-out is conducted only after completing an analysis of the learner and the educational setting. The initial assessment outcome should be the identification of the primary objective of the time-out procedure, which should include the reduction of one or more disruptive responses. Other objectives should include the development of alternative prosocial responses. These may be achieved through modeling, behavior rehearsal, and differential reinforcement procedures.

We have emphasized that time-out is the contingent removal from all sources of reinforcement. Under the principle of least restrictive alternative, if the specific source of reinforcement that motivates a disruptive behavior can be identified, only that specific reinforcer should be withdrawn (e.g., attention, peer approval, removal of unpleasant assignments). Time-out is only used when specific sources of reinforcement cannot be identified or individually withdrawn.

Equally important, the teacher should confirm that the time-out condition is likely to be substantially less desirable than the time-in condition. We are sometimes faced with students for whom time-out appears to be ineffective. This is actually a misnomer because time-out is defined, in part, by its effectiveness. If a student's disruptive behaviors do not diminish, the procedure did not actually result in a deprivation of reinforcing activities to a nonreinforcing condition. For example, a withdrawn child may not be responsive to a "time-out" condition because he or she is not actually being deprived of reinforcing activities. The child would rather sit alone and daydream than play with other students.

A time-out condition is made more effective by ensuring that the child or youth is aware of highly enjoyable reinforcing activities that are being missed. We have advocated the use of a consistent classroom schedule with potentially reinforcing activities occurring intermittently throughout the day (Schloss, Holt, Mulvaney, & Green, 1988). This approach ensures that the student is aware of what is being missed and that the missed activity is substantially more desirable than the time-out activity.

The initial analysis should also indicate that time-out is the least restrictive procedure that will produce a reductive effect. Clear evidence should be provided that other methods (e.g., DRI, response cost, extinction) were tried and proven to be ineffective. When exclusion time-out is used, evidence should be provided to indicate the ineffectiveness of nonexclusion time-out.

Finally, consistent with the replacement objective, the analysis should indicate alternative prosocial behaviors that are expected to substitute for the disruptive behavior. Modeling and behavior rehearsal may be used to teach these behaviors. DRI or DRA may also be used to ensure that the student is motivated to use the prosocial response.

Since time-out is a restrictive procedure that includes possible undesirable negative side effects, such as an escalation of aggressive behavior and a loss of social contact, you should obtain appropriate permissions prior to actually implementing the procedure. Also, the courts have held that placement in a time-out room each day for up to a week does not constitute a change in placement (*Hayes v. Unified School District No. 377*, 1987). However, conscientious professionals may recognize that extended time in a restricted setting may substantially alter the instructional conditions originally intended by the multidisciplinary team. Given these considerations, we recommend using the multidisciplinary team, including family members and the student when appropriate, to review and approve the procedure. We also recommend that this group meet occasionally during implementation of the time-out program to review its effectiveness.

Following review and approval, you should initiate the time-out program by demonstrating the time-out rules to the student. Inform the student of: settings in which the time-out program is in effect, specific responses that should produce the time-out consequence, alternative prosocial responses expected along with their associated reinforcers, the location of the time-out room or the nonexclusion time-out method, the duration of each time-out application, and other criteria required for a student to leave the time-out condition.

The literature is unclear on the optimum duration of time-out periods. In general, however, most authorities agree that brief time-out periods of three to fifteen minutes are preferred over extended time-out sessions (Gast & Nelson, 1977). Longer periods are not only problematic for ethical reasons, but because of the effect they may have in teaching the student to acclimate to isolation, thereby making future time-out sessions less effective (Gast & Nelson, 1977).

Regardless of the duration in the time-out condition, there is consistent acknowledgment of the need for specific behavioral criteria to be met prior to returning to the time-in setting. We recommend that the student be relaxed (breathing deeply, talking in a normal conversational tone, keeping hands limp, proper facial tone, etc.) prior to returning to the time-in condition. One approach to accomplishing this objective is to require that the brief time-out duration be timed from the moment that relaxation responses are begun. You can also return the student to time-in when the time-out duration has passed and 30 seconds of relaxation have been demonstrated.

Evaluating Time-Out Programs

There is an increased responsibility for teachers to evaluate restrictive applied behavior analysis programs (Christian & Hannah, 1983; Thompson, Thornhill, Realon, & Ervin, 1991). In the case of time-out, continuing ineffective seclusion results in the continued isolation of the student with no alternative benefit. However, if the procedure is effective, seclusion will cease as a function of the behavioral reduction.

Observation and recording procedures discussed in Chapter 11 should be used in conjunction with the time-out program. Time-out generally has an immediate effect on the target response. If you do not detect a reduction on observational data, modify the procedure (e.g., making the time-in condition more predictable and attractive, reducing stimulation in the time-out condition, arranging for a highly satisfying DRO component, etc.). If these modifications do not produce an immediate effect, discontinue the procedure.

Observation and recording procedures may also focus on the extent of negative side effects. You may monitor the rate of time engaged in academic instruction, the duration of emotional outbursts, and so on. Again, the persistence of negative side effects that are not supported by benefits to the individual from the intervention may suggest the modification or discontinuation of the intervention.

Overcorrection

Overcorrection is a series of procedures that include several social learning strategies. The two major types of overcorrection include restitutional overcorrection and positive practice overcorrection (Foxx & Azrin, 1972).

Restitutional overcorrection requires that a disruptive student correct all results of his or her misbehavior by restoring the immediate environment to a state that is substantially improved over its original condition (Foxx & Azrin, 1973). Returning the environment to the state prior to the incident would be *simple correction* (Azrin & Besalel, 1980). An example of restitutional overcorrection is the child who throws food at lunch and is required to clean the floor of the lunch room, or the youth who swears at another individual and is required to apologize in writing and orally. Restitutional overcorrection may not be used with responses that have no adverse effect on the social setting.

Positive practice overcorrection requires that a student engage in an appropriate alternative or incompatible response, and it is expected to have an educative effect. The student is expected to learn to use this alternative response over the disruptive behavior. You may ask a child to complete a test after he or she has torn it up. The child is expected to learn that completing a test is preferred to destroying tests. Similarly, a student may be required to walk down the hallway after being punished for running. Your goal is to help him recognize that walking is preferred to running.

Both positive practice and restitution have the preceding secondary purposes. However, it is important to know that the primary purpose of each is to serve as an aversive consequence to deter future occurrences of the target behavior. Consequently, overcorrection meets the functional definition of punishment presented in the introduction to this chapter. A punishing consequence follows a response and decreases the likelihood that it will recur in the future.

Overcorrection uses consequences that are directly related to the disruptive response. This is preferred to consequences such as time-out or response costs that have no logical connection to the behavior (Foxx & Bechtel, 1983).

Designing and Implementing an Overcorrection Program

You should base the development of an overcorrection program on a careful analysis of the student. Be particularly concerned about whether or not less restrictive procedures have been demonstrated to be ineffective. If they have, is the specific overcorrection activity the minimally intrusive technique necessary to produce a reduction in disruptive behavior (e.g., simple correction is preferred to overcorrection if both may be effective)?

You should specify both reductive and replacement objectives for the overcorrection program. The reductive objective will specify responses that will occur less often as a result of the aversive overcorrection activity. The replacement objective will describe alternative prosocial responses. In most cases, the prosocial response will be the positive practice activity.

The analysis should also suggest specific overcorrection restitutional and positive practice activities. Foxx (1982) suggested that you use your own experiences to match an activity to a disruptive response. Specifically, you may ask, "If I broke a pencil, what would I have to do to correct the situation (restitution)?" "How would I perform in the future to avoid negative consequences (positive practice)?"

If answered correctly, the suggested activities would be functionally and topographically related to the disruptive response.

To maximize the replacement function of the positive practice activity, you should use a differential reinforcement procedure whenever the student uses the alternative or incompatible behavior over a disruptive response. An exception is that the positive practice response should not be reinforced during the overcorrection activity because this practice may reduce the aversive nature of the consequence.

You should identify a back-up procedure if the student refuses to participate in the overcorrection activity. This procedure may include planned ignoring or placement in a time-out condition until the student agrees to cooperate.

The plan should be reviewed by the multidisciplinary team if the restitution and/or positive practice activity involves removal from the classroom setting (interpreted as a change in placement), or if it presents possible dangers to the student. The major questions you should address in this review are: Have less restrictive procedures been ruled out? Is the overcorrection procedure a logical consequence of the disruptive response? What negative side effects can be anticipated from implementation of the program (e.g., increased aggression and removal from learning setting)? Do the benefits of the program outweigh the potential risks?

To implement the plan, you should inform the student of the overcorrection rule. You should also discuss and/or role-play the setting in which overcorrection is to be used, specific responses that result in overcorrection, and the overcorrection activity. Also, inform the student of the backup procedures to be used if she or he declines to voluntarily participate in the overcorrection procedure.

We strongly suggest that you use differential reinforcement for alternative or incompatible behaviors demonstrated outside of the immediate application of the overcorrection procedure. It is very important for you to avoid all reinforcement during the overcorrection exercise. Extra attention, physical contact, or removal from a provoking situation may all serve to diminish the effectiveness of overcorrection. Indications that inadvertent events may reinforce the student should suggest modifications in the plan.

Evaluating Overcorrection Programs

As was discussed with time-out, you must be careful to evaluate restrictive applied behavior analysis programs. Ineffective overcorrection procedures should be modified or discontinued. Continuing the activity may simply reinforce the student's disruptive behavior or expose her to ongoing aversive conditions with no collateral benefits.

Observation and recording procedures discussed in Chapter 11 should be used to evaluate overcorrection programs. To be effective, overcorrection must produce a rapid reduction in the target response and the procedure should be discontinued.

Possible negative side effects may also be the focus of observation and recording procedures. Resistance to the overcorrection exercise, time away from instruction, and negative emotional reactions may be evaluated along with the target behavior. Documented benefits to the individual must outweigh negative side effects.

Presentation of Aversive Stimuli (PAC)

Aversive stimuli are generally offensive sights, sounds, smells, tastes, or physical sensations. As noted above, they are punishing if they result in a reduction in a target response. As discussed in a previous chapter, they are negative reinforcers if behavior strength increases through their removal. They may be neutral if no effect on behavior is observed. Aversive stimuli can also be classified as unconditioned or conditioned. This section is limited to the use of PAC as a functional punisher.

Unconditioned Aversive Stimulus

An unconditioned aversive event is unpleasant to the individual through no effect of previous learning. Newborn infants have adverse reactions to these stimuli even though no mediating experiences with these events have occurred. Unconditioned aversive events include extreme temperature, food/water deprivation, physical irritants, strenuous physical activity, physical trauma, loud noise, noxious odors, and sour/bitter foods.

Because we have acquired emotional properties throughout biological endowment, unconditioned aversive stimuli are common to all of us. Since they require no previous learning, they are generally used in punishment programs for very young children, persons with severe developmental delays, or others for whom conditioned aversive stimuli cannot be identified.

Conditioned Aversive Stimulus

A conditioned aversive event acquires its negative emotional properties through the students' experiences. As we discussed in Chapter 6, the repeated pairing of any neutral event with an unconditioned aversive stimulus will result in the unconditioned stimulus acquiring aversive properties. For example, yelling at a child while employing corporal punishment may result in yelling alone producing the aversive reaction. Bad grades are not likely to initially produce aversive reactions. Pairing bad grades with other aversive events, however, will eventually result in the grades acquiring aversive properties.

Events may acquire aversive properties through higher order conditioning in which previously learned aversive events are paired with neutral events. For example, a parent may scold and spank a child simultaneously, but the results in scolding produce the same emotional reaction as spanking. Scolding may then be paired with bad grades. Consequently, bad grades develop the same emotional reaction as scolding and spanking.

Conditioned aversive stimuli are generally used over unconditioned aversives for most behavioral problems. They are generally less intrusive and unpleasant, but still may have a punishing effect for a majority of behavior problems. Conditioned aversives most commonly used in public schools include verbal reprimands, failing grades, detention, and posting of names and offenses.

Limitations of PAC

Several authors have addressed the limitations of PAC procedures (Gardner, 1977; Kazdin, 1989; Matson & DiLorenzo, 1984; Tobin & Sugai, 1993). Each author emphasizes that the potential adverse effects associated with PAC are enough to raise questions about their appropriateness for use in educational programs. Specific concerns include the following:

1. PAC is unpleasant for both the teacher and the student. The use of PAC in educational programs reduces the general attractiveness of the educational setting for all concerned.

2. As a consequence of unpleasant aspects of PAC, students (and possibly teachers) may be motivated to avoid settings in which it is employed. This may lead to truancy, dropping out, and professional burnout.

3. PAC is likely to produce a heightened state of negative emotionality. Students who receive the noxious stimulus are likely to respond with high rates of anxious, aggressive, or depressed affect. In some cases this affective reaction may be more severe than the behavior problem that initiated the PAC program.

4. The effect of PAC may be temporary. Although students may respond under the immediate threat of the aversive stimuli (e.g., in class with the teacher present), they may resort to the disruptive response when PAC conditions are no longer present (e.g., in the restroom or after school).

5. Effects of PAC may be highly specific. You may not expect the effects of PAC to generalize to related responses. If a child is punished for saying a specific swear word, she may not refrain from using alternate profanities.

6. Professionals may be motivated to overuse PAC. When effective, PAC produces a rapid reduction in disruptive responses. As you may recall from our discussion of negative reinforcement, responses that produce the removal of unpleasant stimuli are likely to recur. Consequently, a strong negative reinforcement relationship may be produced between PAC and the removal of noxious behaviors.

7. PAC may not be effective for students with severe behavior disorders. Many of these students have acclimated to extreme aversives that have been present in dysfunctional homes. PACs that may be used ethically in educational settings may not be viewed as being unpleasant when contrasted with other conditions that the child or youth has faced. Consequently, the PAC used in school may fail to produce a reductive effect.

8. PAC does not include educational components. The student may learn to avoid the punisher or punishment but fail to learn prosocial responses.

In view of these limitations, as well as the position of PAC on our restrictiveness hierarchy, we recommend using aversive consequences only as a last resort. PAC programs should always be developed through careful planning and should be implemented only after thorough review by the multidisciplinary team. Finally, the program should be carefully monitored with careful attention to both the direct effects and side effects.

Maximizing the Effectiveness of PAC

In a comprehensive review of available literature, Gardner (1977) identified a series of principles that influence the effectiveness of PAC procedures:

1. Use PAC infrequently and only in combination with differential reinforcement procedures.

2. Determine in advance the conditions under which PAC will be used as well as a precise definition for the target behavior.

3. Teach the student the punishment rule and consequences in advance.

4. Identify alternative behaviors that are expected to replace the behaviors being diminished by the PAC contingencies along with the teaching and differential reinforcement contingencies.

5. Make sure that the student is aware of specific behaviors that will produce aversive consequences and prosocial behaviors that will be differentially reinforced.

6. Implement the PAC rules consistently and immediately.

7. State the PAC contingency each time it is administered (e.g., "You were late for gym. According to our agreement, you must run five laps around the gym after school.").

8. Present the aversive consequence at a level that is expected to be immediately effective. Presenting the PAC at a lower intensity and gradually increasing its strength may result in the student acclimating to the progressively noxious condition.

9. Make sure that the aversive event is undesirable enough to offset desirable consequences that result from the disruptive behavior.

10. Avoid threatening or warning the student about the PAC contingency. Consistent and immediate implementation should be sufficient to make him or her aware of program procedures.

11. Monitor both the target behavior and collateral behaviors to make sure that desirable effects are achieved. Remember that the benefits produced by the procedure should outweigh negative effects.

12. Avoid the unauthorized escape from the aversive event (e.g., highly emotional outbursts may be negatively reinforced if they produce the withdrawal of the aversive consequence).

13. Discontinue the PAC procedure if results are not evidenced relatively soon after implementation.

14. If the reductive effect is present only in the punishment setting, the procedure should be used in other relevant situations (e.g., home, playground).

15. Phase the PAC procedure out of the educational setting as soon as possible.

One final point on the use of PAC is necessary. The appropriateness of PAC for any specific behavior problem rests with the results of a prebaseline analysis of the student and learning environment. No other factor in developing a PAC program is as important as this analysis. Information that must be obtained includes evidence that: all less restrictive procedures have been demonstrated to be ineffective, the rigors and possible negative side effects of the program are offset by the eventual benefits to the student, the aversive consequence is functionally punishing, and you can prevent the unauthorized escape or avoidance of the PAC.

It is important to note that authors generally agree that the PAC should be presented at an optimum level expected to be effective (Azrin & Holtz, 1966; Gardner, 1977). Effectiveness, however, is not necessarily a function of intensity of the aversive event. Carr and Lovaas (1983), for example, have reported that infrequent electric shocks of moderated intensity are as effective or more effective as frequent high intensity shocks. Finally, longer time-out durations are not necessarily more effective than short durations (Brantner & Doherty, 1983).

Summary

Four major sections in this chapter describe punishment procedures most often used in general and special education settings. These include response cost, time-out, overcorrection, and PAC. Within each section we described the basic procedure, discussed its advantages and disadvantages, and suggested guidelines for implementing the punishment procedure.

Just as important as knowing how to use these procedures is knowing when they should be used. We emphasized the principle of least restrictive alternative. This principle argues for the selection of the minimally intrusive approach that is likely to result in the desired behavior reduction. We recommend stimulus control, differential reinforcement, and extinction as methods of first resort. Approaches described in this chapter should be used only when the less intrusive strategies have been demonstrated to be ineffective.

Even when selecting from procedures within this chapter, we recommend using the least restrictive approach likely to be effective. Response cost is generally preferred over time-out. Time-out may be tried prior to using overcorrection. PAC is generally reserved for responses that have not been influenced by the other methods.

It is important to note that each of the procedures described here can differ substantially in restrictiveness depending on the manner in which they are implemented. PAC may range from a mild private reprimand to contingent electric shock. Time-out may occur in the classroom setting and be very brief, or it may occur in an isolated room for an extended period of time. Therefore, generalizations made in this chapter about the restrictiveness of procedures are based on common applications found in the professional literature. The restrictiveness of any procedure must be judged from an objective description of the procedure and the extent to which it restricts the student from normal participation in the educational setting.

Finally, it is tempting to argue against the use of punishment. Those arguments may hinge on the possible negative side effects, the possibility of the procedure being abused, and the unpleasant conditions that it establishes in what should be an enriching environment.

We, like other authors (Baer, 1971), believe that such an argument is not warranted. Rather, we suggest that those using punishment must be both kind and wise. *Kindness* ensures that the teacher has the best interests of the student at heart. The punishment procedure is implemented in a conscientious and thoughtful attempt to improve the quality of life for the learner. Kindness goes beyond simply looking toward what the student would like in the short term.

The kind practitioner weighs the benefits of a behavior change program to a student throughout a lifetime. You may use a response cost out of kindness, knowing that the immediate inconvenience may result in a student being able to obtain passing grades, graduate from high school, and obtain a lifetime of economic benefits.

Kindness precludes using punishment out of convenience or to simply exert control and authority over a recalcitrant learner. This practice would fail the cost-benefit test discussed throughout this chapter. Specifically, are the costs of the program (e.g. professional and student effort, risks associated with negative side effects, and physical discomfort) outweighed by the potential rewards (e.g., enhanced achievement and enhanced social relations)?

Wisdom ensures that the punishment procedure is used in the most effective and efficient manner. The major goal of any punishment procedure is to produce conditions that avoid the use of the procedure. An effective punishment becomes a deterrent that results in the punishment seldom being implemented. This goal is achieved only when educators use punishment and other applied behavior analysis procedures wisely.

Based on information contained in this chapter, the wise use of punishment involves developing the program only after a careful analysis of learning and behavioral characteristics, ruling out all less restrictive approaches, combining punishment with educative and differential reinforcement procedures, teaching all punishment rules, implementing punishment consistently and immediately, monitoring the effects and side effects of the punishment procedure, implementing the punishment procedure at an intensity that is likely to be immediately effective, and fading the punishment procedure out of the educational program as soon as possible.

We have repeatedly emphasized the importance of a careful analysis prior to designing and implementing a punishment program. We also stressed the need for continuous monitoring of the program's effects and side effects. Chapters 11 and 12 include methods for conducting this analysis and evaluation.

References

Azrin, N. H., & Besalel, V. A. (1980). *How to use overcorrection.* Austin, TX: PRO-ED.

Azrin, N. H., & Holtz, W. C. (1966). Punishment. In W. K. Honig (Ed.), *Operant behavior: Areas of research and application.* New York: Appleton-Century-Crofts.

Azrin, N. H., & Powers, M. A. (1975). Eliminating classroom disturbances of emotionally disturbed children by positive practice procedures. *Behavior Therapy and Experimental Psychiatry, 6,* 145–148.

Baer, D. M. (1971). Let's take another look at punishment. *Psychology Today, 5,* 5–23.

Brantner, J. P., & Doherty, M. A. (1983). A review of time out: A conceptual and methodological analysis. In S. Axelrod, & J. Apsche (Eds.), *The effects of punishment on human behavior* (pp. 87–132). New York: Academic Press.

Carr, E. G., & Lovaas, O. I. (1983). Contingent electric shock as a treatment for severe behavior problems. In S. Axelrod & J. Apsche (Eds.), *The effects of punishment on human behavior* (pp. 221–246). New York: Academic Press.

Cavalier, A. R., & Ferretti, R. P. (1980). Stereotyped behaviour, alternative behaviour, and collateral effects: A comparison of four intervention procedures. *Journal of Mental Deficiency Research, 24,* 219–230.

Christian, W. P., & Hannah, G. T. (1983). *Effective management in human services.* Englewood Cliffs, NJ: Prentice Hall.

Cole v. Greenfield-Central Community Schools, 657 F. Supp. 56 (S.D. Ind. 1986).

Cooper, J. O., Heron, T. E., & Heward, W. L. (1987). *Applied behavior analysis.* Columbus, OH: Merrill.

Costenbader, V., & Reading-Brown, M. (1995). Isolation timeout used with students with emotional disturbance. *Exceptional Children, 61,* 353–363.

Dickens v. Johnson County Board of Education, 661 F. Supp. 155 (E.D. Tenn. 1987).

Doke, L. A., Wolery, M., & Sumberg, C. (1983). Treating chronic aggression. *Behavior Modification, 7,* 531–556.

Durand, V. M., & Carr, E. (1987). Social influences on self-stimulatory behavior: Analysis and treatment application. *Journal of Applied Behavior Analysis, 11,* 225–241.

Foxx, R. M. (1982). *Decreasing behaviors of severely retarded and autistic persons.* Champaign, IL: Research Press.

Foxx, R. M., & Azrin, N. H. (1972). Restitution: A method of eliminating aggressive-disruptive behavior of retarded and brain damaged patients. *Behavior Research and Therapy, 10,* 15–27.

Foxx, R. M., & Azrin, N. H. (1973). The elimination of autistic self-stimulatory behavior by overcorrection. *Journal of Applied Behavior Analysis, 6,* 1–14.

Foxx, R. M., & Bechtel, D. R. (1983). Overcorrection: A review and analysis. In S. Axelrod & J. Apsche (Eds.), *The effects of punishment on human behavior* (pp. 133–220). New York: Academic Press.

Foxx, R. M., & Shapiro, S. T. (1978). The timeout ribbon: A non-exclusionary timeout procedure. *Journal of Applied Behavior Analysis, 11,* 125–143.

Gardner, W. I. (1977). *Learning and behavior characteristics of exceptional children and youth: A humanistic behavioral approach.* Boston: Allyn and Bacon.

Gast, D. L., & Nelson, C. M. (1977). Legal and ethical considerations for the use of timeout in special education settings. *Journal of Special Education, 11,* 457–467.

Hayes v. Unified School District No. 377, 669 F. Supp. 1519 (D. Kan. 1987).

Kazdin, A. E. (1989). *Behavior modification in applied settings.* Pacific Grove, CA: Brooks/Cole.

Luce, S. C., & Hall, R. V. (1981). Contingent exercise: A procedure used with differential reinforcement to reduce bizarre verbal behavior. *Education and Treatment of Children, 3,* 309–327.

Mace, F. C., & Heller, M. (1990). A comparison of exclusion time out and contingent observation for reducing severe disruptive behavior in a 7-year-old boy. *Child & Family Behavior Therapy, 12,* 57–69.

Matson, J. L., & DiLorenzo, T. M. (1984). *Punishment and its alternatives: A new perspective for behavior modification.* New York: Springer.

Mayhew, G., & Harris, F. (1979). Decreasing self-injurious behavior. *Behavior Modification, 3,* 322–326.

Misra, A. (1991). Behavior management: The importance of communication. *LD Forum, 11,* 26–28.

Morales v. Turman, 364 F. Supp. 166 (E.D. Tx. 1973).

Porterfield, J. K., Herbert-Jackson, E., & Risley, T. R. (1976). Contingent observation: An effective and acceptable procedure for reducing disruptive behavior of young children in a group setting. *Journal of Applied Behavior Analysis, 9,* 55–64.

Repp, A. E., & Dietz, S. M. (1978). On the selective use of punishment: Suggested guidelines for administrators. *Mental Retardation, 16,* 250–254.

Schloss, P. J. (1984). *Social development of handicapped children and youth.* Rockville, MD: Aspen.

Schloss, P. J., Holt, J., Mulvaney, M., & Green, J. (1988). The Franklin Jefferson Program: Demonstration of an integrated social learning approach to educational services for behaviorally disordered students. *Teaching: Behaviorally Disordered Youth, 4,* 7–15.

Schloss, P. J., Smith, M. A., & Schloss, C. N. (1995). *Instructional methods for handicapped adolescents* (2nd ed.). Boston: Allyn and Bacon.

Singh, J., Beale, I., & Dawson, M. (1981). Duration of facial screening and suppression of self injurious behavior: Analysis using an alternating treatments design. *Behavioral Assessment, 3,* 411–420.

Tanner, B. A., & Zeiler, M. (1975). Punishment of self-injurious behavior using aromatic ammonia as the aversive stimulus. *Jounal of Applied Behavior Analysis, 8,* 53–57.

Thompson, T. J., Thornhill, C. A., Realon, R. E., & Ervin, K. M. (1991). Improving accuracy in documentation of restrictive interventions by direct-care personnel. *Mental Retardation, 29,* 201–205.

Tobin, T. J., & Sugai, G. (1993). Intervention aversiveness: Educators' perceptions of the need for restrictions on aversive interventions. *Behavioral Disorders, 18,* 110–17.

White, A. G., & Bailey, J. S. (1990). Reducing disruptive behaviors of elementary physical education students with sit and watch. *Journal of Applied Behavior Analysis, 23,* 353–359.

10

WORKING WITH LARGE GROUPS

Used correctly, the techniques we described in Chapter 7, 8, and 9 are powerful ways to increase a student's appropriate behavior. Unfortunately, implementing an applied behavior analytic program to change the behavior of one or two students in your class may require a considerable investment of time and energy. We are convinced, however, that it takes even more time and energy to deal with inappropriate behavior in an ineffective manner. Nonetheless, we are not surprised by Naslund and L'Homme's (1979) observation regarding teachers' complaint that many management techniques are based on the assumption that there is only one student in the class rather than thirty. Further complicating the professional lives of busy teachers is the inclusion movement. More students with greater behavior management needs are receiving educational services in the general education classroom. Teachers who need a behavior management program may prefer to use one that will efficiently address the needs of more than one student and allow them to devote more time to meeting the academic needs of all the students in their class.

Another problem with individually administered contingencies is that students who are not involved in the program may feel left out or jealous of the attention that one or two classmates receive from the teacher (Gola, Holmes, & Holmes, 1979). Moreover, some teachers have expressed ethical concerns over implementing a program for one student who demonstrates inappropriate behavior while doing nothing special for those students whose behavior is appropriate (Martin, 1975).

In light of these problems, a teacher may find it beneficial to implement applied behavior management techniques to the entire class. Techniques presented in Chapters 7, 8, and 9 can be used to develop an applied behavior analytic program suitable for use with the entire class. The purpose of this chapter is to present two group procedures that incorporate many separate techniques: group contingencies and levels systems.

Group Contingencies

Behavior management systems that involve individually tailored token economies or response cost systems may fail to take into account the dynamics of a group setting such as a classroom (Kerr & Nelson, 1989). This failure can occur in three ways. First, some students may act inappropriately for the benefit of their peers regardless of the potential for teacher-imposed consequences. For example, a student in your class may act out to get attention. Although you may see through this and attempt to ignore such behavior, other students in the class may attend to it by looking at the student, smiling, or giggling (Rhode, Jenson, & Reavis, 1993). Such peer encouragement may be all a student needs to continue acting out. Second, as we mentioned before, even if other students are not contributing to the problem, they may be jealous of the student who is earning rewards through a specially designed applied behavior analysis program. Finally, you may have a few students who are demonstrating similar problem behaviors. The task of managing separate individually designed programs may be overwhelming.

One way to get around these problems is to use a **group contingency** that applies consequences to the class as a whole. The behavior of one or more classmates determines the consequences received by other classmates (Speltz, Shimamura, & McReynolds, 1982). This technique allows all students to participate and benefit from a program, not just the one student or small group of students whose behavior needs to be changed. You should note, however, that a group contingency can also penalize all students on the basis of the behavior of one or two. Thus, it is not surprising that the fairness of a group contingency has been debated. Rhode, Jenson, and Reavis (1993) maintained that the use of group contingencies in educational settings is fair if peers are contributing to the inappropriate behavior committed by one or two students. Smith and Misra (1994) suggested that group contingencies are a fact of life. On the down side, many members of a society pay the price for the irresponsible acts of one or two people. Our insurance premiums reflect the cost of fraudulent claims. Shoplifting increases the cost of items we purchase at our favorite department stores. On the up side, we all benefit when a single person's medical or technological breakthrough enhances the quality of life for everyone.

A substantial body of literature supports the use of group contingencies to address a variety of problems demonstrated at home (Gresham, 1983), and at school by students in both general (Brantley & Webster, 1993) and special education settings (Brigham, Bakken, Scruggs, & Mastropieri, 1992; Gresham & Gresham, 1982; Kohler, Strain, Hoyson, Davis, Donina, & Rapp, 1995; Salend, Whittaker, & Reeder, 1992). The basic premise of a group contingency is that desired rewards will be provided to the group as a whole if students within that group demonstrate a set of appropriate behaviors (Vogler & French, 1983). Group contingencies exert control over student behavior by capitalizing on peers as an important influence on classroom behavior (Gresham & Gresham, 1982). As students grow older, peer influence may be a more powerful motivator than the influence of adults such as teachers.

TABLE 10.1   Types of Group Contingencies

Type	Definition	Example
Dependent	The performance of one student or a small group of students determines the consequences received by the entire group.	The entire class receives free time if Tom brings in homework that is complete and 90% accurate.
Independent	The contingency that is in effect for all group members is applied on an individual basis.	Each student must bring in his or her homework and it must be complete and 90% accurate.
Interdependent	The same contingency applies to all group members, but final evaluation is based on a specified level of group performance.	The class is divided into teams. All teammates must bring in homework that is complete and 90% accurate so that the team is eligible to earn a reward.

Generally, there are three types of group contingencies: dependent, independent, and interdependent (Litow & Pumroy, 1975). They are summarized in Table 10.1. The major difference between them is the manner in which students earn the reinforcement (Brantley & Webster, 1993). We will discuss each type separately.

A Dependent Group Contingency

In a dependent group contingency, the same response contingency is in effect for all group members; however, the performance of one student or a small group of students determines the consequences received by the entire group (Gresham, 1983). You can use this type of group contingency if classmates are somehow contributing to the inappropriate behavior demonstrated by one student. For example, a student in your class named Pete is out of his seat a lot, chatting with his neighbors. As a result, he is not getting his work done and is falling behind academically. You can arrange a contingency so that Pete receives a point after completing each assignment. At the end of the day, if Pete has five points, the whole class can have ten minutes of free time. This contingency is public in that all the students know that the reward is contingent upon Pete's behavior. Classmates are less likely to allow Pete to be out of his seat chatting with them. Pete's motivation to behave is increased because he knows that all the others are depending on him for their reward. Should he earn five points, Pete gets to be a "star" among his classmates as they share in the reward.

Perhaps Pete isn't the only student in your class who is out of his or her seat a lot. Perhaps you may think it is unfair to put too much pressure on Pete to perform. In these situations, simply select one or more student names at random and keep them confidential. This option keeps all students on their toes. Since no one knows whose behavior is going to count, all are more motivated to remain in their seats and finish their work. Should the criterion be met, you can announce the names of students responsible and reward the class. If the criterion is not met, you can simply say that there will be no reward today and not identify the students who were responsible. This option may keep a healthy dose of peer influence from becoming an overwhelming amount of peer pressure (Hayes, 1976; Rhode, Jenson, & Reavis, 1993).

Gresham and Gresham (1982) used teams in their dependent group contingency. They divided an elementary class of students with retardation into two teams. Team captains were the two students whose baseline behavior was the most disruptive. Reinforcement for each team was contingent upon the captain's behavior—that is, the team whose captain displayed the smaller frequency of disruptive behavior earned the reward.

Gresham (1983) used a dependent group contingency to eliminate the destructive behavior demonstrated at home by an eight-year-old boy who was mildly retarded. Billy's mother gave him a "good note" from home the morning after each day that he did not commit a destructive act. He brought the note to school, where he was rewarded with five tokens, access to juice time, and recess. Five good notes in a row resulted in a "Billy Party" on Friday. Billy was the host of each party and distributed snacks that he had earned and prizes to his classmates.

An Independent Group Contingency

In an independent group contingency, the contingency that is in effect for all group members is applied on an individual basis. Thus, each child in the class can earn reinforcement based on his or her own appropriate behavior (Gresham, 1983) without affecting the consequences experienced by other group members (Wolery, Bailey, & Sugai, 1988). An independent group contingency can address academic skills. For example, each student must have nine out of ten spelling words correct to earn points. Similarly, each student must have at least 80 percent on his or her social studies quiz to earn ten minutes of free time at the end of the day. An independent group contingency can also address nonacademic skills. Perhaps your students do not always remember to bring school supplies to class every day. You can arrange an independent group contingency in which students are required to bring their books, paper, and writing utensils. You check every morning to see if each student has brought the necessary supplies and award points to those who do. Points can be exchanged at a later time. The fact that one or two students are unprepared has no bearing on whether the others receive and exchange points.

This type of group contingency does not single out any particular student from his or her peers. Each student whose performance meets the criterion is eligible for the reward regardless of the performance of the group. As such, an independent group contingency may not be a true group contingency because students do not depend on each other's behavior to earn rewards. There is no incentive to try to influence another person's behavior (Sulzer-Azaroff & Mayer, 1992).

An Interdependent Group Contingency

In an interdependent group contingency, the same contingency applies to all group members, but final evaluation is based on a specified level of group performance (Wolery, Bailey, & Sugai, 1988). Sulzer-Azaroff and Mayer (1992) suggested that a class be divided into two or three smaller groups or teams; each team is treated as though it were a single person. Points for appropriate behaviors are awarded to team members and totaled up at the end of the day. The group with the most points earns a special reward. Conversely, a team can receive a mark each time any one of its members misbehaves. At the end of the day, the team with fewest marks earns the reinforcers. An interdependent group contingency may also involve a comparison of each group's total to a predetermined criterion. All groups who meet or exceed the criterion receive the reinforcement. Similarly, if groups are being penalized with marks, then all groups who do not exceed a predetermined number of marks receive the reinforcement.

A classic example of an interdependent group contingency is the Good Behavior Game described by Barrish, Saunders, and Wolf (1969). Members of a fourth grade classroom were divided into two teams and told by their teacher that they were going to play the "Good Behavior Game." The teacher identified rules that students were to follow, including no out-of-seat behavior or talking with peers without teacher permission. Each team received a mark for any rule violation committed by any of its group members. At the end of day, the team with the fewest marks received reinforcement in the form of stars, victory tags, free time, or being first in line.

There are variations within an interdependent group contingency. In one variation, all group members must meet a predetermined criterion so that all can receive the reward. For example, perhaps several students in your class are using obscenities. Break your class into teams. Write on the board the name of any student who swears. Your contingency may be that no more than three names per team can appear or none of the students on that team receives the reward. Early in the group contingency, you can have a lower criterion; it can be raised over time so that students misbehave less often.

A second variation requires that the average performance of randomly selected students be matched to a preset standard. For example, several of your students may be calling out without raising their hands. You want to reduce calling out and increase hand raising. Record all call-outs for each student, then randomly select a predetermined number of students from the class. If 80 percent of these students did not call out, then all students receive a reward. Again, you can shift the criterion so that a higher percentage of students must not call out.

Implementing a Group Contingency

Smith and Misra (1994) reviewed the research and compiled a list of steps that should be followed when using a group contingency. They include the following:

1. Clearly define the target behavior. Before implementing any group contingency, you will need to explain to your students which behaviors are being changed. A good place to start is with the behaviors included in classroom rules. Teachers who have adhered to the guidelines for rules that we presented in Chapter 4 already have clearly defined their behavioral expectations for their students.

2. Collect data on target behaviors. This is the only way you will be able to judge the effectiveness of your program. (We will discuss data collection procedures in Chapter 11.)

3. Determine which type of group contingency you will use. If you decide to use the interdependent group contingency, arrange groups with individuals who have similar behavioral and academic characteristics.

4. Define the criterion for performance. You may want to use the total number of behaviors, a classroom average, or the performance of a particular student or a student selected at random. Remember, the criterion can become more stringent as student performance improves.

5. Encourage student participation through activities such as setting goals, monitoring behaviors, awarding points, tutoring, and keeping records. This step increases the likelihood that students will have a vested interest in the program. It also shifts the responsibilities of program management from you to them.

6. Make sure students possess the skills needed to meet the criterion. Group contingencies are more effective for students who have the necessary skills but are not motivated to use them. Address skill deficits through instruction in academics or social skills, or through the use of respondent conditioning.

7. Identify items or events that you are sure will be reinforcing to students. Using the reinforcement preference sheet presented in Chapter 7 may be helpful.

8. Explain the contingency to your students.

9. Assign students to groups.

10. Implement the contingency and collect data to monitor its effectiveness. You may have to dismantle a group contingency in favor of individualized programs if the data indicate that it is not having the desired effect.

Advantages of Group Contingencies

Used correctly, group contingencies offer several advantages to students and their busy teachers. First, they use peer influence to increase student motivation to behave. As we noted earlier, peer influence becomes more important as students get older. Capitalize on this influence and use it to your advantage. Second, students can serve as models for each other, which promotes positive peer relationships. Third, the emphasis on group behavior means that individual students are not singled out for teacher attention. This advantage addresses ethical concerns over individualized programs expressed by teachers. Fourth, group contingencies are very efficient. A teacher can plan, implement, and monitor one program rather than several individualized programs. The teacher does not have to maintain separate records on a variety of individually based contingencies. More time can be devoted to instruction (Gresham & Gresham, 1982). Fifth, research has shown that group-oriented procedures are just as effective as individually administered programs in changing behaviors (Kerr & Nelson, 1989). Sixth, research has also shown that they can be used to address a wide variety of behaviors. Group contingencies have increased academic productivity (Speltz, Shimamura, & McReynolds, 1982) and social interactions (Kohler et al., 1995), and reduced or eliminated a variety of disruptive behaviors including talking out or being out of seat without permission (Barrish, Saunders, & Wolf, 1969), laughing inappropriately, verbal and physical aggression (Gresham & Gresham, 1982), and vandalism (Gresham, 1983). Seventh, students may demonstrate positive behaviors not originally targeted by the group contingency. For example, in their review of the literature, Kohler et al. (1995) reported that students who participated in group contingencies used prompts, encouraged, expressed approval, offered assistance, and tutored.

Disadvantages of Group Contingencies

There are some disadvantages associated with group contingencies. First, one or more members of a particular group may take delight in sabotaging the group's efforts (Crouch, Gresham, & Wright, 1985). Rather than earning the predetermined reinforcer, these students may find it more rewarding to spoil others' opportunity to earn the reward. Rhode, Jenson, and Reavis (1993) recommended that such students be assigned to their own group, even if it is a group of one, to eliminate the satisfaction they feel. We also encourage you to reexamine the reinforcers you included in the group contingency. Perhaps they are not strong enough to outweigh the satisfaction some students may experience by undermining the group's efforts. A second disadvantage is that group members who realize they have lost their chance to earn a reinforcer may demonstrate higher levels of inappropriate behavior for the remainder of the day (Crouch, Gresham, & Wright, 1985). For example, you may have selected no more than five call-outs as the daily criterion. Members of a group who have called out six times may realize that they are ineligible for the reinforcer and continue to call out. Brantley and Webster (1995) noted this problem when they used an independent group contingency with fourth graders. Students who failed to earn a check during a specified time period became unruly short afterwards. Students who realized that they were going to be ineligible for a weekly reward accounted for most of the inappropriate behavior that occurred during the intervention.

Third, students whose inappropriate behavior results in the failure to earn the reward may be ridiculed by their peers. As a result, inappropriate behavior may increase. You may prevent this problem when explaining the contingency prior to its implementation by warning students about teasing and ridicule.

Troubleshooting a Group Contingency

It does take time and effort to plan, implement, and monitor a group contingency. Switching from individually based programs to classwide behavior management programs still requires an initial investment of thought, time, and energy. Despite careful planning, however, you may still encounter a few problems when implementing a group contingency. Wolery, Bailey, and Sugai (1988) described some potential trouble spots and suggested solutions. First, a student may repeatedly fail to meet the criterion despite a genuine interest in the program. Two factors may account for this problem. First, the student may not have the skills necessary to meet the criterion. Use systematic instruction procedures to teach the skills and behaviors necessary for success. Second, you may have selected a criterion that is too high. Temporarily reduce the criterion, then gradually increase it as student performance improves.

A second problem is that a student may fail after experiencing success early in the group contingency. There are two reasons for this problem. First, the rewards may have lost some of their power. Review them carefully and make necessary changes. Second, negative peer influence may have occurred or increased. Assign these peers to a separate group.

Third, your data may suggest that the group contingency isn't working. Review every step you took to develop and administer the program, including the clarity of the goals, the suitability of the type of group contingency, the severity of the criterion, the rewards, prerequisite skills, and consistency of implementation.

Finally, you may hear complaints that the contingency is unfair. You can reduce the number of complaints from parents by sharing the program and its rationale before implementation and inviting parents to discuss their concerns. Ultimately, you may have to allow parents to withdraw their child from the group contingency. If students are complaining, you can tell them responsibility and cooperation are expected in your class and that threats or aggression will not be tolerated. Afterwards, ignore complainers and praise those who cooperate. When the complaining student does cooperate, reinforce his or her behavior.

Levels Systems

In the previous section, we described a set of contingencies you can use if one student or a small number of students are demonstrating inappropriate behavior. You may have a class in which there are several particularly difficult students for whom a group contingency may not be strong enough. Another group management system you can use to address the variety of problems that a large number of students may be demonstrating is called a levels system. This system originated in residential facilities for students with severe emotional disturbance but has been adapted for use in public school classrooms. A levels system is a "method for organizing desired social and academic behavior and related consequences into a hierarchical sequence of skills and privileges" (Scheuermann, Webber, Partin, & Knies, 1994, p. 205). It provides "a framework through which various behavioral management strategies are applied to shape students' social, communicative, and academic behaviors to preestablished levels" (Bauer, Shea, & Keppler, 1986, p. 28). The specific behavior management strategies included in a levels system are techniques we described in previous chapters, such as social reinforcement, activity reinforcement, token economies, contracts, reprimands, response cost, and time out. The combination of these techniques increases the power of levels systems (Smith & Farrell, 1993). The rate at which students pass through the levels within the system depends on their progress toward academic and behavior goals. Movement toward a higher level is associated with higher expectations for performance and greater access to privileges. Ultimately, a levels system should shape students so that they can self-manage their own behaviors, develop personal responsibility for their own behaviors, and function successfully in general education environments (Smith & Farrell, 1993).

Characteristics of Levels Systems

Various levels systems have been described in the professional literature. Each system has been designed to meet the needs of a particular group of students. Nonetheless, as Bauer and Shea (1988) pointed out, these systems have several characteristics or elements in common. They are listed in Table 10.2 and discussed separately below.

Levels

The levels within any system provide students with the support they need to regulate their behavior and arrange their environment (Hood, McDermott, & Cole, 1980). Each level is associated with specific expectations and consequences, and is designed to help students capitalize on their current ability levels. A level at the lower end of the system provides students with greater amounts of structure and fewer choices for, or less access to, rewards and privileges. There can be a minimum amount of time during which a student must stay at each level. As motivation increases and abilities develop, a student moves to higher levels, each of which provides less structure and more choices of, or greater access to, rewards and privileges. The highest level, of course, reflects standard classroom conditions. Initial placement can automatically be at Level 1 for all students. Also, placement within a specific level can be determined by examining data from permanent products and systematic observations (discussed in Chapter 11).

TABLE 10.2   Elements of a Levels System

Bauer and Shea (1988) identified the following elements of a levels system.

1. Levels—A system contains several levels, each of which contains specific expectations and consequences.
2. Criteria—Students need to adhere to specific standards of behavior before they can move to a different level.
3. Explanation of behavior and expectations—Behaviors and criteria are clearly explained to the participants.
4. Privileges—Identify rewards and privileges that students can earn at each level.
5. Restrictions—Consequences for inappropriate behavior should be identified at each level.
6. Individualization—A levels system can be tailored to meet the unique needs of any student.

Criteria

Students need to demonstrate specific levels of behaviors for a specified amount of time before they can change levels. For example, within a three-week period, Level 2 may require a student to complete three out of five homework assignments per week with at least 90 percent accuracy, comply with all teacher directives within 30 seconds, and require time-out for physical aggression no more than three times. A student who meets these criteria can move up to the next level, which has higher expectations for homework completion, compliance, and self-control. A student who does not meet the criteria remains at Level 2.

Explanation of Behavior and Expectations

Be explicit when describing the system so that students clearly understand the behaviors being increased and decreased, how they can move from one level to the next, and the positive and punitive consequences involved. A variety of behavior can be addressed by a levels system including attendance, verbal and physical aggression, noncompliance, and task completion. You may develop a handbook that clearly defines and illustrates behaviors and expectations.

Privileges

Access to special rewards and privileges is based on student behavior. A levels system frequently includes a token economy in which points earned for appropriate behaviors are exchanged for special items, activities, and privileges.

Restrictions

Access to reinforcers can also be curtailed or denied when students involved in a levels system demonstrate inappropriate behavior. There may be a response cost for certain behaviors, which means that access to special items, activities, and privileges may be delayed or denied. In addition, demonstration of some behaviors may warrant placement in time-out or removal to a lower level in the system. This movement can serve as a probationary period. The student can stay at the lower level for a short period of time, perhaps a week. If, during this time, the student earns a predetermined percentage of points, he or she can move back up to the next level. This movement can also require the student to start all over again at the new, lower level and earn his or her way up by meeting criteria established for that level.

Individualization

Although a levels system is typically designed for a group, you can and should tailor it for individual students. For special education students, individualized programming is mandated by the Individuals with Disabilities Education Act (IDEA). Initial placement into a levels systems can be determined with the assistance of the student's multidisciplinary team. Target behaviors can be added to or deleted from the levels system, and criteria for movement between levels can be adjusted to meet the unique needs of individual students.

Designing a Levels System

Bauer and Shea (1988) have described the steps you should follow to design a levels system (see Table 10.3). First, you need to determine the current entry level behaviors of the students in your class in academic, social, and behavioral areas. For example, do your students have difficulty attending to their work? Do they complete their assignments? Do they arrive on time for class or school? Are they prepared with the necessary supplies? Do they interact appropriately with their peers and authority figures? Do they commit acts of verbal or physical aggression? Do they steal? Do they comply with requests in a reasonable amount of time? Use positive terminology to identify clearly what students will do at each level of your system. As we have said many times, your students already know what they should not be doing. Therefore, your levels system should identify appropriate alternative behaviors.

Second, you need to decide what your standards will be for students when they complete the levels system. A general guideline is that your students should display standards of behavior that will allow them to be successful in the next less restrictive environment. For example, the standards for students enrolled in a self-contained special education school should be the levels of performance necessary to function effectively in a self-contained class in a public school. The standards for performance for students in a self-contained class in a public school should be the levels of performance necessary for integration in the general education classroom. The measures of social comparison and subjective evaluation that we discussed in Chapter 3 will help you establish reasonable, socially valid standards of performance. For example, your students, who are enrolled in a separate school for students with disabilities, turn in completed homework assignments 40 percent of the time. After visiting a self-contained special education classroom in a nearby public school, you learn that students complete their homework 80 percent of the time. Therefore, your students will need to be motivated to complete and turn in their

TABLE 10.3 Steps in Designing a Levels System

Bauer and Shea (1988) identified the steps to follow when designing a levels system.

1. Identify target behaviors in academic, social, and behavioral areas.
2. Identify the terminal outcome or standards for your students' behavior.
3. Identify interim behaviors between students' current performance level and the anticipated outcomes.
4. Identify rewards for each level.
5. Identify consequences for inappropriate behavior.
6. Determine how students will move through levels.
7. Share information about the levels system with all interested parties.
8. Monitor the system.
9. Plan for transition and follow-up.

homework at least 80 percent of the time to enhance their success in the less restrictive environment.

Third, determine interim behaviors between the standards your students currently display and the standards they should display upon completion of the levels system. These interim behaviors serve as the basis for the number of levels in your system. Bauer and Shea (1988) recommended listing at least two but no more than four interim levels. Establish interim standards for every behavior targeted for development or improvement. Assign one standard per behavior to a level in the system. For example, let's say your students are currently turning in two out of five homework assignments per week and are noncompliant nearly every day. Students at Level 1 will be required to turn in completed homework assignments twice a week and be compliant 60 percent of the time. Students at Level 2 will be required to turn in completed homework three times per week and be compliant 70 percent of the time. Students at Level 3 will be required to turn in completed homework four times per week and be compliant 80 percent of the time. Students at Level 4 will be required to turn in all of the homework assignments and be compliant 90 percent of the time.

By the way, you don't have to use numbers to differentiate among the levels in your system. You can use colors, the names of sports teams, or any other categorization system you think is appropriate given your students' ages and ability levels. Bauer and Shea (1988) cleverly suggested using freshman, sophomore, junior, and senior for a system containing four levels.

Fourth, identify privileges or rewards that students can earn at each level. The nature, amount, and freedom to choose from among privileges should increase as students move through the levels system. Each level should require less structure and less direct staff supervision. The lowest level in your system should provide students with the opportunity to earn a few carefully supervised rewards. The highest level in your system should provide your students with the opportunity to chose from a variety of unsupervised freedoms and rewards. Ultimately, students learn that accepting greater responsibility for their academic, social, and behavioral performance and meeting higher expectations for success give them greater access to reinforcers. Table 10.4 provides examples of the reinforcers that can be assigned to each level.

TABLE 10.4   Examples of Privileges for a Levels System

Level 1: Free time in the room supervised by the teacher, special activities with staff members, items purchased at the class store

Level 2: Unescorted movement through the building, choice of table for lunch, breaks in a lounge area contingent upon points, greater variety of items available for purchase at the class store

Level 3: Unescorted movement throughout the building, lunch off campus, self-selected scheduling, noncontingent breaks, escorted field trips

Level 4: All privileges associated with a general education classroom

Fifth, identify fair and reasonable consequences for inappropriate behavior. Not all students are likely to progress through a levels system without experiencing the occasional setback. You can have two types of consequences for inappropriate behavior. First, you can assign specific consequences for each level. For example, students who do not turn in a homework assignment can be required to complete it rather than participate in a preferred activity such as recess. (Make sure that you do not deny access to a class that is mandated by your school district or by the IEP of a student with disabilities.) The second type of consequences is for a student who commits a major violation at a particular level. You may want to assign him or her to the next lowest level for a period of time. Should the student adhere to those standards successfully, he or she can be moved back up to the original level. For example, a student at Level 4, the highest level in your system, is expected to go through each day without any physical aggression. One episode of this behavior will result in a temporary reassignment to Level 3 for one week. If the expectations of this level are met for a week, the student can be moved back up to Level 4; if not, the student remains at Level 3 until established criteria for that level are met.

Sixth, identify how students will move through the levels. A common stipulation is to require that students remain at a particular level for a minimum period of time. Your knowledge of individual students and of the group should help you decide on the minimum length of time they will stay at a level. For example, you may decide that students must be at Level 1 for at least three weeks. This period of time will give them the structure, support, and close supervision necessary to gain some control over their academic, social, and behavioral performance. However, just because students have been at Level 1 for three weeks does not automatically mean they have developed the control they need to move to Level 2. Therefore, it is also common to require that expectations within a given level be consistently met before moving up to the next level. This measure keeps students from moving to a less structured level before they are ready. For example, students in Level 1 can earn points for homework completion and compliance. While these points can be exchanged daily for positive rewards, they can also be used to keep track of how consistently students met expectations. Students who have been at Level 1 for three weeks and who have earned 100 percent of their homework points and 90 percent of their compliance points can move up to the next level. Students who have not met these expectations remain at Level 1. You and your students will need to document and review performance on a regular basis to determine if assignment to a new level is warranted.

Seventh, develop a system for disseminating information about the levels system to all interested parties. For example, you can develop a handbook; give copies to students, parents, colleagues, and administrative personnel; and review it at conferences.

Eighth, make sure you develop a way to monitor your system. Create point sheets and self-monitoring logs, review them daily or weekly, and keep them on file. It is especially important to get students involved in recording and evaluating their own behavior. Their efforts reduce the amount of work you have to do and increase their involvement and investment in the levels system. Students can also develop important self-management skills needed to structure their school and personal lives independently.

Ninth, consider transition and follow-up levels. As a student reaches the highest level in your class, you may want to consider a shared placement. Such a placement allows the student time to experience and adjust to another setting within the structure provided by the levels system. For example, a student in a self-contained program could attend a self-contained class in a public school for part of the day or the week. A student in a self-contained class could start spending time in the regular class. Features of the levels system can be faded gradually as interactions with the new teachers and peers develop and as the student becomes adjusted to the academic and behavioral standards.

Advantages of Levels Systems

The development and implementation of a levels system offer several advantages. First, a levels systems can be designed to address a variety of student needs and ability levels. While it requires time and effort from a busy teacher, it may be the only program needed to help all the students in your class. A levels system allows students to progress at a gradual pace toward the achievement of long-term academic, social, and behavioral goals. Expectations for performance increase at a pace commensurate with the students' ability to meet them. Thus, a levels system offers the second advantage of not overwhelming students with the need to change a variety of behaviors quickly. Also, building in the opportunity to self-record and self-monitor contributes to the development of self-management skills. Students who can self-manage are more likely to maintain and generalize from treatment gains, a third advantage of a levels system. Fourth, as your students move up through the levels system, they are becoming less dependent on more intrusive contingency management procedures such as token economies (Bauer & Shea, 1988).

Disadvantages of a Levels System

We have already mentioned that it takes time to develop and implement a levels system, although the nature and severity of your students' problems may warrant such an investment of time and energy. Also, you should be aware that the use of levels systems has been the source of some controversy. For example, while there are some data-based articles verifying their use (cf., Schloss, Holt, Mulvaney, & Green, 1988; Schloss, Alper, & Green, 1994), Scheuermann and colleagues (1994) pointed out that much of the literature on levels systems simply describes their use without offering data to document their effectiveness. We recommend that you collect data and systematically evaluate the impact of this technique on your students' performance. The information provided in Chapters 11, 12, and 13 will be helpful. A third problem identified by Scheuermann and colleagues (1994) is that access to the general education classroom could be treated as a privilege. You should be aware that for a substantial number of students with disabilities, the general education classroom is considered to be the least restrictive environment. Making access to this setting a privilege rather than a guarantee is a violation of the provisions of IDEA. The committee responsible for monitoring a particular special education student should be involved in the creation of the levels system.

An Example of a Comprehensive Levels System

In this section, we present a brief description of a levels system designed by Schloss, Holt, Mulvaney, and Green (1988) for students enrolled in the Franklin-Jefferson Special Education School District in Benton, Illinois. The district included two self-contained high school classrooms, two self-contained elementary classes, and one separate special education school for intermediate and high school students. We describe this levels system to illustrate how the components discussed separately in Chapters 4 through 9 can be combined into a levels system to reduce disruptive social behaviors and promote self-control. The levels system includes eight components, each of which is described separately.

The School Note
The school note, illustrated in Figure 10.1, is the focal point of the program as it binds together all elements of the levels system. It is both a planning system that ensures that all IEP goals are addressed, and an implementation instrument that is carried by the students throughout the instructional day. The school note contains the following elements.

   1. Scheduled periods—On the left-hand side of the school note are the time periods during which instruction occurs. In keeping with the guidelines for schedule development discussed in Chapter 4, the length of the time periods reflects the students' age and ability levels. Shorter instructional periods can be scheduled for younger, less able students. Two or three time periods can be devoted to an instructional activity designed for older or more able students. Ultimately, the length of instruction can match the time that nonhandicapped students of a comparable age engage in an activity.
   2. Scheduled breaks for reinforcement—Three breaks lasting 15 minutes each are scheduled daily. As we will discuss shortly, students can earn a break by completing a predetermined amount of work, staying in their assigned areas, and not demonstrating socially disruptive behaviors. Students who do not earn breaks remain in their seats completing enrichment activities that do not require teacher assistance.
   3. Goal areas—Goal areas such as reading and math that correspond with IEP goals are listed in the second column. Initially, the teacher establishes nonnegotiable activities and/or times. Other time blocks can be filled in by the student after consultation with the teacher. This activity encourages students to begin managing their own day.
   4. Assignments—In the next column, the teacher identifies specific products that should result from completion of each scheduled activity.
   5. Dockage areas—Behaviors that could result in the student's failure to earn breaks are listed in the upper right-hand corner of the school note. We have listed

SCHOOL NOTE			DOCKAGE				AWARD	
			NONCOMPLIANCE	VERBAL AGGRESSION	OBJECT AGGRESSION	PHYSICAL AGGRESSION	ASSIGNED AREA	WORK COMPLETION
NAME _____ DATE _____								
PERIOD	GOAL AREA	ASSIGNMENT						
1　8:30			5	10	10	60	5	5
2　9:00			5	10	10	60	5	5
3　9:30			5	10	10	60	5	5
4　10:00			5	10	10	60	5	5
B　10:15		BREAK						
5　10:30			5	10	10	60	5	5
6　11:00			5	10	10	60	5	5
7　11:30			5	10	10	60	5	5
8　12:00			5	10	10	60	5	5
B　12:15		BREAK						
9　12:30			5	10	10	60	5	5
10　1:00			5	10	10	60	5	5
11　1:30			5	10	10	60	5	5
12　2:00			5	10	10	60	5	5
B　2:15		BREAK						
		#					c/c	

FIGURE 10.1　The School Note Used by Schloss, Holt, Mulvaney, and Green (1988)

Used with permission of the Council for Exceptional Children.

four areas that were problematic for many of the students; however, teachers interested in adopting this system can tailor these dockage areas to meet the needs of individual students.

6. Award areas—Behaviors that will result in a student earning break points are identified in the upper right-hand corner of the school note. These behaviors reflect the goals included on the student's IEP. The behaviors included in Figure 10.1 are those most frequently targeted for development by students in the program; however, you can adapt these as needed for use in your classroom.

7. Point values—Points that can be lost or earned are listed under the dockage and award areas. An economy was developed that balanced awards with dockages. Students can earn a maximum of 40 points during the four periods that precede

break by remaining in their assigned areas and completing their work. Students can earn a break by having any amount of points and then use these points to purchase additional privileges. For example, students spend 5 points if they want to play a computer game or 5 to 20 points if they want to purchase snacks. Students will lose points for displaying any of the behaviors listed under the dockage area. Problems such as verbal aggression cost 10 points; more serious offenses such as physical aggression result in a loss of 40 points. In keeping with the guidelines for a token economy and a response cost, points cannot be carried over from one break period to the next, nor can a student drop below zero points.

Rules for using the school note are taught to the professional and paraprofessional staff, and all are expected to abide by them. In addition, all students receive a handbook and instruction that describe the note and all contingencies.

Break Activities
Break is the most pleasant noninstructional activity available during the day. Students in the lower levels can participate in a break only after they have earned it. Students in the higher levels of the system receive break noncontingently. This procedure reflects the fact than typical elementary and high school students are allowed to participate in pleasant school activities automatically. During break, students can have free time to participate in special activities or buy special privileges.

Aggression Management Strategy
The Prosocial Response Formation Technique (Schloss, 1984), informally called the 10 Rs, is used as a backup procedure to ensure that students do not use disruptive behaviors to gain satisfying events or avoid unpleasant consequences. The steps included in this technique are listed in Table 10.5 and described separately on page 213.

TABLE 10.5   **The Prosocial Response Formation Technique (Schloss, 1984)**

The Prosocial Response Formation Technique, or the 10 Rs, includes the following steps:

1. Response cost
2. Relaxation
3. Rectify
4. Recognize
5. Rehearse
6. Reinforce
7. Reflect
8. Reenter
9. Record
10. Repeat

Note that students can become disruptive at any point during this procedure. Should this happen, start again at Step 2.

1. Response cost—A predetermined number of points are deducted.

2. Relaxation—The individual is instructed to use relaxation training techniques. With the exception of this directive, no other interaction occurs, as it may inadvertently reinforce the student.

3. Rectify—The student must correct any physical or emotional damage.

4. Recognize—The student identifies discrete, observable events that led to the inappropriate behavior, then identifies alternative responses.

5. Rehearse—Having identified the alternative, the student rehearses it.

6. Reinforce—The teacher praises the student for behavior rehearsal.

7. Reflect—The student identifies the consequences of inappropriate behaviors and compares them to the consequences that would have been available for appropriate behavior.

8. Reenter—The student reenters the schedule at the point of disruption. This step reduces the likelihood that the student will use inappropriate behavior to escape an unpleasant scheduled activity.

9. Record—The teacher should document the behavior and use of the 10 Rs.

10. Repeat—Every person who comes into contact with the student should use the 10 Rs correctly and consistently.

Use of the 10 Rs ensures that students make restitution for any emotional or physical damage they have caused. In addition, the Ten Rs requires the students to identify and practice appropriate alternative behavior.

Relaxation Training
The Franklin Jefferson program uses the relaxation training procedures described in Chapter 6.

Social Skill Instruction
Some students do not possess the interpersonal skills needed for success in educational and community settings. Therefore, direct instruction in social skills is scheduled every other school day using the procedures described in Chapter 5. A new social skill from the social skill matrix presented in Chapter 5 becomes the focus of instruction every two weeks of the school year. In addition, staff consistently identify and praise students throughout the day for using socially skillful behavior.

Fading Procedures
Features of the school note and use of the 10 Rs are faded as students demonstrate that they can benefit from more traditional classroom conditions. Ultimately, it is expected that students will make the transition to less restrictive classrooms in the school district. Therefore, the program includes the following three levels of structure.

1. Level 1: Standard Program—Level 1 incorporates all program features including the school note, the 10 Rs, social skills training, relaxation training, the token economy, and the response cost. All students enter the program at Level 1 and move to Level 2, depending on their behavior.

2. Level 2: Unrestricted Program—Level 2 involves the same program procedures as Level 1 except that all dockage and award areas are removed from the

school note. Breaks and privileges are given automatically. Students enter Level 2 by achieving 80 percent of their points in Level 1 for three consecutive weeks.

3. Level 3: Mainstream Class—Level 3 is integration into one or more general education classes at the local schools. Students are eligible for Level 3 when they have completed 80 percent of their assignments within a two-week period and have had no occurrences of any of the behaviors previously included in the dockage areas.

Restriction Room
Any student who commits an act of aggression against a staff member is assigned to a restriction room that contains none of the amenities. All procedures are in effect except that the student is ineligible for breaks regardless of the number of points earned. Social interactions are limited to direct instruction from the teacher. To leave the restriction room and return to the classroom, the student must earn all assigned area points and 80 percent of the work points and commit no acts of noncompliance or aggression.

Monitoring System
The daily percentages of earned and lost points are recorded on separate graphs for each student in the class. These data indicate whether a student is ready to move to the next level.

As you can see, the Franklin Jefferson program exemplifies a comprehensive applied behavior analytic intervention that includes all the points of the multifaceted model we described in Chapter 2. It has been implemented successfully across several settings and can be used in schools, group homes, supported living employment sites, and supported living arrangements. For example, the Franklin Jefferson program has been adapted for use in a group home. Known as Integration Plus (I+), it is a supported living program developed by Schloss, Alper, and Green (1994) for youths between 8 and 21 years of age with retardation and challenging behaviors such as physical aggression.

Summary

In Chapter 2, we discussed the concept of power and how it applies to the development of applied behavior analytic interventions. We encouraged you to consider how a multifaceted program can give you more power in changing students' academic and social behaviors. Toward that end, Chapters 4 through 9 provided detailed information on how you can prevent problems through antecedent control, develop students' repertoires through social skills and emotional learning, increase their motivation to use newly acquired skills through positive reinforcement, and decrease inappropriate behavior through differential reinforcement and, if necessary, punishment.

A recurring theme throughout these discussions is the need to attend to all points in the multifaceted model. Procedures such as group contingencies and levels systems provide ideal opportunities to develop comprehensive programs that can be used with an entire classroom. In this chapter, we discussed three types of group contingencies, including dependent, independent, and interdependent. Group contingencies take advantage of the powerful influence peers can have on each other's behavior. They are ideal for use in a variety of behavior problems demonstrated by one or several members of your class.

We also described another more potent procedure for managing disruptive behaviors demonstrated by large groups of students. You can use a levels system to organize appropriate social and academic behaviors and their consequences into a hierarchical sequence and create opportunities for students to gain control over their own behavior.

Because both of these group procedures have generated some controversy, we suggested guidelines to ensure their appropriate, ethical use. Central to their appropriate use are the collection and evaluation of data, topics we will cover in the next three chapters.

References

Barrish, H. H., Saunders, M., & Wolf, M. M. (1969). Good behavior game: Effects of individuals contingencies for group consequences on disruptive behavior in a classroom. *Journal of Applied Behavior Analysis, 12*, 199–210.

Bauer, A. M., & Shea, T. M. (1988). Structuring classroom through levels systems. *Focus on Exceptional Children, 21*(3), 1–12.

Bauer, A. M., Shea, T. M., & Keppler, R. (1986). Levels systems: A framework for the individualization of behavior management. *Behavioral Disorders, 11*, 28–35.

Brantley, D. C., & Webster, R. E. (1993). Use of an independent group contingency management system in a regular classroom setting. *Psychology in the Schools, 30*, 60–66.

Brigham, F. J., Bakken, J. P., Scruggs, T. E., & Mastropieri, M. A. (1992). Cooperative behavior management: Strategies promoting a positive classroom environment. *Education and Training in Mental Retardation, 27*, 3–12.

Crouch, P. L., Gresham, F. M., & Wright, W. R. (1985). Interdependent and dependent group contingencies with immediate and delayed reinforcement for controlling classroom behavior. *Journal of School Psychology, 23*, 177–187.

Gola, T. L., Holmes, P. A., & Holmes, N. K. (1979). Effectiveness of a group contingency procedure for increasing prevocational behavior of profoundly mentally retarded residents. *Mental Retardation, 20*, 26–29.

Gresham, F. M. (1983). Use of a home-based dependent group contingency system in controlling destructive behavior: A case study. *School Psychology Review, 12*, 195–199.

Gresham, F. M., & Gresham, G. N. (1982). Interdependent, dependent, and independent group contingencies for controlling disruptive behavior. *Journal of Special Education, 16*, 101–110.

Hayes, L. A. (1976). The use of group contingencies for behavioral control: A review. *Psychological Bulletin, 83*, 628–648.

Hood, L., McDermott, R., & Cole, M. (1980). "Let's try to make it a good day"—Some not so simple ways. *Discourse Processes, 3*, 155–168.

Kerr, M. M., & Nelson, C. M. (1989). *Strategies for managing behavioral problems in the classroom* (2nd ed.). Columbus, OH: Merrill.

Kohler, F. W., Strain P., Hoyson, M., Davis, L., Donina, W. M., & Rapp, N. (1995). Using a group-oriented contingency to increase social interactions between children with autism and their peers. *Behavior Modification, 19*, 10–32.

Litow, L., & Pumroy, D. K. (1975). A brief review of classroom group oriented contingencies. *Journal of Applied Behavior Analysis, 8*, 341–347.

Martin, R. (1975). *Legal challenges to behavior modification: Trends in school, corrections, and mental health.* Champaign, IL: Research Press.

Naslund, S. R., & L'Homme, B. P. (1979). Creating a group management system. *Pointer, 24*(1), 82–87.

Rhode, G., Jenson, W. R., & Reavis, H. K. (1993). *The tough kid book.* Longmont, CO: Sopris West.

Salend, S. J., Whittaker, C. R., & Reeder, E. (1992). Group evaluation: A collaborative, peer mediated behavior management system. *Exceptional Children, 59,* 203–209.

Scheuermann, B., Webber, J., Partin, M., & Knies, W. C. (1994). Level systems and the law: Are they compatible? *Behavioral Disorders, 19,* 205–220.

Schloss, P. J. (1984). *Social development of handicapped children and youth.* Rockville, MD: Aspen.

Schloss, P. J., Alper, S., & Green, C. (1994). Integration PLUS: A community based social learning program for youth with mental retardation and physical aggression. *Issues in Special Education and Rehabilitation, 9,* 51–60.

Schloss, P. J., Holt, J., Mulvaney, M., & Green, J. (1988). The Franklin-Jefferson Program: Demonstration of an integrated social learning approach to educational services for behaviorally disordered students. *TEACHING Behaviorally Disordered Youth, 4,* 7–15.

Smith, M. A., & Misra, A. (1994). Using group contingencies with students with learning disabilities. *LD Forum, 20*(1), 17–20.

Smith, W. S., & Farrell, D. T. (1993). Level system use in special education: Classroom intervention with prima facie appeal. *Behavioral Disorders, 18,* 251–264.

Speltz, M. L., Shimamura, J. W., & McReynolds, W. T. (1982). Procedural variations in group contingencies: Effects on children's academic and social behaviors. *Journal of Applied Behavior Analysis, 15,* 533–544.

Sulzer-Azaroff, B., & Mayer, G. R., (1992). *Behavior analysis for lasting change.* Ft. Worth, TX: Holt, Rinehart, and Winston, Inc.

Vogler, E. W., & French, R. W. (1983). The effects of a group contingency strategy on behaviorally disordered students in physical education. *Research Quarterly for Exercise and Sport, 54,* 273–277.

Wolery, M., Bailey, D. B., & Sugai, G. (1988). *Effective teaching: Principles and procedures of applied behavior analysis with exceptional students.* Boston: Allyn and Bacon.

11

DATA COLLECTION

Regardless of our capabilities as teachers or human beings, we are all prone to make mistakes. Errors in reading people and anticipating their reactions occur with surprising regularity. We often attribute these mistakes to the unpredictability of the human species. Teachers' errors of judgment are particularly troublesome. Incorrectly predicting that a student would not be able to keep pace with a regular math class may set into motion a self-fulfilling prophecy that retards math development. Judging that a child would be able to benefit from an unstructured recess time may be equally troublesome if this situation actually leads to severe aggressive behavior and subsequent suspension from school.

These examples are fairly dramatic. More critical, however, may be the total effect of teachers' routine decisions. What assignment should be given? What are the grading criteria? What incentives should be used? Should assistance be provided? The answers to each of these questions, as well as the myriad of questions raised throughout the instructional day, will eventually determine the quality of the educational experience for each student.

Numerous authors have debated whether the teaching profession is an art or a science. Those favoring the "art" position highlight the importance of innate ability in reading students and planning accordingly. They suggest that the capable teacher does not need to operationally define when student characteristics trigger specific instructional decisions. Those favoring the "science" position emphasize the importance of teachers following specific principles of instruction based on the careful study of the individual. They argue that the rule-governed behavior of teachers can easily be evaluated and taught to other teachers.

Both positions may be inappropriate when taken to an extreme. The "artist" teacher who ignores basic empirical principles relating to teaching and learning may not be providing the best educational program for students. The "scientist" who studies and applies broad principles to specific individuals for whom the principles may not apply runs a similar risk.

An issue of *Money* magazine highlighted people's poor judgment in making financial decisions. The article emphasizes that "no matter how smart we are, we all make dumb mistakes…The culprits: a series of mental blind spots and knee jerk reactions" (Willis, 1990, p. 84). Several of these blind spots and knee jerk reactions also cloud our educational system.

Consider the following questions:

1. *There are roughly 25,000 movie theaters in the United States. How many are there in Russia? Provide a high estimate, a low estimate, and your estimation of the actual number. Attempt to be 90 percent certain that your range includes the actual number.*

Most people are overly confident about their ability to make judgments in the absence of empirical support. Even though United States citizens generally know little about the Russian theater business, they are likely to begin by estimating the actual number and then producing a range based on their level of confidence. When this problem was posed to business executives, almost one half of the respondents did not include a range sufficiently large to include the actual number—150,000. We recognize the temptation to be overly confident in our abilities to make judgments about student behavior. Consequently, we seek to obtain as much information as possible prior to developing and initiating program changes. Once the program change is made, we are not fully assured that it will be effective. Consequently, we continue to collect information to confirm that the approach is having a desirable effect.

Another insight that can be drawn from the preceding question is that we often use irrelevant information to make judgments. Differences in culture, economy, and population make this information only marginally relevant to the number of theaters in Russia. Similarly, educational and sociological research highlights the influence of irrelevant variables such as physical attractiveness, sex, socioeconomic status, race, and disability labels on teachers' decisions. The "scientist" teacher recognizes these distractions and seeks to confirm judgments about individual students with as much *relevant* information as possible. Consider another question.

2. *Is suicide or murder more common in the United States?*

We tend to ascribe too much importance to dramatic and memorable events. The child who is chronically careless in completing assignments and is pervasively unhappy may not receive the attention and support provided to a child who commits infrequent but serious acts of aggression. In balance, however, the careless and unhappy child may have more significant special educational needs.

As you might guess from this point, the suicide rate of approximately 31,000 is significantly larger than the murder rate of approximately 23,000. Equally interesting, there were more suicides among Vietnam veterans following the war than there were casualties during the war. One can speculate that the tendency to place a higher estimate on the murder rate or casualty rate is due to attention paid in the media to these events. Little attention is given to more frequent but less dramatic suicides.

As conscientious teachers, we seek to obtain comprehensive information about the social and academic development of our students. We recognize that continuous information about daily events is more important than written or verbal anecdotal accounts of one or two major events. The next question provides additional insights into the need for well-focused data collection efforts.

   3. *Judy is a 19-year-old graduate from a rural high school. She is considering postsecondary education for a future career. Judy is somewhat reserved and has few friends. She shows little interest in establishing friendships. Despite her meek and timid nature, she is very helpful. She is compulsive about detail and has a passion for order and structure. Given the two choices, how confident would you be that Judy will eventually become a librarian instead of a salesperson?*

   As noted above, we often fail to obtain sufficient information from which to make educational decisions. Most individuals would be quick to recommend that Judy seek a position as a librarian in view of her personality characteristics. Equally important is the availability of full-time paid positions in libraries or sales. There are currently fewer than 200,000 librarians in the United States. Conversely, there are over 14 million people in sales.

   As noted earlier, teachers must obtain all relevant information from which to make an informed decision. Simply knowing the learning and behavioral features of a student may not be sufficient. We must also know the environmental context in which the student is expected to perform. In the preceding example, Judy's characteristics suggest that she would be better suited for a position in a library. Knowing that few such positions exist, however, may alter the educational decisions that we make. The next question expands upon this idea.

   4. *A collegiate golfer averages 72 strokes per round with a range from 68 to 78 in competitive events. Prior to a meet with a rival university, he states that he does not feel like he will be able to perform well. He expresses a severe lack of confidence. Based on this information, what do you predict will be his score for the event?*

   We are often confused by behavioral samples that are not relevant to critical decisions. In the preceding question, one is tempted to conclude based on a sample of "verbal behavior" that the golfer's performance will be above the 72 average if not at the top of the range. In fact, however, the best predictor of future behavior is past behavior of the same type. Given the preceding information, one may assume that the golfer's performance would be near the average regardless of his verbal behavior.

   We are often tempted to make judgments based on what students say as opposed to what they do. For example, many of us are disappointed when we see that a student continues having aggressive episodes even after vowing convincingly that he will act in a more responsible manner. After observing this pattern it is best to conclude that without intervention, the student is likely to continue to behave aggressively. One may also conclude that he is likely to continue to pledge to change his ways.

   Knowing this tendency, effective teachers strive to collect information directly relevant to decisions being made. When questions relate to overt social behavior, the overt social behavior should be measured. For example, if one is concerned with a student's aggressive conduct, aggression incidences and associated events should be recorded. Questions relating to verbal behavior such as students' self-perceptions, spelling achievement, interpersonal skill, and so on should be assessed using related verbal measures.

The preceding questions and the accompanying explanations provide a rationale for collecting student performance data. We clearly cannot trust instruction and management decisions to *intuition*. There must be an objective foundation for our decisions. This chapter includes descriptions of the major data collection procedures used by applied behavior analysts. Equally important, it provides guidelines for the development and selection of recording procedures. Specific recording methods include anecdotal, permanent products, task analysis, frequency recording, interval recording, duration recording, and group monitoring procedures.

Anecdotal Recording

An **anecdotal record** is a written narrative describing critical incidents. The anecdotal record is similar to a personal diary, except that diaries recount all significant events in an individual's life along with the time and place of their occurrence. While the time and place of events are equally important in the anecdotal record, the focus of entries is limited to specific types of events.

Anecdotal records may be used for four major purposes. First, they can confirm the existence of a hypothesized problem. The entries note both the frequency with which problems occur and the intensity or severity of reactions. Second, they can reveal conditions that provoke or cause the problem behavior. Time of day, professionals responsible, peers present, instructional demands, and other factors may be identified in the narrative. Third, the narrative may indicate events that reinforce or punish the problem behavior. Finally, the anecdotal record may help identify alternative positive social behaviors that may be used to replace disruptive responses.

A basic method for keeping an anecdotal record involves identifying and defining the behaviors that are to be studied using the record. A notebook or writing pad is kept handy, and a narrative is written whenever the target behavior occurs. The narrative generally includes an objective description of the student's reaction, the time and place of the reaction, professionals and peers involved with the student at the time of the reaction, and significant events associated with the reaction.

As with all recording methods, it is important that recording be accomplished during or immediately after the event. The longer you wait to complete the entry, the more information you will forget. Similarly, information in the log should be factual and objective. The log should report only the discrete details of the incident. Speculation about motives, anticipated consequences, or other subjective opinions should either be clearly labeled as such or not included in the log.

An alternative method for collecting anecdotal information involves using a specially designed form. The form may include column headings that correspond to the specific assessment questions. For example, one question may be whether

Student _____ Date _____

Teacher _____

Student Behavior	Location	Peers Present	Peer Reaction

FIGURE 11.1 Sample Form for Collecting Anecdotal Information

specific peers are present more frequently when aggressive behaviors occur. A column may indicate peers present during aggressive incidents. A second question may address the specific location of incidents and the column heading may indicate location of incidents. A third question may focus on the reactions of peers following a disturbance and the column heading may indicate peer reactions. Figure 11.1 depicts the form suggested in the preceding example. Remember, however, that the number and type of column headings are limited only by the questions that the teacher wishes to answer.

Antecedent Behavior Consequence (ABC) Recording

Antecedent behavior consequence recording is another method for structuring anecdotal accounts. ABC recording is most directly useful for obtaining diagnostic information prior to constructing an intervention program. As noted in earlier chapters, applied behavior analysis interventions generally rely on three major activities: the modification of antecedents, or conditions that precede the target behaviors and influence the probability of their initial occurrence; the modification of consequences, or events that follow a target behavior and influence the likelihood that the response will reoccur; and the development of specific skills (e.g., social skills, relaxation skills, self-management skills, etc.) that allow the individual to act appropriately when faced with provoking antecedents.

The ABC recording form presented in Figure 11.2 may be used as a source of information for developing applied behavior analysis interventions. The student's name, the time when observations are made, the teacher's name, and the observation setting are identified on the top of the form. Specific target behaviors are identified in the middle column, and antecedents and consequences are described in relationship to the target behaviors.

The ABC recording form is used by observing a student for all or a portion of the school day (e.g., during math class, recess, and unstructured time) depending on the expected scope of the intervention program. It may be useful to include the student's parents in using the ABC recording form after school hours if the eventual goal is to extend benefits of behavior change to home and community settings.

Student _____   Time _____

Teacher _____   Setting _____

Antecedent	Behavior	Consequence

FIGURE 11.2   Antecedent Behavior Consequence (ABC) Recording Form

Finally, more adaptive students may be taught to record their own behavior. This may be an effective self-management strategy because it encourages the student to study the conditions under which problem behavior occurs. The student may subsequently be advised to avoid these conditions.

There are three major activities involved in ABC recording. First, the target behaviors are identified. Each time the student engages in one of the behaviors, a precise and objective description of the response is entered into the **target behavior** section. These descriptions can later be used to refine a definition for program planning and implementation purposes. Second, the antecedent section is filled in by identifying and recording objective events that immediately preceded the target behavior. Finally, the **consequence** section is filled in by identifying and recording objective events immediately following the target behavior.

Frequency and Rate Recording

Frequency recording may be the most useful and least time-consuming method for monitoring classroom behavior. Performance levels are determined by tallying and counting each occurrence of a behavior over a specified period of time. For example, you may record the frequency of verbal aggression by making a tally each time a negative statement is uttered. The frequency at the end of the day is determined by adding tallies. Other examples of responses that can be measured using frequency recording methods include compliance, punctuality, work completed, positive statements, and laps run.

Frequency recording is appropriate when the beginning and end of the behavior are easily discernible. It is often difficult to identify exactly when "unhappy affect" or "crying" begin and end. Consequently, one observer may record several episodes while another observer records one longer episode. Balls caught, letters folded, and words uttered have a distinct start and stop so that multiple occurrences within a brief time can easily be distinguished.

Frequency recording also requires that the behavior have a relatively consistent duration. Frequency counts of behaviors such as strokes made, questions answered, or greetings made can be accurately interpreted because each count represents relatively the same level of performance. However, tantrums may last from one minute to several hours. The length of Scott's aggressive responses to words with a negative connotation varied across episodes. For example, he may have been aggressive four times each on Monday and Tuesday. However, Monday's episodes may have lasted 4 minutes, 35 minutes, 7 minutes, and 90 minutes. Tuesday's episodes may have lasted 1 minute, 5 minutes, 2 minutes, and 6 minutes. Because of the substantial differences in the duration of episodes, it would be misleading to tally the amount of episodes each day and simply report four.

In addition, simple frequency records made from one day to the next may not be directly comparable because of varying times available for the responses to occur. For example, Andrew swears 10 times on Monday but only 8 times on Tuesday. On the surface, it looks as though his behavior is improving. However, Tuesday was a half day of school. Frequency data that are based on unequal observation periods cannot be compared. When the observational time is variable, frequency of response should be converted to rate of response. This transformation produces comparable data regardless of the time available for the behavior to occur. Response rate is established from frequency data by dividing the number of occurrences (frequency) by the duration of the observation (time). For example, ten instances of swearing divided by five hours (the length of Andrew's school day) yields a rate of two times per hour. Eight instances of swearing divided by a two-and-one-half-hour school day yields a rate of 2.12 times per hour.

Although many researchers use recording sheets or charts to tally frequency (Mathur & Rutherford, 1994; Smith, Siegel, O'Connor, & Thomas, 1994), numerous devices have been demonstrated for increasing the ease and efficiency of frequency and rate recording; Mahoney (1974) used an abacus watchband and Lindsley

Student _____   Teacher _____

Behavior_____   Setting _____

Definition _____

_____

Date	Observation Time	Frequency	Rate

FIGURE 11.3   Form for Collecting Rate Data

(1968) used a golf counter. In a self-monitoring demonstration for preschool students, Holman and Baer (1979) used a bracelet made of a pipe cleaner and snug-fitting beads. Frequency was tallied by sliding a bead from one side of the bracelet to the other. Football officials use a rubber band placed around the wrist and the first through fourth finger to record downs. These mechanical counting devices are especially useful to teachers because they can be used with a single hand, are portable, and can be operated while conducting other professional activities.

Beyond the instrument used to tally information during the observation period, a recording sheet that stores data from one day to the next should be prepared. Figure 11.3 depicts a commonly used data sheet for rate data.

Recording Permanent Products

One of the most efficient, yet reliable methods for monitoring students' behavior is to record tangible results of their efforts. Self-care skills can be recorded by monitoring the permanent results of these skills such as hands being clean, hair being combed, and nails being trimmed. On-task behavior can be recorded by monitoring the quantity and quality of work that is actually completed. While directly monitoring the target behavior (e.g., on-task) and evaluating permanent products (e.g., work completion) generally produce comparable results, permanent product assessment is often more efficient and reliable. Direct observation of on-task behavior, for example, requires that the teacher observe the student during instructional time. Permanent product recording, on the other hand, can be conducted at any time during the day.

Permanent product recording methods can be very simple, as demonstrated by Wacker and Berg's (1985) recording of vocational task assembly and packaging. The authors simply recorded the number of items completed and packaged correctly. Permanent product recording methods can also be very complex. Helwig, Johns, Norman, and Cooper (1976), for example, reported a comprehensive scoring procedure for students' writing. Their recording method is summarized in the following passage:

1. The total stroke must be within the confines of the line of the overlay.
2. Each stroke that is not a complete circle must begin and end between the small slash mark and in the line forming the confines of the letter.
3. All circles in the letters *a, b, d, g, o p, q,* and the top of the letter *e* must be closed curves.
4. All strokes must intersect each successive stroke at one point except for the dot above the *i* and *j.*
5. The letter must be complete with all strokes present.
6. The horizontal stroke in the *t* and *f* must intersect the other stroke within the confines of the ellipse near the center of the vertical stroke. (p. 232)

It should also be noted that technology can make less tangible behaviors permanent. Audio recording has been used to measure sight-word learning rates (Skinner,

Smith, & McLean, 1994). Similarly, videotaping equipment has allowed researchers to produce permanent records of students' social skills (Mathur & Rutherford, 1994).

Accurate comparisons of permanent product data from one day to the next can only be made if the requirements of the task remain relatively constant. Changing the amount of assistance or substantially altering the difficulty of assignments may reduce the validity of comparisons from one day to the next. As with frequency data, the amount of work completed during varying periods of time can be controlled by dividing the number of products or units completed by the amount of time available for work completion.

Task Analysis Recording

As was discussed in Chapter 4, task analysis is a procedure for reducing complex behaviors into component parts or skills for the purpose of systematizing instruction. Learning is facilitated by the student acquiring and chaining together component skills that comprise the complex skill. Task analysis instruction may include forward or backward chaining. You use forward chaining by developing the first component skill to the point of mastery, then beginning instruction on the second component skill. Once mastery is achieved on the second skill, instruction begins on the third skill. This process continues until all component skills are mastered and the complex behavior is performed without hesitation or error. The process is reversed in backward chaining. You develop the last component skill, then the second to the last, and so on until all component skills are mastered.

The quality and effectiveness of task analysis instruction depends on the use of continuous recording of student performance. The teacher must be able to assess when mastery of each component skill is achieved prior to moving to the next component skill. Introducing a component skill prior to mastery of the previous skill is likely to produce frustration and failure. Conversely, delaying the introduction of a new component skill well after the mastery of a previous skill is likely to produce boredom and wasted instructional time.

Figure 11.4 illustrates a form used for collecting task analysis data. Four major elements of *task analysis recording* are depicted on the form.

1. The overall objective or complex skill is identified at the top of the form. As discussed in Chapter 3, the objective statement should include the student's name, the complex skill, the conditions under which the skill will be performed, and the criterion for successful performance.

2. The component skills, or tasks, are listed sequentially from first to last (in forward chaining), or last to first (in backward chaining). These skills should be described in clear and complete terms so that all observers are able to agree on their acceptable performance.

3. Spaces are provided for recording a series of trials for each component skill. Task analysis assessment is not static. Data collected during a session should rep-

Student _____   Date Initiated _____

Teacher _____   Setting _____

Skill _____

Conditions _____

Success Criterion _____

Task	Trial					
	1	2	3	4	5	6
1						
2						
3						
4						
5						
6						
7						
8						
9						
10						

Prompt Key: S = self-initiate   M = modeling
                V = verbal   P = physical

FIGURE 11.4   Form for Collecting Task Analysis Data

resent several opportunities for the student to perform. These recording opportunities should reveal progress toward mastery.

4. Each component skill in each trial is recorded using the prompt key. In our example (Figure 11.4), the key includes the level of prompt used at the point of successful performance. This may include: *self-initiating*, in which the student performs the skill without teacher assistance; *verbal prompt*, in which the student performs the skill following verbal instruction from the teacher; a *modeling prompt*, in which the student performs the skill following a teacher demonstration; and a *physical prompt*, in which the teacher manually guides the student through the skill.

A less complex task analysis recording form is depicted in Figure 11.5. on page 228. This form includes the four major elements discussed for the preceding form.

Student _____   Date Initiated _____

Teacher _____   Setting _____

Skill _____

Conditions _____

Success Criterion _____

Task	Class Period					
	1	2	3	4	5	6
1						
2						
3						
4						
5						
6						
7 .						
8						
9						
10						

Prompt Key: + = skill performed to criteria

− = skill not performed to criteria

FIGURE 11.5   Simplified Form for Collecting Task Analysis Data

The major difference is that rather than recording performance for multiple trials each day, one observation is made each class period. In addition, rather than scoring prompt levels, you note that the component skill was or was not performed without assistance. It is important to note that while this form is more easily used, it provides substantially less diagnostic information. You are able to determine whether or not a component skill is performed independently on a given day, but you cannot determine the consistency of performance or the amount of assistance that would have produced successful performance.

Task analysis data can be summarized in a number of ways depending on the actual recording method. For task analysis recording in which prompt levels are indicated, you report the average prompt level for each session or on the final trial of a session. For task analysis recording in which only independent performance is noted, the teacher may report the average number of subskills performed successfully each day.

Duration and Latency Recording

Duration recording is used to monitor increases or decreases in the amount of time an individual spends engaged in a response. For example, you may wish to increase the amount of time a student spends working on math worksheets. Similarly, you may wish to decrease the amount of time spent in transition from one class period to another. Duration recording is effective only when the target behavior has a discrete and easily identified beginning and end. Duration recording was ideal for monitoring Scott's aggressive behavior. Although it did have a discrete beginning and ending time, the episodes varied in length. Duration recording was sensitive to these variations. However, the beginning and end to other behaviors such as "happy affect" may be difficult to identify. Consequently, observers would fail to agree on the duration due to differing standards for beginning and ending the measure of duration.

Latency recording is a variation of duration recording in which the time elapsed between a specific event and a student response is monitored. Examples of latency recording include identifying time that elapses from the ringing of a bell signal to being seated in class, asking a question to getting a student's response, or giving a directive and student compliance. As with duration recording, the end of the signal and start of the response should be discrete and easily identified.

Figure 11.6 includes a form commonly used to collect duration data. Enter the time each response begins and ends. In the far right column, note the duration for the event (ending time minus the beginning time). Finally, sum the total duration for each day. The form is used to record latency data by changing the column headings from "time beginning" to "time of signal" and "time ending" to "behavior initiation." This form can be modified for use in latency recording. The columns labeled "Begin" and "End" would be renamed "Time of Cue" and "Time of Response" respectively.

Of all the recording methods identified in this chapter, duration and latency data may be the most difficult to use. You must attend both to the student's behavior and to the time. These demands provide little time for you to conduct other instructional activities. Because of these practical matters, you may prefer to use rate or permanent product measures of related behaviors. For example, you may avoid monitoring the duration of on-task behavior by recording assignments completed. Similarly, you may avoid determining the duration of hall travel by noting the frequency with which a student is tardy. While these strategies produce different raw results, their results are highly correlated. As on-task behavior increases so do assignments completed. As the duration of hall travel decreases so will the number of classes in which the learner is tardy.

Student _____   Teacher _____

Behavior _____   Setting _____

Definition _____

_____

_____

	Observation Time		Cumulative Duration
Date	Begin	End	

FIGURE 11.6   Duration Recording Form

Interval Recording

Interval recording may present a more efficient alternative to duration and latency recording. It also provides temporal information not assessed through frequency recording. Interval recording can also be used with responses that do not have discrete start or stop times and that vary in length.

Interval recording involves breaking the school day into brief time periods (e.g., from 10 seconds to 60 minutes). Responses are subsequently measured in relation to their occurrence at the start of or during the interval. Since it is often not convenient to monitor responses through the entire day, interval data are frequently collected during relatively brief periods interspersed throughout the day. Figure 11.7 is a general form for collecting interval data. Plus signs are inserted in boxes that indicate the correspondence with the occurrence of a behavior.

Student _____   Teacher _____

Behavior_____   Setting _____

Definition _____
_____
_____

Interval Length _____

Date	Time	1	2	3	4	5	6	7	8	9	10	# Scored +

FIGURE 11.7   Interval Scoring Format

Two approaches may be used to record interval data. A given approach is selected based on the instructional conditions and the nature of the target behavior. *Whole-interval recording* is conducted by noting if the target response occurs throughout the interval (e.g., 5 seconds of on-task performance during a 5-second interval). *Partial-interval recording* is conducted by scoring the target response if it occurs any time during the interval (e.g., a profane statement during a 30-second interval).

Use of interval data is illustrated in the following example. A high school math teacher randomly selects from her 40-minute period two 5-minute periods. Each 5-minute period is further divided into thirty 10-second intervals. The teacher could use whole-interval recording to score each interval in which the student is fully engaged in assigned seat work. She could use partial-interval recording and score each interval in which the student spends any time engaged in the assignment. In either case, the daily measure of seat work is computed by dividing the number of intervals scored with a plus sign by the 60 intervals possible. The resulting fraction or decimal is multiplied by 100 to produce the percentage of time the student spent engaged in seat work.

Several critical judgments must be made prior to developing an interval recording procedure. First, you must identify the target behavior(s). Interval recording requires the same standards for clear and complete descriptions of the response(s) that are required in other recording methods.

Second, you may consider whether to observe for a long or short period. The longer the period, the more likely the behavioral sample will reflect the actual level of behavior throughout the day. This is particularly true for highly variable responses. Mudford, Beale, and Singh (1990) reported an analysis of varying observation periods for high- and low-frequency responses. They concluded that sampling slightly less than one-third of the time available in the instructional day may produce less than 20 percent error for a behavior that occurs in half of all intervals throughout the day. For a low-frequency behavior (1.5 to 3.0 intervals throughout the day), error levels exceeding 50 percent occurred when sampled from half of the instructional day.

Third, you may consider whether to use brief or long intervals during the observation period. As noted earlier, the general standard in the applied behavior analysis literature is for intervals to be from 10 to 60 seconds. The longer the interval, the less sensitive the monitoring procedure. For example, aggressive actions that occur throughout a 60-second period would be scored as only one interval in a 60-second interval method. On the other hand, it would be registered as six intervals in a 10-second interval method. The 10-second method requires substantially more effort and recording skill on the part of the teacher when compared to the 60-second method. Consequently, we recommend using as long a period as possible while still retaining an appropriate level of sensitivity.

Fourth, consider the feasibility of using noncontinuous observational control. Tawney and Gast (1984) recommended this procedure as a way to reduce difficulties associated with scoring complex behaviors in brief intervals. In this procedure, you observe and score on alternate intervals. As illustrated in Figure 11.8, for example, you observe during an initial 15-second interval and score during the following 5-second interval. The next 15-second interval is for observation while the

15"	5"	15"	5"	15"	5"
Score	Record	Score	Record	Score	Record

FIGURE 11.8   Interval Recording Using Noncontinuous Observations

subsequent 5-second interval is for scoring. Alternate observation and scoring intervals throughout the observation period. As with all interval observational methods, you can adjust the lengths of the observation period and observation/scoring intervals to suit the target response and assessment conditions.

Finally, you may judge whether to observe for many or few periods each day. A large number of observation periods interspersed throughout the day will provide greater sensitivity than one or two periods. As suggested above, you should use the fewest number of periods possible while retaining acceptable sensitivity.

Time Sampling

Very closely related to interval recording is *time sampling,* sometimes called *momentary time sampling.* The procedure for using it is nearly identical to the procedures for using interval recording, and the same recording sheet can be used. Break the school day into brief time periods. At the moment when the time period ends, score whether or not the target behavior is occurring. For example, you may be interested in recording a student's on-task behavior during 30-minute independent activities. Break the activity into thirty 1-minute intervals. At the end of the interval, look at the student and decide if she is or is not on task. Time sampling does compromise the accuracy of your data to some extent. A student could be off-task for the first 59 seconds of the interval but become engaged at the moment you are observing. Conversely, a student could be on-task for 59 seconds then distracted from her work at the precise moment you are recording her behavior. You can see how several such intervals can compromise the accuracy of your data. The opposite is also true. If you believe your data are not accurate, then you need to adjust the size of your observation period. A 30-second time period may be more sensitive to the level of true performance.

Time sampling can be adapted to allow for observations of multiple students or multiple behaviors of one student. Figure 11.9 on page 234 illustrates a time/sampling form used to measure multiple responses. A similar form can be constructed to monitor the same behavior for multiple individuals. To use the multiple response form with momentary time sampling, look at the student the moment the interval ends. Score each response down the initial interval column. To use the multiple student form with momentary time sampling, look at a group of students the moment the interval ends. Score each student using the initial interval column.

Technology in Recording

Old and new technologies provide opportunities to record student behavior efficiently with minimum teacher effort. Microcomputer programs, for example, provide an objective and reliable measure of student performance in a number of areas. One such area is keyboarding skills. Upon completion of a practice period, the

Student _____   Teacher _____

Behavior A   = _____

Definition A   = _____

_____

Behavior B   = _____

Definition B   = _____

_____

Behavior C   = _____

Definition C   = _____

_____

Interval Length   _____

Date	Time	Beh.	1	2	3	4	5	6	7	8	9	10	# Scored +
		A											
		B											
		C											
		A											
		B											
		C											
		A											
		B											
		C											
		A											
		B											
		C											

FIGURE 11.9   Portion of an Interval Recording Form for Multiple Responses

microcomputer may produce a record of letters typed correctly within a specified period following a cue, words typed correctly per minute, errors per word, and so forth.

Halle, Schloss, and Schloss (1989) used a microcomputer program to record the clerical productivity of an individual with autism. The file-system program kept a running total of the number of individual files entered. It also recorded the percentage of disk space occupied by file data. Finally, it kept a reliable count of the number of keystrokes of information entered into the file. These data were used to demonstrate that changing criteria for reinforcement associated with the daily production of files increased the young man's performance to 34 percent of a floppy disk per day.

Finally, a videotape camera may be used as an effective adjunct to direct observation procedures (Broome & White, 1995; Mathur & Rutherford, 1994; Moore, Cartledge, & Heckaman, 1995). We have found videotape to be particularly effective in correcting unexpected deficiencies in an observation system (Schloss, Smith, Santora, & Bryant, 1989). The videotape record allows you to rescore data when new information suggests that the response definition or observational procedure should be revised. Without the videotape record, you would need to reinitiate data collection upon revision of the observation or scoring procedure.

Also, because the videotape record can be stopped and restarted, complex recording systems that require subtle or multiple discrimination decisions can be used reliably. Similar systems could not be used effectively without the ability to "stop action" to enter tallies, note durations, or mark intervals.

Finally, the fast forward capability of the videotape can economize effort when conducting all forms of data collection. For momentary time sampling, you need only view the tape when the counter hits the specified interval. Frequencies can be assessed while observing the tape in the "fast forward while viewing" mode.

Reliability

In the beginning of this chapter, we discussed the limited confidence that one may have in subjective judgments. Data collection procedures described later in the chapter may provide a more objective and accurate appraisal of student performance. It is important to note, however, that even data collection systems can yield inaccurate or biased results.

Kazdin (1982) has identified several sources of error that are relevant to teachers who collect observational data. The most common is **expectancy error,** which is the tendency for teachers to identify anticipated changes regardless of whether they actually occurred. This variability may result from changing standards in defining/ identifying the target behavior or changing vigilance for the target behavior. For example, you may record a reduction in aggression following the implementation of a special management plan. The reduction is actually noted, however, because you did not record borderline aggressive acts. Similarly, you may not watch the student as closely, and thus may miss aggressive behaviors that would have been recorded under other circumstances.

The second source of error involves the *complexity or difficulties inherent in applying the observational system.* We noted earlier that duration recording may be difficult to use while teaching. Similarly, some interval methods may be so complex that judgment errors or omissions of target behaviors occur. In general, the more students and responses being observed in the same period of time, the greater the chances of error. Also, the more subtle the judgments required when recording (e.g., "being mad at others" versus "hitting others"), the more likely the chances of error.

The third source of error is *observer drift*. Drift is the gradual change in the stringency with which the target behavior is defined/identified. Observer drift may result from changes in your expectations as data collection proceeds. It may also result from varying levels of attention to the data collection process. For example, early in the program, you may be highly vigilant for any occurrence of the target behavior. As the program progresses and the student improves, you may no longer watch the student as closely. Subsequent behavior records may then reveal a substantial decline in the target behavior when, in fact, only a modest decline has actually occurred.

These sources of error can be minimized by following several general recommendations. First, *response definitions should be clear*. The more objective and specific the response definition, the less likely that judgment errors will occur. Second, *recording procedures should be as simple and practical as possible*. As was emphasized above, complex recording systems are more likely to produce observer error. Third, *observers should be trained in using the observation system*. They should possess a thorough understanding of the response definition and procedures used in its measurement. Finally, *observers should be evaluated periodically to determine the actual reliability of their observations*. The following section describes procedures for evaluating the reliability of observations.

Procedures for Evaluating Reliability

The principal method for testing the reliability of observations involves establishing the level of interobserver agreement. **Interobserver agreement** is the extent to which independent individuals agree on the occurrence or duration of a specific behavior. Procedures for collecting and reporting the level of interobserver agreement vary depending on the measure of behavior strength. Each procedure will be discussed separately.

Reliability of Frequency and Rate Data

The level of interobserver agreement for frequency and rate data is established by two individuals (e.g., a teacher and a paraprofessional) independently observing a student over the same period of time and in the same setting. Each maintains an independent frequency count on the standard recording form. At the end of the observation period, the reliability level or rate of agreement is determined by dividing the lower frequency by the higher frequency.

For example, you and a colleague recorded "talk outs" for a student over a 40-minute lab period. You identified 14 incidents while your colleague identified 12. As shown below, a reliability level of .86 is established by dividing the smaller number (12) by the larger number (14).

Smaller frequency / Larger frequency = 12 / 14 = .86

Reliability of Permanent Product Data

The reliability of permanent product data is established in a similar fashion. Upon completion of the assignment, collect and evaluate the student's work. Request that another individual evaluate the work using the same standard. In general, the rate of agreement is determined by dividing the smaller score by the larger score.

For example, record the number of problems completed accurately during math class. Provide an unscored copy to your paraprofessional and ask him or her to indicate the number of correctly completed problems. In this case, you both may indicate that 20 of 20 problems were completed correctly. The rate of agreement would be 1.0.

Reliability of Task Analysis Data

Slightly more effort is required to establish the reliability of task analysis data. Similar to the preceding procedures, two independent observers record the student's performance over one or more attempts at the task sequence. The rate of agreement is established by dividing the number of subskills in the task sequence on which both observers agreed by the total number of subskills in the task sequence.

For example, two paraprofessionals may observe a student tie his shoes. The paraprofessionals score each step of a task analysis for shoe tying as being performed independently or requiring assistance. Over the 14-step task analysis one paraprofessional indicates that 12 steps were performed correctly without assistance. The other indicates that 10 were performed correctly without assistance. The rate of agreement as indicated below is .83.

Smaller # steps / Larger # steps = 10 / 12 = .83

Duration and Latency Recording

Reliability for duration and latency recording is established simply by dividing the shorter time by the longer time reported by independent observers. For example, two students may record the duration of the chemical reaction that occurs when vinegar is added to baking soda. One student reports a duration of 43 seconds and the other reports a duration of 48 seconds. The rate of agreement, .90, is determined by dividing the shorter duration (43) by the longer duration (48).

Shorter duration / Longer duration = 43 / 48 = .90

Interval Recording and Time Sampling

Reliability for interval recording and time sampling is established by dividing the number of intervals in which two independent observers score an occurrence of the target behavior by the total number of intervals. Depending on the behavior being observed, intervals not scored as an occurrence by at least one of the observers may be excluded from the analysis. For example, two paraprofessionals score "on-task behavior" using a whole-interval recording method. Their independent records appear as follows:

Teacher 1 + + + + + − − + − − − + − − + + + − − +
Teacher 2 − − + + + − − − − − − + − − − + + − + +

Using the less conservative method, in which all intervals are included in the denominator, they agreed on 15 of 20 intervals for a reliability level of .75. Using the more conservative method, in which intervals not scored as an occurrence by at least one observer, they agreed on 7 of 12 intervals (eight were scored as nonoccurrences by both observers) for a reliability level of .58.

Agreements / All intervals = 15 / 20 = .75

or

Agreements / Intervals scored by teacher A or B = 7 / 12 = .58

To be considered reliable, interobserver agreement rates should exceed .70 for more subtle responses (e.g., "pleasant disposition," "polite comment," or "remaining on task"). More obvious responses such as the number of "balls thrown," "papers written," or "classes attended" should produce reliability rates exceeding .80. Rates of agreement can usually be improved by clarifying the response definition (e.g., clarifying vague references, including qualifying statements, or adding discrete examples of target responses). They can also be increased by providing additional training in recognizing target behaviors and using the observational system. Finally, they can often be improved by simplifying the observational system (e.g., including fewer target responses, longer intervals during which to record, or using frequency counts rather than monitoring duration).

Initial reliability checks should be made prior to the initiation of formal data collection. This initial evaluation will provide evidence that the data collection procedure is potentially reliable during actual instructional conditions. It will also provide an estimate of the amount of time that will be required to collect data.

Reliability checks should also be made periodically during baseline and in each program condition. For most instructional purposes, it is sufficient to include reliability checks for one sixth to one tenth of all observations. If high reliability rates are noted, fewer checks may be made. Low reliability rates suggest the need for more frequent checks.

It is important to note that reliability checks should be made with each separate target behavior when more than one is used. They should also be conducted with each individual when multiple students are observed. An observational procedure that is reliable with a student who engages in the target response in a very obvious manner may not be reliable with a student whose display of the target response is more subtle. Similarly, some responses in an observational system focusing on multiple behaviors may be reliably assessed while others may yield less accurate records.

Finally, research has suggested that observers produce higher rates of agreement when they are aware that a reliability check is being made (Kent, O'Leary, Dretz, & Diament, 1979). Therefore, more conservative estimates of reliability may be obtained by arranging for covert reliability checks. Given that practical constraints may make this difficult to impossible, more frequent reliability checks may accomplish the same goal (Taplin & Reid, 1973).

Summary

It is important that we recognize that intuition is not an effective tool in making instructional decisions. Rather, when significant decisions are involved, we must act on comprehensive, objective, and reliable information. This chapter has provided a number of strategies for obtaining this information.

Data collection strategies presented in the chapter include anecdotal recording, antecedent behavior consequence recording, frequency and rate recording, permanent product recording, task analysis recording, duration and latency recording, and interval recording and time sampling. Also discussed were procedures for ensuring the reliability of observations.

Information presented in this chapter offers a range of options for collecting observational data. The predominant criterion for selecting from these options involves balancing the desirable level of precision with the cost. If a major decision will be made based on obtained data (e.g., change in placement, classification, retention, referral for pharmacological intervention), more costly and sensitive data collection procedures should be used. If decisions are less significant (e.g., assigning quarterly conduct grades, determining seating assignments, selecting instructional materials), less costly data collection procedures may be selected.

In conclusion, this chapter has provided a wide range of options for assessing student behavior. The actual procedure used by a teacher will depend on the questions he or she wishes to ask and the resources that are available.

References

Broome, S. A., & White, R. B. (1995). The many uses of videotape in classrooms serving youth with behavioral disorders. *Teaching Exceptional Children, 27*(3), 10–12.

Halle, J. W., Schloss, P. J., & Schloss, C. N. (1989). Using changing-criterion methodology to enhance the vocational performance of a developmentally disabled adult: A home-based demonstration. *Career Development of Exceptional Individuals, 12*(2), 83–95.

Helwig, J. J., Johns, J. C., Norman, J. E., & Cooper, J. O. (1976). The measurement of manuscript letter strokes. *Journal of Applied Behavior Analysis, 9*(2), 231–236.

Holman, J., & Baer, D. M. (1979). Facilitating generalization of on-task behavior through self-monitoring of academic tasks. *Journal of Autism and Developmental Disorders, 9*, 429–445.

Kazdin, A. E. (1982). *Single case research designs: Methods for clinical and applied settings.* New York: Oxford University Press.

Kent, R. N., O'Leary, D. K., Dretz, A., & Diament, C. (1979). Comparison of observational recordings in view, via mirror and via television.

Journal of Applied Behavior Analysis, 12(4), 517–522.

Lindsley, O. R. (1968). Technical note: A reliable wrist counter for recording behavior rates. *Journal of Applied Behavior Analysis, 1*, 77–78.

Mahoney, M. J. (1974). *Cognition and behavior modification.* Cambridge, MA: Ballinger.

Mathur, S. R., & Rutherford, R. B. (1994). Teaching conversational social skills to delinquent youth. *Behavioral Disorders, 19*, 294–305.

Moore, R. J., Cartledge, G., & Heckaman, K. (1995). The effects of social skill instruction and self-monitoring on game-related behaviors of adolescents with emotional or behavioral problems. *Behavioral Disorders, 20*, 253–266.

Mudford, O. C., Beale, I. L., & Singh, N. N. (1990). The representativeness of observational samples of different durations. *Journal of Applied Behavior Analysis, 23*(3), 323–333.

Schloss, P. J., Smith, M., Santora, C., & Bryant, R. (1989). A respondent conditioning approach to reducing anger responses of a dually diagnosed man with mental retardation. *Behavior Therapy, 20*(4), 459–464.

Skinner, C. H., Smith, E. S., & McLean, J. E. (1994). The effects of intertrial interval duration on sight-word learning rates in children with behavior disorders. *Behavioral Disorders, 19*, 98–107.

Smith, S. W., Siegel, E. M., O'Connor, A. M., & Thomas, S. B. (1994). Effects of cognitive-behavioral training on angry behavior and aggression of three elementary-aged students. *Behavioral Disorders, 19*, 126–135.

Taplin, P. S., & Reid, J. B. (1973). Effects of instructional set and experimenter influence on observer reliability. *Child Development, 44*, 547–554.

Tawney, J., & Gast, D. (1984). *Single subject research in special education.* Columbus, OH: Charles E. Merrill.

Wacker, D. P., & Berg, W. K. (1985). Use of peers to train and monitor the performance of adolescents with severe handicaps. *Education and Training of the Mentally Retarded, 20*(2), 109–123.

Willis, C. (1990, June). The ten mistakes to avoid with your money. *Money*, 84–94.

12

GRAPHING

It is important that you gain an understanding of each student in the classroom. This understanding enables you to anticipate your students' reactions to typical academic and social situations, as well as identify the causes of these reactions. You are also able to plan instruction and structure the classroom in a way that consistently produces achievement. Not understanding a particular child makes it difficult to match instructional plans with student interests and abilities.

Unfortunately, educational literature and policy of the past several decades may have done more to confuse our understanding of individual students than to enhance it. Theories have proliferated that offer few testable constructs. Many of these theories are not based on the actual study of individual students. As a consequence, they cloud the real relationships between specific classroom events and individual student reactions.

Prudent teachers have recognized that the only valid way to understand students is through the direct observation of their behavior. While a popular theory may be a useful starting point from which you may form hypotheses about an individual student's behavior, there is no substitute for confirming these impressions through direct observation.

Preceding chapters have provided numerous options for collecting observational data with individual students. Frequency recording, duration recording, interval recording, task analysis assessment, and other methods produce raw data from which judgments can be made. Used alone, however, these methods may fall short of providing the level of understanding sought by effective teachers.

Analyzing the effects of an applied behavior analytic intervention is at best difficult when your evidence lies in a pile of completed recording sheets. Your task becomes much easier if the data on your recording sheets are displayed in a graphic form. As the saying goes, one picture is worth a thousand words. Having graphed your data, you can then draw conclusions regarding program effectiveness. This chapter covers two very important skills. First, we discuss methods for summarizing your data graphically. Having "created the picture," we then discuss four methods by which to analyze the data to determine program effectiveness.

Methods of Graphic Display

The line graph is the most common approach for depicting applied behavior analysis data. Line graphs show the relationship between an intervention (the independent variable), which is plotted on a horizontal axis, and the target behavior (or dependent variable), which is plotted on a vertical axis.

Preparing a Line Graph

A review of applied behavior analysis research studies reveals a wide variety of approaches for constructing **line graphs.** Despite this variability, several conventions exist for charting behavioral data. The following discussion, along with Figure 12.1 reviews major conventions used in constructing simple line graphs.

X Axis

This horizontal axis generally identifies the time during which observations were made as well as the presence or absence of independent variables. Tic marks, or points along the axis, should be of equal length. This allows you to evaluate changes in student performance within a standard time frame. In the example, each tic mark represents the passage of one day. Generally, each tic mark is labeled by a number that corresponds to each data collection session. We have noticed that many teachers make one mistake. They leave spaces on the x axis to account for weekends and holidays. For example, if the first day of data collection were Monday, they would use "1" to refer to Monday, "2" to refer to Tuesday, and so on until the weekend. They would use "6" and "7" for Saturday and Sunday respectively. They leave these sessions blank on the graph since most interventions are school based and there are no data for the weekend. There is no need to leave blanks; instead, use "6" to refer to the next Monday, "7" to refer to the next Tuesday, and so on.

Y Axis

This vertical axis generally identifies the strength of the target behavior or dependent variable. As with the x axis, tic marks along the y axis should be of equal length so that changes in the scale do not obscure the visual representation of behavior strength within the scale continuum. Each tic mark on the y axis in the accompanying example represents five math problems completed correctly.

It is important to note that the y axis suggests data are comparable. We have noticed that some teachers neglect this point. To review briefly our discussion in Chapter 11, we noted that a change in the total observation time may mean your data are not comparable from day to day. For example, you may be using frequency recording to monitor the number of call-outs during school hours. You record 10 instances each on Thursday and Friday. However, Thursday was a full day of school while Friday was a half day. Because the length of the observation

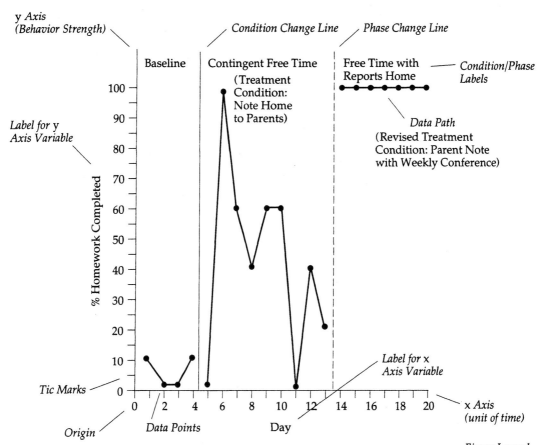

Figure 1. Percentage of Homework Completed During Baseline and Treatment Conditions

FIGURE 12.1 Conventions Used in Constructing Simple Line Graphs

changed, Thursday's data are not comparable to Friday's data. A change in the length of the observation period affects the comparability of all data, regardless of how they are collected. Bear in mind that you may need to convert all of your data to rate, percentages, or averages before graphing. As you can see in Figure 12.1, the label on the *y* axis suggests that all the permanent product data have been converted to a percentage to facilitate comparisons from one day to the next.

Origin
The point at which the *x* and *y* axes intersect is usually 0 on each scale. This point is referred to as the *origin*. In our example, the origin is the point at which 0 days intersects with 0 math problems completed correctly.

Condition or Phase Changes

Vertical lines are generally drawn separating data points collected under different conditions. Solid lines are used to note major changes in program conditions, while broken lines are used to note more subtle changes in procedures within a given condition. In our example, data collected under general instructional conditions, also referred to as **Baseline,** are separated by a solid vertical line from data collected under more specialized *Treatment Conditions.* A broken line is used to separate two variations of the treatment.

Condition or Phase Labels

These brief notations highlight the nature of the intervention or condition. In our example, the label "Baseline" is used to identify use of general instructional procedures. "Contingent Free Time" is used to identify the first phase of the new treatment. "Free Time with Reports Home" is used to identify the second phase.

Data Points

Each data point indicates the strength of the target behavior during each observation period. The first observation in our example, for example, occurred on day 1 and indicated that 10 math problems had been completed correctly. The next observation, occurring on day 2, produced 10 correct math problems.

Data Path

Contiguous data points within a phase are connected with straight lines. The data path is discontinued immediately prior to phase and condition changes. (Continuing a data path across a phase change line is another error we see teachers make frequently.) Also, a broken line may be used to connect data points separated by missing observations. The data path is the best estimate of the overall strength of behavior during a phase or condition. The more observations you conduct, the more accurately the data path represents the strength of the behavior. A data path composed of weekly samples of social behavior, for example, would not provide the same level of confidence as a data path composed of daily samples.

Supplemental Mean Lines

As an aid in interpretation, you may compute the average behavior strength for each phase or condition. Calculate the mean by summing the mean of the behavior strength in each observation and dividing by the number of observations. This value can be displayed using a horizontal line in the corresponding phase or condition, as shown on page 248.

Supplemental Trend Lines

Trend lines may also be displayed within each phase or condition to facilitate interpretation. The trend line is the best fitting straight line between points in the condition or phase. A method for producing trend lines is described later in this chapter, as shown on page 252).

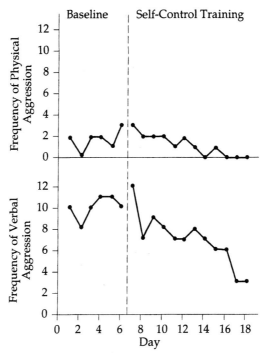

Figure 1. Effect of Self-Control Program on Physical Aggression and Verbal Aggression

FIGURE 12.2   Using Separate *Y* Axes to Chart Multiple Data Paths

Figure Key
As shown in Figures 12.2 and 12.3, graphs may include more than one type of data point and data path. For example, separate data paths may be produced on the same graph for more than one student. Also, different data paths may depict several different behaviors or observation settings for the same student. A figure key may be used to indicate differences in the data paths (see Figure 12.3 on page 246).

Legend
Applied behavior analysis graphs should include a figure legend to aid interpretation. The legend usually includes a statement of the measure used in the vertical and horizontal axis as well as any unique features in the graph.

Multielement Graphs

Line graphs can be used to compare two or more data paths over the same period. This approach is particularly useful for evaluating the relative effects of an educational procedure on two or more distinct behaviors. It may also be used to compare

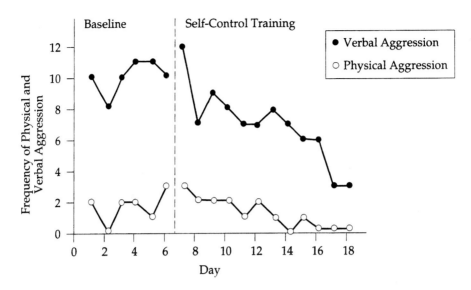

Figure 1. Effect of Self-Control Program on Physical and Verbal Aggression

FIGURE 12.3   Using a Common Y Axis to Chart Multiple Data Paths

the effects of an intervention on the same behavior in multiple settings. Finally, multiple data paths may be used to compare the performance of two or more students over the same period of time.

Two formats are commonly used to chart multiple data paths. The first is illustrated in Figure 12.2. This format involves producing separate *y* axes. Each axis includes a separate baseline for the distinct behavior, setting, or individual being monitored. The baselines each share a common *x* axis so that vertically aligned points were produced during the same data collection period. The second format involves plotting separate data paths for distinct behaviors, settings, or individuals within the same *x* and *y* axes. This format, illustrated in Figure 12.3, uses distinctive data points for each separate data path. A figure key identifies differences between the data paths.

Interpreting Graphic Displays

We noted early in this chapter that raw data are displayed graphically to aid in analysis and interpretation. Differences in baseline and treatment data may be so extreme that a casual glance at the graphic display convinces you of the efficacy of treatment. It is more likely, however, that differences are so subtle that some degree of subjective judgment must occur. Kazdin (1982) has described four criteria that can be used to analyze graphic data. Each criterion will be discussed separately.

Level

Level is the most basic method for visually inspecting graphic data. Level is determined by comparing the data point immediately preceding the phase change with the data point immediately following the phase change. Figure 12.4 illustrates the use of level. The data point immediately preceding the introduction of a punishment program denotes a high rate of self-abusive behavior. After the initiation of the punishment procedure, the behavior decreases to three occurrences. Although the behavior has not been reduced to zero, there are strong changes in the desired direction.

Measure of Central Tendency

Measures of central tendency summarize behavior strength for all individual observations within a phase. The measure of central tendency used most often is the mean, or average, which is computed by adding the individual observations in a phase and dividing by the number of observations. As shown in Figure 12.5 on page 248, the resulting value is indicated within a phase on a graph by a horizontal line. Comparing the mean performance across phases (e.g., baseline and treatment) provides an indication of the magnitude of behavior change in the phases. It is among the most objective and clear means of identifying performance differences between phases.

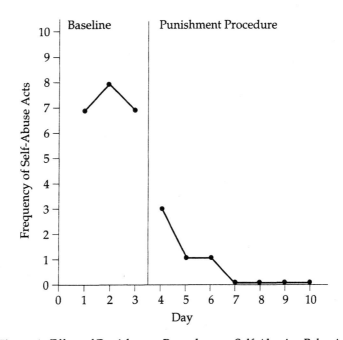

Figure 1. Effect of Punishment Procedure on Self-Abusive Behavior

FIGURE 12.4   Use of Level to Interpret a Graphic Display

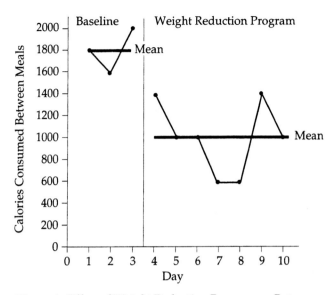

Figure 1. Effect of Weight Reduction Program on Between-Meal Calories

FIGURE 12.5 Use of Mean to Interpret a Graphic Display

Mean comparisons are particularly appropriate when data within each phase are stable and are neither ascending nor descending. Instability of data may allow one or two uncharacteristic data points to exert an excessively strong influence over the mean for the phase. A student may complete 90 percent of all assignments in each of four days. A family emergency may result in 0 percent of assignments being completed on the fifth day. Use of mean would indicate that only 72 percent of assignments were completed for the phase. This figure may not be an accurate reflection of overall performance in the phase.

The median is an alternate measure of central tendency used when data are highly variable or unstable. The median line is established by rank ordering all observation values in the phase. The number of observations is divided by two and the value for the observation occurring at that middle rank is the median observation value. In the preceding example, the median value would be 90 percent.

Ascending or descending trends in a phase present a more serious and less easily resolved problem. In one example, homework completion rates over a five-day baseline were 70, 65, 50, 65, and 50. Five observations during intervention were 45, 65, 65, 70, and 85. The difference between the 60 percent baseline mean and 66 percent intervention mean was only 6 percent. A brief review of individual data within each phase indicates that the problem was becoming more severe during baseline but improving substantially as the intervention progressed.

Measures of central tendency are not sensitive to changes in behavior strength that occur during a phase. Consequently, other methods of visual analysis must supplement measures of central tendency when changes within a phase are suspected.

Trend

Trend refers to the slope of the data path within each phase. As displayed in Figure 12.6, a data path that moves upward from left to right has an ascending trend. A data path that remains horizontal has a neutral or zero trend. A data path that moves downward from left to right has a descending trend. Data comprising either

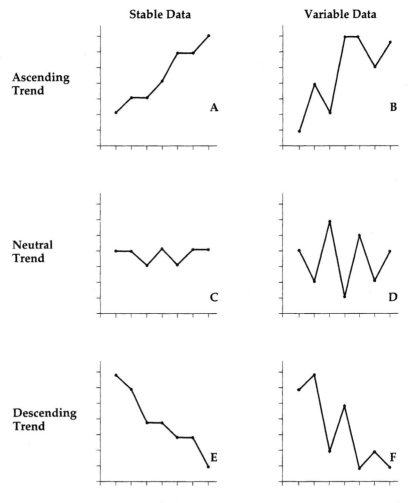

FIGURE 12.6 **Examples of Ascending, Descending, and Neutral Trends for Variable and Stable Data**

trend can be highly variable to highly stable. Variable data are dispersed widely around the trend line. Stable data fall uniformly on or around the trend line.

Consideration of the target behavior is essential if a trend line is to be interpreted correctly. For example, Scott, our young man who reacted aggressively to words with a negative connotation, was increasing his level of aggression during baseline. His data path indicated an ascending trend and resembled section A in Figure 12.6. An ascending trend for a behavior that we want to decrease indicates that an intervention is warranted. On the other hand, the number of social interactions initiated by Charlie during baseline may be increasing. There is an ascending trend evident in a behavior we hope to increase; thus, no intervention is necessary.

Similarly, you must consider the implications of a descending trend. Baseline data describing Jimmy's accuracy on homework assignments may look like section E on Figure 12.6. A descending trend for a behavior we hope to increase suggests intervention is warranted. A graph of Andrew's frequency of swearing during baseline may also illustrate a descending trend. In this example, however, no intervention is needed because Andrew's behavior is changing in the desired direction.

Even stable trend lines have implications for treatment. A high but stable baseline for a student who is self-abusing or a low but stable baseline for on-task behavior indicates that intervention programs are needed.

We compare trend lines across conditions to determine if an intervention is having the desired effect. If Scott's data paths change from an ascending trend in baseline to a descending trend in treatment, then we can have confidence in the potency of our intervention program for aggression. If Jimmy's data paths change from a descending trend during baseline to an ascending trend in treatment, then we have evidence of the success of our program to increase homework accuracy.

Sections B, D, and F in Figure 12.6 display data that are variable. In such cases, trend lines may be difficult to discern.

White and Haring (1980) described a technique for objectively charting the trend of a data path that includes the following steps:

1. Draw a vertical line through the midpoint of the phase. If an odd number of points is included in the phase, the line will cross a point. If an even number of points is included in the phase, the line will divide two points.

2. Draw a vertical line through the midpoint of each half phase created in the first step. At this point, the phase should be divided into quarters.

3. Draw horizontal lines through the median data point for the first half of the phase and the second half of the phase. If an even number of points exists in the half phases, the line will fall between two data points. If an odd number of points exists, the line will cross a single point. Data points of equal value should be treated as separate values. At this point, there should be three vertical lines (i.e., the midpoint for the phase and two midpoints for the half phases). There should also be two horizontal lines (i.e., median points for each half phase). The two midpoints for the half phases should intersect at a right angle with the two median points for each half phase.

4. Draw a slope line through the intersections of the midpoints of the half phases and the median points for the half phases.

5. The *quarter intersect line* (Koening, 1972) just completed provides an accurate assessment of the trend within the phase. To also indicate the entry and exit level of performance in the phase, White and Haring (1980) suggest constructing a split middle line. This line is parallel to the quarter intersect line and has an equal number of points above and below.

Figure 12.7 on page 252 illustrates the steps used to construct a split middle line for establishing the trend of a data path.

Latency

Latency is the period of time that elapses between the start of intervention and the start of a performance change. A brief latency is indicated by an immediate change in level upon introduction of the intervention. A longer latency is indicated by an extended period of time elapsing from the onset of intervention to a change in trend or level. Figure 12.8 on page 253 illustrates both a brief latency and an extended latency.

Charting Social Comparison Data

It is often important to know not only how well a particular student is performing, but how he or she compares to others. Knowing that a preschooler has reduced soiling incidents from daily to an average of once in nine days is useful. Equally useful, however, is the rate of soiling expected for a child her age. Social comparison procedures discussed in Chapter 3 provide an avenue through which teachers can establish and graphically depict performance comparisons between a target student and his or her peers.

The following steps are used to chart social comparison data on a line graph:

1. Graphically display the target student's performance using a line graph.

2. Identify a small sample (6 to 20) of students against which the target student's performance is to be compared. These may be age-matched peers in regular education, or other individuals whose performance provides a standard for appropriate performance.

3. Collect data on each of the sample students for one or more observation periods. Behavior that occurs more frequently and with greater stability permits a smaller sample and fewer observations. Behavior that occurs less frequency and with greater variability requires a larger sample and more frequent observations. To demonstrate the procedure, we collected the following weekly participation frequencies for nine high-school students in an algebra class: 6, 10, 12, 12, 14, 18, 22, 24, and 26.

4. Compute the mean performance level for the sample by adding the value for each observation and dividing by the number of observations. In our example, the sum of the observation values is 144 and the mean is 16.

5. Compute the mean deviation by subtracting each observation value from the mean, adding the absolute value of these numbers, and dividing by the number of

1. Vertical Line through Midpoint of Phase

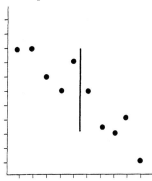

2. Vertical Line through Midpoint of Half Phase

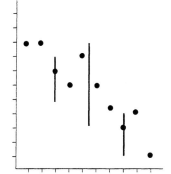

3. Horizontal Line through Median of Half Phase

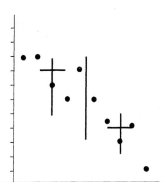

4. Slope Line through Intersection of Midpoint Line and Median Point Line

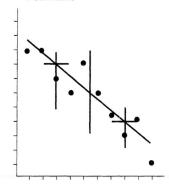

5. Split Middle Line Constructed Parallel to Slope Line

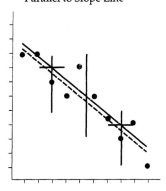

FIGURE 12.7   Procedures for Constructing a Split Middle Line Used in Establishing the Trend in a Data Path

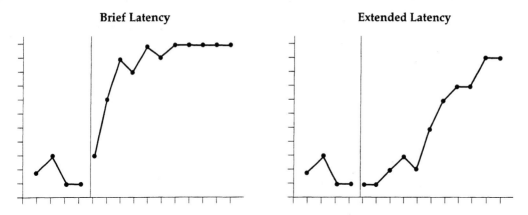

Brief Latency   Extended Latency

FIGURE 12.8   Examples of a Brief and Extended Latency between Phases
of an Intervention Program

observations. In our example, the absolute values for the difference between the
mean and each observation are as follows: 10, 6, 4, 4, 2, 2, 6, 8, and 10. The sum of
the deviations from the mean is 52 and the mean deviation is 5.8.

  6. Graphically display the mean and mean deviation for the sample by drawing
solid horizontal lines on the graph at the mean (16) and broken lines at the mean plus
one mean deviation (21.8), and the mean minus one deviation (10.2). Figure 12.9 on
page 254 illustrates the graphic display of these data.

A Sample Analysis of Graphed Data

We have discussed four methods you can use to determine the effectiveness of an
applied behavior analytic program. Although we presented them separately, we
believe all four methods should be applied jointly when evaluating graphed data.
You would probably be very upset if your grade in a course were determined by a
final exam that contained only one item. Similarly, it is unfair to judge the effectiveness of an applied behavior analytic program based on any single method. We recommend that you consider the nature of the target behavior (should it increase or
decrease?) and the specific applied behavior analytic techniques you are using
(e.g., a shaping program will take time to work; PAC should work very quickly) as
you use all four methods. It is possible that these procedures will yield inconsistent
results that must be interpreted carefully. For example, in Chapter 8 we discussed
extinction and warned that its use may temporarily increase rather than decrease
a target behavior. This extinction burst will probably mean that the level of treatment will be higher when it should have been lower. It may result in the mean of
treatment exceeding the mean of baseline. It will also increase latency, indicating
that the program took a long time to start working. These three outcomes may suggest that extinction is not working. It is only through an analysis of trend that the

Figure 1. Frequency of Algebra Participation for Mainstreamed Students and Social Comparison Data

FIGURE 12.9   Graphic Display of Social Comparison Data

effectiveness of an extinction program will be confirmed. The baseline trend will probably be ascending in the wrong direction while the intervention trend will be descending in the desired direction

Let's evaluate the data presented in Figure 12.10 for an intervention designed for Gary. He called out rather than raising his hand, a behavior we want to decrease. A DRO and a token economy were used to change his behavior.

Level

We can see that the data point preceding the implementation of DRO was 7. The data point following the intervention was 3. As we had hoped, behavior decreased upon implementation of the program.

Mean

During baseline, there was an average rate of 5 call-outs per hour. During treatment, this average decreased to an average rate of 1.75 call-outs per hour. Again, we hoped for this outcome.

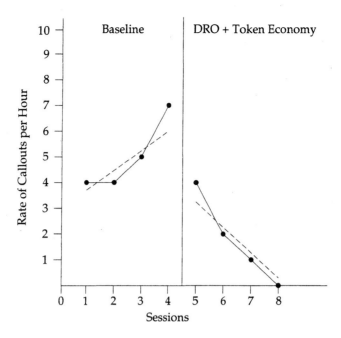

FIGURE 12.10 Hypothetical Data for Gary

Trend

There is an ascending trend in the baseline data, indicating that the behavior is getting worse in the absence of an intervention. The treatment phase is characterized by a descending trend, further evidence of the program's success. We can also draw a best fitting straight line for each phase (indicated on Figure 12.10 by a broken line, for clarity).

Latency

Two opinions may be voiced regarding the results of an analysis of latency. On day 5, the first day of treatment, there is an immediate change in behavior in the desired direction. It could be argued that latency is short, that is, one day. On the other hand, it could be argued that two days were required before the treatment data were lower than baseline data. This latter method is a more conservative interpretation.

Summary

Early in this chapter we highlighted the importance of understanding each student in a classroom. We noted that observational procedures and the raw data they produce represent an effective step in gaining this understanding. We also noted that graphic displays of the raw data assist the teacher in summarizing and interpreting the data. Based on this rationale, the balance of the chapter included a discussion of conventions used in displaying observational data.

The line graph was described as having the greatest utility for graphing observational data. Although numerous variations exist, the simple line graph includes the following elements: a horizontal or *x* axis on which the time and program condition is plotted; a vertical or *y* axis on which the measure of behavior strength is plotted; condition or phase change lines and labels; data points comprising the data path; mean and trend lines; a figure key; and legend. More complex line graphs may include multiple data paths, with each representing a different behavior, setting, or individual. They may also include multiple *y* axes for distinct behaviors, settings, or individuals. For a majority of classroom applications the *y* axis is best scaled using equal units.

Four variables were discussed for interpreting graphic data. Level involves comparing data points immediately before and after the phase change. Measures of central tendency summarize behavior strength within each phase. Mean may be used when data are stable. When data are highly variable, median may produce a more accurate summary of behavior strength within the phase. Trend is the slope of the data within a phase; it indicates if the response being graphed is improving, worsening, or remaining neutral within the phase. Finally, latency is the period of time from the start of a phase to evidence of change in the target behavior. It is important to highlight that accurate interpretation of graphic data requires that all four criteria be considered simultaneously. The strongest evidence of an effect is available when all criteria indicate the effect.

Finally, we emphasized the importance of knowing how a particular student's performance compares to a socially significant standard. We described a method for obtaining and displaying social comparison data. The method involves briefly observing a sample of more capable students. Data from the sample are summarized using mean and mean deviation. The mean for the group is plotted on the *y* axis of the target student's performance graph. Also, a range of plus and minus one mean deviation is plotted.

We have described major strategies for displaying observational data. Methods for visually inspecting and interpreting these data were highlighted so that differences in performance across phases could be identified. Finally, we emphasized the interpretation of changes in performance within the context of its social importance.

References

Kazdin, A. E. (1982). *Single-case research designs: Methods for clinical and applied settings.* New York: Oxford University Press.

Koening, C. H. (1972). *Charting the future course of behavior.* Unpublished doctoral dissertation, University of Kansas.

White, O. R., & Haring, N. G. (1980). *Exceptional teaching* (2nd ed.). Columbus, OH: Merrill.

13

SINGLE-CASE EXPERIMENTAL DESIGNS

The preceding chapters provide a method for assessing the effects of educational interventions on the behavior of students. Chapter 11 identified a number of data collection methods that objectively report the strength of student behavior under certain conditions. Chapter 12 included a discussion of methods for displaying and interpreting data. The focus of both chapters was limited to case study or baseline-treatment methodology.

Baseline-treatment methods are effective in demonstrating that one or more students are meeting performance objectives. They are not effective, however, in determining whether the specific educational program was responsible for the change. A number of single-case experimental designs have been developed that overcome problems with baseline-treatment methodology. These designs allow us to be confident of the effect of an intervention on the target behavior. The most widely used single-case experimental designs will be discussed following a more detailed analysis of case study methodology.

Case Study Methodology

Case study methodology involves observing and recording the responses of an individual during a no-treatment phase. This phase is called a baseline (A) and it is similar to a pretest. Data are collected for a period of days until they are stable and give a picture of the individual's current level of performance. Once the baseline is stable, an intervention (B) phase is initiated (Hersen & Barlow, 1976). You expect performance to have improved in the intervention phase when contrasted with the baseline phase.

Several factors recommend the case study method for most educational purposes. First, case study is an objective method for assessing performance changes. Reliability tests of the measurement system assure you that graphs actually depict the strength of student responses over time. Second, case study is an efficient means of assessing student performance changes. In most cases, data can be collected with little effort. Charting requires no special skills, and the resulting graphs can be easily interpreted. Third, the case study method is well suited to a variety of academic and social performance problems. You can record the results of daily assignments, disruptive social responses, attendance checks, or any other response of importance to a student's adjustment. Finally, the case study method can serve as a foundation for more complex analytic methods. Results of a case study analysis can suggest additional questions to be addressed using expanded observation and intervention methods.

Internal Validity and Case Study Methodology

The major limitation of case study methodology is its ineffectiveness in establishing the internal validity of results. **Internal validity** allows direct and causal relationships to be established between implementation of an intervention program and subsequent changes in student performance (Cook & Campbell, 1979). Well-designed applied behavior analysis demonstrations rule out **threats to internal validity,** or alternative explanations for performance changes. More simply, they allow you to establish a functional relationship and verify that the only reason a student's behavior changed was because an intervention program was implemented. The designs that will be discussed later are effective in ruling out threats to internal validity and increasing your confidence in the impact of your program.

Case study data permit us to determine the rate of student progress and the extent of gain over baseline. Case studies, however, do not control for threats to internal validity. Therefore, we cannot confidently state that changes in student performance were solely the result of the intervention procedure. Any number of alternative explanations may have been responsible for the change in student performance.

Campbell and Stanley (1963) have offered an extensive discussion of possible threats to internal validity, which are listed in Table 13.1. The first two threats are particularly relevant to applied behavior analysis interventions.

History

Kazdin (1980) has defined history "as any event...other than the treatment approach, that may account for the results" (p. 34). Examples of history cited by Kazdin include a power failure, medical emergency, fire drill, or a change in classroom. In general, any condition that may alter performance and be mistaken for treatment effects can be categorized under the heading of history. It is important to note that history does not include experiences of the individual prior to treatment.

We know a teacher who developed an intervention program that included differential reinforcement and restitution for a youth who had assaulted another individual. Baseline data revealed a high rate of both physical and verbal aggression. Shortly after intervention, the rate of aggression dropped to near zero occurrences. The teacher attributed the results to the intervention program. Unknown to the teacher, however, the youth's parents provided severe restrictions as a result of the initial incident. In addition, the youth's father beat him severely and threatened

TABLE 13.1   Threats to Internal Validity

Campbell and Stanley (1963) described the following threats to internal validity.

History: Events other than intervention that may account for the results.

Maturation: Factors within the individual (e.g., growth, development, etc.) that may account for the results.

Testing: Effects that occur as a result of repeated assessment.

Instrumentation: Results attributable to changing standards of measurement.

Regression: Changes due to movement of extreme scores to the mean.

Selection bias: Results that can be attributed to unfair selection procedures.

Attrition: Results that are influenced by select subjects dropping out of the program.

Treatment diffusion: Obscuring results by inadvertently providing treatment when general conditions should prevail.

similar treatment if future bad reports were received at home. Although the differential reinforcement and restitution program may have had an impact, it is likely that the parents' treatment of the child was at least partially responsible for changes associated with the onset of intervention. This case illustrates how the effects of history can obscure the relationship between treatment and a behavior change.

Maturation

Christensen (1980) has defined maturation as "changes in the internal conditions of the individual as a function of the passage of time...including both biological and psychological processes such as age, learning, fatigue, boredom, and hunger, which are not related to specific external events but reside within the individual" (p. 97). As noted by Kazdin (1980), history and maturation frequently operate together to mask apparent treatment effects.

We know a teacher who had been working with a preschooler on a variety of fine motor skills. She provided many opportunities for the student to use her hands, including drawing, painting, working with clay, and limited handwriting. The following September, the paraprofessional assigned to the teacher noticed that the student's manuscript writing had improved enormously. She attributed these gains to the teacher's efforts the previous academic year. As much as the teacher would like to have taken credit for the student's progress, she recognized that the gains probably had more to do with Mother Nature than any instructional program. The preschooler had simply matured over the summer break.

Case Study versus Experimental Designs

Single-case experimental designs, also referred to as *intrasubject replication designs* or single-subject designs, have been developed to exclude threats to internal validity. Intrasubject replication is derived from the method through which internal validity is established. A case study method includes one baseline phase and one treatment phase. At best, it can only suggest the possibility that a change in behavior occurred because an intervention was provided. For example, Bill works harder when provided specific incentives. The certainty of this relationship is not assured because of threats to internal validity. Bill may work harder because he has matured during treatment. He may also work harder because of extra attention provided by the teacher.

Replication can rule out the threats to internal validity. During the initial baseline, Bill worked very slowly. After incentives were provided, his work rate increased. To replicate, the teacher removed the incentives and noted that Bill's work rate decreased. The teacher again provided incentives and observed Bill's work rate increase. In this example, the two replications of the effect of incentives over baseline reduce the likelihood that maturation, history, or other factors influenced Bill's performance. The more replications that occur, the more confidence the teacher may have in the effectiveness of incentives.

A number of intrasubject replication designs have been described in the professional literature. The selection of a given design may be based on the instructional setting, student, target behavior, and specific questions being addressed by the investigation. Four major intrasubject replication designs will be briefly described in the following sections. The reader is encouraged to refer to a text dedicated exclusively to intrasubject replication designs for a more detailed discussion (Kazdin, 1980; Neuman & McCormick, 1995).

Reversal Designs

The **reversal design** is also designated by the letters A-B-A or A-B-A-B in which A represents baseline and B represents intervention. As is shown in Figure 13.1, replication occurs by systematically introducing and removing the treatment. The reversal design provides the most pragmatic and compelling demonstration of the effect of treatment over baseline. As will be discussed later, it provides the strongest defense against threats to internal validity when multiple reversals are used (e.g., A-B-A-B-A-B...).

A convincing A-B-A pattern begins with the A phase. Ideally, there is a stable level of behavior during baseline. This level can be high and stable for an undesirable behavior, or low and stable for a desirable behavior. When the intervention program is implemented during the B phase, the behavior should change in the desired direction. The trend should ascend for a behavior we want to increase or it should descend for a behavior we want to decrease.

The next phase, the second baseline phase, includes a return to the initial baseline response rate. The final phase, the second treatment phase, produces a return to the level of responding noted in the initial treatment phase. Repeated demonstrations of the influence of the intervention increase our confidence in its effectiveness.

Internal Validity and the Reversal Design

The reversal design rules out the effects of maturation and history by showing that the behavior change *only* occurs with the introduction or withdrawal of treatment. The more times this effect is replicated, the less likely that maturation and history are

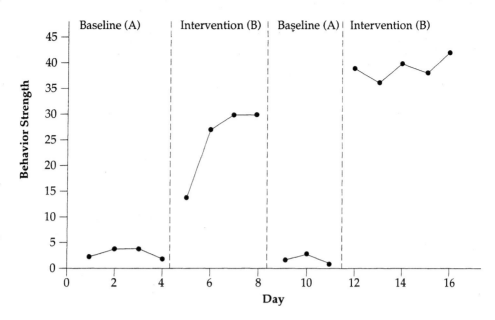

FIGURE 13.1   Reversal Design

causing the effects. Internal validity is further strengthened by dramatic changes in the trend, level, and mean of the dependent variable or target behavior following each phase change. A change that is subtle or that has a longer latency makes the results difficult to interpret. It is possible that any change could be the result of other factors.

Procedures

As noted above, the reversal design can include three or more phases. The minimum requirement of one replication occurs in an A-B-A design as the effect of treatment is contrasted with two separate baselines. The applied literature, however, emphasizes the importance of returning to a second treatment phase (A-B-A-B) because of the increased confidence that results from the added replication. More important, the A-B-A-B design concludes during an effective treatment while the A-B-A design concludes during a countertherapeutic baseline (Kazdin, 1982). Few teachers would agree to let a behavior reverse to and stay at baseline levels.

The first step in an A-B-A-B design requires you to conduct a prebaseline assessment of the student to identify a treatment that is likely to be effective. Prebaseline assessment may include the development of an effective task analysis, the identification of contingency relationships that are likely to be reinforcing or punishing, and the identification of provoking or supportive antecedents. The prebaseline assessment should also produce objectives for the intervention. Since the reversal design generally includes only one target behavior, there is likely to be only one objective (e.g., reduction of verbal aggression or increase in homework completion).

Second, you need to define behavior objectively and develop a recording system. Procedures were described in Chapter 11 for constructing and using a recording system. Special attention is given to assessing the reliability of measurement. A reliable observation system rules out instrumentation as a threat to internal validity. Also, data must be collected continuously, that is, before and during implementation of your program.

Third, you collect baseline data. Kazdin (1982) recommended that baseline data be collected until there is clear evidence of the natural strength of the target behavior. In most cases, three to five baseline days are sufficient. Ideally, the data should be relatively stable or going in the undesired direction. For example, you may record 10, 9, 12, 13, and 14 instances of swearing by Andrew during five days of baseline. If you were to graph these data, you would see an ascending trend. This trend is acceptable during baseline because it is contratherapeutic, that is, going in the wrong direction. However, 14, 13, 12, 10, and 9 instances of swearing over a five-day period would produce a descending trend when graphed. If you intervened on the sixth day, you would have no way of knowing if any additional improvements were the result of your program or the natural progression of Andrew's behavior. If your data are not stable or if they are moving in a therapeutic direction during baseline, simply collect more data.

Once you are satisfied that baseline data accurately represent the natural strength of the target behavior, you may begin the fourth step and intervene. As with baseline, this treatment phase should continue until the strength of the target response under treatment is apparent. The effect of intervention on the target response may be clear after only a few days of treatment. The treatment phase should continue until data are stable or moving in the desired direction.

Fifth, you need to return to baseline. To the extent possible, conditions during this baseline should be identical to those in the initial baseline period. Changes not directly related to the study (e.g., using new curriculum materials, introducing new staff members, changing diet) should occur in the middle of a baseline or treatment phase so that their effects (if any) are not confused with the effects of the phase change.

Applications of the A-B-A-B Design

The professional literature contains numerous examples of the use of the A-B-A-B design. It has been used to show the relationships between the application of a variety of independent variables and subsequent changes in dependent variables.

An A-B-A-B design can be used with ease in the classroom. We have mentioned Andrew's penchant for swearing. This behavior does not shock you but it does disrupt your class and you know that someday he will encounter an adult who is not as understanding. In accordance with the steps we just discussed, you conduct a prebaseline analysis, noting that Andrew swears when he is frustrated or angry. You also note that Andrew enjoys playing computer games. After considering all the options, you decide to combine a DRO program with praise and a token economy to reinforce periods of no swearing, and reprimands and response cost to punish each instance of swearing. The tokens that he earns for periods of no swearing can be exchanged for computer time. Next, you establish an objective and select frequency recording as the measurement system. Third, you collect baseline data, and note that he swore 10, 9, 12, 13, and 14 times over five consecutive days. Your graph illustrates an ascending trend in the data, which is acceptable during baseline because it is contratherapeutic. You implement the intervention package on the sixth day, continuing to collect and graph data. Seven days later, Andrew is no longer swearing. To verify the functional relationship between the application of the intervention program and the reduction in swearing, you withdraw the intervention program and return to baseline conditions. Within four days, Andrew is swearing again. This is sufficient evidence of a functional relationship. Not wanting to leave Andrew in baseline condition, however, you again start using the intervention program. The frequency of swearing decreases to zero.

You can also use an A-B-A-B design to evaluate the effectiveness of an applied behavior analytic program that increases behavior. For example, you could test the impact of a contract on homework completion.

Advantages and Disadvantages

The major advantage of the A-B-A-B design is its strength in ruling out threats to internal validity. As noted previously, it may be the most convincing applied behavior analysis design (Hersen & Barlow, 1976). Also, the reversal design is very practical. The design is employed by simply applying and removing a specific intervention. Conclusions are drawn by noting the effect of these manipulations on the target behavior.

Despite the strength and simplicity of the design, other factors limit its usefulness in educational settings. Most notably, withdrawing a potentially effective intervention may not serve the best interests of the learner. In more extreme cases, reversal to baseline may not be ethical. For example, the initial intervention phase may reduce the rate of self-abusive behaviors of a learner with severe disabilities from an average of eight a day to no occurrences. Since the self-abusive responses threaten the health and safety of the student, returning to baseline with an associated increase in self-abusive behavior may result in unwarranted injury.

A second limitation is that many responses developed through applied behavior analysis interventions may not be subject to reversal. A student who learns to use social skills during an initial intervention phase is likely to continue to use these behaviors even when training is discontinued and baseline reinstated. While you may be pleased that the new responses maintain in the absence of intervention, failure to replicate (e.g., demonstrate a convincing pattern of high rates of social skills during intervention and low rates during baseline) reduces confidence that the social skill training strategy was responsible for the effect.

Extensions

Reversal designs include any demonstration in which one set of conditions (e.g., a baseline) is alternated with other sets of conditions. The number of replications and order of replications can be varied to suit the purpose of the demonstration. As we noted earlier, the basic design may include only three phases (A-B-A). Montee, Miltenberger, and Wittrock (1995) used this design to conduct an experimental analysis of facilitated communication. Since ending a potentially effective intervention in baseline is of questionable social validity, the design is generally extended to an additional treatment phase (A-B-A-B). In areas where the effects of treatment are very modest, additional replications may be used to strengthen the case against threats to internal validity (A-B-A-B-A-B). Finally, you may initiate the intervention with treatment and reverse to baseline with a subsequent return to treatment (B-A-B). This modification is particularly appropriate for evaluating the effect of existing interventions.

Multiple Baseline Designs

The **multiple baseline design** is effective in overcoming the two major limitations of the reversal design since a return to baseline is not required to demonstrate experimental control. As depicted in Figure 13.2, replication in the multiple baseline design occurs by repeatedly demonstrating the effect of a program on several responses or people, or in several settings (Kazdin, 1980, 1982).

The multiple baseline across behaviors design is used by collecting baseline data for three or more responses at the same time with the same individual. For example, you may want to see how social skills training influences a student's ability to give compliments, accept criticisms, or ask questions. Once stability is achieved in all baselines, an intervention is initiated with one of the responses. The other two continue under baseline conditions. It is assumed that the strength of the first behavior will increase (or decrease) under treatment. Once it reaches the desired level and is again stable, the treatment is applied to the second behavior (this forms the first replication). When the second response reaches the desired level and is stable, the treatment is applied to the third response (this forms the second replication). The more responses included in the multiple baseline, the more replications are possible and the stronger the demonstration.

The multiple baseline across students design is similar except that baseline data are collected for one response each with three or more students. For example, you may want to measure the impact of DRO on three students who swear. Once stability in each baseline is achieved, treatment is initiated with one learner. The other students continue under baseline conditions. When the response level of the first student reaches the desired level, treatment is applied to the second student (this forms the first replication). When the behavior of the second student reaches the desired level, treatment is applied to the third student (this forms the second replication). The more students included in the demonstration, the more replications possible and the stronger the demonstration.

The multiple baseline across settings design follows the same pattern established for other multiple baseline designs except that the same response of one individual is observed in three or more settings. For example, you may want to see

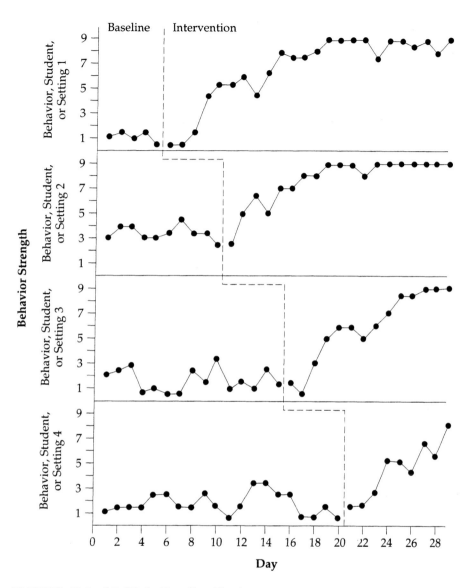

FIGURE 13.2   Multiple Baseline Design

if a self-monitoring program works in study hall, the school library, and the resource room. Initial intervention focuses on the response in the first setting and then shifts to the second setting. Finally, intervention is focused on the behavior in the third setting. As with the other variations, three settings provide for two replications of the effect occurring in the first settings. Additional settings provide for more replications and increase the strength of the demonstration.

Internal Validity and the Multiple Baseline Design

The effects of maturation and history are ruled out in the multiple baseline across students and settings designs by demonstrating that behavior strength changes only when treatment is introduced with the new individual or skill or in the new setting. Maturation and history are ruled out in the multiple baseline across behaviors design by demonstrating that the effect of a procedure is replicated with other responses. As noted earlier, the greater the number of replications across students, settings, or responses, the stronger the demonstration. Also, the more sizable the change in trend, level, and mean for the target response, the less likely that maturation and history are responsible for the behavior changes.

Procedures

As noted previously, the multiple baseline design should include three or more baselines. It can technically include only two baselines; however, the single replication produced by this version of the design provides limited evidence of a functional relationship (Hersen & Barlow, 1976).

The initial step in developing a multiple baseline design involves conducting a prebaseline assessment, which should suggest one or more specific target behaviors that require intervention, settings in which the behavior change is desirable, or additional individuals that would benefit from treatment. The prebaseline analysis should also suggest specific intervention approaches that are likely to be effective. These may include modeling and prompting procedures, reinforcement or punishment procedures, or other social learning methods.

The preceding analysis will help you decide which variation of the multiple baseline design will be most efficient. For example, a multiple baseline across students design may be used when several individuals need the same intervention. A multiple baseline across settings design may be selected when it is desirable to modify a student's responses in several classes or areas. Finally, a multiple baseline across behaviors design may be selected when it appears necessary to influence several objectives.

Having completed the prebaseline analysis, you next need to develop a recording system matched to the behaviors, settings, and/or individuals to be studied. You should ensure that the system produces a reliable record of behavior strength by using procedures described in Chapter 11. Equally important, the recording system must be applied continuously through the investigation. Failing to collect data for even brief intervals through the study may introduce threats to internal validity. This is particularly true if missing data appear immediately prior to or following the introduction of treatment in one of the baselines.

Third, collect baseline data. The same considerations for collecting baseline data in the reversal design apply to the multiple baseline design. Specifically, at least three observations must be made. Observations should continue until zero acceleration exists (i.e., neither an ascending nor descending trend). In some cases, intervention may begin during a countertherapeutic trend. Finally, when the response strength is highly variable, additional observations should be made.

Fourth, apply the intervention to the first leg of the multiple baseline. Depending on design, this may be the first behavior, setting, or individual. Generally, the first application of the intervention involves the person, behavior, or setting for which the target behavior is most problematic. Once the impact of the intervention on the target behavior in the first leg is clear (i.e., behavior strength in the first leg increases as evidenced by a change in level, mean, and/or trend), intervention may be applied to the second leg. Again, once the impact of intervention on this leg is apparent, intervention may be applied to the third leg.

It is important that changes in the educational program not directly related to the intervention approach not be initiated at the same time as intervention is introduced in any legs of the multiple baseline. These changes can occur in the middle of baseline or treatment phases as their effects will not be evidenced at the same time as the expected effects resulting from treatment.

An Example of Multiple Baseline Designs

A multiple baseline across behaviors design was used by Moore, Cartledge, and Heckaman (1995) to evaluate the effects of social skill training an a variety of game-related behaviors. A multiple baseline across settings design has been used by Smith, Siegel, O'Connor, and Thomas (1994) used a multiple baseline across students design to evaluate the impact of cognitive-behavioral training on angry behavior and aggression.

We have made many references throughout this text to a student named Scott. Scott's teacher used a multiple baseline design to show the impact of a DRO program on his aggressive responses to words with a negative connotation. First, she conducted a prebaseline analysis during which she noticed that Scott displayed this behavior in the evenings and weekends at the dorm of the residential center where he lived. The problem was even worse on the weekends because fewer staff were available to deal with the aggression. Medical sedation was used frequently. After her observations, his teacher made several adjustments in her classroom, such as revising her rules and developing a schedule. She also decided to teach social skills and relaxation training. She developed a consequence control package that included DRO, social reinforcement, a token economy, response cost, and the 10 Rs (see Chapters 9 and 10). Finally, she decided to use a multiple baseline across settings intervention and obtained the cooperation of residential staff.

Second, Scott's teacher developed a duration recording system. She and the residential staff used it to collect data for several days in all three settings. Third, after examining the data, school was selected as the first setting for intervention. The program was put into place only at school; however, Scott's teacher and the staff continued to collect data in all three settings. After a short period of time, aggression decreased during school hours. It continued to be high at the dorm after school and on weekends. At this point, Scott's teacher had some indication of a functional relationship, but stronger evidence was needed. The program was then used in the dorm after school hours. A short time later, a decrease in aggression was noted in this setting as well, although it still occurred frequently on the weekends. Finally, the intervention program was implemented by the weekend staff and a decrease in aggression was noted. Visual inspection of the graphed data indicated to Scott's teacher that there was a functional relationship between implementation of the applied behavior analytic program and a decrease in aggression. Specifically, aggression decreased in each setting only after the program was implemented.

As is the case for A-B-A-B designs, multiple baseline designs can be used to increase behavior. For example, you can use a multiple baseline design to evaluate the impact of assertiveness training on three different students.

Advantages and Disadvantages

The multiple baseline design is effective in ruling out threats to internal validity without requiring the withdrawal of treatment. As emphasized above, replication occurs by repeated demonstration of an effect on several behaviors or people. Repeated demonstrations may also occur in several settings.

A related advantage is that the multiple baseline design is well suited to complex educational problems in which gradual progress is expected. You may plan to reduce aggressive responses of a disruptive youth over a period of several months by beginning with verbal aggression, moving to object aggression, and concluding with physical aggression. Also, the multiple baseline across settings design allows you to "pilot" a method prior to encouraging others in additional settings to use the method.

A major limitation of a multiple baseline design relates to its complexity. Failure to produce an effect in any leg of the multiple baseline design can reduce confidence that threats to internal validity have been ruled out. These failures often occur because of factors outside of your control. For example, a student selected for a multiple baseline across students design may withdraw midway through the study. While two other students may have benefited from the experimental method, loss of the third learner results in only a single replication. Similarly, another teacher responsible for implementing treatment in one setting of a multiple baseline across settings design may fail to conscientiously administer the experimental procedure. Again, while two other teachers/settings were effective, loss of the third limits the analysis. As will be discussed in the next section, use of four or more legs in the multiple baseline may guard against this problem.

A second limitation is that the multiple baseline design requires a student to spend an extended period of time under baseline conditions. Assuming six days in baseline for a multiple baseline across students design with four legs, the final student will remain in baseline for 18 days prior to intervention. Erratic baseline patterns or therapeutic trends during baseline may further extend this period.

A final limitation is that some responses may generalize across legs of the multiple baseline. Improvement that occurs prior to the introduction of treatment may be viewed as being the result of history or maturation. Using the preceding example, initial attention to verbal aggression may also reduce the other forms of aggression. While you may believe that the treatment of verbal aggression had a more general effect than anticipated, a critic may suggest that changes in all three baselines were the result of factors outside of the experimental treatment such as increased attention or the child growing older.

Extensions

The most obvious extension of the multiple baseline design involves the number of legs that may be included in the analysis. We have suggested that you use a minimum of three legs. It is desirable, however, for you to include four or more legs to add strength to the demonstration. They also serve as a hedge against the loss of one or more individuals in an across students design; the failure of a behavior to change in alternate classes in an across settings design; or the failure of the treatment to impact a response in an across behaviors design. Several investigators have used more than three legs when using multiple baseline designs, including Lockart and Law (1994), Miller and Kelley (1994), and Shapiro and McCurdy (1989).

A reversal may be included in one or more legs of the design when less than convincing replications occur (Dapcich-Miura & Hovel, 1979). We noted earlier that a return to baseline may not be desirable for some responses. However, when appropriate, the use of a reversal within a leg of the multiple baseline design adds a replication and increases confidence that threats to internal validity have been ruled out.

Changing Criterion Design

The **changing criterion design** rules out threats to internal validity by repeatedly demonstrating that a student's responses improve each time the criterion for reinforcement is elevated. In general, you establish baseline for the target behavior and then set a criterion for reinforcement slightly higher than that level. As the behavior consistently meets the established level, choose a second more stringent level for reinforcement. This constitutes the first replication. Once the student's performance meets the second criterion, choose a third, more stringent criterion. This process continues, with each criterion change representing a new replication. The study is completed when the strength of the student's behavior meets or exceeds the goal level for the intervention program. A changing criterion design with six replications is presented in Figure 13.3 on page 270.

Internal Validity and the Changing Criterion Design

The changing criterion design rules out the effects of maturation and history by showing that the behavior repeatedly increased to meet successively more stringent criteria for reinforcement. The more times the behavior is elevated in response to a criterion change, the more convincing the demonstration. Other elements of the changing criterion design support the control of the educational procedure over the target behavior. The larger the criterion changes and the closer the corresponding response level over the preceding response level, the more evident the

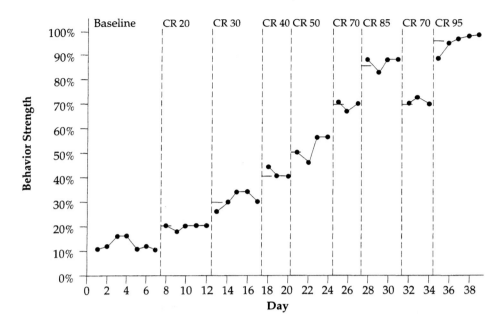

FIGURE 13.3   Changing Criterion Design

effect of the intervention. Also, the more irregular the pattern of criterion changes and corresponding behavior levels, the stronger the demonstration.

Procedures

As with all single-case experimental methods, the changing criterion design is initiated by conducting a prebaseline analysis. Of particular concern is the identification of a target behavior and the overall goal for the intervention program. Once identified, you can develop an observation system using frequency, duration, interval or other recording methods described in Chapter 11 to record the target behavior. The prebaseline analysis should also suggest reinforcers that are likely to promote the target response. Since the changing criterion design requires the repeated demonstration of the effect of reinforcement on successively higher levels of responding, the identification of a potent reinforcer is critical to the success of the design. Finally, the prebaseline analysis may suggest the size of each criterion change.

The second step in using the changing criterion design involves collecting baseline data for three to five days. Substantial variability in the target behavior suggests that observations should continue until a stable baseline is achieved.

Third, an interim criterion should be selected. The first criterion should be established once baseline accurately reflects the target behavior's natural strength. Depending on the desired outcome, the criterion should be higher or lower than the overall mean for baseline as well as the last several data points prior to the criterion change. In general, the greater the change in the criterion over the baseline level, the stronger the demonstration.

Fourth, implement the applied behavior analytic program. Once the student's responses are stable with zero acceleration and continuously meet or exceed the first criterion, a second criterion can be introduced. Again, this criterion should be substantially different from the mean response level for the preceding criterion. It should also be substantially different from the last several points under the initial criterion. This process should continue until the level of the behavior reaches the preestablished goal. As noted earlier, the larger the number of criterion changes, the stronger the demonstration.

Hartmann and Hall (1976) provide several procedures for enhancing the internal and external validity of the design. First, consistent with the preceding recommendations, phase changes should be of sufficient length to demonstrate stability in the level of responding. Second, baseline data should be longer than each separate treatment phase, and the treatment phase lengths should be variable. This provision ensures that behavior changes can be attributed to stepwise changes in the criterion and not the result of serendipitous synchronization of the natural behavior rate to criterion changes. Third, larger criterion shifts and longer phases should be used when response levels are highly variable. Finally, you may return to a less stringent criterion prior to the final criterion change. The corresponding response reduction and the subsequent increase when a higher criterion is reinstated add strength to conclusions.

An Example of the Changing Criterion Design

Many investigators have used a changing criterion design to evaluate the effectiveness of a program (Johnson & McLaughlin, 1982; Schloss, Sedlak, Elliot, & Smothers, 1982). It can be used to evaluate many classroom programs as well, such as differential reinforcement of lower rates (DRL) or diminishing rates (DRD). In Chapter 8, we said that one of Mr. MacDonald's students, Caroline, was out of her seat frequently during independent activities. Mr. MacDonald can use a changing criterion design to evaluate the effectiveness of the DRD program he developed. First, he conducts a prebaseline analysis during which he establishes an objective. After conducting some social comparison, he selects as his terminal criterion that Caroline be out of her seat no more than two times in a 30-minute period and only with permission. He decides to use a token economy in the form of tickets that may be exchanged for free time. Mr. MacDonald also develops a frequency recording system. Second, he gathers baseline data for three days and notes that Caroline is out of her seat 10, 12, and 14 times. Third, he chooses 11 times as his first interim criterion. Next, he implements his program. Caroline is given 12 tickets. She is told that she must return a ticket each time she leaves her seat. If she has one or more tickets left over at the end of the activity, she can exchange it for free time. Mr. MacDonald gathers data during this interim phase until Caroline has two out of three days during which she is out of her seat no more than 11 times. He continues to adjust the criterion downward and collect data until, finally, Caroline meets the criterion.

Changing criterion designs can also be used to increase behavior. For example, Smith, Schloss, and Israelite (1986) used this design to evaluate a program targeting use of idioms by youth with hearing impairments.

Advantages and Disadvantages

The major advantage of this design lies in its consistency with effective educational interventions. Both task analysis and shaping methods are easily evaluated using the changing criterion design. Task analysis instruction can be evaluated by establishing criteria based on the number of steps in the task sequence that the student is expected to complete. As he or she becomes more proficient, the number of steps to be completed is increased. Shaping procedures are evaluated by expecting responses that more closely approximated the final goal response. In both cases, data in the changing criterion design guide educational decisions and provide evidence of the effectiveness of the educational procedures.

The changing criterion design is not appropriate for intervention procedures expected to produce substantial and relatively immediate changes in behavior. You may not wish to provide an extended period of time for a student to reduce physical aggression and increase compliance. Also, the steps involved in reinforcing approximations of zero aggression may be viewed by the student and others as actually reinforcing aggression (albeit at a lower rate).

Some responses are likely to increase to the goal level independent of the criterion changes. A student may become interested and motivated to achieve in specific independence of reinforcers offered by the teacher. As a result, the student's performance may consistently exceed the criterion levels. While this effect is desirable as judged by its impact on the development of the learner, failure of behavior changes to meet criterion only when they are introduced reduces experimental control. Consequently, despite being confident that the student improved, you are unable to attribute that improvement to the educational intervention.

Extensions

The changing criterion design may be combined with multiple baseline designs to further increase opportunities for replication. This is accomplished by systematically changing the criteria for reinforcement within each leg of a multiple baseline. In this case, two legs of a multiple baseline may be sufficient where a minimum of three were recommended without changing criteria within the design.

Multielement Designs

Each of the preceding designs is limited to an evaluation of a single intervention. There was substantial need and interest in simply demonstrating the viability of an intervention early in the history of applied behavior analysis. More recently, however, attention has shifted to evaluations of rival procedures. We are confident of the efficacy of modeling based on early research. Of current interest, however, are strategies that enhance the effectiveness of modeling. Is peer modeling superior to adult modeling? Must models demonstrate attainable performance levels to be effective? Does reinforcement paired with modeling produce better effects than modeling alone?

Single-case approaches that compare various procedures are described under the general heading of multielement designs (Martin & Pear, 1996) and comparative intervention design (Gast, Thomas, & Tawney, 1984). Under these general headings, specific authors have described multielement baseline designs (Sidman, 1960), multiple schedule designs (Hersen & Barlow, 1976), simultaneous treatment designs (Kazdin & Hartmann, 1978), and alternating treatment designs (Barlow & Hersen, 1984). As is suggested by the variety of names, substantial diversity exists in these research strategies. The two common features are that each design compares two or more interventions and each relies on intrasubject replication to rule out threats to internal validity.

Because of the variety of comparison methods and the complexity of each, we will limit our discussion to the alternating treatment design described by Barlow and Hersen (1984). The **alternating treatments design** relies on rapid shifts from one treatment to another. These shifts can occur on alternate half sessions, sessions, half days, or days. Essential to this approach is the student's ability to discern what approach is in effect at a particular time. Prompts, instruction, modeling, or other methods may be used to ensure that the student recognizes the specific intervention being employed.

As an example of the alternating treatments design, a punishment procedure may be used to reduce aggression on selected mornings or evenings while a differential reinforcement procedure is used on alternate mornings or evenings. Clear verbal instructions outlining contingencies in effect precede each period. As is shown in Figure 13.4 on page 274, data collected by morning and afternoon and grouped by intervention demonstrate the differential effect of the two approaches.

Internal Validity and the Alternating Treatments Design

As with each of the preceding single-case experimental designs, the alternating treatments design relies on replication of an effect to rule out history and maturation as threats to internal validity. Each session may produce two separate data points accounted for by half sessions in which alternate treatments are employed. Repeated demonstrations that one treatment produces a higher response level than the other eliminate alternative explanations. This is particularly true when the order of treatment (e.g., first or second half session) is alternated or randomly assigned to a given treatment. Also, the larger the distance between data points for respective conditions, and the less frequent the occasions in which data points overlap, the stronger the demonstration.

It is important to note that the basic alternating treatments design is effective in ruling out threats to internal validity for the comparison of treatments. However,

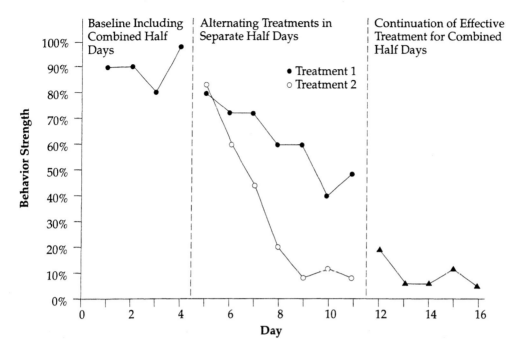

FIGURE 13.4   Alternating Treatments Design

design elements do not demonstrate that either treatment is effective over a baseline. As can be noted from Figure 13.4, baseline is followed by alternating treatments. The strength of each treatment over baseline is demonstrated in a single A-B comparison. There is no replication of this comparison. Therefore, while you can confidently state that one treatment is superior to the other, the effect of both treatments over baseline can be attributed to history, maturation, and other threats to internal validity.

Procedures

As with all single-case designs, planning for the alternating treatments design begins with a prebaseline analysis. This assessment should result in an objectively defined and reliably measured target behavior. It should also produce two rival intervention procedures that are likely to be effective. The prebaseline analysis should also result in a method for ensuring that the student is aware of experimental conditions in effect at a particular time. Failure of the student to discriminate between conditions may result in interference between treatments that obscures differential effects. The prebaseline analysis should also yield an objective and reliable data collection system. As with all single-case designs, continuous measurement is required throughout the alternating treatments design.

Next, collect baseline data during both half sessions. These may be reported as a single response level for the session. Third, once the response strength is stable, the two treatments may be initiated on alternate half sessions. The order of treatments must be counterbalanced throughout the study to avoid the possibility that one treatment is effective over another only when followed or preceded by the other. Counterbalancing can be accomplished by either alternating order (e.g., treatment A preceding treatment B on even days and following treatment B on odd days), or by randomly selecting order each day (e.g., tossing a coin daily to determine if treatment A occurs first or second).

Regardless of order, the treatment that is in effect in a given half session should be clearly identified to the student prior to each half session. As was noted earlier, prompts, cues, modeling, instruction, and other guidance should be used to ensure that the learner clearly understands what contingencies are in effect.

Alternating treatments should continue until the superiority of one treatment is clearly established. This is judged by differences in data measuring the two conditions. The larger the differences and less frequent the overlap in data for the two conditions, the stronger the differences. Finally, once you are confident that one treatment is superior to the other, you may merge both half phases into a single phase in which only the superior treatment is employed.

An Example of an Alternating Treatments Design

Many authors have reported using alternating treatments design to choose which of two intervention programs is more effective. Cuvo, Ashley, Marso, Zhang, and Fry (1995) compared different instructional methods for spelling. Skinner, Smith, and McLean (1994) compared two methods for increasing oral reading of sight words. When trying to change behavior, we have advised you to consider all of the options available within an applied behavior analytic approach. For example, Ms. Lawrence wanted to develop a program to teach Evelyn to take care of property rather than damage it. After serious consideration, she narrowed her choices down to two techniques: a response cost with a time-out and overcorrection. An alternating treatment approach will help her in the final selection. Because she conducted a prebaseline analysis, Ms. Lawrence has developed an objective definition of this behavior and has measured it reliably using frequency recording. Next, she collected baseline data regarding property destruction in the morning and afternoon. She scheduled the interventions by selecting "morning" or "afternoon" randomly from a hat, then selecting time-out or overcorrection randomly. Each treatment was available an equal number of times. Third, she began the treatments, adhering to the schedule. She began each part of the school day with a reminder to Evelyn of the rules and an explanation of the contingencies that were in effect for that time period. She continued implementation of both procedures until the data indicated that overcorrection decreased property destruction to a greater degree than time-out. Finally, she continued to use only the overcorrection procedure.

Advantages and Disadvantages

The principal advantage of this design is its effectiveness in comparing separate treatments. Other single-case designs are effective only in comparing a single treatment to baseline. Many educational questions relate to the relative merits of comparable approaches. The alternating treatments design is a viable method for answering these questions.

The first disadvantage of this design is that the effect of one treatment on the target behavior may contaminate the effect of the second treatment. This is referred to as an *induction effect* (Barlow & Hayes, 1979). For example, you may wish to compare a self-control procedure to an aversive technique. Even though you clearly stated that the aversive technique will not be used on alternate periods, your student may act as though the aversion might be used continuously. Consequently, the self-control strategy may appear to be more effective than it would be if the aversive technique were not being used on alternate sessions.

Similarly, some responses are not subject to fluctuation based on transient conditions. For example, alternating treatments used to increase spelling skills may not have a clear differential effect. Once spelling is acquired under one condition, it is likely to continue to be practiced even under alternate educational conditions. Separate word sets may be used for the two treatments. However, you must ensure that the sets are of comparable difficulty. Failure to do so may produce differences attributable to word difficulty rather than to the strength of the educational procedure.

A related concern is that the alternating treatments design is somewhat unnatural. It is not expected that you will rapidly alternate instructional or motivational procedures within a given day. Doing so may be confusing to students participating in the study. As noted earlier, this confusion can obscure the independent effectiveness of either treatment.

Finally, the alternating treatments design may not be sensitive to small differences in treatment effects on behaviors that are naturally variable. Variability is likely to produce overlaps in trend lines even when differences exist. These overlaps may obscure actual differences.

Extensions

The difficulty of establishing experimental control of both treatments over baseline can be overcome with two possible design modifications. First, the baseline can be carried throughout the study. That is, the two interventions can be conducted in counterbalanced 1/3 phases with a baseline phase occupying a third counterbalanced 1/3 phase (Rose & Beattie, 1986). Alternately, you can begin the study with a reversal design with the B phase being the most promising treatment. After the return to baseline, you can initiate alternating treatments. This approach would allow for the demonstration of the effect of one treatment over baseline followed by a comparison of that treatment to another treatment.

Summary

It is sufficient for us to simply record student progress for most educational purposes. Occasionally, however, it is important that we establish the specific effectiveness of a particular strategy. For example, approaches that are aversive to the student or costly to the school district should be continued only if they are established to be independently responsible for the student's improvement. Continuing to use such an intervention is unwarranted when alternate strategies, history, and/or maturation alone produce comparable effects. Single-case experimental designs are able to determine that the intervention is necessary beyond these alternate strategies.

We described four major single-case experimental designs. Common to each is the use of intrasubject replication to rule out threats to internal validity. Each design establishes the possibility that a treatment is effective through a case study demonstration. They go beyond this, however, by replicating the effect one or more times. In the case of a reversal design, replication occurs by repeatedly introducing and removing the special treatment. Evidence that, regardless of phase, the target response is uniformly higher or lower during treatment when compared to baseline rules out alternative explanations for student success. The multiple baseline design establishes experimental control by replicating an effect across individuals, settings, or responses. Regardless of these variables, each time the intervention is introduced, the response improves when compared to baseline levels. The changing criterion design relies on repeated demonstrations that a response improves to meet a new criterion for reinforcement. Each phase in which the level of response rises to meet a new criterion adds confidence that the intervention procedure is solely responsible for the performance change. Finally, the alternating treatments design is uniquely suited to comparing rival treatments. Experimental control is established through replications in which the teacher rapidly alternates methods. Regardless of order, the method that consistently produces the higher level of the target behavior can be described as being most effective.

References

Barlow, D. H., & Hayes, S. C. (1979). Alternating treatments design: One strategy for comparing the effects of two treatments in a single subject. *Journal of Applied Behavior Analysis, 12,* 199–210.

Barlow, D. H., & Hersen, M. (1984). *Single case experimental design: Strategies for studying behavior change* (2nd ed.). New York: Pergamon.

Campbell, D. T., & Stanley, J. C. (1963). *Experimental and quasi-experimental designs for research.* Chicago: Rand McNally.

Christensen, L. B. (1980). *Experimental methodology.* Boston: Allyn and Bacon.

Cook, T. D., & Campbell, D. T. (1979). *Quasi-experimentation: Design & analysis issues for field settings.* Chicago: Rand McNally.

Cuvo, A. J., Ashley, K. M., Marso, K. J., Zhang, B. L., Fry, T. A. (1995). Effects of response practice variables on learning spelling and sight vocabulary. *Journal of Applied Behavior Analysis, 28,* 155–173.

Dapcich-Miura, E., & Hovel, M. F. (1979). Contingency management of adherence to a complex medical regimen in an elderly heart patient. *Behavior Therapy, 10,* 193–201.

Gast, D. L., Thomas, C. C., & Tawney, J. W. (1984). Comparative intervention designs. In J. W. Tawney and D. L. Gast (Eds.), *Single subject research in special education* (pp. 300–341). Columbus, OH: Merrill.

Hartmann, D. P., & Hall, R. V. (1976). The changing criterion design. *Journal of Applied Behavior Analysis, 9,* 527–532.

Hersen, M., & Barlow, D. H. (1976). *Single case experimental designs: Strategies for studying behavior change.* New York: Pergamon Press.

Johnson, R. J., & McLaughlin, T. F. (1982). The effects of free time on assignment completion and accuracy in arithmetic: A case study. *Education and Treatment of Children, 5,* 33–40.

Kazdin, A. E. (1980). *Research design in clinical psychology.* New York: Harper & Row.

Kazdin, A. E. (1982). *Single case research designs: Methods for clinical and applied settings.* New York: Oxford Press.

Kazdin, A. E., & Hartmann, D. P. (1978). The simultaneous treatment design. *Behavior Therapy, 9,* 912–922.

Lockhart, J., & Law, M. (1994). The effectiveness of a multisensory writing programme for improving cursive writing ability in children with sensori-motor difficulties. *Canadian Journal of Occupational Therapy, 61,* 206–214.

Martin, B., & Pear, J. (1996). *Behavior modification: What it is and how to do it.* Englewood Cliffs, NJ: Prentice-Hall.

Miller, D. L., & Kelley, M. L. (1994). The use of goal setting and contingency contracting for improving children's homework performance. *Journal of Applied Behavior Analysis, 27,* 73–84.

Montee, B. B., Miltenberger, R. G., & Wittrock, D. (1995). An experimental analysis of facilitated communication. *Journal of Applied Behavior Analysis, 28,* 189–200.

Moore, R. J., Cartledge, G., & Heckaman, K. (1995). The effects of social skill instruction and self-monitoring on game-related behaviors of adolescents with emotional or behavioral disorders. *Behavioral Disorders, 20,* 253–266.

Neuman, S. B., & McCormick, S. (1995). *Single-subject experimental research.* Newark, DE: International Reading Association.

Rose, T. L., & Beattie, J. R. (1986). Relative effects of teacher-directed and taped previewing on oral reading. *Learning Disability Quarterly, 9,* 193–199.

Schloss, P. J., Sedlak, R. A., Elliot, C., & Smothers, M. (1982). Application of the changing criterion design in special education. *Journal of Special Education, 16,* 359–367.

Shapiro, E. S., & McCurdy B. L. (1989). Effects of a taped-words treatment on reading proficiency. *Exceptional Children, 55,* 321–325.

Sidman, M. (1960). *Tactics of scientific research.* New York: Basic Books.

Skinner, C. H., Smith, E. S., & McLean, J. E. (1994). The effects of intertrial interval duration on sight-word learning rates in children with behavioral disorders. *Behavioral Disorders, 19,* 98–107.

Smith, M. A., Schloss, P. J., & Israelite, N. K. (1986). Evaluation of a simile recognition treatment program for hearing impaired students. *Journal of Speech and Hearing Disorders, 51,* 134–139.

Smith, S. W., Siegel, E. M., O'Connor, A. M., & Thomas, S. B. (1994). Effects of cognitive-behavioral training on angry behavior and aggression of three elementary-aged students. *Behavioral Disorders, 19,* 126–135.

14

GENERALIZING AND MAINTAINING CHANGES IN STUDENT BEHAVIOR: PART 1—EXTERNAL AGENTS

Every school day you plan and teach lessons designed to change some aspect of your students' academic behavior. By June, you may be able to look back with pride at how much material you and your students have covered. Unfortunately, this feeling of accomplishment may fade during the first few weeks of September when students demonstrate difficulties with material covered previously. Some of you may not have to wait three months before questioning the effectiveness of your teaching methods and materials. Perhaps you have taught phonics to enable students to decode unknown words and comprehend material in a basal series reader. Or maybe you have taught the names, values, and various combinations of coins so that students can use money correctly. Although you are understandably gratified when your students score well on reading tests or math worksheets, you are concerned when they do not use their decoding skills to figure out words in their science textbook or when they mishandle money while purchasing items in the school cafeteria. Such difficulties are not limited to the academic arena. Substitute teachers and paraprofessionals in general and special education settings can provide numerous anecdotes of how students behave when the "real" teacher is absent for a day.

Even though these academic and behavioral problems are frustrating, they are common. Students who are not able to keep up their skill levels over an extended period of time or who do not use newly learned skills in unique situations are experiencing difficulties with generalization. In addition to teacher and student frustration, limited generalization of newly acquired skills has financial implications.

Our students are coming to school in desperate need of skills that will enable them to handle the demands of an increasingly diverse society (Carnine, 1992). In response, school officials must use effective and economical teaching methods that will produce important and durable changes in students' behavior. Such efforts can be expensive, adding to the burden of school districts already facing massive reductions in financial support (Fantuzzo & Atkins, 1992). We must be careful to use our dwindling resources wisely.

Previous chapters in this text have provided ample documentation of the effects of applied behavior analysis techniques on a host of behaviors demonstrated by students in general and special education classrooms. However, as Rutherford and Nelson (1988) have noted, the lack of generalization to settings where therapeutic contingencies were not in effect imposes "critical limitations" on the research. In fact, as we discussed in Chapter 1, limited generalization and maintenance of newly acquired skills are major criticisms surrounding the use of applied behavior analysis.

Other applied behavior analysts have also recognized that a therapeutic change must be enduring and pervasive if it is to be truly effective (Stokes & Baer, 1977). We can no longer assume that the generalization of skills will occur automatically, simply as a result of good teaching (Anderson-Inman, 1986; Stokes, Baer, & Jackson, 1974; Stokes & Baer, 1977). Our methods to help students retain and appropriately use skills must be planned as systematically as the methods we used to bring about positive change in the first place. We have available to us two bodies of techniques to assist students in the generalization of important skills: use of external agents and use of internal agents. Teachers and other significant individuals serve as external agents by carefully managing a variety of environmental factors with which the students come in contact. Students themselves serve as internal agents, using an assortment of techniques to monitor and evaluate their own academic and social behavior. In this chapter, we focus on techniques that rely on external agents. Teaching students to manage their own behavior will be addressed in Chapter 15.

Definitions

In their classic article, Stokes and Baer (1977) defined *generalization* "to be the occurrence of relevant behavior under different, nontraining conditions (i.e., across subjects, settings, people, behaviors, and/or time) without the scheduling of the same events in those conditions as had been scheduled in the training conditions" (p. 350). This definition suggests there are different types of generalization and, accordingly, many ways to measure it. Other authors have identified, defined, and illustrated each type. We have listed and illustrated each in Table 14.1 and now discuss each one separately below.

Response Maintenance

Rutherford and Nelson (1988) defined **response maintenance** as "the continuation of behavior in treatment settings following the withdrawal of an intervention program" (p. 278). This type of generalization is extremely important for teachers because it means that students are capable of using skills in the absence of the conditions required to teach them. A teacher who is introducing a unit on regroup-

TABLE 14.1   Types of Generalization

Type	Definition	Examples
Response Maintenance	The behavior continues to be used in training settings after the instructional program has been completed	Students no longer swear in class Students continue to regroup in math in the resource room
Stimulus Generalization	Transfer of training to a setting not included in the original intervention program	Students no longer swear in the cafeteria Students use regrouping skills in the regular class
Response Generalization	A change in one class of behavior affects behaviors not specifically addressed in the original intervention program	Students no longer use verbal threats Students regroup when multiplying

ing does not continue to teach basic addition and subtraction facts in every lesson. It is assumed that students will remember and use these skills without constant teacher reminders. While occasional reviewing and reteaching is standard practice, a daily summary of all concepts leading up to the lesson at hand would be extremely inefficient, leaving little or no time for the introduction of new concepts and skills.

For example, as resource room teacher, you may have used a token economy for a month to promote homework completion skills in students. Being aware of the importance of the rate of success upon the selection of homework tasks, you only assigned work within their ability level, and they have completed it consistently and accurately for several days. Because nonhandicapped students can and do finish their homework in the absence of a token economy, you decided it was time the resource students worked under similar circumstances. You phased out the token economy but continued to record the consistency and accuracy with which assignments are completed. Students who have continued to complete assigned tasks accurately without the reward of tokens demonstrate response maintenance.

Stimulus Generalization

Stimulus generalization refers to transfer of training, that is, the student's ability to use a skill in learning situations that differ from the one in which he or she was previously taught. A learning situation can differ by setting (i.e., special education class versus general education class) or by personnel (i.e., the special educator versus the general educator). Rhode, Morgan, and Young (1983) stated that this type of generalization is often used as a measure of the success of a special education program. Specifically, professionals are concerned with the degree to which academic and behavioral skills mastered by students in special classrooms are demonstrated in mainstream settings (Haring & Liberty, 1990). Use of a newly acquired skill should not be a function of the setting in which it was learned or the teacher who taught it. Students in the resource room who start to complete homework assignments regularly and correctly in the general education setting are demonstrating stimulus generalization.

You are probably quite familiar with stimulus generalization, or, as in the following case, the lack of it. We have referred frequently to Andrew, a young student in your class who swears frequently. When you bring this problem to his parents' attention, they may exclaim, "He never talks like that at home!" He probably does not. He simply has not transferred to the school setting the standards he adheres to at home. For another example, we will refer back to the resource room described earlier. Students assigned to a resource room learned to complete appropriate homework assignments consistently and accurately even when the token economy was dismantled. Working cooperatively with the general educator, you should gather data to see if students are doing homework in other content areas assigned in mainstream settings. Students completing such assignments are demonstrating stimulus generalization.

Response Generalization

Response generalization refers to a spread of effects (Salzer-Azaroff & Mayer, 1991), that is, a change in one class of behavior may affect behaviors not specifically addressed in the original intervention program. Students may demonstrate positive gains in areas related to, but not the same as, the skills initially targeted for change. We will refer again to the resource room example. Assigning independent work to students not involved in a reading lesson is a common classroom practice. The teacher may note that resource room students who participated in the token economy to increase homework completion are now finishing independent assignments with greater regularity and more accuracy.

Techniques for Promoting Generalization

Stokes and Baer (1977) conducted a thorough critique of the literature in applied behavior analysis and identified nine techniques for enhancing generalization. No discussion of this topic is complete without a review of their suggestions. Since 1977, other authors studying this area in depth (e.g., Ellis, Lenz, & Sabornie, 1987; Haring & Liberty, 1990) have supported Stokes and Baer's original conclusions and have supplemented their list with additional techniques. In addition, they have offered frameworks that categorize generalization techniques according to when they can be used in an instructional sequence. Table 14.2 lists and illustrates each generalization technique within four major categories.

Generalization Techniques That Precede Instruction

Ellis, Lenz, and Sabornie (1987) and Haring and Liberty (1990) both used the term *antecedent* to describe activities that should occur before instruction begins on a

TABLE 14.2   Categories of Generalization Techniques

Category	Type	Definition
Antecedent	Program common stimuli	Teaching elements common to natural settings
	General case programming	Identifying and teaching positive, negative, and irrelevant stimuli
	Train sufficient examplars	Teach several examples of the target behavior
Concurrent	Train and hope	Generalization is probed but not trained
	Train in the natural setting	Teach in settings in which students are expected to generalize
	Train loosely	Vary the setting and prompts to avoid inflexible responding
Subsequent	Sequential modification	Training is provided within a series of settings
	Introduce to naturally maintaining contingencies	Teach functional skills to a high level of proficiency
	Use indiscriminate contingencies	Alter the schedule of reinforcement
Independent	Train to generalize	Reinforce generalized instances of the skill
	Mediate generalization	Teach strategies that enable students to determine when a skill is used

new skill. You will remember how we used this term in Chapter 4 to describe a group of techniques teachers can implement prior to instruction to increase the probability that appropriate behaviors will occur and inappropriate behaviors will not. In a similar vein, these authors offered suggestions teachers can use prior to instruction to increase the probability that students will generalize newly acquired skills. Ellis, Lenz, and Sabornie recommended that teachers increase their students' commitment to learning the skill or concept. Highlighting its importance and discussing how it can be useful immediately or in the near future can impress upon students the need to retain and use a skill or concept. For example, before beginning a unit on measuring with older learners, you can point out how skills in this area can enhance independent living skills such as cooking and decorating. Haring and Liberty (1990) examined Stokes and Baer's (1977) original list of generalization techniques and identified how they can be used prior to actual instruction.

Program Common Stimuli
Stokes and Baer (1977) defined *programming common stimuli* as the use of a stimulus that is found in both the instructional setting and the natural setting to which a skill is expected to generalize. Two strategies can assist teachers trying to program common stimuli. First, they can make the classroom resemble important aspects of the natural environment in which the skill is required. This does not mean you must constantly redecorate your classroom; time and financial constraints do not permit such drastic measures. However, small and easily managed adjustments can make a substantial difference. Use real coins and bills to teach money skills.

Use applications obtained from local employers rather than the practice exercises provided in a workbook to enhance job-seeking skills. Deshler, Alley, Warner, and Schumaker (1981) used this strategy by first teaching reading skills to special education students using high-interest low-vocabulary materials and then providing additional practice on materials obtained from the general education classroom. Students continued to use their skills outside the special education setting.

Larger scale modifications do not have to be expensive. For example, paper tablecloths and napkins, dishes and utensils borrowed from the cafeteria, and a re-arrangement of desks and chairs can change your classroom into a small restaurant. Students can learn and practice skills such as reading menus, making conversation, and paying for purchases. We know a young man who was participating in a work study program that allowed him to attend school in the morning and work at a local supermarket in the afternoon. His primary responsibilities involved stocking the shelves, but when business picked up, the ringing of a bell was supposed to prompt him to go to the register area to assist with bagging groceries. Unfortunately, the young man had difficulty attending to the bell and responding appropriately. Because his teacher maintained close contact with the employer, she was aware of the problem and developed a solution. She collected empty food containers and paper bags and placed them on a table in a corner of her classroom. Occasionally, during school hours, she rang a bell. The young man learned to stop what he was doing and go to the table to bag groceries, and his work performance improved.

The second strategy for programming common stimuli is the reverse of the first strategy. Rather than bringing elements of the natural setting into the classroom, teachers can bring elements from the classroom into natural settings. For example, a kitchen timer used in the classroom as part of a token economy program can be taken on field trips. Despite his aggressive reaction to words with a negative connotation, Scott's teacher was able to include him in nearly all trips into the community. She simply brought with her the timer, his index card, and a hole puncher. Such portability made it possible for the program to be in place at all times. We also knew another young man with multiple handicaps who displayed highly aggressive behavior toward anyone who sat near him. His behavior was brought under control in a very restrictive one-to-one setting. Before placing him in a less restrictive special education classroom, his teacher brought features of that classroom to the one-to-one setting. Standard classroom equipment was moved in, another teacher provided instruction, and peers were slowly introduced. Eventually, the student was participating in a traditional special education setting.

Provide General Case Programming

Haring and Liberty (1990) defined *general case programming* as an analysis of the setting to which behaviors are to generalize. Such an analysis should identify instances that represent (1) positive examples that prompt the behavior, (2) negative examples where the behavior should not be used, and (3) irrelevant examples that should not prompt the behavior, but may inappropriately do so. You use general case programming to identify appropriate examples that can be included in an instructional activity. A good example of this technique is the classic spelling rule "*i* before *e* except after *c* or when sounded like *a* as in neighbor or weigh." Prior to teaching the rule, review spelling books, basal readers, content area textbooks, and written language samples to identify words students should know that follow this rule. Such a list could include "receive," "belief," and "freight." This list of words constitutes positive examples and should be introduced to students in the early stages of instruction. Your review should also identify a list of negative instances where the rule should not be applied. Words on this list may include "science." This list should be discussed with the students in later stages of instruction so that they do not overgeneralize and inappropriately apply the rule. Finally, your review should have resulted in a list of words that do not contain all the necessary letters but may prompt use of the rule anyway. Words on this list could include "long *e*" sounds such as "scene" and "long *a*" words such as "away" or "bait."

General case programming can be very useful in developing social repertoires. For example, you may want to increase the social greeting skills of the seven- and eight-year-old students in your special class. Study the social settings in which your students participate and identify a list of people they should greet. This list may include known adults, friends, shopkeepers, and community helpers. You should also identify people they should ignore or avoid, including strangers offering treats or requesting help finding a lost puppy, or anyone who makes them feel uncomfortable or unsafe. Finally, you should identify instances in which a greeting is irrelevant, such as saying hello the second time a person is seen within a short period of time. Each of these items should be discussed and illustrated over the course of several instructional activities. Horner, Sprague, and Wilcox (1982) described a sequence of activities teachers can complete to enhance instruction through general case programming. These activities are described and illustrated in Table 14.3.

TABLE 14.3 Steps in Using General Case Programming

Horner, Sprague, and Wilcox (1982) identified a sequence of activities you can complete to enhance instruction through general case programming.

1. Carefully define the instructional universe. Identify the range of situations to which students should generalize. For example, the student will be able to use all fast food restaurants within a mile of his home.
2. Identify the relevant stimuli and response variations in the instructional universe. For example, does the student need to wait to be seated? Does he go to a counter to place an order, or are servers available?
3. Select examples for teaching and probe testing. Which restaurant skills will be directly taught? Which will serve as sites for measuring generalization?
4. Develop a sequence for teaching.
5. Teach.
6. Probe for generalization.

Train Sufficient Exemplars

Stokes and Baer (1977) warned that teaching one example of a skill may not be enough to promote generalization. They did not call for teaching all possible examples of a skill; such actions are economically unfeasible and unnecessary. They advised teachers to present a sufficient number of exemplars (or examples) to students until they consistently demonstrate competence in natural settings. Stokes and Baer believed that training sufficient exemplars could be one of the most valuable techniques for promoting generalization; it ensures that students receive enough examples to generalize a skill but still allows the teacher enough time to address other important curricular areas.

Although you may not be familiar with this label, you would probably agree that training sufficient exemplars is a technique used frequently when preparing lessons. You recognize that a single explanation or demonstration will not provide students with sufficient opportunity to master a skill. Accordingly, identify numerous relevant examples or plan several related lessons to provide students with sufficient exposure to a topic. It is hoped that, with sufficient practice, students will handle similar problems they may encounter. For example, a single teacher demonstration of regrouping in subtraction will probably not be enough for students to obtain 80 percent or higher on an exam. Therefore, you will typically plan several problems so students can receive an explanation as often as necessary and practice several examples under close teacher supervision. Similarly, it is doubtful that a single lesson in which students complete one employment application will be enough to ensure they can complete the variety of forms used in the job market. You should obtain forms from those employers whom students are likely to contact for a job and plan several lessons for instruction and practice.

Not only can an "exemplar" refer to an example of a skill, but it can also describe specific conditions of the material, setting, or the people with whom the student interacts. Schloss and his colleagues (Schloss, Alexander, Horning, Parker, & Wright, 1993; Schloss, Alper, Watkins, & Petrechko, 1995; Schloss, Schloss, & Misra, 1985; Schloss, Smith, & Boyd, 1988; Smith & Schloss, 1986) have gathered hundreds of items that represent a single domain of skills and task analyzed them. They have developed a list of the specific tasks or items that, once mastered, enable students to demonstrate a success rate of least of 80 percent on novel, related tasks. For example, they developed one employment application that was based on an analysis of the vocabulary and questions contained in over 200 applications for entry-level positions. Students who were exposed to this application during teaching were able to complete applications that were not part of instruction.

Generalization Techniques That Are Concurrent to Instruction

The preceding section discussed techniques that you can use during your instructional planning to enhance generalization. The next category includes generalization techniques you can use while you are teaching skills and concepts. Ellis, Lenz, and Sabornie (1987) describe these techniques as being concurrent to instruction.

Their use assumes that you are using effective and efficient instructional practices that allow students to learn a skill well enough to be generalized.

Train and Hope

Stokes and Baer (1977) identified *train and hope* as the most frequently used method for promoting generalization, accounting for nearly half of the studies in which generalization was measured. Actually, train and hope describes a situation in which the occurrence of generalization is tested despite the lack of specific plans to promote it. This technique requires no special effort beyond that used to develop and implement lesson plans. It assumes that generalization will occur because you have identified and fully described the skill or concept, explained its importance, provided a demonstration or an illustration, and allowed students ample opportunities for practice or discussion. After instruction has been completed, either test at a later date to see if response maintenance has occurred, or observe to see if students are using the concept or skill in other settings or with other people. Stokes and Baer (1977) pointed out that teachers who do not plan for generalization still take a step in the right direction by probing for it after instruction. Documentation of the occurrence of generalization enhances the efficiency and effectiveness of their instructional strategies. Lack of generalization can prompt teachers to implement techniques after instruction has been completed.

Throughout this text, we have discussed a number of ideas that can enhance skill generalization. In Chapter 3, we strongly recommended that you measure the social validity of your objectives and teaching procedures. In Chapter 4, we discussed antecedent control techniques, including the selection and teaching of functional skills with age-appropriate materials. Following these recommendations should increase the likelihood that generalization will occur without specifically planning for it. Skills perceived by students as functional and rated as important by significant others in the community will be demonstrated and reinforced without extraordinary efforts from you. Similarly, skills that increase students' ability to gain access to positive reinforcers, either immediately or in the near future, are more likely to be used long after instruction has ended. Nutter and Reid (1978) used these principles to teach clothing selection skills to young women who were retarded. They developed their objectives and criteria after conducting observations of 649 women in community settings frequented by the participants in their study (e.g., malls and restaurants). Follow-up measures with real articles of clothing indicated that participants were still able to color-coordinate their outfits after the training program concluded.

Train in the Natural Setting

Training in the natural setting is a generalization technique added by Haring and Liberty (1990) to Stokes and Baer's (1977) original list. Its use requires that a targeted skill be taught directly in at least one of the settings in which it is expected to be used. Student performance is evaluated in nontraining settings to determine if generalization has occurred. For example, if you want to increase your students' ability to use public transportation, actually arrange for instruction on a bus route.

Later, probe for generalization by arranging for students to be observed as they take bus routes to other destinations.

Training in the natural setting offers many advantages. You do not have to conduct extensive observations of community settings to ensure that you can accommodate every variation within a classroom simulation. You do not have to make any modifications to your classrooms to reflect naturally occurring events. Real materials are readily available. Finally, students can experience naturally occurring reinforcers for their accomplishments. Unfortunately, several disadvantages associated with training in the natural setting have been identified. Page, Iwata, and Neef (1976) taught pedestrian skills to individuals with retardation and reported that inclement weather, the need for additional staff, transportation to and from a training site, and limited opportunities to correct student errors can undermine the usefulness of instruction in natural settings. Haring, Kennedy, Adams, and Pitts-Conway (1987) suggested that teachers developing simulations include slides, scale models, and photographs. Technological innovations have also made videotaping a popular option (Broome & White, 1995). We caution, however, that students can benefit from a simulation only if they are capable of observational learning and imitation.

It appears that increases in generalization can be offset by disadvantages associated with training in natural settings. We suggest a compromise. Our own work in the areas of social skill development involved a combination of simulation training and instruction in the natural environment. Students participated in role-plays of situations typically encountered in consumer settings, such as asking for more information or making a complaint. After reaching a predetermined criterion, training was then conducted briefly in actual consumer settings. Store managers and personnel were advised of our plans and agreed to "arrange" events to prompt student behavior. For example, a waitress in a fast food restaurant made an arithmetic error in the bill. Results indicated that careful use of simulation and training in natural settings efficiently and effectively promoted the development and generalization of social skills (Schloss, Smith, & Schloss, 1984; Smith, Schloss, & Schloss, 1984).

Train Loosely

Stokes and Baer's (1977) suggestion to enhance generalization by training loosely may appear to contradict earlier assertions. In previous chapters, we emphasized the importance of precision. Target behaviors must be defined clearly and concisely. Intervention procedures must be described completely and delivered consistently. Teacher precision is essential, particularly for initial skill acquisition. Such attention to detail enables us to document any changes in student performance and establish a functional link between those changes and the intervention program. Unfortunately, this emphasis on precision may undermine your students' ability to generalize their newly acquired skills. Your presentations may be so structured that students fail to recognize slight variations for which the new response is still appropriate.

Once skills have been acquired, you need to train loosely by changing aspects of your instruction that are irrelevant to the skill or concept you are teaching. For example, during early lessons in a social skills unit, you may have taught a very precise order for responding to compliments about possessions that included saying thank you, identifying the person by name, and extending the conversation. During instruction later in the sequence, order of the components is no longer emphasized. In addition, the manner in which students extend the conversation could be expanded from a description of how they obtained it to how much they enjoy having and using it.

In a sense, training loosely requires that you use a great deal of precision. Only through analysis can you determine those aspects of your objectives, procedures, and settings that you must structure to enhance skill acquisition and those you can vary to enhance generalization.

Generalization Techniques That Are Subsequent to Instruction

Ellis, Lenz, and Sabornie (1987) identified a category of generalization techniques that you can use after instruction is concluded. Informal testing or observations at the end of an instructional unit may verify that a skill was mastered; however, testing at a later date may indicate that a student has not used the skill in different settings or with different people. Perhaps there was no evidence of the skill at all. The generalization techniques we now present will help you to promote generalization in different contexts.

Conduct Sequential Modification

Stokes and Baer (1977) recommended that teachers probe for generalization after a skill or concept has been taught. Limited or absent generalization can be developed by modifying behavior systematically within the appropriate settings using the exact intervention program responsible for the initial change. This technique may remind you of the multiple baseline design presented in Chapter 13. As you may recall, the impact of an intervention program is demonstrated by applying it systematically across three distinct persons, settings, or behaviors.

Sequential modification has many educational applications. A student who uses legible handwriting only during handwriting instruction can be taught with the same procedures to use this skill during spelling, then written expression, and then any of the other content areas. A student who has been taught to greet one teacher appropriately can be taught using the same social skills program to greet a second teacher, then a third, and so on. A token economy that increased homework completion in the resource room can be implemented within the general classroom. Herbert and Baer (1972) used sequential modification to extend behavioral gains made in school to home settings. They gave golfers' wrist counters to mothers of two preschool special education students and instructed them to record the number of times they attended to their child's appropriate behavior. Substantial improvements in child behavior were reported at home. Evans and Evans (1983) outlined guidelines teachers can use with parents interested in replicating a school-based program at home. We believe their suggestions are helpful to anyone using sequential modification to enhance generalization. Their steps included:

1. an exact description of the target behavior,
2. an exact description of the intervention procedure,
3. a data collection system,
4. the development of a log,
5. the scheduling of review sessions, and
6. demonstrations of the intervention procedure.

Teachers who are trying to extend positive changes in student behaviors to other settings should combine consistency with flexibility. It is important to recognize that features of some settings may make the exact replication of an intervention program highly improbable. For example, the general educator may want to adopt a token economy responsible for the increase in homework completion. The resource room teacher should recognize that the general educator must keep track of several homework assignments completed by 25 students; therefore, slight adaptations to the original program may be required.

Introduce to Natural Maintaining Contingencies

Stokes and Baer (1977) referred to the use of natural maintaining contingencies as the most dependable of all the generalization techniques. They encouraged teachers to identify stable, natural contingencies that are already available in settings in which students are expected to participate. The desire to experience these contingencies should be sufficient for students to demonstrate continued use of newly acquired skills. For example, a student who learns computer skills has a competitive edge in the job market. The possibility of a better job at a higher salary is a naturally occurring contingency that should prompt continued use of computer skills. An individual who has completed a program to improve personal hygiene may be receiving positive attention from members of the opposite sex. This attention should sufficiently reward continued use of good personal hygiene skills.

Haring and Liberty (1990) identified four methods that ensure that students experience natural maintaining contingencies. Two of their ideas may sound familiar. First, they recommended teaching a functional skill that is expected and reinforced by significant others in natural settings. We discussed this topic in Chapter 3. For example, social greetings are reinforced by the responses of others in the community. Expertise in managing money is reinforced by being able to purchase desired items and knowing the correct change was given. Second, Haring and Liberty (1990) suggested training a skill to a level of proficiency that is truly useful, a practice that reflects the importance of social validity. We recommended use of social comparison in Chapter 3 as a way to select criterion levels that reflect community standards, and in Chapter 12 as a way to ensure that students have met them. Third, they encouraged teachers to make sure students really experience natural consequences. This does not mean that you should place a student at risk for bodily harm during a unit on pedestrian skills. Occasionally teaching in the natural environment and pointing out newspaper articles describing accidents should suffice. Finally, Haring and Liberty (1990) advised teaching students to recruit reinforcement from individuals in natural settings. Deshler, Alley, Warner, and Schumaker (1981) taught learning disabled adolescents to show completed work to their general teachers to prompt social reinforcement of their efforts.

Use Indiscriminate Contingencies

Once a student has mastered a skill, Stokes and Baer (1977) recommend altering the schedule of reinforcement to make it more difficult for students to recognize when reinforcement will occur. The inability to predict the precise moment the contingency will be awarded forces students to behave as though it were always available.

Schedules of reinforcement were discussed in detail in Chapter 7. You may recall that teachers can move from reinforcement contingent upon every instance of the target behavior to a fixed or variable schedule that reinforces students based on either the number of occurrences or the time period involved. Teacher judgment based on adequate data collection is a crucial factor. Reinforcing behaviors too frequently can make students dependent upon rewards; however, a schedule that is thinned too quickly may not reinforce appropriate behaviors often enough to promote skill maintenance and generalization.

Techniques That Promote Independent Generalization

The fourth category of generalization techniques discussed by Ellis, Lenz, and Sabornie (1987) requires students to assume responsibility for extending the benefits of an intervention program. Stokes and Baer (1977) identified two techniques that fall into this category; however, we will only discuss them briefly. Teaching students to manage their own behavior is discussed in depth in the next chapter.

Train to Generalize

Stokes and Baer (1977) suggested that teachers reinforce only those behaviors that indicate generalization, just as they reinforced the behavior that represented the targeted objective during the original intervention program. For example, a social skill training program may have involved teaching interactive play skills to a limited number of students. After a while, students are no longer reinforced for playing with peers in the original group. Instead, you reinforce them for playing with other students not included in the training program.

Mediate Generalization

Finally, Stokes and Baer (1977) advised teachers to include in the original intervention package a skill, such as language, that will be used in other situations as well. Such a skill emphasizes elements common to the training situation and novel settings that may in turn prompt generalization. Another skill that mediates generalization is self-management, a topic that will be addressed in Chapter 15.

Factors That Limit Generalization

In the preceding sections, we identified and illustrated several categories of generalization techniques that can promote consistent use of newly learned skills. The careful reader may have noticed that use of some of these techniques actually contradicts information provided in previous chapters. For example, we suggested that you use sequential modification if follow-up data indicate that behaviors trained in one setting have not generalized to other settings. This recommendation is contrary to the logic supporting the use of the multiple baseline design across settings (discussed in Chapter 13). By using this design you can establish a functional relationship by showing that improvements in behavior were dependent solely on the introduction of the instructional program. Basically, you hope that students will not show spontaneous improvements in settings where instruction has not occurred; otherwise, the conclusions drawn about the value of the program are suspect. Rutherford and Nelson (1988) and Haring and Liberty (1990) have identified features essential to the correct use of applied behavior analysis that may in fact undermine generalization. We summarize their work here to make you aware of the relationship between techniques that promote initial skill acquisition and techniques that promote generalization. Teachers who are aware of potential conflicts can design and implement more efficient and effective behavior change programs.

Stimulus Discrimination

Many of the instructional practices described in this text were designed to teach students stimulus discrimination, that is, the ability to respond in a certain manner to a discrete class of stimuli and not to respond in the absence of those stimuli. Generalization techniques such as training loosely require you to vary settings, cues, and prompts so that students do not become rigid and inflexible. The clash is obvious: discrimination training requires precision whereas training loosely requires versatility. This dilemma is resolved by distinguishing between the purpose each serves. Applied behavior analysis techniques that promote stimulus discrimination should be used during the early stages of instruction to ensure that students have acquired the skill. Once the basics have been mastered, you can vary the stimulus to ensure that behavior occurs in the presence of relevant stimuli.

Consider the following example. Students are taught to cross the street when the "walk" light appears, but to remain on the sidewalk when the "don't walk" light appears. This is an important discrimination; students who fail to make it risk serious injury. You wisely include this discrimination early in a program to develop pedestrian skills. Unfortunately, students who can make only this discrimination may not be adequately prepared to walk about their community. Subsequent training should address other indicators that it is safe to cross a street. For example, the "walk" sign could be flashing rather than constant, or it could have a human shape. The "don't walk" sign could be in the shape of an outstretched hand. In addition, a police officer directing traffic may indicate whether it is safe to cross the street. Carefully sequencing the use of techniques that enhance stimulus discrimination and those that promote generalization enables students to acquire important skills and use them in all relevant settings.

Reinforcement Procedures

In Chapter 7 we discussed the importance of using positive reinforcers to develop a skill or increase its use by students. It was noted that some students may require frequent, primary reinforcers (such as edibles) due to their age or the severity or duration of their problem behavior. However, a steady diet of primary reinforcers contradicts generalization techniques requiring use of contingencies that are naturally maintaining and indiscriminable. Once again, the clash is obvious. Students demonstrate behaviors to obtain reinforcers; unfortunately, these reinforcers are not readily available in natural settings. The solution is to use primary reinforcers during initial skill acquisition and pair them with other, more natural consequences. Once the behavior is demonstrated at an acceptable level, you can alter the schedule of reinforcement. Over time, you increase the value and effectiveness of natural contingencies while decreasing the frequency with which they are used.

For example, you may use a sweetened cereal to reinforce eye contact in a young, severely disabled student. You pair presentation of the cereal with a smile and praise. After the student reaches criterion, continue to praise and smile when eye contact is established but only use the cereal occasionally. Eventually, you discontinue use of the cereal altogether and rely solely on frequent social reinforcement. Finally, you reduce the use of praise and smiles to rates used with nondisabled children in the same age group. As in the example in the previous section, careful sequencing of teaching and generalization techniques can facilitate the use of natural contingencies at levels found in natural settings.

Design Features

We already alluded to the generalization difficulties associated with the use of one single-subject design. The problem with the multiple baseline design is that you must hope generalization does not occur in behaviors, settings, or people that have not been exposed to the intervention program. Improvements in the absence of treatment suggest that other factors may be influencing performance. Another design that mitigates against generalization is the A-B-A-B design. This design requires that the intervention program be withdrawn for a short period of time. It is anticipated that behavior will regress toward baseline levels. Once again, you must hope that generalization, specifically response generalization, has not occurred. Behaviors that maintain or continue to improve in the absence of treatment suggest that something other than the intervention program was responsible for the change.

Data Collection

Determining the extent to which generalization has occurred in natural settings requires you to gather data during follow-up observations. Unfortunately, you may have neither the time nor the financial resources to personally conduct such observations. In addition, your presence may appear "unnatural" to students in some natural settings. Student suspicion will no doubt be aroused if you constantly "pop up" in community settings. Such appearances may also prompt certain student behaviors, casting doubt on the degree to which generalization has occurred. We recommend that you request the assistance of significant others in settings in which students function. Colleagues, parents, siblings, peers, employers, and service providers can observe students covertly and report their findings to you. While establishing such a network requires some time and effort, we believe the information received will be valuable in determining the overall effectiveness of an intervention program.

Summary

The preceding discussion identified and illustrated generalization techniques used prior to, during, and following instruction. Careful selection and application of these techniques should extend the benefits of an instructional program that changes academic or behavioral skills. Merely using them, however, is insufficient. Just as the correct use of applied behavior analysis techniques demands an evaluation of their effectiveness, so too must you measure the extent to which the application of generalization techniques actually promoted consistent use of newly acquired skills upon the completion of instruction.

The need to assess for generalization was fairly obvious in our discussion of techniques used subsequent to instruction. You would not know to use techniques from this category until your follow-up observations of student behavior indicated that generalization had not occurred. However, we want to point out that probing for generalization must always occur. Using techniques included in the antecedent and concurrent categories does not guarantee that they will have the desired effect in the absence of supporting data. Regardless of the exact technique chosen, we strongly encourage you to assess skill generalization. Methods for conducting such probes are the same as those used to measure and record the original target behavior. For example, the time sampling procedure used to measure on-task behavior in the resource room can be used in the general classroom. The frequency recording procedure used to measure noncompliant behavior in the special education classroom can be used at home. Granted, you may have to explain and demonstrate the data collection methods to those significant others conducting observations in natural settings. We realize that such training places another responsibility on the shoulders of overburdened teachers; however, we believe the value of the information regarding generalization makes the effort worthwhile. Developing or changing a behavior has already required substantial investment of time and effort from both you and your students. All this hard work would be worth very little if you did not take the final step toward ensuring that positive changes occur in applied settings. If you find little or no evidence of generalization, take specific steps to ensure that targeted skills are used consistently in relevant settings. The flow chart in Figure 14.1 is based on the work of Liberty (1988) and Haring and Liberty

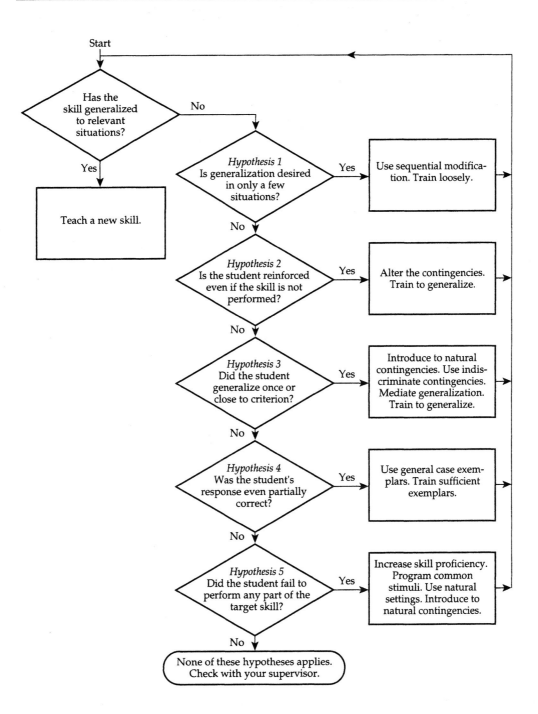

FIGURE 14.1   A Flow Chart to Help Teachers Identify Appropriate Generalization Techniques

(1990). It was developed for teachers probing for generalization upon the completion of instruction, and it offers a systematic strategy for identifying problematic areas and generating solutions.

References

Anderson-Inman, L. (1986). Bridging the gap: Student-centered strategies for promoting the transfer of learning. *Exceptional Children, 52,* 562–572.

Broome, S. A., & White, R. B. (1995). The many uses of videotape in classrooms serving youth with behavioral disorders. *Teaching Exceptional Children, 27*(3), 10–12.

Carnine, D. (1992). Expanding the notion of teachers' rights: Access to tools that work. *Journal of Applied Behavior Analysis, 25,* 13–19.

Deshler, D. D., Alley, G. R., Warner, M. M., & Schumaker, J. B. (1981). Instructional practices for promoting skill acquisition and generalization in severely learning-disabled adolescents. *Learning Disability Quarterly, 4,* 415–421.

Ellis, E. S., Lenz, B. K., & Sabornie, E. J. (1987). Generalization and adaptation of learning strategies in natural environments: Part 1: Critical agents. *Remedial and Special Education, 8,* 6–20.

Evans, W. H., & Evans, S. S. (1983). Using parents in behavior management. *Academic Therapy, 19,* 37–41.

Fantuzzo, J., & Atkins, M. (1992). Applied behavior analysis for educators: Teacher centered and classroom based. *Journal of Applied Behavior Analysis, 25,* 37–42.

Haring, N. G., & Liberty, K. A. (1990). Matching strategies with performance in facilitating generalization. *Focus on Exceptional Children, 22*(8), 1–16.

Haring, T. G., Kennedy, C. H., Adams, M. J., & Pitts-Conway, V. (1987). Teaching generalization of purchasing skills across community settings to autistic youth using videotape modeling. *Journal of Applied Behavior Analysis, 20,* 89–96.

Herbert, E. W., & Baer, D. M. (1972). Training parents as behavior modifiers: Self-recording of contingent attention. *Journal of Applied Behavior Analysis, 5,* 139–149.

Horner, R., Sprague, J., & Wilcox, B (1982). General case programming for community activities. In B. Wilcox & G. Bellamy (Eds.), *Design of high school programs for severely handicapped persons* (pp. 61–98). Baltimore: Paul H. Brookes.

Lagomarcino, A., Reid, D. H., Ivancic, M. T., & Faw, G. D. (1984). Leisure-dance instructions for severely and profoundly retarded persons: Teaching an intermediate community-living skill. *Journal of Applied Behavior Analysis, 17,* 71–84.

Liberty, K. A. (1988). Decision rules and procedures for generalization. In N. Haring (Ed.), *Generalization for students with severe handicaps: Strategies and solutions.* Seattle, WA: University of Washington Press.

Nutter, D., & Reid, D. H. (1978). Teaching retarded women a clothing selection skill using community norms. *Journal of Applied Behavior Analysis, 11,* 475–487.

Page, T. J., Iwata, B. A., & Neef, N. A. (1976). Teaching pedestrian skills to retarded persons: Generalization from the classroom to the natural environment. *Journal of Applied Behavior Analysis, 9,* 433–444.

Rhode, G., Morgan, D. P., & Young, K. R. (1983). Generalization and maintenance of treatment gains of behaviorally handicapped students from resource rooms to regular classrooms using self-evaluation procedures. *Journal of Applied Behavior Analysis, 16,* 171–188.

Rutherford, R. B., & Nelson, C. M. (1988). Generalization and maintenance of treatment effects. In J. C. Witt, S. N. Elliot, & F. M. Gresham (Eds.), *Handbook of behavior therapy in education* (pp. 277–324). New York: Plenum Press.

Schloss, P. J., Alexander, N., Horning, E., Parker, K., & Wright, B. (1993). Teaching meal preparation vocabulary and procedures to individuals with mental retardation. *Teaching Exceptional Children, 25*(3), 7–12.

Schloss, P. J., Alper, S., Watkins, C., Petrechko, L. (1995). I can cook! A template for teaching meal preparation skills. *Teaching Exceptional Children, 28*(4), 39–42.

Schloss, P. J., Schloss, C. N., & Misra, A. (1985). Analysis of application forms used by special needs youths applying for entry-level jobs. *Career Development for Exceptional Individuals, 8,* 80–89.

Schloss, P. J., Smith, M. A., & Boyd, S. (1988). Influence of forms containing multiple versus few common elements upon application completion skills of hearing impaired learners. *Career Development of Exceptional Individuals, 11,* 71–79.

Schloss, P. J., Smith, M. A., & Schloss, C. N. (1984). Empirical analysis of a card game designed to promote consumer-related social competence among hearing impaired youth. *American Annals of the Deaf, 129,* 417–423.

Smith, M. A., & Schloss, P. J. (1986). SUPERFORM: A form for enhancing generalized competence in completing employment applications. *Teaching Exceptional Children, 18,* 277–280.

Smith, M. A., Schloss, P. J., & Schloss, C. N. (1984). Empirical analysis of a social skills program used with hearing impaired youth. *Journal of Rehabilitation of the Deaf, 18*(2), 7–14.

Stokes, T. F., & Baer, D. M. (1977). An implicit technology of generalization. *Journal of Applied Behavior Analysis, 10,* 349–367.

Stokes, T. F., Baer, D. M., & Jackson, R. L. (1974). Programming the generalization of a greeting response in four retarded children. *Journal of Applied Behavior Analysis, 7,* 599–610.

Sulzer-Azaroff, B., & Mayer, G. R. (1991). *Behavior analysis for lasting change.* Fort Worth: Holt, Rinehart, and Winston.

15

GENERALIZING AND MAINTAINING CHANGES IN STUDENT BEHAVIOR: PART 2—INTERNAL AGENTS

In the previous chapter, we described four categories of generalization techniques that can be used to maximize the benefits of students' academic or behavioral change programs. Careful selection and implementation of these techniques should result in the consistent use of newly acquired skills across time and in novel settings with people not involved in the original training program. With two exceptions (train to generalize and mediate generalization), all the techniques included in Chapter 14 required extensive involvement of external agents. To promote generalization, you decided which technique to use, planned for its implementation, and conducted follow-up observations to document success. You were not the only external agents available; colleagues, parents, and significant members of the community played supporting roles in generalization efforts. The point is that someone other than the student was taking responsibility for extending the benefits of an instructional program. While external agents are a powerful resource, many authors have cautioned against sole reliance on their efforts for initiating and maintaining positive changes in student behavior (Browder & Shapiro, 1985; Hughes, Ruhl, & Misra, 1989).

Kazdin (1975) identified some of the disadvantages associated with the use of external agents. First, he noted that external agents are not present in the environment where the desired behavior should occur. Second, he pointed out that many student behaviors may go undetected, particularly in a crowded setting such as the general classroom. The busy teacher may not notice and reinforce behaviors that represent generalization. Similarly, typical classroom activities may make it difficult to observe behaviors that indicate students are regressing toward preinstructional levels. Third, Kazdin argued that external agents such as teachers may become discriminative cues for student performance. It is possible that students will use newly acquired skills only if their teachers are present. Finally, poor communication between external agents in different settings may limit the success of an instructional program.

In response to these concerns, professionals have turned their attention to the development of self-management techniques that are implemented and controlled by students themselves. Thus, students become internal agents for change. They assume responsibility for identifying behaviors, arranging their environment, and managing the consequences. They benefit by experiencing greater success in developing, maintaining, and generalizing skills expected and reinforced by members of the community in which they participate.

Managing one's own behavior has long been recognized as a primary goal of education (Dewey, 1939; Glynn, Thomas, & Shee, 1973; Lovitt & Curtiss, 1969). Many daily events indicate that most of us succeed in controlling our own behavior. For example, you set your clock so that you can get up in the morning. You keep a checklist of things to do during the day. You may "talk yourself through" a difficult or complex task. Occasionally, you may arrange a special event such as a shopping trip, a night on the town, or a vacation as a reward for a lengthy, intensive period of work. Other daily events highlight how difficult it can be to control your own behavior. If you have tried to increase physical activity, limit caffeine or alcohol consumption, quit smoking, or lose weight, then you understand how hard it can be to control your own behavior. Perhaps you joined a group of people with similar interests to learn better ways to manage daily events.

Students can also benefit from such instruction. We already know that they may not continue to use a new skill once instruction is completed; we also know that teachers cannot be present 100 percent of the time to offer reminders and reinforcers. Therefore, we can extend the benefits of an instructional program by teaching self-management skills to students so that they can assume responsibility for their own behavior. The purpose of this chapter is to define self-management, and to describe and illustrate the techniques it encompasses.

Definition

A variety of terms have been used synonymously with **self-management,** including *self-control* and *self-regulation*. Similarly, a number of definitions have been offered. Dickerson and Creedon (1981) defined self-management as "any response made by an individual to maintain or change his or her own behavior" (p. 425). Similarly, Browder and Shapiro (1985) described self-management as "all processes used by an individual to influence his or her own behavior" (p. 200). As these definitions suggest, there are a number of behaviors encompassed by self-management. They are identified and illustrated in Table 15.1 on page 300. We must point out that some of the techniques listed in the table have been described by more than one label and have been used frequently in combination with each other.

TABLE 15.1   Self-Management Techniques and Definitions

Technique	Definition
Self-determined criteria	Setting standards for performance prior to engaging in a task (O'Leary & Dubey, 1979).
Self-determined content for performance	Choosing what to learn or what behavior to change (Browder & Shapiro, 1985).
Self-determination of reinforcement	Determining the nature and the amount of reinforcer to be administered contingent upon performance (McLaughlin, 1976).
Self-evaluation	Examining one's own behavior to determine if a specific behavior or standard has been achieved. This term is synonymous with self-assessment (Hughes, Ruhl, & Misra, 1989; McLaughlin, 1976).
Self-instruction	Giving oneself a verbal statement to prompt, direct, or maintain behavior (O'Leary & Dubey, 1979).
Self-monitoring	Assessing and recording one's own behavior. This term is synonymous with self-observing and self-recording (Hughes, Ruhl, & Misra, 1989; McLaughlin, 1976; Rosenbaum & Drabman, 1979).
Self-punishment	Administering an unpleasant consequence contingent upon performance (Browder & Shapiro, 1985).
Self-reinforcement	Administering a positive consequence contingent upon performance (Bandura, 1976; Kanfer, 1980).
Self-scheduling	Establishing the sequence of daily events (Lovitt, 1973).

Advantages of Self-Management Techniques

We realize that teaching self-management skills to students requires additional time and effort from very busy teachers. Already overwhelmed by the demands of the typical school day, you may reasonably wonder if the effort to teach self-management skills is worthwhile. The professional literature provides ample evidence that self-management skills do indeed offer several advantages to both you and your students. These advantages are listed in Table 15.2 and are described in the following sections.

Self-Management Is Practical

As we mentioned elsewhere, economic concerns make it unreasonable, if not impossible, for teachers or trained observers to monitor students in every relevant community setting. For example, teachers who are working with students on the development of job-seeking skills or positive work habits cannot accompany their students to every personnel office or employment site to ensure that skills are being used. Generally, teachers are hired to provide instruction in traditional classroom

TABLE 15.2   Advantages of Self-Management

The following is a list of benefits enjoyed by teachers and students that can be attributed to self-management:

1. Self-management is practical, economical, and ethical.
2. Self-management is a powerful tool for changing behavior.
3. Self-management is a powerful tool for promoting generalization.
4. Self-management frees you to teach students other important skills.
5. Self-management increases student independence by making them responsible for their own behavior.
6. Self-management is inexpensive and requires only slight modification of existing information and materials.
7. Self-management is easily adapted to meet the needs of student in any setting.
8. Self-management can be used with a variety of behaviors.
9. Self-management can be used with students with diverse abilities.

settings, and they find there is little time available for such extended observations. Some school district officials have arranged for the occasional delivery of instruction and supervision of students in natural settings; however, you are probably obligated to conduct the majority of their instruction and evaluation in the classroom.

Another concern associated with prolonged observation in natural settings is ethics. Even if financially possible, it is simply inappropriate to observe, record, and reinforce students in all the community settings they frequent. For example, you may have completed a social skills instruction unit related to dating behavior. Your need to measure the extent of skill generalization is secondary to your students' right to privacy. Your appearance during a student's date would be awkward at the very least.

Self-management is a practical alternative. Fixsen, Phillips, and Wolf (1972) suggested that students self-record their behavior in natural settings and share the results with their teacher. Granted, without proper instruction, students can self-record inaccurately or falsify the results. Adequate instruction coupled with sporadic covert use of trained observers (when ethical) in natural settings can minimize errors and reduce the number of false reports.

Self-Management Is a Powerful Tool for Changing Behavior

When trying to change a bad habit, you may have begun by making note of each time you engaged in it. For example, if you ever tried to give up smoking you may have counted the number of cigarettes you had during the day. If you have tried to cut down on caffeine consumption, you may have written down the number of cups of coffee you consumed. The final tally at the end of the day may have been such a jolt that the next day you smoked fewer cigarettes or drank less coffee. This example highlights the potential use of self-management techniques as components in a behavior change program. Particularly useful during and after intervention are self-monitoring and self-instruction.

Although we are presenting self-management as a technique for enhancing generalization, we are aware of the substantial literature supporting its use as a primary tool for changing behavior. It seems that making a person aware of his or her current level of performance may be sufficient to produce significant changes in the desired direction (Webber, Scheuermann, McCall, & Coleman, 1993).

Self-Management Is a Powerful Generalization Tool

As suggested earlier, it is possible that generalization of newly acquired skills can be attributed to the presence of the person who is primarily responsible for the change. Traditionally, this person has been the teacher. Unfortunately, if your presence is the only reason why a skill was demonstrated, then it is logical to assume that, in your absence, the skill will be weak or missing. This situation is exemplified by students who behave appropriately for their teacher, but misbehave for the substitute or the paraprofessional.

Proponents of self-management argue that improvements in behavior can be generalized more effectively and efficiently if students become their own agents for change (Webber, Scheuermann, McCall, & Coleman, 1993). Rather than being cued by the presence of other people, students who self-manage can monitor, evaluate, and observe the result of the appropriateness of their behavior on a continuing basis. More information on the impact of self-management on generalization will be provided in the second half of this chapter.

Self-Management Frees the Treatment Provider

You do not need to call in sick to appreciate the effect you have on your students' behavior. The amount of instructional time typically spent reinforcing and correcting academic and social behavior is probably sufficient to give you an indication of events that transpire in your absence. At the end of a particularly frustrating day, you might hear yourself say, "I could get so much more done if only I didn't have to spend so much time with discipline!"

Self-management techniques offer you the opportunity to increase the time you can devote to teaching important skills without losing control of student behavior (Webber, Scheuermann, McCall, & Coleman, 1993; Workman & Katz, 1995). You can spend more time developing and implementing instruction because students who self-manage can monitor, evaluate, record, and reinforce their own behavior. Similar advantages have been experienced by parents of children using self-evaluation to control disruptive and noncompliant behavior (O'Brien, Riner, & Budd, 1983).

Self-Management Increases Student Independence

We have just noted that teachers directly benefit when students self-manage their behavior. Strongly related to this is another advantage enjoyed by students. Self-management increases students' ability to act independently, a characteristic that is expected and reinforced by our society (O'Leary & Dubey, 1979). As we said in the introduction of this chapter, a primary goal of our educational system is to develop students' ability to control their own behavior. Providing instruction in self-management can assist students in achieving this goal.

Self-Management Is Inexpensive

Promoting generalization through the use of external agents may require some investment of time, energy, and money. For example, programming common stimuli, identifying sufficient exemplars, and training in the natural environment may involve observations of appropriate settings and purchasing or developing relevant materials. There may be the additional cost of recruiting, training, and using observers to conduct generalization probes in natural settings. We believe the value of the information obtained is worth the expenditures.

Nonetheless, self-management techniques can also promote generalization and may exhaust fewer resources (Bolstad & Johnson, 1972). Having already developed and implemented instructional programs, you will be able to present to students much of the information and materials they require to self-manage. Operational definitions of target behaviors have been developed, a recording system is in place, and reinforcers have been obtained. Obviously, some of this information and material will have to be adapted to facilitate student use. For example, rather than use a complex time-sampling procedure to measure on-task behavior, students can put slashes under columns marked "+" and "–" that have been drawn on a paper taped to their desks.

Self-Management Is Adapted Easily

Activities in which students should be using newly acquired skills may occur at different times and in a variety of locations, making the scheduling of observations in natural settings challenging. Self-management techniques such as self-monitoring can make it easier to gather information about performance in natural settings (Koegel & Koegel, 1990). Students can be taught a simple, unobtrusive system to record behavior anywhere and anytime. We know a young man with moderate disabilities who was learning to give appropriate compliments. He carried a library counter in his pocket and recorded the frequency with which he offered compliments. Initially, another observer gathered data simultaneously, but this practice was discontinued in favor of sporadic reliability checks once the young man self-recorded accurately.

Self-Management Is Useful for a Variety of Behaviors

Self-management techniques have been used to solve many problem behaviors found in general and special education settings. These techniques have successfully reduced disruptive behaviors (Kern, Dunlap, Childs, & Clarke, 1994), noncompliance, tantruming (Fowler & Baer, 1981; O'Brien, Riner, & Budd, 1983), inappropriate verbalization, out-of-seat behavior, and aggression (Rhode, Morgan, & Young, 1983). Self-management techniques have also increased attention to task (Maag, Rutherford, & DiGangi, 1992), cooperative classroom behaviors (Lonnecker, Brady, McPherson, & Hawkins 1994), the completion of academic tasks such as history (Broden, Hall, & Mitts, 1971; Glynn, 1970), geography (Glynn, 1970), writing and math (Dickerson & Creedon, 1981; Lazarus, 1993; Leon & Pepe, 1983), homework (Trammel, Schloss, & Alper, 1994), and schedule management (Newman, Buffington, O'Grady, McDonald, Poulson & Hemmes, 1995).

Self-Management Is Suitable for Students with Diverse Abilities

The success of self-management relies on the ability of students to use it. If you work with very young or more disabled learners you may believe this technology has very little to offer. Actually, numerous authors have reported effective use of self-management techniques by students with diverse abilities. Self-monitoring, self-reinforcement, self-determination of reinforcement, and self-selection of standards have been used by students in regular education (Bolstad & Johnson, 1972; Broden, Hall, & Mitts, 1971; Dickerson & Creedon, 1981; Glynn, 1970). Self-instruction has been used by four-year-old students enrolled in a Head Start program (Bornstein & Quevillon, 1976) and by elementary students with behavior disorders and learning disabilities (Leon & Pepe, 1983). Self-monitoring has been used by students with learning disabilities (Maag, Rutherford, & DiGangi, 1992; Trammell, Schloss, & Alper, 1994), emotional disorders (Kern, Dunlap, Childs, & Clarke, 1994), and autism (Koegel & Koegel, 1990; Newman et al., 1995). Self-evaluation has also been used by students with emotional disturbances (Wood & Flynn, 1978).

Thus, it appears that the majority of students can benefit from some form of self-management. For most students, these skills did not develop incidentally. Their ability to self-manage was developed through systematic instruction. In the next section, we present sequences of instructional activities and suggestions for developing specific self-management skills.

Strategies for Teaching Self-Management Techniques

Just as there are steps for teaching an academic skill, so too are there sequences of instructional activities you can use to develop specific self-management skills. Unfortunately, the techniques listed in Table 15.1 have not received equal attention in the professional literature. Further complicating the issue is that many authors fail to describe fully the exact procedures they used to teach self-management skills. Therefore, our discussion reviews only those self-management techniques that have been described adequately in the professional literature. They include self-monitoring, self-instruction, and self-reinforcement. As you read, you will no doubt notice that many instructional activities are similar to those used to teach academic skills. We believe this similarity makes teaching self-management skills a more attractive proposition. While doing so may require some extra time, you may find you already possess the necessary skills. Additional training should not be required.

Teaching Self-Monitoring

Self-monitoring has also been referred to as *self-recording* and *self-observation*. Students who self-monitor examine their own behavior and record whether or not they have met a predetermined standard. Self-monitoring is an excellent example of the interrelated nature of self-management techniques. As you can see, correct self-monitoring requires students to self-evaluate behavior by comparing it to an established criterion and then making a permanent record of it (Nelson, 1977).

Some special preparation is required prior to introducing students to self-monitoring. Of particular concern is the instrument students will use to record their behavior. No doubt, you have already developed and used a data collection system to record student progress under instructional conditions; however, it is likely that the system is too complex for students to use correctly. Therefore, you will have to modify the self-monitoring instrument.

Modify Data Collection Using Frequency Recording

Generally, a frequency recording system already used before and during an intervention program by a teacher can be taught to students with relative ease. Simply provide students with an appropriate form and instruct them to make a mark each time a behavior has occurred. For example, if you recorded every instance of swearing, simply instruct students to do likewise during specific time periods. Paper and pencil are not the only ways students can count the number of times they displayed a behavior. Frith and Armstrong (1986) suggested that students can place tokens in a box, transfer objects from one place to another, or use a golf counter.

If you have conducted observations using either an interval recording or a time sampling procedure, you can transform it into a frequency recording system that students can use to monitor the same behavior. Perhaps you used time sampling to record student attention to task every two minutes before and during an intervention program. Students are now attending at acceptable rates and you want to make them responsible for maintaining treatment gains. Rather than teaching them to fill in a complex form every two minutes, students will simply record a plus sign or a minus sign every time they think about whether they are paying attention. Figure 15.1 on page 306 illustrates a suitable form that could be taped to a student's desk, and Figures 15.2 on page 307 and 15.3 on page 308 illustrate variations of this form. Broden, Hall, and Mitts (1971) used this type of frequency recording with an eighth grader who needed to practice better study habits in a history class. The student was instructed to record her study behavior whenever she thought about it, using a "+" or a "–".

Name: _____   **Date:** _____

Stay on Target

Directions: When you think about it, make a " " in the box if you are working. Make a " "—if you are not working. Remember, don't fill in all the boxes at one time!

I am working on _____ .

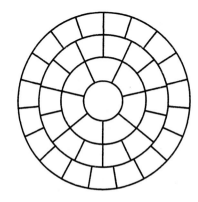

I am working on _____ .

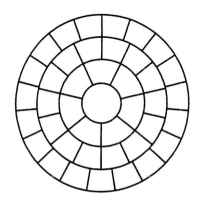

FIGURE 15.1   A Self-Monitoring Sheet for Frequency Recording

Name: _____   **Date:** _____

Are you working hard? Make a smile if you are. Make a frown if you aren't.

FIGURE 15.2   A Self-Monitoring Sheet for Younger or Less Able Students

Name: _____   **Date:** _____

Are you working hard? Circle the happy face.

Are you not working hard? Circle the sad face.

FIGURE 15.3   Another Self-Monitoring Sheet for Younger or Less Able Students

Name: _____   **Date:** _____

Directions:

1. Get a timer.
2. Set it for 15 minutes
3. Start working.
4. When the bell goes off, decide if you are working. If yes, write a "$+$" in the box. If no, write a "$-$".
5. Repeat.

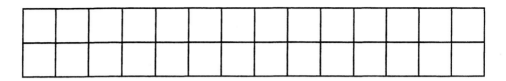

FIGURE 15.4   A Self-Monitoring Sheet for Time Sampling

Modify Data Collection Using Time Sampling
As is the case for most teachers, the use of time sampling may be one of the easiest methods for students to record their own behavior. You only need to explain the form students will use, identify the length of the observation interval, and demonstrate how they will know the interval is up. You can further simplify time sampling procedures by extending the length of the observation interval. For example, the teacher who collected data at the end of five minutes may decide that students should self-monitor every fifteen minutes or at the end of each lesson. Such modifications reduce the intrusiveness of self-monitoring while still providing you and your students with valuable information regarding behavior strength. Figure 15.4 contains an example of a time sampling sheet that can be used to self-monitor.

Modify Data Collection Using Permanent Product Recording
Permanent product recording is another data collection method used easily by students who are self-monitoring. You need only to instruct students to count and record the number of work samples they completed during an assigned activity. Work samples can include the number of math problems solved, workbook pages completed, sight vocabulary words read, or essays written. You can also modify permanent product recording to include levels of accuracy. This modification encourages students to attend not only to the quantity of the work they produce, but to its quality as well. Figure 15.5 on page 310 is a sample sheet students can use to monitor permanent products.

Name: _____   **Date:** _____

Subject	Page(s)	Numbers	How many are finished?	How many are right?

FIGURE 15.5   A Self-Monitoring Sheet for Permanent Product Recording

With this preparation, you can present self-monitoring to students. The sequence of instructional activities we recommend for teaching self-monitoring skills includes the five steps listed in Table 15.3, which is a compilation of the work of several authors.

*Clearly Define the Behavior That Will
Be Self-Managed*
A precise definition of the behavior students will monitor makes observations easier and recording more accurate. If you are presenting self-monitoring as a tech-

TABLE 15.3   Procedures for Teaching Self-Monitoring

Make sure you include the following steps when teaching your students to self-monitor:

1. Clearly define the behavior that will be self-managed.
2. Explain the purpose of self-monitoring.
3. Model the recording procedure.
4. Practice with role-play.
5. Practice responding to a cue.

nique to enhance gains made during instruction, you should already have suitable definitions of the target behavior. Discussion of the target behavior should include all relevant examples. For example, White and Koorland (1996) developed a very comprehensive definition of swearing that addressed several categories including curses, epithets, insults and slurs, and scatology. They also provided clear examples of words and phrases for each category.

Such precision leaves little doubt regarding the behavior in question. Explanations can be supplemented by modeling instances and noninstances of the target behavior (Montague, 1987; Osborne, Kosiewicz, Crumley, & Lee, 1987) and having students generate additional examples (Safran & Safran, 1984). Broome and White (1995) suggested viewing videotapes.

Explain the Purpose of the Self-Monitoring
Highlighting its functional utility may enhance the attractiveness of self-monitoring for students and increase their motivation to use it (Montague, 1987; Osbourne, Kosiewicz, Crumley, & Lee, 1987).

Model
You must demonstrate how to use a self-monitoring instrument. (Remember that instruments should be simple to enhance accuracy and increase the likelihood they will be used.) Students can observe while instances and noninstances of the target behavior are recorded. Follow-up discussions allow you to identify and clear up confusion with either the definition or the recording instrument.

Practice with Role-Play
Students must have sufficient opportunity to practice using the recording instrument (Montague, 1987; Osbourne, Kosiewicz, Crumley, & Lee, 1987). Initially, have students observe and record just one role-played instance or noninstance of the behavior at a time. During follow-up discussion, students can explain their decisions, ask any questions, and receive clarification of any vague areas. Next, present combinations of two instances and noninstances of the target behavior, then three, and so on, until students can accurately record behavior over a period of time.

Practice Responding to a Cue
Students who will be using time sampling will need to practice self-monitoring in response to a cue (Montague, 1987; Osbourne, Kosiewicz, Crumley, & Lee, 1987). Explain how students will know it is time to self-monitor. For example, let students listen to the device used to mark the end of the interval, such as a bell, a kitchen timer, or a tape with prerecorded cues. Students should practice self-monitoring when they hear the predetermined signal.

Teaching Self-Instruction

Self-instruction is defined as "an adult-generated strategy used by those who cannot generate a strategy when approaching a task. It cues a behavior students have but do not think to use" (Leon & Pepe, 1983, p. 54). People occasionally talk to

TABLE 15.4   Procedures for Teaching Self-Instruction

Make sure you include the following steps when teaching your students to self-instruct:

1. Model the behavior while talking aloud.
2. Talk aloud while the student performs the behavior.
3. Whisper while the student talks aloud and performs the behavior.
4. Mouth the words while the student whispers and performs the behavior.
5. Have the student perform the task while covertly self-instructing.

themselves while solving a difficult problem or engaging in a complex behavior. When you were learning to regroup in math, you may have said, "Nine plus nine is eighteen. Put down the eight, carry the one." Even now, when balancing your checkbook, you may mutter, "O.K., I add new deposits to the amount listed on the front page. Done. Now, I subtract the outstanding checks from the new total." Similarly, students can be taught to prompt or cue their own behavior when teachers are unavailable. Students who have learned to self-instruct in one setting may generalize this skill to other settings or conditions. For example, a student whose spelling accuracy improves because she reminded herself to "change -y to i and add -es" is likely to use this rule in other situations, such as story writing.

Much of the work in this area was pioneered by Meichenbaum and Goodman (1971) through their work with impulsive children. The five steps listed in Table 15.4 are necessary to train students to self-instruct.

Model the Behavior While Talking Aloud
Perform the targeted behavior, describing each step as it is completed. At this point the student is only an observer. For example, while regrouping to solve a subtraction problem, start in the ones column and say, "I can't take away 9 from 2. Go to the next column, borrow 10, cross out the 50 and make it 40. Make the 2 a 12. Take away 9. Write down 3." Continue until the problem is solved.

Talk Aloud While the Student Performs the Behavior
Referring to the previous example, present another problem to the student. Describe the procedure to be followed while the student demonstrates.

Whisper While the Student Talks Aloud and Performs the Behavior
Another problem is assigned to the student, who completes it while describing the necessary steps. The only form of assistance is the instructions you have whispered.

Mouth the Words While the Student Whispers and Performs the Behavior
The student completes another problem, using whispers to guide behavior. You "lip-sync" directions for completing the task.

Have the Student Perform the Task While Covertly Self-Instructing

Finally, assign another problem and have the student complete it. Encourage the student to "think it through." While it is easy to see whether a behavior is being performed, covert self-instruction, or private speech (Luria, 1961), is not observable.

Teaching Self-Reinforcement

Self-reinforcement enables individuals to increase or maintain levels of performance by rewarding themselves whenever they reach a predetermined criterion (Bandura, 1976). Examples of self-reinforcement occur daily. You may decide that you cannot take a break until after you have read a certain number of pages in a chapter. You may decide to buy a new suit only after you have lost 15 pounds. It is also possible to teach students self-reinforcement skills so that they too can arrange satisfying consequences in the absence of their teachers or in other community settings. Research indicates that students using self-reinforcement were just as successful in changing behaviors as were students exposed to teacher-controlled reinforcement. In fact, Bolstad and Johnson (1972) reported that first and second grade students controlling their own reinforcement were slightly more successful in reducing disruptive classroom behavior than students who were reinforced by their teacher.

Assumptions associated with the use of self-reinforcement can affect its success. These assumptions refer to two other self-management techniques. One is self-determined criteria, defined by O'Leary and Dubey (1979) as a procedure in which the standards for performance are established prior to engaging in a task. It is likely that students will be very liberal when asked to set their own standards for acceptable behavior; at the very least, their standards will probably not be as rigorous as those you establish. The other technique is self-determination of reinforcement, which requires that the exact nature and amount of reinforcement be established (McLaughlin, 1976). It is not surprising that people selecting their own reinforcers tend to reward themselves more generously. Self-determined criteria and self-determined reinforcers have implications for the training procedures used to teach self-reinforcement skills.

Table 15.5 on page 314 lists the steps we recommend for teaching self-reinforcement skills. They reflect the efforts of Felixbrod and O'Leary (1974), O'Brien, Riner, and Budd (1983), and Rhode, Morgan, and Young (1983).

Bring Behavior under the Control of Externally Managed Contingencies

Students cannot self-reinforce academic or behavioral skills they do not have in their repertoires. Skills that are nonexistent or occurring at very low rates need to be developed and increased. In addition, inappropriate behaviors that interfere with the development of target skills must be eliminated. Externally managed contingencies, such as those discussed in Chapters 7, 8, 9, and 10, are the most efficient way to ensure that these goals are accomplished.

TABLE 15.5 Procedures for Teaching Self-Reinforcement

Include the following steps to increase your students' ability to use self-reinforcement:

1. Bring student behavior under the control of externally managed contingencies.
2. Emphasize the importance of doing their best work in the classroom, just as they would for an employer who is paying them.
3. Let the students determine the criterion for reinforcement.
4. Let the students determine the amount and nature of reinforcement.
5. Match student evaluations of performance against teacher evaluations, reinforcing accurate recording.
6. Gradually fade matching requirements.

Discuss the Importance of Doing a Job Well
Felixbrod and O'Leary (1974) urged teachers to draw an analogy between work that students will do eventually on the job for money and the work they do in school for rewards.

Let the Students Determine the Criterion
for Reinforcement
Because higher expectations produce higher levels of performance, encourage students to establish rigorous standards for reinforcement.

Let the Students Determine the Amount and Nature
of Reinforcement
You can encourage students to be realistic about the exact nature and amount of the reinforcers they will award themselves. Reinforcers available during the externally managed contingency should reflect their preferences; thus, they are a good place to start when developing reward options. You can also reduce the tendency to be generous by pointing out that a fair day of work deserves a fair wage.

Match Student Evaluations of Performance
against Teacher Evaluations
It is possible that students will not self-monitor accurately so that they can secure a greater reward for themselves. To counteract this, you and your students can develop a bonus system that rewards correct self-monitoring. Using newly established criteria, you and your students should monitor performance simultaneously and compare their results at the end of the observation interval. Students can obtain extra rewards if their evaluations match yours.

Fade Matching Gradually
As students improve their ability to self-monitor, you can fade matching requirements. Occasional use with students chosen at random should maintain accuracy.

The Influence of Self-Management on Generalization

A primary purpose for teaching self-management skills is to extend the benefits of an intervention program by making students responsible for their own behavior. We now turn our attention to a brief discussion of how various self-management techniques have promoted generalization.

Response Maintenance

In Chapter 14, response maintenance was defined as "the continuation of behavior in treatment settings following the withdrawal of an intervention program" (Rutherford & Nelson, 1988, p. 278). Students demonstrate response maintenance by continuing to use newly acquired skills after the intervention program designed to teach them has been dismantled. Researchers using self-management techniques have documented response maintenance in their follow-ups on student performance. Self-instruction enabled the 7- to 9-year-old students in Meichenbaum and Goodman 's (1971) investigation to maintain low rates of impulsive behavior four weeks after training. The self-monitoring package used by Kaufman and O'Leary (1972) resulted in the maintenance of low rates of disruptive behavior in their 15-year-old participants. Self-monitoring was also used by 10- and 12-year-old participants in a study conducted by McLaughlin, Burgess, and Sackville-West (1982). Their low rates of aggression were maintained over a 70-day follow-up period.

Stimulus Generalization

Stimulus generalization refers to a student's ability to use a skill in learning situations that differ from the one in which he or she was previously taught. A student demonstrates stimulus generalization by using a skill either in a setting completely different from the one in which it was taught or in the presence of someone other than the original trainer. Holman and Baer (1979) reported that self-monitoring increased the on-task behavior of three students across settings over a three-month follow-up period. McLaughlin (1983) also used self-monitoring to help 8- and 9-year-old students generalize their use of appropriate on-task and academic behavior across persons. Students continued to use their skills for nearly a year after training was terminated. Finally, Koegel and Koegel (1990) reported that self-monitoring enabled 9- to 14-year-old students with autism to reduce the use of stereotypic behavior in nontreated community settings.

Response Generalization

Response generalization refers to change in one class of behavior that affects behaviors not specifically addressed in the original intervention program (Sulzer-Azaroff & Mayer, 1991). Students demonstrate response generalization if they improve in areas related to, but not the same as, the skills initially targeted for change.

This form of generalization is not as frequently reported in the professional literature on self-management. Leon and Pepe (1983) did note that students used self-instruction with computation skills not included in their training program. Shapiro, Browder, and D'Huyvetters (1984) noticed that the autistic children in their investigation increased productivity on academic tasks not included in the original training program.

In summary, it appears that using self-management to make students responsible for their own behavior is an effective means for promoting all types of generalization. In light of these results, we strongly encourage you to plan and implement self-management strategies with your students.

Summary

In this chapter, we discussed the substantial contribution self-management can make to the development and use of important academic and behavior skills by students regardless of the nature and severity of their learning problems. We identified, described, and illustrated several self-management techniques, most notably self-monitoring, self-instruction, and self-reinforcement. We recognize that teaching self-management skills to students requires extra effort, but we strongly encourage you to consider adding them to your arsenal of instructional methods. The amount of time required to teach self-instruction skills is offset somewhat by the fact that you have developed many of the required elements just by using other applied behavior analysis techniques. You also benefit greatly when students use self-management skills. Your constant attention is no longer required, leaving you more time to teach other important skills. In addition, you may find that you need to review and reteach skills less often.

We offer a few other suggestions to increase the effectiveness of self-management skills.

1. Introduce self-control training early in the students' academic careers. Students will use self-control more effectively and for more purposes when training is begun early (Frith & Armstrong, 1986).
2. Just as you would for any academic task, allow sufficient time for students to practice newly acquired self-management skills (Frith & Armstrong, 1986).
3. Set aside enough time to use self-management skills (Anderson-Inman, 1986). Completing self-monitoring sheets or matching performance to your records requires that some time be added to a lesson.
4. Establish time limits. Don't expect students to use self-management for extended periods, particularly when they are just learning it (Frith & Armstrong, 1986).
5. Conduct random checks on student use of self-management techniques (Wood & Flynn, 1978). Such checks keep students on their toes.

References

Anderson-Inman, L. (1986). Bridging the gap: Student-centered strategies for promoting the transfer of learning. *Exceptional Children, 52,* 562–572.

Bandura, A. (1976). Self-reinforcement: Theoretical and methodological considerations. *Behaviorism, 4,* 135–155.

Bolstad, O. D., & Johnson, S. M. (1972). Self-regulation in the modification of disruptive classroom behavior. *Journal of Applied Behavior Analysis, 5,* 443–454.

Bornstein, P. H., & Quevillon, R. P. (1976). The effects of a self-instructional package on overactive preschool boys. *Journal of Applied Behavior Analysis, 9,* 179–188.

Broden, M., Hall, R. V., & Mitts, B. (1971). The effect of self-recording on the classroom behavior of two eighth-grade students. *Journal of Applied Behavior Analysis, 4,* 191–199.

Broome, S. A., & White, R. B. (1995). The many uses of videotape in classrooms serving youth with behavioral disorders. *Teaching Exceptional Children, 27*(3), 10–12.

Browder, D. M., & Shapiro, E. S. (1985). Applications of self-management to individuals with severe handicaps: A review. *Journal for the Association of the Severely Handicapped, 10,* 200–208.

Dewey, J. (1939). *Experience and education.* New York: Macmillan.

Dickerson, E. A., & Creedon, C. F. (1981). Self-selection of standards by children: The relative effectiveness of pupil-selected and teacher-selected standards of performance. *Journal of Applied Behavior Analysis, 14,* 425–433.

Felixbrod, J. J., & O'Leary, K. D. (1974). Self-determination of academic standards by children: Toward freedom from external control. *Journal of Educational Psychology, 66,* 845–850.

Fixsen, D. L., Phillips, E. L., & Wolf, M. M. (1972). "Achievement Place." The reliability of self-reporting and peer-reporting and the effects on behavior. *Journal of Applied Behavior Analysis, 5,* 19–30.

Fowler, S. A., & Baer, D. M. (1981). "Do I have to be good all day?" The timing of delayed reinforcement as factor in generalization. *Journal of Applied Behavior Analysis, 14,* 13–24.

Frith, G. H., & Armstrong, S. W. (1986). Self-monitoring for behavior disordered students. *Teaching Exceptional Children, 18,* 144–148.

Glynn, E. L. (1970). Classroom applications of self-determined reinforcements. *Journal of Applied Behavior Analysis, 3,* 123–132.

Glynn, E. L., Thomas, J. D., & Shee, S. M. (1973). Behavioral self-control of on task behavior in an elementary classroom. *Journal of Applied Behavior Analysis, 6,* 105–113.

Holman, J., & Baer, D. M. (1979). Facilitating generalization of on-task behavior through self-monitoring of academic tasks. *Journal of Autism and Developmental Disorders, 9,* 429–446.

Hughes, C. A., Ruhl, K. L., & Misra, A. (1989). Self-management with behaviorally disordered students in school settings: A promise unfulfilled? *Behavioral Disorders, 14,* 250–262.

Kanfer, F. H. (1980). Self-management methods. In F. H. Kanfer & A. P. Goldstein (Eds.), *Helping people change* (2nd ed.) (pp. 334–389). New York: Pergamon Press.

Kaufman, K. F., & O'Leary, K. D. (1972). Reward, cost, and self-evaluation procedures for disruptive adolescents in a psychiatric hospital school. *Journal of Applied Behavior Analysis, 5,* 293–309.

Kazdin, A. E. (1975). *Behavior modification in applied settings.* Homewood, IL: Dorsey Press.

Kern, L., Dunlap, G., Childs, K. E., & Clarke, S. (1994). Use of a classwide self-management program to improve the behavior of students with emotional and behavioral disorders. *Education and Treatment of Children, 17,* 445–458.

Koegel, R. L., & Koegel, L. K. (1990). Extended reductions in stereotypic behavior of students with autism through a self-management treatment package. *Journal of Applied Behavior Analysis, 23,* 119–127.

Lazarus, B. D. (1993). Self-management and achievement of students with behavior disorders. *Psychology in the Schools, 30,* 67–74.

Leon, J. A., & Pepe, H. J. (1983). Self-instructional training: Cognitive behavior modification for remediating arithmetic deficits. *Exceptional Children, 50,* 54–60.

Lonnecker, C., Brady, M. P., McPherson, R., & Hawkins, J. (1994). Video self-monitoring and cooperative classroom behavior in children with learning and behavior problems: Training and generalization effects. *Behavioral Disorders, 20,* 24–34.

Lovitt, T. C. (1973). Self-management projects with children with behavioral disabilities. *Journal of Learning Disabilities, 6,* 15–28.

Lovitt, T. C., & Curtiss, K. A. (1969). Academic response rate as a function of teacher and self-imposed contingencies. *Journal of Applied Behavior Analysis, 2,* 49–53.

Luria, A. R. (1961). *The role of speech in the regulation of normal and abnormal behavior.* New York: Liveright.

Maag, J. W., Rutherford, R. B., & DiGangi, S. A. (1992). Effects of self-monitoring and contingent reinforcement on on-task behavior and academic productivity of learning disabled students: A social validation study. *Psychology in the Schools, 29,* 157–172.

McLaughlin, T. F. (1976). Self-control in the classroom. *Review of Educational Research, 46,* 631–663.

McLaughlin, T. F. (1983). Effects of self-recording for on-task and academic responding: A long term analysis. *Journal of Special Education Technology, 6,* 5–12.

McLaughlin, T. F., Burgess, N., & Sackville-West, L. (1982). Effects of self-recording and matching on academic performance. *Child Behavior Therapy, 3,* 17–27.

Meichenbaum, D., & Goodman, J. (1971). Training impulsive children to talk to themselves: A means of developing self-control. *Journal of Abnormal Psychology, 77,* 115–126.

Montague, M. (1987). Self-management strategies for job success. *Teaching Exceptional Children, 19*(2), 74–76.

Nelson, R. O. (1977). Assessment and therapeutic function of self-monitoring. In M. Hersen, R. M. Eisler, & P. M. Miller (Eds.), *Progress in behavior modification* (Vol. 5). New York: Academic Press.

Newman, B., Buffington, D. M., O'Grady, M. A., McDonald, M. E., Poulson, C. L., & Hemmes, N. S. (1995). Self-management of schedule following in three teenagers with autism. *Behavioral Disorders, 20,* 190–196.

O'Brien, T. P., Riner, L., & Budd, K. S. (1983). The effects of a child's self-evaluation program on compliance with parental instructions in the home. *Journal of Applied Behavior Analysis, 16,* 69–79.

O'Leary, S. G., & Dubey, D. R. (1979). Application of self-control procedures by children: A review. *Journal of Applied Behavior Analysis, 12,* 449–465.

Osborne, S. S., Kosiewicz, M. M., Crumley, E. B., & Lee, C. (1987). Distractible students use self-monitoring. *Teaching Exceptional Children, 19*(2), 66–69.

Rhode, G., Morgan, D. P., & Young. K. R. (1983). Generalization and maintenance of treatment gains of behaviorally handicapped students from resource rooms to regular classroom using self-evaluation procedures. *Journal of Applied Behavior Analysis, 16,* 171–188.

Rosenbaum, M. S., & Drabman, R. S. (1979). Self-control training in the classroom: A review and critique. *Journal of Applied Behavior Analysis, 12,* 467–485.

Rutherford, R. B., & Nelson, C. M. (1988). Generalization and maintenance of treatment effects. In J. C. Witt, S. N. Elliot, & F. M. Gresham (Eds.), *Handbook of behavior therapy in education* (pp. 277–324). New York: Plenum Press.

Safran, S., & Safran, J. (1984). The self-monitoring mood chart: Measuring affect in the classroom. *Teaching Exceptional Children, 16*(3), 172–175.

Shapiro, E. S., Browder, D. M., & D'Huyvetters, K. K. (1984). Increasing academic productivity of severely multi-handicapped children with self-management: Idiosyncratic effects. *Analysis and Intervention in Developmental Disabilities, 4,* 171–188.

Sulzer-Azaroff B., & Mayer, G. R. (1991). *Behavior analysis for lasting change.* Fort Worth, TX: Holt, Rinehart, and Winston, Inc.

Trammel, D. L., Schloss, P. J., & Alper, S. (1994). Using self-recording, evaluation, and graphing to increase completion of homework assignments. *Journal of Learning Disabilities, 27,* 75–81.

Webber J., Scheuermann, B., McCall, C., & Coleman, M. (1993). Research on self-monitoring as a behavior management technique in special education classrooms: A descriptive review. *Remedial and Special Education, 14*(2), 38–56.

White, R. B., & Koorland, M. A. (1996). Curses! What can we do about cursing? *Teaching Exceptional Children, 28*(4), 48–52.

Wood, R., & Flynn, J. M. (1978). A self-evaluation token system versus an external evaluation system alone in a residential setting with predelinquent youth. *Journal of Applied Behavior Analysis, 11*, 503–512.

Workman, E. A., & Katz, A. M. (1995). *Teaching behavioral self-control to students.* Austin, TX: PRO-ED.

16

WORKING WITH PARENTS

Chapters 4 through 10 provided you with the information you need to increase the likelihood that students in your class will demonstrate appropriate behavior. Chapters 11, 12, and 13 provided the information you need to verify that desired changes have taken place and that these changes occurred solely as a result of the applied behavior analytic program you implemented. By carefully selecting and implementing these techniques and monitoring student performance, you will observe changes in the behavior of the students in your classroom. It is very likely, however, that the classroom is not the only setting in which students are experiencing difficulty. For example, you may have implemented a program that reduced or eliminated physical aggression in your classroom. Unfortunately, when you are in the school hall, you overhear a student describing or even boasting about the fistfight he had with his siblings at home last night. It certainly comes as no surprise to you that student misbehavior is not limited to the school grounds. It is extremely likely that the difficulties students present in class are also problematic at home for their parents.

On a related note, your applied behavior management program may have produced a change in the desired direction of a targeted behavior. For example, you may have been able to increase the frequency with which the majority of your students turn in homework assignments that are complete and 90 percent accurate. Even so, you are not receiving all assignments consistently and there are a few students who have made little progress at all. Obviously, there is still room for improvement in your students' performance, although you may feel you have exhausted all of your resources. Have you considered asking parents for their assistance?

These two examples illustrate the benefits that working with parents can offer you, the parents, and the students. Parents receive valuable assistance in dealing with problems at home that have a strong resemblance to behaviors your students used to have in class. As a teacher, you can use parental influence to change or improve student performance at school. Finally, students benefit as they develop and generalize skills that will allow them to function more effectively in school, at home, and in the community.

The purpose of this chapter is to present three methods for involving parents in their child's educational program. These methods include parent training, conferences, and home–school communication. We first discuss barriers to effective partnerships, including how to overcome them, and we conclude with the advantages of parental involvement and discussion of some further potential problems in the relationships.

Barriers to Working Effectively with Parents

Let's say you have a student in your class named Clare who has a great deal of difficulty doing ability-level tasks independently. Her numerous requests for attention and her frequent failure to turn in complete assignments are a constant drain on your time, energy, and patience. Following the procedures we have described in previous chapters, you develop a multifaceted program of antecedents, related personal characteristics, and consequences to increase independent behavior. Although she is slow, you have documented that Clare is making progress. How would you feel if you discovered that Clare has few or no responsibilities at home, that she depends on parents or siblings to help her do everything? No doubt you would be frustrated, possibly angry, that your efforts are being undermined.

In another example, let's say that David, another student in your class, has a very messy desk and locker. This doesn't particularly bother you, as long as the mess is confined to his personal space. At open house, however, David's parents may express dismay over the condition of his desk and locker. They both work outside the home and expect that David will be able to help out around the house by keeping his room in order and picking up after himself. He is not consistently performing these chores, and his parents are concerned that the home and school environments are sending mixed messages about standards for tidiness.

These examples highlight the need for teachers and parents to communicate and work together toward the same goals for a particular child. A child will make greater progress more quickly when his or her parents and teacher are "on the same page." Both parties should have the same expectations for appropriate behavior and neither should inadvertently reinforce a behavior that the other is trying to eliminate. Not only is parent involvement a good idea, but for the parents of students with special needs it's the law. The Individuals with Disabilities Education Act (IDEA) guarantees parents of children and youth with disabilities the right to have an active role in the development and implementation of educational programming.

Despite the desire to work together, or a legal mandate, effective teacher–parent partnerships don't always happen. Although well worth the effort, the establishment of effective teacher–parent partnerships is not easy as a result of several barriers, which are listed in Table 16.1 on page 322. Major problems have resulted from several changes in American society. Many of your students now come from homes in which there is only one parent, who is solely responsible for the day-to-day operation of the family. This parent is probably holding down a full-time job, while

TABLE 16.1   Barriers to Effective Teacher–Parent Partnerships

There are several barriers that undermine positive relationships between teachers and parents. They include:

1. The changing configurations of the family
2. The mobility of the family
3. Ethnic and cultural diversity of families
4. Increased poverty
5. Teacher belief that parents are responsible for their child's poor performance
6. Parental history of negative interactions with school personnel
7. The mistaken belief that teachers know what is best for the child
8. The failure to recognize the serious nature of behaviors some parents have to deal with
9. Ineffective parent training practices
10. Constraints on teacher time

juggling the responsibilities of raising more than one child and managing the home. No matter how concerned the parent is, taking the time to meet with teachers may sorely test an overextended schedule. Even two-parent homes have their share of problems. It may be necessary for both parents to work outside the home, reducing the amount of time they can devote to family issues. Some two-parent homes may in fact be blended families. There may be friction between stepparents and stepchildren or between the stepchildren. In addition, families are much more mobile today than in the past. The enrollment roster a teacher started out with in September may be vastly different in June. It is discouraging to devote time and energy to building partnerships with parents who are unable to remain in the area, and it takes more time and effort to start all over again as new sets of parents move into the district. This mobility has also contributed greatly to the increased cultural, ethnic, and value-system diversity of the students enrolled in public schools. Working effectively with these students and their families can be challenging. Finally, changes in family structure and the economy have contributed to greater numbers of families who are living in poverty. These families may have more pressing things to worry about than a child's misbehavior in the school (Simpson & Carter, 1993).

Teacher attitude can be another barrier to building effective partnerships with parents. Unfortunately, teachers tend to regard parents and parental involvement in negative terms. The problems we described earlier may cause teachers to view parents as obstacles rather than partners in producing student change (Williams & Chavkin, 1985). In addition, teachers may make the parents feel that they are the cause of the problems their children are experiencing. Dawson and McHugh (1987) have identified the presumption that a parent is to blame for a child's problem as "the most fundamental stumbling block to any successful partnership" (p. 119–120).

In addition to being justifiably angered by teacher attitude, many parents have experienced only negative interactions with school personnel. Although it is a good idea, not all teachers call students' homes or send notes that describe positive aspects of children's behavior. Chances are that most calls and notes to parents whose children demonstrate inappropriate behavior at school are complaints and requests for meetings. A teacher adds to parents' stress and anxiety when he or she shares only bad news about a child's performance and behaviors. After a while, parents just don't see the point of staying in close contact with the teacher. They may not attend parent conferences, participate in multidisciplinary meetings or IEP meetings, or even respond to notes. While teachers need to be honest about a student's current academic, social, and behavioral abilities, it is important to identify strengths in these areas as well. Rather than being made to feel responsible for inappropriate behavior, parents need to feel comfortable and that they are a valued part of a coordinated team that works between the home and the classroom to help their child.

Even if teachers have a positive attitude, another barrier to effective teacher–parent partnerships is the belief that they know what is best for a child. Turnbull and Turnbull (1997) maintained that teachers commit a grievous error by assuming that parents should automatically defer to their decisions about their child because they know what is best. Such attitudes may intimidate and anger parents. Remember that parents are an extremely valuable resource because, when it comes to their child, they are the experts. Therefore, it behooves teachers to make parents equal partners when making decisions about their child. Close cooperation between parents and teachers that is characterized by mutual respect increases the likelihood that students will develop and maintain skills essential for success.

Another barrier to the development of a cooperative relationship is the occasional failure by teachers to recognize the seriousness of the problems that parents face at home and to offer real solutions. A teacher needs to be ready to assist parents—not only with minor problems they may be experiencing with their children, but with the major issues as well. Chances are that any problem a teacher notes during a five-hour school day is probably just as annoying or severe a problem at home. Parenting a typical child is difficult; parenting a child with behavior problems can be overwhelming (Zirpoli & Melloy, 1997). These parents may be very interested in learning ways to help their children improve their academic performance and be more compliant and less aggressive. Teachers must be prepared to work with them to identify and implement suitably strong intervention programs.

Unfortunately, it is possible that, during parent training, professionals don't teach correctly or they use the wrong materials. While teachers may have the education and credentials needed to work with children and youth of various ages and abilities, few may have completed coursework pertaining to working effectively with parents as partners. Teachers may confuse parents by using technical jargon to explain applied behavior analytic concepts and procedures. They may not take the time necessary to explain or demonstrate behavior management techniques. As a result, parents may be poorly prepared to implement a behavior change project at home or to assist you with a cooperative effort between home and school. It is important that parents know what they are doing or they won't succeed in bringing about anticipated changes. Such outcomes may cast a shadow over one's competence as a teacher in particular and the effectiveness of applied behavior analysis in general.

A final barrier to good teacher–parent partnerships is the hectic nature of most teachers' professional lives. Just developing and implementing educational programs necessary to enhance students' academic and behavioral progress is enough to keep teachers very busy. Although well worth the effort, developing and maintaining good relationships with parents adds significantly to the workload.

Parent Training

As we have illustrated in this chapter, there may be occasions in which you want to help parents extend the benefits of a school-based intervention to the home setting. On other occasions, you may need parents to help you maximize the potential of a school-based program by reinforcing your efforts at home. In either case, you will need to plan and implement training for parents that will enable them to work directly with their children or follow through on your behavior change program. Rhode, Jenson, and Reavis (1993) noted that, unfortunately, nearly 50 percent of parents enrolled in training programs drop out. A possible reason for this statistic, as we noted earlier, is that few teachers have completed specific coursework related to developing cooperative teacher–parent partnerships and providing parent training. This is a troubling circumstance because poor training will adversely affect the quality of the intervention and limit the child's progress at home and in school. Such outcomes jeopardize the future of cooperative ventures between teachers and parents. To avoid this problem, we devote this section to a description of parent training.

Goals for Parent Training

Kerr and Nelson (1989) identified two general objectives for working with parents. The first is to assist parents in developing the skills they need to manage their child's problem behavior at home. This objective can be met through parent training either in groups or on an individual basis. The second is to obtain parental support for classroom goals. You can accomplish this objective by holding conferences with parents and using home–school communication systems.

Parent Training in Groups

You may want to consider working with a group of parents. If your goal is to help parents develop the skills they need to implement applied behavior analytic procedures at home, then they may feel less self-conscious or defensive in a group situation. As people start sharing their stories and concerns, parents may see that others have problems similar to those experienced by their children. If your goal is to convince parents to assist you in maximizing the benefits of an existing program, then group training is an economical use of your time.

TABLE 16.2 Children's Problem Behaviors Reported at Home

Parents of typical children and children with disabilities can demonstrate several problems at home. After training, parents have used applied behavior analytic techniques to deal with the following behaviors:

Parents of Typical Children	Parents of Children with Disabilities
Defying authority	Temper tantrums
Noncompliance	Inability to concentrate on one thing
Temper tantrums	Short attention spans
Lying	Failure to complete tasks
Arguing about rules	Distractibility
Not obeying house rules under own initiative	Inappropriate choice of companions
	Vandalism
Refusal to go to bed on time	Curfew violations
Failure to complete tasks	Attention seeking
Yelling or screaming	Interrupting
Teasing other children	Fighting with siblings
Fighting with siblings	Whining
Verbal abuse	Stereotypic behaviors
	Self-injury

Behaviors

You can use group training to help parents address a variety of excessive or deficit behaviors demonstrated by their child at home. Table 16.2 is a list of the behaviors that parents of typical children and children with disabilities have addressed after participating in parent training sessions. Many of these behaviors reflect problems you may be having at school.

Components of Parent Training

Several authors have described the training procedures they used to teach skills to parents. Although programs varied according to the children's needs and the exact nature of the applied behavior analytic procedure being discussed, the components of the training programs were very similar (Anastopoulos, DuPaul, & Barkley, 1991; Love, Matson, & West, 1990; Mullin, Oulton, & James, 1995; Nangle, Carr-Nangle, & Hansen, 1994; Patterson, 1982; Patterson, Reid, Jones, & Conger, 1975; Sloane, Endo, Hawkes, & Jenson, 1991).

The majority of these authors reported that they conducted parent training in groups. Alberto and Troutman (1995) suggested having two leaders for the group, one a parent and the other a professional. If you have worked successfully with a parent to change a child's behavior at home, then it may help to have him or her present. This measure enhances your credibility with other parents. Both group leaders should maintain a sense of humor, which can break down parents' barriers and make training sessions more enjoyable (Rhode, Jenson, & Reavis, 1993).

Group size can range anywhere from 12 to 30 people. You can't require attendance, so chances are that the parents who attend training sessions are volunteering to be present. If you are working with parents of typical children, you may want to arrange groups according to their children's ages or the difficulty of the problem. If you are working with the parents of children receiving special education services, then you may want to arrange groups according to severity of the children's disabilities. While it is possible that parents will report a range of behaviors, it is more likely that parents of children with severe disabilities experience problems that are substantially different from those experienced by those whose children are typical or only mildly disabled (Alberto & Troutman, 1995). Similarly, it is likely that parents of young children will experience problems that are different from those reported by parents of older children.

Choose a Training Site

Training sessions can be held in any convenient location. Depending on group size, you may consider alternating among the homes of group members. However, a more formal location may be more conducive to the functioning of the group. Also, you may want to avoid meeting at school if some members of the group have a history of negative interactions with school personnel. Perhaps you can take advantage of a meeting room in a community center or at a public library.

Schedule Training Sessions

Authors report that their groups met for 60 to 90 minutes once a week over a period of 10 to 12 weeks (Alberto & Troutman, 1995; Mullin, Oulton, & James, 1995).

Select Training Topics

By the end of your training program, you want parents to have developed basic skills in the use of several aspects of applied behavior analysis. Choose your topics carefully so that you include those that they will need in order to intervene in their own programs or to extend a school-based program to the home environment. Based on parents' needs, devote one or more sessions to each topic. You may want to consider accomplishing the following in the training program:

1. Develop the ability to describe problem behavior in specific, measurable, observable terms. Focus on meaningful behaviors that are of interest to parents, such as those we presented in Table 16.2. Cover the range of problems parents are likely to be experiencing such as compliance, arguing, fighting with siblings, and homework completion. Parents can start by describing what they see their children doing, identifying major concerns about their children's behaviors, rank ordering them from most to least troublesome, then selecting one behavior to work on. On a related note, you may also encourage parents to think about when the behavior does and does not occur. They may want to consider antecedents such as who is

present when the behavior occurs, what activities are occurring, and when and where the behavior happens (Mullin, Oulton, & James, 1995). In keeping with the guidelines presented in Chapter 3 for writing behavioral objectives, help parents state target behaviors in positive terms by identifying what they want their child to do in place of the misbehavior. Finally, ask parents to describe previous attempts at dealing with problem behaviors. Some of the things parents have tried may in fact have been good ideas, although perhaps they were not implemented entirely correctly. Their experiences may provide you with a starting point as you choose which intervention techniques to present in subsequent training sessions.

2. Identify a way to keep track of the behavior. Parents need to measure the strength of behaviors before and during the time they try an intervention so that they can see the progress their child is making. Parents can learn to use the systematic observation techniques presented in Chapter 11 to collect frequency data, duration data, task analytic data, and samples of permanent products.

3. Present antecedent control techniques. Just as you would prefer to prevent problem behavior in school, so too would parents prefer to prevent problems at home. Discuss ways to prevent or minimize problem behaviors through the use of antecedent control techniques. Many of the techniques we presented in Chapter 4 are ideal for use in the home, particularly establishing rules and routines, developing schedules, and enhancing adult–child interactions.

4. Teach parents how to meet their child's needs. Rather than their simply telling the child to do something, discuss the importance of modeling for a child exactly what the parent wants him or her to do. Parents can learn how to use task analysis so that difficult steps are broken into smaller ones that are more easily completed by children.

5. Teach strategies for responding to children's appropriate and inappropriate behavior. You may need to devote several sessions to consequences, because there are so many options from which to choose and it is vital that parents understand the use of each. In addition, techniques such as token economies, contracts, and response cost require that consideration be given to positive and negative consequences. Parents may include the items listed in Table 16.3 on page 328 among their consequences.

The techniques you cover should reflect the nature and severity of problem behaviors demonstrated by the children as well as their ages and ability levels. For each technique you present, you may wish to do the following:

1. Identify the technical term for the technique but take the time necessary to define it thoroughly.

2. Explain exactly how to use the technique.

3. Identify its advantages, limitations, and how to troubleshoot any problems.

4. Modify a technique slightly if necessary to make it more useful at home.

5. Include in training sessions those techniques that are practical, economical, feasible, realistic, and effective (Kerr & Nelson, 1989).

**TABLE 16.3   Examples of Positive and Punitive Consequences
That Can Be Used at Home**

Parents should be encouraged to use as positive and negative consequences
those items or activities to which they already have easy access.

Positive Consequences	Negative Consequences
Praise	Extra chores
Special snacks and desserts	Short-term privilege removal
Choosing the dinner menu	Brief time-out periods
Selecting a rental movie	Early bedtime
Access to video games	No bedtime snack
Trips to the local mall	Reprimands
Small amounts of money	
Stickers	
Later bedtime	
Having a friend spend the night	

6. Point out how the technique may already be at work in the environment. For
example, parents may be reluctant to use a response cost system, thinking it is
overly harsh. You may want to point out that response cost systems are already
present in everyday life. Traffic tickets, library fines, directory assistance charges,
and late payment charges are all examples of response cost systems, although society does not typically refer to them as such.

7. Describe exactly how the technique can be used at home with their children,
including what they will say to explain the program.

8. Consider how acceptable each technique will be to the parents. Reimers and
his colleagues (1992, 1995) discussed factors that contribute to treatment acceptability, including the amount of time it takes to implement the procedure, the side
effects, whether it is a positive or negative approach, the severity of the problem
behavior, and its effectiveness. The more severe the problem behavior, the more acceptable a particular technique may be to a parent. You should be advised that parents who attribute the cause of their children's problems to physical factors (e.g., a
medical condition, general health problems, or genetic factors) are less accepting
of environmentally based treatments than parents who attribute causes to the environment (e.g., stressful life events, discipline methods, influence of a peer group,
or school/home situation).

9. Discuss the importance of developing and adhering to a sequence of steps
during the implementation of any technique. Warn parents that not using the technique in the prescribed manner will reduce the effectiveness of the intervention.
Parents can use their newly developed data collection skills to verify treatment integrity. Encourage parents to stick with an intervention plan. Be consistent because
it will take time for their child to unlearn inappropriate behaviors and develop
new skills.

Develop Training Materials

Create handouts that include written instructions with detailed explanations of all the topics or procedures being discussed (Smith, 1994). You may also consider printing posters listing rules or a sequence of steps required by a technique. Just as you display rules and schedules, so too can parents hang these posters in highly visible locations such as the refrigerator. Distributing laminated, wallet-sized descriptions of techniques is useful as parents can refer to the cards and place a check next to each part of the technique as they complete it (Powers, 1992).

Select Training Procedures

The techniques you use to teach a new skill to students will be successful when teaching applied behavior analytic procedures to parents. We summarized these techniques in Table 16.4. In each session, you should do the following:

1. Establish the purpose of the session and outline the topics that will be covered.

2. Demonstrate the skill using numerous examples. Use videotapes (Broome & White, 1995), films, overheads, and cartoons (Rhode, Jenson, & Reavis, 1993) to illustrate your point.

3. Allow parents to share their own knowledge of and experience with a concept or skill.

4. Provide numerous opportunities to practice. For example, parents can pinpoint target behaviors and describe them in measurable, observable terms. They can practice recording the strength of behaviors with a variety of data collection methods.

5. Provide opportunities to role-play. Having parents telling you what they should do is not the same as doing it. Role-playing is particularly useful when learning to implement positive and negative consequences (Love, Matson, & West, 1990).

6. Provide feedback on their performance. Make sure you tell parents what aspects of their performance were correct during practice activities or role-play. If necessary, provide suggestions for improvement.

TABLE 16.4   Parent Training Strategies

The following teaching techniques should be included in parent training sessions:

1. Establish the purpose of the session.
2. Demonstrate new concepts or skills.
3. Discuss.
4. Conduct practice activities.
5. Arrange for role-playing.
6. Provide feedback on performance.
7. Respond to parent questions.
8. Assign homework.

7. Encourage parents to ask questions.

8. Assign homework and review it at the beginning of the next training session. The nature of the homework activity can vary. It can be an informal observation of their child to identify situations, environments, and circumstances that contribute to the misbehavior. It can be practice with a systematic recording technique. It can be charting or graphing preintervention behavior, implementing the program, measuring treatment integrity, or analyzing the results.

Increasing Attendance at Parent Training Groups

Parents may be unwilling or unable to attend group meetings for a variety of reasons such as illness, home responsibilities, a sudden crisis, transportation difficulties, conflicting appointments, or simply forgetting. Poor attendance can reduce the quality of care available to children. It also wastes precious staff time and effort. Finally, there are fewer training benefits and, ultimately, the risk that the child's problem will get worse (Kolko, Parrish, & Wilson, 1985). Some measures you can take to increase attendance include calling to remind parents of a meeting, arranging to have child care available at the training site, and arranging the meeting in a mutually convenient place for group members. You can also make sure that the group is working on problems that are important and that learning solutions are reasonable.

Individual Parent Training

Parents who are unable or unwilling to attend group sessions may need to have the option of participating in individual training sessions. Each session can last for about one hour and occur once a week, for several weeks, in the parents' home. Content is the same as it is for group training sessions, although individualized sessions offer the advantage of allowing you to tailor intervention programs to meet the unique needs of a particular child and his or her family. Teaching techniques include all the strategies listed in Table 16.4. Individual sessions can also be conducted in a clinic setting, which may offer the advantage of one-way mirrors through which the teacher and the parent can observe each other working with the child (McMahon & Forehand, 1984).

Obtaining Parental Support

Beyond formal parent training, you will have the opportunity to meet with parents at open house and during informal conferences. If the student is receiving special education services, you will work with parents during multidisciplinary meetings and IEP meetings that focus on the development of goals and objectives for their child's educational program. You can use these occasions to share information about your program and gain parent support.

Parent Conferences

Parents can't help you if they don't know about or don't understand all aspects of their child's educational program. You can use a conference to keep parents informed of their child's progress and to increase their involvement (Boutte, Keepler, Tyler, & Terry, 1992). You can share positive aspects of their child's performance and then identify concerns, get their perspective, develop or share a draft of a plan, and ask for their input. As we discussed in Chapter 3, you can increase the social validity of a program by asking for parents' input on standards for their child's behavior. As we emphasized in Chapters 9 and 10, depending on the intrusiveness of the procedure, you may need to obtain parental permission before implementing a program. It has been our experience that most parents are enthusiastic when you present them with a draft of your plan and ask for their input. More than likely, they know that their child is experiencing difficulty and want to do something so that their child will not continue to fail (Sulzer-Azaroff & Mayer, 1991). You can also use subsequent conferences to keep parents informed of the effects that the program is having on their child's performance. If you have attended carefully to all the details of planning, implementing, and evaluating an applied behavior analytic approach, then your updates should feature improvements in their child's academic and social behaviors. Such information could be a refreshing change of pace, particularly for parents with a history of negative interactions with school personnel.

Home–School Communication

Frequent, meaningful communication between the home and the school should not be left to chance. Developing a system of ongoing communication with families offers you the opportunity to convey information about positive and negative events and to address student needs in a timely manner. Parents benefit by receiving up-to-date information, having the opportunity to maintain or increase their level of involvement, and receiving support from other people involved in their child's life (Bischoff, 1994).

Traditional report cards are not issued often enough and don't contain enough information about behavior to be really useful. Sulzer-Azaroff and Mayer (1991) suggested use of a daily report card. This card is a contingency arrangement between the teacher at school and the parents at home. At school, the teacher provides a rating or makes notes on the card as soon as a target behavior occurs. Later, at home, a consequence occurs that is typically related to an activity. For example, the teacher makes note of the fact that a child walked away from a confrontation rather than becoming physically aggressive. At home, the child gets to choose which video the family will rent and watch together. Similarly, students can receive a sticker after every class period during which their behavior was appropriate. Specific numbers of stickers are associated with special privileges granted at home, such as an extra dessert, having a friend over to visit, or going to the mall. Bear in mind that a home–school communication system can support appropriate behavior in the home. For example, Gresham (1983) reported that the mother of an eight-year-old boy with a history of destructive behavior sent a note to school each morning. This note indicated whether or not inappropriate behavior occurred the evening or the weekend before. Based on the content of the note, the child was able to choose from a variety of reinforcers available at school.

Rhode, Jenson, and Reavis (1993) identified the Home Note Program as one of the most effective techniques for increasing students' motivation and behavior (see Table 16.5).

We recommend that you develop a system that encourages daily or weekly communication and provides parents with the opportunity to respond. You should work out the details of your communication program together with parents well in advance of using it. This way, parents will know what to expect (e.g., note, charts, or a point total), when to expect it (e.g., every day or every Friday), how to respond to their child (e.g., praise or carry out a predetermined contingency), and whether they should respond (e.g., sign it and send it back to school with their child). Parents should also know what to do if their child does not bring home the communication device. Gaushell and Lawson (1989) advised parents to accept no excuses for a missing report. Kerr and Nelson (1989) recommended treating the absence of the product as if it were a negative report and implementing the predetermined contingencies.

TABLE 16.5   Using a Home Note Program

Rhode, Jenson, and Reavis (1993) identified the steps you should follow to implement a Home Note Program:

1. Choose or design a simple home note. You can purchase commercially prepared carbonless notes at most teacher supply stores.
2. Identify no more than five behaviors that you want to change.
3. Contact the student's parents and explain the system.
   a. Work together to identify both rewards and mild negative consequences that the parents are willing and able to administer at home. These usually take the form of permitting or withholding activity reinforcers.
   b. Ask parents to read each note, sign and date it, and give it to their child to return to school.
   c. Ask them to accept no excuses for a missing note.
4. Decide when the program will start and how often a note will be sent home. Initially, you may want to send a note home every day. Fade over time to sending one note home on Friday, then discontinue the program completely.
5. Explain the program to the student and answer any questions.
6. Implement the program, making sure to give the student feedback after you mark the note.
7. Early in the program, contact the parents occasionally to discuss and resolve difficulties.
8. Keep track of progress and share it with the parents and their child.

Kerr and Nelson (1989) described advantages of home–school communication systems. First, they increase the likelihood that home contingencies for school behavior will be carried out, which should have a positive effect on academic, social, and behavioral performance. Second, parents are informed of and involved in their child's progress. Third, parents will learn that not all reports from school are negative. They can be proud of both their child's increasing competence and their own contribution to his or her progress.

Outcomes Associated with Teacher–Parent Partnerships

Providing parent training, the planning of conferencing, and using a communication system between the home and the school require time and effort from both parents and teachers. As summarized in Table 16.6, their hard works pays off in a variety of ways.

Advantages of Positive Teacher–Parent Partnerships

From your perspective as a teacher, these measures can improve your relationship with parents and increase their support for your activities. Second, parents who are familiar with what you are doing, and why, are less likely to complain, making your job a lot easier. Third, you will find that you are able to deal with problems consistently, making a program work faster. Fourth, when students do their homework, arrive on time and fully prepared for school with all the necessary supplies, and behave during lessons, you can devote more time to academic instruction (Sheridan & Kratochwill, 1992). That your students are making greater academic gains should be a very satisfying outcome for you. Fifth, the time you invest in developing solid teacher–parent relationships ultimately saves time as parents become active, purposeful trainers.

TABLE 16.6 Benefits of Cooperative Teacher–Parent Partnerships

Solid teacher–parent partnerships offer many advantages. Below are the benefits associated with different groups of people.

Teachers	Students	Parents
Improved relationships with parents	Changes in a variety of behaviors	More positive attitudes
Fewer complaints	Increase in self-esteem	More self-confidence
Faster results	Effectiveness across age/ability levels	Improved parenting skills
More instructional time	Generalization	
Efficiency		

Good teacher–parent relationships benefit students as well. First, these techniques can change a variety of behaviors. Through parent support, teachers have been able to increase homework accuracy (Miller & Kelley, 1994) and completion (Miller & Kelly, 1994; Smith, 1994), attention to task (Smith, 1994); and decrease verbal aggression and fighting (Smith, 1994). With proper instruction, parents have been able to help their children overcome fear and avoidance behavior (Love, Matson, & West, 1990), increase compliance and positive family interactions (Nangle, Carr-Nangle, & Hansen, 1994); and decrease interruptions (Sloane, Endo, Hawkes, & Jenson, 1991) and destructive behavior (Gresham, 1983). Second, increasing parental praise may possibly increase the child's self-esteem. Third, teacher–parent partnerships assist students across the age range including elementary learners (Love, Matson, & West, 1990) and adolescents (Nangle, Carr-Nangle, & Hansen, 1994); and across ability levels including nonhandicapped children (Mullin, Oulton, & James, 1995) and children with autism (Love, Matson, & West, 1990; Powers, 1992), physical disabilities (Mullin, Oulton, & James, 1995), emotional disorders (Nangle, Carr-Nangle, & Hansen, 1994), retardation and multiple disabilities (Powers, 1992), learning disabilities (Evans & Evans, 1983), and attention deficit hyperactivity disorder (Anastopoulos, DuPaul, & Barkley, 1991). Finally, generalization of newly acquired skills is enhanced because the students learn that expectations for appropriate behavior do not change just because they are in a different setting (Kelley & Carper, 1988).

Advantages of cooperative teacher–parent relationships for parents include development of more positive attitudes about themselves, the school, and school personnel. Second, they may experience an increase in the confidence they have in their own parenting skills (Becher, 1986; Mullin, Oulton, & James, 1995). Third, parents can develop skills such as identifying specific measurable goals (Smith, 1994); modeling; prompting; using positive reinforcement procedures such as praise and tangible rewards (Love, Matson, & West, 1992), contracts (Miller & Kelley, 1994; Smith, 1994), and group contingencies (Gresham, 1983); and implementing negative consequences such as response costs (Nangle, Carr-Nangle, & Hansen, 1994), extinction, and time-out (Evans & Evans, 1983; Powers, 1992).

Problems in Working with Parents

Despite your best efforts, some parents may be difficult to reach and keep informed, but that doesn't excuse you from making the effort. Making no attempt to establish a cooperative relationship with parents may mean the child may not reach his or her optimal development.

Boutte et al. (1992) identified six categories of behavior that make interactions with some parents difficult. They offered general suggestions for dealing with all six categories, including encouraging the parents to attend a meeting, being well prepared before the meeting starts, and clearly identifying the purpose of the meeting. They also offered specific suggestions for dealing with parents within particular categories, two of which were particularly relevant to our discussion. They characterized as "negative" those parents who are usually disagreeable, unwilling to try, and have an excuse for everything. They recommended that you can make optimistic, but realistic, statements about past successes, encourage the parent to make suggestions, and praise when appropriate. Don't push the parent to act before he or she is ready, as this will only result in more negativism. It may help to limit the number of tasks you ask the parent to complete.

You may also be dealing with parents who are shy or unresponsive. You can determine their understanding by asking open-ended questions that require more than a simple "yes" or "no" response, allowing enough time for a response, and not dominating the conversation.

Summary

As their child's first teacher, parents know more about a student than anyone else. Their involvement can greatly enhance the effectiveness of an intervention program. For example, with proper training, parents can target socially relevant goals and objectives, identify suitable reinforcers and mild punishers for a contingency management program, share and reward the same standards of performance, and provide information on generalization.

The level of parent cooperation varies widely. Some parents take a very active role in their child's program, essentially becoming partners with you and their child. Others are content to go along with the flow. The vast majority of parents with whom we have dealt fell into these categories. Unfortunately, we are also familiar with other parents whose role has been primarily adversarial. We acknowledge that teachers must shoulder some of the responsibility for this problem. Typically, intervention programs are designed to increase deficits or decrease excesses. Either way, they demonstrate to parents that their child is experiencing difficulties. It is no wonder that parents of children with severe or long-standing difficulties react negatively to a request for a conference or assistance. Such requests may be perceived as another opportunity to criticize and find fault.

You can take specific steps to minimize hostility. As we mentioned, IDEA mandates that an IEP be established for all students enrolled in special education. This IEP must be developed cooperatively with parents and include a statement that describes the student's strengths. Thus, the IEP meeting is an ideal time to share positive aspects regarding student performance, solicit opinions and concerns about problem areas, identify a plan of action, and discuss how you can all work cooperatively to bring about improvements. Although you are not legally mandated to do so, you are advised to extend these opportunities also to the parents of a child who has no formal special education label but who has been experiencing social and behavioral difficulties in school or at home.

You can meet with all parents at the conferences that are held a few times during the year. The topics for discussion are similar to those addressed at an IEP meeting. Strengths can be shared and problem areas identified and prioritized. You can explain general classroom management systems or specific programs and the rationale for their use. You can also offer suggestions for ways in which parents can enhance the child's success.

A Final Note

Please remember that reading a book and completing a course are important steps in mastering applied behavior analysis. Obviously, actual integration and use of the techniques we described are better ways to discover the advantages that applied behavior analysis offers to teachers and their students. We continue to learn with each application of this technology, and we encourage you to continue developing, practicing, and refining your skills. Good techniques in the hands of caring, competent professionals can make a substantial difference in the quality of our students' lives.

References

Alberto, P. A., & Troutman, A. C. (1995). *Applied behavior analysis for teachers* (4th ed.). Englewood Cliffs, NJ: Merrill/Prentice-Hall.

Anastopoulos, A. D., DuPaul, G. J., & Barkley, R. A. (1991). Stimulant medication and parent training therapies for attention deficit–hyperactivity disorder. *Journal of Learning Disabilities, 24,* 210–218.

Becher, R. M. (1986). Parent involvement: A review of research and principles of successful practice. In L. G. Katz (Ed.), *Current topics in early childhood education* (Vol. 6), (pp. 85–122). Norwood, NJ: Ablex.

Bischoff, L. G. (1994). Families of children with emotional and behavioral disabilities: Issues and strategies for educators. *Contemporary Education, 65,* 145–147.

Boutte, G. S., Keepler, D. L., Tyler, V. S., & Terry, B. Z. (1992). Effective techniques for involving "difficult" parents. *Young Children, 47*(3), 19–22.

Broome, S. A., & White, R. B. (1995). The many uses of videotape in classrooms serving youth with behavioral disorders. *Teaching Exceptional Children, 27*(3), 10–13.

Dawson, N., & McHugh, B. (1987). Learning to talk to parents. *British Journal of Special Education, 14,* 119–121.

Evans, W. H., & Evans, S. S. (1983). Using parents in behavior management. *Academic Therapy, 19,* 37–43.

Gaushell, W. H., & Lawson, D. M. (1989). Using a checksheet with misbehaviors in school: Parent involvement. *The School Counselor, 36,* 208–213.

Gresham, F. M. (1983). Use of a home-based dependent group contingency system in controlling destructive behavior: A case study. *School Psychology Review, 12,* 195–199.

Kelley, M. L., & Carper, L. B. (1988). Home-based reinforcement procedures. In C. Witt, S. Elliot, & F. M. Gresham (Eds.), *Handbook of behavior therapy in education.* New York: Plenum.

Kerr, M. M., & Nelson, C. M. (1989). *Strategies for managing behavior problems in the classroom.* Columbus, OH: Merrill.

Kolko, D. J., Parrish, J. M., & Wilson, F. E. (1985). Obstacles to appointment-keeping in a child behavior management clinic. *Child and Family Behavior Therapy, 7,* 9–15.

Love, S. R., Matson, J. L., & West, D. (1990). Mothers as effective therapists for autistic children's phobias. *Journal of Applied Behavior Analysis, 23,* 379–385.

McMahon, R. J., & Forehand, R. (1984). Parent training for the noncompliant child: Treatment outcomes, generalization, and adjunctive therapy procedures. In R. F. Dangel & R. A. Polster (Eds.), *Parent training: Foundations of research and practice* (pp. 298–328). New York: Guilford Press.

Miller, D. L., & Kelley, M. L. (1994). The use of goal setting and contingency contracting for improving children's homework performance. *Journal of Applied Behavior Analysis, 27,* 73–84.

Mullin, E., Oulton, K., & James, T. (1995). Skills training with parents of physically disabled persons. *International Journal of Rehabilitation Research, 18,* 142–145.

Nangle, D. W., Carr-Nangle, R. E., & Hansen, D. J. (1994). Enhancing generalization of a contingency-management intervention through the use of Family Problem Solving Strategy: Evaluation with a severely conduct-disordered adolescent. *Child and Family Behavior Therapy, 16,* 65–76.

Patterson, G. R. (1982). *Coercive family process.* Eugene, OR: Castalia.

Patterson, G. R., Reid, J. B., Jones, R. R., & Conger, R. W. (1975). *A social learning approach to family intervention* (Vol. 1). Eugene, OR: Castalia.

Powers, L. E. (1992). Behavioral parent training in home and community generalization settings. *Education and Treatment in Mental Retardation, 27,* 13–27.

Reimers, T. M., Wacker, D. P., Cooper, L. J., & De-Raad, A. O. (1992). Clinical evaluation of the variables associated with treatment acceptability and their relation to compliance. *Behavioral Disorders, 18,* 67–76.

Reimers, T. M., Wacker, D. P., Derby, K. M., & Cooper, L. J. (1995). Relation between parental attributions and the acceptability of behavioral treatments for their child's behavior problems. *Behavioral Disorders, 20,* 171–178.

Rhode, G., Jenson, W. R., & Reavis, H. K. (1993). *The tough kid book.* Longmont, CO: Sopris West.

Sheridan, S. M., & Kratochwill, T. R. (1992). Behavioral parent-teacher consultation: Conceptual and research considerations. *Journal of School Psychology, 30,* 117–139.

Simpson, R. L., & Carter, W. J. (1993). Comprehensive, inexpensive, and convenient services for parents and families of students with behavior disorders: If only Sam Walton had been an educator. *Preventing School Failure, 37*(2), 21–25.

Sloane, H. N., Endo, G. T., Hawkes, T. W., & Jenson, W. R. (1991). Reducing children's interrupting through self-instructional parent training materials. *Education and Treatment of Children, 14,* 38–52.

Smith, S. E. (1994). Parent-initiated contracts: An intervention for school-related behaviors. *Elementary School Journal, 20,* 182–187.

Sulzer-Azaroff, B., & Mayer, G. R. (1991). *Behavior analysis for lasting change.* Fort Worth, TX: Holt, Rinehart and Winston.

Turnbull, A. P., & Turnbull, H. R. (1997). *Families, professionals, and exceptionality.* Upper Saddle River, NJ: Merrill/Prentice-Hall.

Williams, D., & Chavkin, N. (1985). *Guidelines and strategies to train teachers for parent involvement.* Austin, TX: Southwestern Educational Development Laboratory.

Zirpoli, T. J., & Melloy, K. J. (1997). *Behavior management: Applications for teachers and parents.* Upper Saddle River, NJ: Merrill/Prentice-Hall.

GLOSSARY

Alternating treatments design.   The only applied behavior analysis design that allows comparison of two or more interventions. Each intervention is associated with a distinctive stimulus so that you know which one is in effect. By rapidly shifting between/among rival interventions, differential effects can be observed.

Anecdotal record.   A written narrative describing critical classroom incidents.

Antecedent control.   The systematic control of preceding events/stimuli over the strength of the behavior. The presence of a discriminative stimulus increases the strength of a behavior, and its absence decreases the strength of the behavior.

Antecedent stimulus.   An event/stimulus that precedes a behavior.

Applied behavior analysis (ABA).   Originally defined by Baer, Wolfe, and Risley (1968). *Applied* refers to responses that are important to society. *Behavior* refers to responses that can be reliably measured. *Analysis* refers to procedures that allow you to establish the effect of an intervention on the target behavior.

Artificial reinforcer.   Any reinforcer that is not typically a consequence of the behavior in the natural environment.

Ascending trend line.   A data path that is accelerating, indicating an increase in strength.

Aversive stimulus.   A stimulus that is perceived as noxious or unpleasant by an individual. It may or may not decrease the strength of a behavior when made a consequence of the behavior. Alternatively, it may or may not increase a behavior when its removal/avoidance is made contingent upon the behavior.

Avoidance behavior.   Behavior that postpones or allows complete avoidance of aversive stimuli.

Backup reinforcer.   An object or event received in exchange for a specified amount of tokens such as points or poker chips.

*We thank David S. Hofius for preparing this glossary. Mr. Hofius was a doctoral candidate in the Department of Special Education at the University of Missouri-Columbia during the preparation of this text.

Baseline. A measure of the strength of a target behavior. Baseline data are generally used to establish the strength of a response before treatment. They are compared to data collected while treatment is in effect.

Behavior. Any act of an organism that is observable and measurable. It is also called a *response.*

Behavior management. A system of procedures designed to promote precise and measurable changes in behavior. Behavior management procedures may address antecedents of existing behavior, consequences of existing behavior, or the establishment of new behavior.

Behavior management review committee. A group of individuals responsible for reviewing and approving behavior management programs.

Behavioral repertoire. All behavior that an individual can perform.

Behavioral sample. A small measure of behavior that is representative of ongoing behavior.

Celeration. A stable response rate, one without an ascending or descending trend.

Chaining. A procedure that progressively reinforces each step in a sequence of responses that form a single complex behavior. *Forward chaining* begins with first response in the sequence. *Backward chaining* begins with the last response in the sequence.

Changing criterion design. An applied behavior analysis design that reinforces behavior when it occurs under successively more stringent criteria. Experimental control is first demonstrated, and then replicated each time the behavior changes to meet but not exceed a criterion change.

Classical conditioning. A procedure by which a neutral stimulus is presented along with a stimulus that naturally elicits an uncontrollable response. With sufficient presentations, the neutral stimulus will become a conditioned stimulus. In some instances, pairing of another neutral stimulus with a strongly conditioned stimulus will extend the effect. It is also called *respondent conditioning* or *Pavlovian conditioning.*

Clinical importance. Changes are clinically important if the selected target behavior and the magnitude of behavior change increase the person's quality of life.

Conditioned reinforcer. A previously neutral stimulus that has acquired reinforcing properties through pairing with an unconditioned reinforcer or a strongly conditioned reinforcer. It is also called a *secondary reinforcer.*

Conditioned stimulus. A previously neutral stimuli that has acquired the ability to elicit an uncontrollable response through a classical conditioning procedure.

Consequence. Any event or stimulus that is contingently presented, subsequent to the occurrence of a particular response.

Consultation. A process whereby one professional with certain expertise (consultant) helps another professional or parent (consultee) to work more effectively with students. Consultation differs from collaboration in that the consultee retains full responsibility for the outcomes.

Continuous behavior. Any behavior that does not have a clearly discernible beginning and/or ending.

Contracting.   Preparing a written document describing the contingency arrangements of a behavior intervention program. Responsibilities are clearly specified, and commitment is demonstrated by signature; all participants are provided their own copy.

Counterconditioning.   A respondent conditioning technique that replaces a disruptive emotional reaction with a more adapative reaction.

Countertherapeutic trend.   Changes in the strength of a behavior during baseline in the direction opposite from that which intervention is designed to achieve.

Covert behavior.   Behavior that is inaccessible to direct observation by others (e.g., thoughts or feelings).

Criterion.   A behavior standard used to determine if an acceptable level of performance has been achieved.

Delay of reinforcement.   Reinforcement that is not provided immediately upon performance of a target behavior. Generally the longer the delay, the weaker the effect on the subsequent strength of the target behavior.

Dependent group contingency.   The same response contingency in effect for all students, but it is applied to an individual or small subset of the larger group.

Dependent variable.   The behavior that an intervention is intended to change.

Deprivation.   A condition in which access to a reinforcer or potential reinforcer is denied or reduced. Establishing a state of deprivation increases the effectiveness of the reinforcer when it is made available.

Descending trend line.   A data path that is decelerating, indicating a decrease in strength.

Differential reinforcement.   Behaviors that meet a certain standard are reinforced, while others not meeting the standard are ignored. The objective is to reduce a less desirable behavior by using reinforcement rather than punishment.

Differential reinforcement of alternative behavior (DRA).   A procedure designed to reduce a target behavior by reinforcing an alternative (not necessarily incompatible) behavior, intended to be its replacement.

Differential reinforcement of diminishing rates of behavior (DRD).   A procedure similar to DRL except that the criteria for reinforcement are gradually reduced rather than fixed at one level throughout the program.

Differential reinforcement of incompatible behavior (DRI).   A procedure designed to reduce a target behavior by reinforcing an incompatible alternative behavior, intended to be its replacement.

Differential reinforcement of low rates of behavior (DRL).   A procedure designed to reduce the frequency of a target behavior to socially appropriate levels by reinforcing the occurrence of the behavior only after a preset interval of time has elapsed during which the behavior did not occur.

Differential reinforcement of other behavior (DRO).   A procedure designed to reduce a target behavior by providing reinforcement for not engaging in the target behavior. Unfortunately, DRO does not replace the target behavior with a more appropriate behavior.

Discrete behavior.   Behavior with a clearly discernible beginning and end.

Discrimination.   Differentiation among stimuli/events.

Discrimination training. Reinforcement of behavior in the presence of one stimulus/event and extinction or punishment of that same behavior in absence of the stimulus/event.

Doctrine of least restrictive alternatives. A philosophy that recognizes the advisability of using the least intrusive intervention that is effective.

Duration. The length of time from the beginning to the end of a behavior.

Escape behavior. Behavior that results in the reduction or removal of aversive stimuli.

Exclusion time-out. A student is physically removed from a potentially reinforcing environment to an environment that is void of reinforcers.

Expectancy error. The tendency to identify anticipated changes regardless of whether they actually occur.

Experimental control. An experimenter's ability to reliably produce specified changes in the target behavior by manipulating an intervention.

External validity. The extent to which an experiment's findings can be generalized to individuals, settings, and/or behaviors not included in the experiment.

Extinction. The reduction of the future probability of a behavior by withholding reinforcement of the behavior.

Extinction burst. An initial elevation of the strength of a response upon implementation of an extinction procedure.

Fading. Systematic, gradual removal of supplementary prompts and/or discriminative stimuli until natural stimuli/events control the target behavior.

Feedback. The process of providing information for the purpose of maintaining or improving future performance.

Frequency. The number of times a behavior occurs during an observation period.

Functional analysis. Methodology used to determine the relationship between behaviors and environmental events.

Generalized reinforcer. A reinforcer (e.g., money) that has acquired reinforcing properties as a result of pairing with primary or other secondary reinforcers. Generalized reinforcers can be exchanged for a variety of other reinforcers.

Group contingency. A behavior change program that applies rewards and reductive consequences to the class as a whole. There are three types: dependent, independent, and interdependent.

Independent group contingency. The response contingency in effect for all group members, applied to students' performance on an individual basis.

Independent variable (IV). The variable that is not manipulated; the intervention procedure.

Individualized Education Plan (IEP). A document mandated by IDEA and created by parents and school representatives. It describes current levels of performance, annual goals, short-term objectives, criteria, evaluation procedures, degree of participation in general education settings, related services, and dates and expected duration of services.

Individuals with Disabilities Education Act (IDEA). A legislative act that defines definitions for several disability categories and includes provisions for services for all students with disabilities.

Informed consent. An individual's ability to make decisions regarding any treatment or services he or she will receive.

Interdependent group contingency. The same contingency applies to all group members, but with final evaluation based on a specified level of group performance.

Internal validity. The degree to which changes in the target behavior can be attributed to the intervention strategy rather than alternative explanations. Campbell and Stanley (1963) offered an extensive discussion of possible threats to internal validity.

Interobserver agreement. The extent to which independent individuals agree on the occurrence or duration of a specific behavior.

Latency. The elapsed time from the presentation of a cue or prompt and the beginning of the response. Latency is also the period of time elapsing from the start of intervention to the start of a performance change.

Least restrictive environment (LRE). A provision within the Individuals with Disabilities Education Act that mandates consideration be given to the placement that is appropriate for the educational needs of students with disabilities and provides access to nonhandicapped peers.

Levels systems. A method for organizing desired social and academic behavior and related consequences into a hierarchical sequence of skills and privileges.

Line graph. A graph that shows the relationship between an independent variable plotted on a horizontal axis and a dependent variable plotted on a vertical axis. It is also known as a *frequency polygon*.

Modeling. A stimulus control procedure that arranges conditions so that a behavior can be observed and imitated.

Multiple baseline design. An applied behavior analysis design that introduces the intervention to different baselines at different points in time. Effects of the intervention are demonstrated as behavior changes in response to each successive introduction across behaviors, settings, or individuals.

Negative reinforcement. A procedure that strengthens a behavior through removal/ avoidance of a noxious stimulus/event as a consequence of performing the behavior.

Nonexclusion time-out. All sources of satisfaction and attention are withdrawn from a student without restricting movement.

Observational recording system. Any of several methods of data collection by which an observer records ongoing behavior. *See* Recording methods.

Observer drift. A gradual change in the stringency with which the target behavior is defined/identified.

Operant. Any behavior that is controlled by its consequences.

Operant conditioning. A procedure by which consequences are used to change the strength of a target behavior. Operant conditioning encompasses both reinforcement and punishment procedures.

Overcorrection. A behavior reduction procedure that includes several social learning strategies. There are two basic forms of overcorrection. *Restitutional overcorrection* requires that the disruptive individual restore the immediate environment to a state that is substantially improved over its original condition.

Positive practice overcorrection requires the disruptive individual to engage in exaggerated practice of an appropriate alternative behavior. In the absence of environmental disruption only positive practice can be used.

Overt behavior.   Behavior that is accessible to direct observation by others.

Pavlovian conditioning.   Learning that results from an emotional response to the environment. It is also called *classical* or *respondent conditioning.*

Permanent product.   The tangible results of a behavior (e.g., completed problems, food stains, or shoes shined).

Planned ignoring.   The deliberate withholding of attention, physical contact, or verbal interaction contingent upon the occurrence of an inappropriate behavior. The time period should be brief and specified. It is also known as *extinction.*

Positive practice overcorrection.   A student engages in an appropriate alternative or incompatible response.

Positive reinforcement.   A procedure that strengthens a behavior through provision of a satisfying stimulus/event as a consequence of performing the behavior.

Premack Principle.   A principle that states that access to any high-frequency behavior can be used as a positive reinforcer for any low-frequency behavior. It is also called "Grandma's Law."

Primary reinforcer.   A stimulus/event, such as food, that has reinforcing properties in the absence of prior learning. It is also called an *unlearned reinforcer* or an *unconditioned reinforcer.*

Prompt.   Any supplementary discriminative stimulus that increases the probability that a given response will occur. *Natural prompts* occur as an ongoing part of the environment. *Engineered prompts* are contrived to encourage initial acquisition of a behavior.

Punishment.   A procedure that reduces the future probability of a behavior by presenting a stimulus contingent upon the occurrence of the behavior.

Rate.   A measure of response that allows comparison of frequency of response when the observational periods are unequal. Rate data are established from frequency data by dividing frequency by time.

Ratio strain.   A decrease in student performance that occurs when the schedule of reinforcement is thinned too quickly.

Recording methods.   Data collection procedures used by applied behavior analysts. The choice of target behaviors and the nature of intervention strategies determine the most appropriate recording method. There are several specific recording methods.

Anecdotal recording is a narrative of preselected events that is recorded.

Antecedent behavior consequence (ABC) recording is a precise description of a target behavior each time it occurs, objective preceding events, and objective following events.

Duration recording is a recording of the amount of time during which the target behavior actually occurs.

Frequency recording requires recording each occurrence of the target behavior.

Interval recording and time sampling require observational periods to be divided into a number of short intervals. The occurrence or nonoccurrence of the target behavior is recorded for each interval. There are several variations. In *momentary time sampling recording,* the target behavior must be occurring at the moment that the interval ends. In *partial-interval recording,* the target behavior must occur during some part of the interval. In *whole-interval recording,* the target must occur throughout the interval. In *latency recording,* the time from a specific event until initiation of the target behavior is recorded. In *permanent product recording,* tangible results of the target behavior are recorded. In *task analysis recording,* the level of prompt required for each component skill in the task analysis is recorded. A simpler, but less precise approach involves recording whether each component skill was performed with or without assistance.

Reinforcement. A process through which a target behavior is strengthened as the result of its consequences.

Reinforcer sampling. Students are allowed to experience various potential reinforcers prior to initiating the formal contingency arrangement. Such exposure helps determine the effectiveness of potential reinforcers and gives students an opportunity to become familiar with previously unfamiliar potential reinforcers.

Related characteristics. Observable and inferred characteristics of the individual that influence the target behavior.

Reliability. Consistency of measurement. *See also* Interobserver agreement.

Reprimand. A verbal statement that can be used by itself or in conjunction with another behavior reduction procedure to decrease a target behavior. It has components—including the student's name, a directive to stop engaging in the behavior, and a rationale for discontinuing the behavior—and is a request for the identification of an appropriate alternative to the behavior.

Respondent conditioning. Learning that results from the environment eliciting an emotional response. It is also called *classical* or *Pavlovian conditioning.*

Response. See Behavior.

Response cost. A behavior reduction procedure in which a specified amount of a reinforcer is removed following each occurrence of the target behavior.

Response generalization. Changes in behaviors not specifically addressed in an intervention program.

Response maintenance. Continuation of changes in behavior after the intervention program has been completed.

Restitutional overcorrection. A student is required to correct any and all results from a misbehavior by restoring the environment to a state that is substantially improved over its original condition.

Reversal design. An applied behavior analysis design that systematically introduces and removes treatment. Treatment effects are demonstrated when changes in the target behavior correspond to these switches. It is also called an A-B-A-B design.

Satiation. The temporary reduction of a reinforcer's effectiveness because receipt of the reinforcer has offset the state of deprivation.

Schedule of reinforcement. The operating response requirements that control the delivery of reinforcement. There are many different schedules of reinforcement. *Continuous reinforcement (CRF)* is administered every time the target behavior occurs. *Fixed reinforcement* is administered according to an unchanging response requirement. *Variable reinforcement* is administered according to a fluctuating response requirement.

Secondary reinforcer.   *See* Conditioned reinforcer.

Self-control.   *See* Self-management.

Self-management.   Any behavior change program in which an individual seeks to change some aspect of his or her own behavior. One or more of several procedures may be involved.

In *self-determination of reinforcement,* the student determines the nature and amount of reinforcer to be administered contingent upon performance. In *self-determined content for performance,* the student chooses what to learn or what behavior to change. In the *self-determined criteria,* the student sets standards for performance prior to engaging in a task. In *self-evaluation,* the student examines his or her own behavior to determine if a specific behavior or standard has been achieved. In *self-instruction,* the student himself or herself gives a verbal statement to prompt, direct, or maintain behavior. In *self-monitoring,* a student assesses and records his or her own behavior, including self-observing and self-recording. In *self-punishment,* the student administers an unpleasant consequence contingent upon performance. In *self-reinforcement,* the student administers a positive consequence contingent upon performance. In *self-scheduling,* the student establishes the sequence of daily events.

Shaping.   A procedure to develop new skills by differentially reinforcing successively closer approximations of the terminal behavior.

Slope.   *See* Trend.

Social comparison.   *See* Social validity of effects.

Social reinforcement.   A special form of secondary reinforcement that involves the use of personal interactions to increase a behavior.

Social validity of effects.   The extent to which the magnitude of change of the target behavior improves the individual's quality of life. There are two measures of social validity of effects.

Social comparison is the use of a peer group, functioning adequately with respect to the target behavior, to provide a basis for evaluating a student's performance level. *Subjective evaluation* is the use of the opinion of others who are familiar with the student to judge or evaluate his or her performance level.

Social validity of goals.   The extent to which the target behavior is relevant to the individual's quality of life.

Social validity of procedures.   The extent to which students, parents, and other significant individuals accept the selected intervention strategies.

Spontaneous recovery.   The recurrence of an extinguished response in the absence of resumption of reinforcement.

Stable trend line.   A data path that is neither accelerating nor decelerating, indicating there is no change in behavior.

Stimulus.   An event or object that triggers or inhibits a response.

Stimulus control.   *See* Antecedent control.

Stimulus discrimination.   The ability to respond in a certain manner to a discrete class of stimuli and not in the absence of those stimuli.

Stimulus generalization.   Changes in the target behaviors that occur under conditions (other times, places, and/or people) not included in the intervention program.

Subjective evaluation.   *See* Social validity of effects.

Target behavior.   Behavior to be changed by an intervention program.

Task analysis.   The process of breaking down a complex behavior into its simplest components.

Thinning of reinforcement.   Reducing the availability of reinforcement by gradually making the performance criteria more stringent.

Threats to internal validity.   Factors other than the intervention that could influence the target behavior.

Time-out.   A behavior reduction procedure that removes as many sources as possible of positive reinforcement contingent upon a specified response. Time-out is enforced for a brief, specified time period. Methods vary in degree of restrictiveness.

Nonexclusion time-out involves withdrawal of all sources of satisfaction and attention without restricting the individual's movement. A *time-out ribbon* involves the removal of a ribbon, worn by all participants, that indicates eligibility to receive social, edible, and activity reinforcers. *Contingent observation time-out* involves requiring the individual to sit outside the circle of activity, while watching others participate. *Exclusion time-out* requires the removal of the individual to placement in a segregated setting (e.g., seated in a corner) within the room or area. *Isolation time-out* involves the removal of the individual to a separate room, void of reinforcers.

Token economy.   A highly structured intervention strategy wherein tokens are immediately provided contingent on the occurrence of target behaviors. Tokens can be exchanged for back-up reinforcers at prescribed times.

Token reinforcer.   A generalized conditioned reinforcer that can be exchanged for back-up reinforcers.

Topography.   The physical form or configuration of a response.

Treatment package.   A behavior change program consisting of more than one intervention procedure.

Trend.   The tendency for performance to increase or decrease systematically over time.

Unconditioned reinforcer.   *See* Primary reinforcer.

AUTHOR INDEX

SUBJECT INDEX

A phase, 257
A-B-A, 260
A-B-A-B, 260–264
academic routines, 61–62
activity reinforcers, 140–141
age-appropriate activities, 78
aggression management strategy, 212–213
allocated time, 66
alternating treatment design, 273–276
  advantages, 275–276
  disadvantages, 275–276
  extensions of, 276
  procedures for, 274–275
analogue modeling, 91
analogue observation, 90
analogue rehearsal, 96
anecdotal recording, 220–221
  purpose, 221
  structuring, 221–223
antecedents, 54, 127, 222, 282–283
  defined, 59
  examples of, 60
Antecedent Behavior Consequences Recording, 221–223
antecedent control, 26, 81, 154
antecedent control techniques, 25, 54–80
  advantages of, 80
  cautions in using, 55–56
  classroom routines, 61–62, 327
  classroom rules, 57–61, 200, 327, 329

classroom schedule, 54–55, 57–61, 141, 210, 327, 329
  functional age appropriate activities, 78–79
  modeling, 71
  peer interactions, 70–71
  physical arrangement, 79
  rate of success, 71–78
  review of educational program, 79
  systematic instruction, 71–77
  teacher–student interactions, 68–70, 327
  time management, 66–67
Applied Behavior Analysis (ABA), 2–16
  advantages of, 7–8
  criticisms of, 9–12
  ethical use of, 13–16
  historical foundations of, 4–8
  sequence of steps, 21–32
artificial reinforcers, 137
ascending trend line, 250
association, 106, 110
attrition, 259
aversive consequences, 28, 152–153
  disadvantages of, 152–153
  side effects of, 152
aversive stimuli, 189
  conditioned, 189
  unconditioned, 189

B phase, 257
back-up reinforcers, 137, 178

backward chaining, 226
baseline, 144, 257, 266
behavioral model, 4–5
behavioral objective, 23. *See also* instructional objective
behavioral theory, 4–5
behavior modification, 1, 4
behavior rehearsal, 96
behavior-to-cost ratio, 180
biological model, 6
bribery, 11, 147, 148

case study methodology, 257–260
central tendency, 247–249
  mean, 247–248, 254, 261
  median, 248
chaining, 143, 226
  backward, 226
  forward, 226
changing criterion design, 163, 269–273
  advantages, disadvantages, 272
  extensions of, 272
  procedures for, 270–271
classical conditioning, 4, 108
classroom routines, 61–62, 327
classroom rules, 57–61, 200, 327, 329
clinically important behaviors, 2–3
condition changes, 244
conditioning, 4–5, 108–110
  classical, 4
  higher-order, 110